ASSISTED SUICIDE AND EUTHANASIA

LIVE QUESTIONS IN ETHICS AND
MORAL PHILOSOPHY

Tom Sorell, University of Birmingham, UK
Norman Bowie, University of Minnesota, USA
and London Business School, UK

The series offers short, accessible studies addressing some of the most topical questions shared by moral philosophy and the social sciences. Written by leading figures who have published extensively in the chosen area, single-author volumes in the series review the most recent literature and identify what the author thinks are the most promising approaches to the live questions selected. The authors are philosophers who appreciate the importance and relevance of empirical work in their area. In addition to single-author volumes, the series will include collections of contributions on live questions. The collections will consist of important published literature and freshly commissioned pieces, with introductions explaining why the contributions represent progress in the treatment of the live questions selected.

Topic areas of focus in this series include: Inequality; Ageing; Minorities; Refugees; Health Care; Childhood; Globalisation; Genocide; Civil Society; Privacy, Secrecy; Sustainability; Public Office; Harm and Offence.

Other titles in the series:

Children, Family and the State
David William Archard

Stakes and Kidneys
Why Markets in Human Body Parts are Morally Imperative
James Stacey Taylor

Is it Rape?
On Acquaintance Rape and Taking Women's Consent Seriously
Joan McGregor

Assisted Suicide and Euthanasia
A Natural Law Ethics Approach

CRAIG PATERSON
An independent scholar

ASHGATE

Published by
Ashgate Publishing Limited
Gower House
Croft Road
Aldershot
Hampshire GU11 3HR
England

Ashgate Publishing Company
Suite 420
101 Cherry Street
Burlington, VT 05401-4405
USA

Ashgate website: http://www.ashgate.com

British Library Cataloguing in Publication Data
Paterson, Craig, 1965–
  Assisted suicide and euthanasia : a natural law ethics
  approach. – (Live questions in ethics and moral philosophy)
  1. Assisted suicide – Moral and ethical aspects
  2. Euthanasia – Moral and ethical aspects
  I. Title
  179.7

Library of Congress Cataloging-in-Publication Data
Paterson, Craig, 1965–
  Assisted suicide and euthanasia : a natural law ethics approach / Craig Paterson.
    p. cm. — (Live questions in ethics and moral philosophy)
  Includes bibliographical references and index.
  ISBN 978-0-7546-5745-3 (hardcover : alk. paper)—ISBN 978-0-7546-5746-0 (pbk. : alk. paper) 1. Assisted suicide—Moral and ethical aspects. 2. Euthanasia—Moral and ethical aspects. 3. Natural law. I. Title. II. Series.
  [DNLM: 1. Suicide, Assisted—ethics. 2. Euthanasia—ethics. WB 60 P296a 2007]
  R726.P39 2007
  179.7—dc22
2007025877

ISBN 978-0-7546-5745-3 (Hbk)
ISBN 978-0-7546-5746-0 (Pbk)

Printed and bound in Great Britain by TJ International Ltd, Padstow, Cornwall.

To Mum and Dad

Contents

Preface and Acknowledgments   *ix*

1	Introduction	1
1.1	Contemporary Debate	1
1.2	Natural Law Ethics	2
1.3	Suicide, Assisted Suicide and Euthanasia	7
1.4	Subsequent Arrangement of the Book	13

2	Justifications for Suicide, Assisted Suicide and Euthanasia	15
2.1	Introduction	15
2.2	Invalid Religious Arguments	16
2.3	Inconsistency in Killing	17
2.4	A Life Worth Living	17
2.5	Arguments from Self-Determination	21
2.6	Rejection of Double Effect Reasoning	27
2.7	Politics, Anti-Perfectionism and Neutrality	32

3	A Revised Natural Law Ethics	41
3.1	Introduction	41
3.2	Secular not Supernatural	41
3.3	Non-natural not Natural	43
3.4	Whose Practical Rationality?	48
3.5	The First Principle of Practical Rationality	48
3.6	The Primary Goods of Persons	50
3.7	Non-Primary or Secondary Goods	55
3.8	Pluralism and Normative Theory	59
3.9	Key Requirements of Practical Rationality	63

4	The Good of Human Life	73
4.1	Introduction	73
4.2	Action Types	74
4.3	Elements of an Action	76
4.4	Normative Demands	77
4.5	Negative Demands and Concrete Moral Absolutes	81
4.6	Killing and Double Effect Reasoning	85
4.7	Disaster Escape Clauses	95

5	Suicide, Assisted Suicide and Voluntary Euthanasia	103
5.1	Introduction	103
5.2	Species of Homicide	103

5.3   Better Off Dead?   105
5.4   Quality-of-Life   106
5.5   Killing and Letting Die   109
5.6   Intentional Killing and Personal Autonomy   112
5.7   Some Interesting Cases from the Literature   120

6   Non-voluntary and Involuntary Euthanasia   129
6.1   Introduction   129
6.2   Already Dead   129
6.3   Not All Humans Beings Are Persons   132
6.4   Anencephalic Infants, PVS Patients and Non-voluntary Euthanasia   139
6.5   Involuntary Euthanasia   148

7   State Intervention and the Common Good   155
7.1   Introduction   155
7.2   Anti-Perfectionism and State Authority   156
7.3   Liberal Perfectionism   165
7.4   Natural Law Ethics and the Common Good   167
7.5   Slippery Slopes   173

Conclusion   *181*
Bibliography   *185*
Index   *211*

Preface and Acknowledgments

I first encountered the topic of assisted suicide and euthanasia while an undergraduate studying social sciences in Scotland in the 1980's. I remember being affected at the time by the way in which arguments presented against the case for legalizing certain forms of assisted death were basically viewed as the product of religious-based ideology. Sweep away the 'cobwebs of superstition' and the secular case for legalizing certain forms of euthanasia was said to become overwhelming. While I was not well enough developed in my own thoughts at the time to argue just why a 'sanctity-of-life' ethic was not merely the product of 'outmoded faith allied to convention,' I was convinced that my own opposition to state-licensed killing was not being underpinned by faith or mere attachment to convention.

When I later went to York University, England to study political philosophy, I made the first real attempt to grapple with a secular natural law ethics that could be used to oppose Western nuclear deterrence policy. By 1989, I became convinced that state policies aimed at justifying the conditional intention to kill millions of people in order to promote peace and security were not policies that could be reconciled with an ethically legitimate framework for collective self-defence. The dissertation culminating from that period of study was my first attempt to address foundational questions of natural law theory and the ethics of state-sanctioned killing.

In the mid 1990's I was offered a scholarship to undertake doctoral studies in Health Care Ethics at Saint Louis University, Missouri. The opportunity to study and teach there helped me further develop my approach to natural law ethics and my appreciation for 'life' questions in a context that was interdisciplinary and seriously engaged with conditions of contemporary pluralism. The culmination was a doctoral dissertation on the topic of assisted suicide.

After leaving Saint Louis in order to teach biomedical ethics at Providence College, Rhode Island, I have had many subsequent opportunities to refine and develop both my natural law methodology and my thinking on assisted suicide and euthanasia. Several articles have subsequently been published in scholarly literature. I sought to write a book length treatise in order to integrate my thoughts more accessibly that would have appeal beyond the confines of scholarly journals. In writing this book as an independent scholar over the course of 2006 and into 2007 and having reread my earlier York dissertation, notwithstanding the developments and refinements of intervening years, I am struck by my continuing commitment to a secular defence of the principle: is it always and everywhere morally wrong to intentionally kill an innocent person as a means to an end, regardless of further appeals to consequences or motive. Then, as now, I defend the importance of this principle to an analysis of deeply challenging life and death issues. Justification for the principle in my revised natural law approach to moral and legal debate over assisted suicide and euthanasia informs the book's applied case against granting physicians the moral or legal right to intentionally procure the death of any patient, even with express consent, in order to end pain and suffering.

The verdict as to whether or not my natural law approach to ethics and politics offers a credible and sustained secular case against the acceptance of assisted suicide and euthanasia, is, of course, for the reader to determine. At the very least, I hope it will be viewed as having offered, in the spirit of open dialogue, a contribution to contemporary debate on this topic from a secular natural law perspective that is, I believe, being underrepresented in the public debate.

I would like to take the opportunity to thank a number of people for their personal and intellectual support over the years. Without their different contributions, my work would not have been possible. My deep gratitude is extended to my family, especially my parents, and my friends, especially Craig Strachan for steadfastly supporting me in my scholarly endeavors. At Glasgow Caledonian University and at York University I would like to thank Hugh McLaughlin and David Edwards respectively. At Saint Louis University my thanks go to Gerard Magill and James Dubois and at Providence College Matthew Pugh and Philip Devine. I would also like to extend my thanks to several writers I have known only through their works, but whose considerable intellectual efforts have significantly contributed to my own intellectual development over the years: John Finnis; Joseph Boyle; T. D. J. Chappell; David S. Oderberg; Robert George; the late G. E. M. Anscombe. They would doubtless disagree with many of my intellectual judgments and turns, both theoretical and applied, but not I hope, with my spirit of engagement. Lastly, my thanks go to Tom Sorell and Norman Bowie, the Ashgate series editors for *Live Questions in Ethics and Moral Philosophy* for including my manuscript in the series, and the editorial staff at Ashgate for their help and assistance in bringing the manuscript to press.

Bearsden, Glasgow
April 2007

Chapter 1

Introduction

1.1 Contemporary Debate

Controversy pervades contemporary debate over the moral and legal status of assisted suicide and euthanasia. If you were asked to compile a top-ten list of hotly contested moral issues, it's a safe guess that assisted suicide and euthanasia would feature prominently on your list. The passionate nature of the current debate and the spirited activities of pressure groups in the UK and US who support or oppose these practices, help ensure that the topic will not disappear from the public spotlight.

If proof were really needed to substantiate the claim that ethical debate over the status of assisted suicide and euthanasia is very intense, to make good the claim I need only draw the reader's attention to two recent high profile legal examples. In the UK, we have seen a flurry of public debate over the voting decision of the House of Lords to block a private member's bill that would have granted terminally ill patients the legal right to avail themselves of assisted suicide, overturning a 1961 statute that currently prohibits the practice. In the US, within the last year or so, we have also witnessed intense media discussion concerning the status of Oregon's physician-assisted suicide statute, and the decision of the US Supreme Court in January 2006 to strike down a former US Attorney-General's attempt to use a federal drug control statute to circumvent the legality of assisted suicide.

The topic has already generated a good deal of scholarly and popular writing, especially after 1984, the watershed event being the Dutch Supreme Court's decision to permit the Netherlands to become the first Western country to give legal sanction to some forms of assisted suicide and euthanasia. Given this body of writing, the reader might well question the need for another book on the topic. What can I expect to add to the nature of the debate that has not already been said? In reply, let me state that I decided to put pen to paper and write a book on the topic because I perceived a gap in the literature that needed to be addressed—an accessible treatise opposing assisted suicide and euthanasia written from a *secular* natural law ethics perspective. The more I delved into the available literature, the more I increasingly began to think that my own ethical position on the moral and legal status of assisted suicide and euthanasia was not being well enough articulated or defended. The kind of natural law approach often encountered in the thrust of contemporary debate, I surmised, was either overtly religious in nature or implicitly traded on revealed theological doctrine (so-called 'baptised reason'[1]). This did not accord well with my own understanding of how a publicly accessible natural law approach should be explained and defended. When faced with the reality of pluralism in contemporary society, I especially thought that the rationale for adopting a natural law approach to moral discourse stood in need of stronger justification.

The reality of pluralism fatally challenges the assumption that we can make ready appeal to the common values of Judaeo-Christian heritage in order to provide us with the shared moral underpinnings for social life together. Further, some think the reality of pluralism fatally undermines any possible appeal to substantive reasoning about goods in order to determine what constitutes the 'good life' for persons. While this second challenge also runs deep, I am convinced that the secular natural law approach I seek to defend in this book can effectively respond to it. My approach, broadly, seeks to demonstrate how a 'polyteleological' notion of the 'good life'—a pluralistic 'good lives' approach—is able to provide a secular framework for shared social life together but is nevertheless decidedly guarded in its grounds for justifying the state use of coercive power over moral questions (roughly, only where the human conduct in question can be seen to clearly imperil compelling goods that the state has a paramount interest to protect and foster).

Since I am aware that 'natural law ethics' may not be an ethical and political approach familiar to the reader (or familiar only in religious or quasi-religious guise), I first turn to the task of sketching out, by way of initial orientation, some useful structural distinctions. Subsequent chapters will endeavor to 'flesh out' the shape of my revised 'non-natural' approach to natural law ethics. After completing this task, I then turn to address some significant questions of scope and meaning concerning the terms 'suicide,' 'assisted suicide,' and 'euthanasia.' Since use of these terms is not unproblematic, it will be helpful to indicate to the reader where I stand on questions of use. Lastly, I will conclude this introductory chapter with a brief conspectus highlighting the subsequent chapter by chapter arrangement of the book.

1.2 Natural Law Ethics

'Natural law' is a phrase that is apt to be misunderstood or misinterpreted in different ways, especially given its long and varied history.[2] Part of the problem is that there is no single theory or thinker that constitutes the 'core' of natural law thought, although the influence of Aquinas's work is often considered central by many who would consider themselves natural law ethicists. Space, alas, will not permit the production of a comprehensive taxonomy of the different kinds of natural law theory. I must instead content myself with the task of mentioning some necessary broad brush distinctions with a view to explaining where I am structurally positioned *viz.* my own revised approach to natural law ethics.

1.2a Moral Law not Law of Nature

Moral natural law should not to be confused with 'the law of nature,' in the scientific sense of that expression. Laws of nature describe how physical entities act. Laws of nature are descriptive not prescriptive. These uniformities or regularities simply are. Physical entities do not 'deliberate' on how they behave; they do not choose to act or not according to laws of nature. Natural law, on the other hand, is concerned with how rational human beings ought to act, and here the key ingredients of human deliberation and choice are crucial. The word 'ought' in that last sentence is important. Human beings have minds and wills capable of reasoned deliberation and choice. We are not bound to behave in a way that a mere physical entity has no choice but to behave (although since 'ought implies can,' as Immanuel Kant pointed out, laws of nature certainly place logical and physical limitations on the powers we have to deliberate and will).[3]

All forms of natural law are concerned with how human beings are obligated to act in the world *if* their willed acts are to conform to the requirements of objectively determined moral standards. Natural law, then, is to be understood as a normative law of reason, not as a law describing a force of physical necessity that autonomically compels all of our actions.

1.2b Secular not Religious

Natural law has become marginalized in the eyes of many due to its perceived dependency on the sources of revealed religion. Revelation and faith are 'privileged sources of information' that cannot be said to function in an open and publicly accessible manner. Natural law is thought to be a kind of 'cloaking device' used in order to 'conceal' the imposition of divine moral imperatives on secular society. I am the first to admit that many varieties of natural law are in fact religious accounts and use the inspiration of divine imperatives as explicit or implied premises in their argumentative strategies. It often seems as if these accounts would be better labeled 'supernatural law' ethics rather than natural law ethics. As my argument unfolds, however, it will become clear why I argue that such an assessment of my revised natural law approach would be unwarranted. My revised approach is secularly grounded. When I say secular I mean that reason cannot be based on appeals to any form of knowledge other than natural human knowledge. Centered on our natural human ability to reason, I seek to argue how a secular natural law approach can credibly claim to be a genuine source of ethical knowledge that is open and (*in principle*) accessible to all. The structure of my approach will not depend upon any prior acceptance of the truth of God's existence or upon anything obtained from special privileged sources of information.

While secularism is often thought of as a notion falling under the near exclusive province of liberal thought, I would contend that there is nothing inherent in the notion of secularism that renders it an exclusively liberal concept, for its ethical significance reaches beyond divisions of political philosophy. Liberal thinkers like John Rawls stress that 'respect for persons' must take the 'fact of pluralism' seriously and that we fail in our duties of respect if this crucial fact is sidelined from our ethical and political thinking.[4] I am in basic agreement that respectful consideration of persons cannot be satisfied by justifying coercive legal restraints on the basis of appeal to thick religious doctrine or to complex and highly abstract lines of metaphysical argumentation quite untethered to any sense of bedrock intuition. Restraints on human conduct, if they are to have justification, must instead be substantiated by appeals to publicly accessible reason. As will become clear, however, where I take issue with Rawls and others is over the question of just what constitutes, under conditions of pluralism, a secular publicly accessible reason capable of justifying and setting limits on certain kinds of human conduct. I challenge some of the limiting mechanisms used to determine just what secular arguments can legitimately be included within the scope of 'publicly reasonable' discourse. For the moment it is sufficient for me to recognize and accept the significance of a plea for secularism as a general condition for inclusion in the ball-park of publicly reasonable discourse.

1.2c Objectivist not Subjectivist

Natural law is rightly classified as an 'objectivist' approach to ethics because it defends the tenet that there is discernible truth to be had in morality—truth that we are all, in principle, able to grasp and appreciate. More exactly, moral truth is held to be grounded in the teleological appeal of humanly fulfilling goods. These goods are understood to be the objective and foundational value sources for the subsequent operation of human reason to work out questions of the good and the right in human conduct.

It is important to bear in mind that natural law stands in basic opposition to the 'subjectivist' position that ethics is simply a matter of expressing our personal feelings about moral opinions. The subjectivist holds that there is no objective truth to be discerned in moral discourse. Thus, when we say that an act is evil—for example, the involuntary euthanasia of an elderly person—we are not stating an objective moral truth; we are simply saying that we have negative feelings towards the execution of such an action.

Commitment to objectivism is central to all varieties of natural law.[5] This emphasis allows us to identify a significant though not exclusive condition that helps make a moral theory a natural law theory, namely, the insistence that moral principles are discernible by reason and are held to be objectively valid. Although natural law differs in some of its elements from other forms of ethical theory, for example, Kantian ethics, natural law at least shares a joint commitment with Kantian ethics that objectively valid principles are to be our guide when discerning how to make moral judgments, not the subjective state of our emotions. Moral judgments and the prescriptions that relate to them are not to be regarded as mere statements of approval or disapproval but rather as truth statements concerning the knowable structure and content of morality.

'Conventionalism' is a related view to subjectivism which considers ethical utterances to represent the shared attitudes of a number of persons in a given culture or society. In opposition to conventionalism, all varieties of natural law subscribe to some form of 'universalism,' the claim that certain basic ethical truths (primary moral principles) are held to be universally valid because they are knowable and applicable to all people (in all societies; at all times) by virtue of their common shared human capacity to reason about the good and the right. Thus, what may be right or just according to the prevalent standards of a given community or society, for example, Dutch acceptance of euthanasia, may still be radically at odds with objectively discernable moral standards.

If natural law transcends current variations in culture, it also transcends variations in culture over time. Slavery is an objective moral evil that is not simply true of contemporary Western society. It has always been objectively wrong no matter how prevalent the view once was that slavery was a morally acceptable practice. Natural law as 'natural' is trans-historical as well as trans-cultural.[6]

Later chapters will attempt to convince the reader just why sound ethical judgments are objectively grounded and not simply the product of subjective feeling (no matter how powerful) or convention (no matter how widespread). In particular, I will seek to explain how my revised natural law approach is capable of establishing the necessary groundwork for an objective morality that: (a) identifies primary and non-primary goods; (b) generates requirements for choosing reasonably in relation to them; and (c) gives rise to a negative moral norm that rules out the intentional killing of all innocent persons (regardless of whether or not the killing is held to be of the 'consensual kind').

1.2d Perfectionist not Anti-Perfectionist

Natural law is an approach to normativity rooted in the idea of 'perfectionism'—the view that morality and politics ought to promote excellence of well-being in both the individual and in society at large. The general idea of perfectionism, pursuit of virtue, is also common to all varieties of natural law. Perfectionism is not merely about the individual pursuing his or her quest to instantiate excellence of virtue in his or her own life. It also represents the notion that political and societal institutions should also be concerned with the ends of promoting virtue in order to advance the common good of society.[7]

Natural law contends that morality, politics and law are ultimately concerned with the promotion of 'good persons' making 'good choices.' The state cannot be thought of as neutral with regard to the central aim of morality and politics—the recognition of virtue and its promotion via the establishment and maintenance of positive conditions that encourage people to pursue virtuous lives. Contrary to the idea of anti-perfectionism, that governments must eschew promoting substantive ideas of goodness, natural law supports the idea that promoting intelligible and important goods (even if contested) is central to the very rationale for legitimate government.

A natural law understanding of persons and what fulfills them is socially mediated. Natural law is not simply about the promotion of human flourishing in our own lives or even in the lives of our 'moral friends.' There are no 'moral strangers.' Its understanding of the role of society in fostering and promoting human flourishing militates against any radical severance between individuals and their basic interconnectedness to one another in and through the common good. For natural law ethics, therefore, the state has a positive role to play in promoting conditions that actively foster, rather than undermine, the authentic well-being of all persons in society.

While natural law is perfectionist, an important word of caution is needed. Perfectionism need not translate into heavy handed justification for the blunt wielding of comprehensive coercive power in order to 'force people to be moral.' Perfectionist ideals have certainly been used in the past to justify grossly unfair impositions on the liberty of people in order to 'save their souls.' Two significant influences in the history of natural law—Aristotle and Aquinas—used the idea of perfection to justify some deeply intolerant practices. Aristotle thought that a person's failure to live up to the 'contemplative ideal' was such a deep blight on the soul that the person could be treated as a kind of 'natural slave.' Aquinas's theological brand of monistic perfectionism effectively granted public authority the duty to legislate for the Roman Catholic faith by punishing heretics and apostates.

In contrast to these visions of the good life—both elitist and corporatist—elitist because of their privileged monistic vision—corporatist because of their tendency to treat the individual as an appendage to the body politic—it is my contention that the 'good lives' approach I seek to defend, eschewing as it does any monistic vision of what can be said to perfect us, and though its commitment to the equal dignity and treatment of all persons, distances itself from any form of perfectionism that would impose undue restrictions over the scope for individual liberty.[8]

A natural law approach can be but need not be monistic (or monolithic) in its understanding of what constitutes an array of worthwhile plans and forms of living. When value pluralism is genuinely appreciated, many ways of life can be understood to be quite compatible with an open and expansive understanding of the goals of human flourishing.[9] Given the meaningful conjunction of perfectionism with support for a worthwhile array of pluralism, it is not an oxymoron to talk of a revised natural law ethics as being committed to the idea of 'pluralistic perfectionism' rather than 'monistic perfectionism.'[10]

1.2e Naturalism and Non-Naturalism

While the phrase 'natural law' may evoke the ready assumption that natural law is necessarily a form of 'ethical naturalism' (a form of analysis that seeks to deduce or derive ethical 'norms' from 'factual' or 'theoretical' statements about human nature), an assumption supported by ample precedent in the tradition of natural law inquiry, it need not be construed as such. I will argue for a revised version of natural law that is 'natural' in the sense that human nature is the ultimate parameter setter for what is considered humanly fulfilling (if human nature were different then so too would be our idea of what the elements of human flourishing are), but 'non-natural' in the sense that reason—specifically insights provided by the operation of practical rationality—and not any direct appeal to natural drives, urges or inclinations— furnishes us with the starting points for normative content.[11]

Non-naturalism holds that normative statements cannot be derived or inferred from non-normative statements. A proposition involving an 'ought' cannot be deduced from non-normative premises. Moral propositions have an irreducible feature that no natural fact could have, namely, their normativity. Normative claims can only be deduced from prior normative claims back to irreducibly foundational normative claims that, so to speak, constitute ethical bedrock. Thus, if action X is deemed wrongful, it is not wrong because of its alleged 'unnaturalness,' for example, assisted suicide is wrong because it is natural to preserve life and unnatural to end it. Rather, action X is deemed wrongful because it dishonors a key requirement of practical rationality never to violate or disrespect any normative demand generated by any primary good of persons (specifically, here, the key negative normative demand of the good of human life never to intentionally kill an innocent person, whether as an end in itself or as a means to another end).

1.3 Suicide, Assisted Suicide and Euthanasia

All too often in applied ethics debates, there is a danger that lack of clarity and precision in the use of key terms serves to cloud and confuse the real nature of the debate being undertaken. My concern here relates to some questions of scope and meaning over use of the terms 'suicide,' 'assisted suicide' and 'euthanasia.' A word of initial caution is necessary. Definitional neutrality, in my view, is not possible when faced with differing and competing accounts of action theory, accounts that differ not merely in incidentals but in fundamentals, especially the validity and significance of distinctions drawn between intention and foresight, intention and motive, act and omission, and act and consequence.[12] Any attempt at defining terms inevitably risks exposure to the charge of engaging in the practice of 'sophistry with words.' Here, I ask the reader to accept 'on trust,' for the time being, my initial deployment of some as yet unsubstantiated assumptions. A promissory note is issued to the effect that the burden of substantiating these assumptions will be addressed in the action analysis of subsequent chapters.

1.3a Usage of Suicide

Initial use of the word 'suicide' is recorded in the *Oxford English Dictionary* as occurring in 1651. Alfred Alvarez, however, has discovered an earlier use of the word that dates from 1635.[13] The definition that occurs from historical usage is 'one who dies by his own hand; one who commits self-murder.' Subsequent usage of the word has reflected, in part, the strong pejorative meaning of earlier phrases used to connote the wrongful killing of oneself, for example, 'self-murder' and 'self-slaughter.'

There are severe problems with the adoption of this definition, however, for it lacks clarity and discrimination with reference to some of the cardinal elements that go into the creation of an act-description. First, too many acts that cannot properly be described as the 'intentional killing of self' would be incorporated under this description, for example, martyrdom or other forms of self-sacrifice. The scope of intent is a crucially important element to consider when determining any act-characterization. Whether a consequence of an act is specifically intended or not is no minor matter and cuts to the heart of subsequent analysis.

Second, the Oxford definition—'by his own hand'—is unsatisfactory because it appears arbitrarily to exclude the possibility of an omission being the attributable means of intentionally killing oneself. By omission I mean the non-performance of an action that was within the scope of a person's power of agency to perform. It should, therefore, remain an open question for subsequent moral assessment as to whether an agent intended to kill himself or herself by means of an omission, say, by refusing life-sustaining treatment.

Third, the overly pejorative connotations of the Oxford usage should be avoided so that we can move beyond any ready appeal to rhetoric. It is highly desirable to avoid the use of terminology of an overly biased nature—terminology that in *a priori* fashion settles the question of wrongfulness.[14] When the word 'suicide' is used, for example, we should not definitionally rule out, by rendering it linguistically absurd, the very notion of a morally acceptable suicide.[15]

On the basis of these criticisms, I think that any satisfactory usage of 'suicide' needs to clearly incorporate both the key elements of intent and omission. The Oxford definition is at once too broad and too narrow: too broad since it does not focus upon the necessary action component of intent that would further clarify the definition; too narrow since it fails to recognize the possibility of bringing about an intentional death by means of an omission.

Turning to the influential usage of the French sociologist Émile Durkheim, his usage (whatever its merits for sociological investigation) lacks precision for moral and legal analysis, concerned as they both are with the apportionment of culpability (if any) for our actions and omissions. Durkheim applies the term suicide to '... all cases of death resulting directly or indirectly from a positive or negative act of the victim himself which he knows will produce this result.'[16]

On a positive note, Durkheim's definition at least gives weight to the idea that an omission, as well as an action, can be suicidal in nature. He avoids such exclusion. Yet, the essential problem with Durkheim's definition is that it is still too vague in its characterization of basic action types. For example, all forms of 'self-sacrifice' would automatically be included under his definition of suicide. Thus, Jesus, for example, would necessarily be said to have committed suicide since he knew of the impending certainty of his earthly death and yet chose not to avert it in any way. Death acceptance becomes suicide in one bold definitional step. Such an interpretation will not do, however, for it fails to give sufficient weight to the importance of intention in determining the proximate objective of a person's action.

Another definition of suicide worth considering is given by Richard Brandt. He defines suicide as:

> ... doing something which results in one's death, either from the intention of ending one's life or the intention to bring about some other state of affairs (such as relief from pain) which one thinks it certain or highly probable can be achieved only by means of death.[17]

Brandt's definition is clearly more precise than the Oxford definition or the definition of Durkheim. Yet, notwithstanding relative precision, his definition will still not suffice, for it introduces, by his secondary use of the word 'intention,' the claim that intention can be read as being equivalent to 'foresight with probability.' Such a definition lacks discrimination in terms of an anatomy of the will. Here I can only state, to be defended later in the book, that for an intentional behavior to be brought under the act-description of suicide, it should require more than mere knowledge or belief that an action may (even certainly) result in death for it to be so identified. Undoubtedly knowledge (cognition) is a crucial element to be considered in the analysis of an action, but it should not be conflated with intention (volition) so as to rule out the possibility of meaningfully saying that the consequence of an action can be certainly known, yet not, as such, be intended.

Finally, I will consider a problematic aspect of Tom Beauchamp's definition of suicide. He seeks to build into his definition of suicide the idea of non-coercion, for 'an act is a suicide if a person brings about his or her own death in circumstances where others do not coerce him or her to action.'[18] Tempting as it is to write into the definition of an action, a 'freedom from coercion' clause, that insertion is unduly restrictive, for coercion is most usually taken into account as a highly significant circumstance pertaining to the degree of responsibility borne by the agent for intentionally acting the way he or she did. It is, of course, possible to envisage circumstances in which responsibility can be diminished significantly, even to the point of exoneration. Anyone having some acquaintance with the history of Anglo-American criminal law will be familiar with the classic case of *Regina v. Dudley and Stephens*. In that case a sick cabin boy was intentionally killed by his two fellow shipwrecked crew members in order to use his body for food. However, while the judge was prepared to exercise leniency in sentencing, he was not prepared to re-describe the conduct of the men on the basis of coercive circumstance.[19] Many actions are performed under conditions of severe pressure but we do not seek to redefine them simply on that basis. Thus, an act of rape (penetrative sexual intercourse with a woman contrary to her will) is still considered an act of rape, even if a gun was held to the head of the agent and he had every reason to believe he would be shot dead unless he behaved as he was bidden.[20]

Beauchamp's definition goes too far in altering our account of basic act-descriptions by building a 'coercion exception clause' into the definition of suicide. The question of an agent's degree of culpability should be regarded as a second-order question, to be assessed once the nature of the intended act undertaken has been determined.

On the basis of my analysis, I will adopt the following usage to signify what I mean when I use the word 'suicide' (or other synonyms). Suicide is to be taken to mean:

> an action (or omission) informed by the intended objective, whether as an end in itself or as a means to some further end, that one's bodily life be terminated.

1.3b Usage of Assisted Suicide

The term 'assisted suicide' attempts to classify the role played by a third party in the suicide of another person. The phrase can receive additional specification, as in the phrase 'physician-assisted suicide' whereby a designated class of person performing the assistance is referred to as a qualifier. The term has come to prominence due to an apprehended difference in act-description between the analysis of an act of assisted suicide and one of voluntary euthanasia. In an act of assisted suicide, the final act of killing, in a chain of acts, is said to be left to the suicide and is not performed by a third party, the assister. A typical case of assisted suicide would entail a physician furnishing a patient with a lethal dose of narcotics in order to end his or her life.

In addition to what I have already said on suicide above, I will confine myself here to making some clarifying remarks on the status of intent. To furnish another person with the necessary means to take his or her own life, following a suicide request, can usually be described as intending that the other person be killed by the provision of those means (since the provision of those means is a condition central to the attainment of the objective). Writers who favor the legalization of assisted suicide sometimes say that the assister need not intend death as an end in itself but only as a means to some further end, for example, the ending of pain and suffering in the context of the physician-patient relationship. It is, however, surely odd to say that an intended end can simply lead to the re-description of a whole class of acts under a phrase like 'mercy killing.' The question is best framed as one of whether it is ever permissible to intentionally provide lethal means to another person so that the other person may terminate his or her life as a means to some further intended end (the end being the collusive motive of eliminating pain and/or suffering).

Questions concerning the intended end of an action—for the sake of which a means is utilized—should be distinguished from questions concerning the intended choice of means. Consider the distinction between means and ends with reference to the following example. A woman seeks a position as an administrator at a local hospital. A friend is the personnel manager. The applicant claims a crucial qualification that she does not have. The proverbial blind eye is turned. The applicant is a single mother with several dependent children to support. She and her friend are both motivated by an altruistic concern to provide for her family. Yet, notwithstanding that motive of altruism, it would render violence to our basic understanding of the relationship between means and ends to claim anything other than that a deliberate deceit was employed as the intended shared means to some further shared end (leaving aside all questions of whether deceit, in the circumstances, could be morally justified). Questions pertaining to the moral assessment of means cannot be avoided by linguistic turns that attempt to re-describe act classifications on the basis of an appeal to the intended end, for means themselves are a distinguishable and highly significant bearer of moral value in their own right.

Some writers argue the point that an assister in a suicide need not be said to intend the death of the other person, even as a means. It appears possible to say that a person provided the means reluctantly and hopes that the other person, intent on committing suicide, does not go through with the final act. Yet, what is being intentionally willed here, even though heartfelt wishes or desires might be expressed to the contrary, is precisely an act intimately and strategically bound to the performance of the final act by the suicide. An agent cannot avoid questions of responsibility by claiming to 'merely' provide the lethal means needed for the actualization of the suicide. Consider the following case. A person sells heroin to a drug addict. The seller may hope that the drug addict may not overdose on the drug. Yet the seller's act of selling the drug was undertaken in the context of knowledge as to the subsequent effects those drugs would likely have on drug users. It can be no defence to state that the seller merely sought to pursue this transaction for money and was not responsible for the subsequent use made of the drugs supplied. The seller intentionally sold drugs to those whom the seller had good reason to believe would run a high risk of overdosing. A physician (or nurse), then, can hardly be said to be absolved from questions of moral culpability for assisting a suicide on the ground that (i) they are merely satisfying the requests of their patients to be provided with the lethal drugs, and (ii) the provision of means will not necessarily result in death because some patients so furnished may yet decide not to kill themselves.

On the basis of my preceding analysis, I will adopt and use the term 'assisted suicide' to mean:

> a third party action informed by the intended objective (at the very least), to furnish a potential suicide with the lethal means necessary to end his or her bodily life.

1.3c Usage of Euthanasia

The *Oxford English Dictionary* points out that in its classic Greek usage the term 'euthanasia' meant 'a gentle and easy death.' It is only within the latter decades of the nineteenth century that we find the term being used in the modern sense of 'the action of inducing a gentle and easy death.' What the Oxford definition does point to is the sense in which motive plays a peculiar role in characterizing this form of homicide. The motive of the third party is said to be the good one of seeking to relieve pain and/or suffering. Death is not sought as an end in itself but instead is sought as a means of putting the person out of their woes.

Such a usage, however, has problems. First, it makes no direct reference to the analysis of a series of similar acts that fall under the broad category of homicide—intentionally killing X for the purpose of Y. This is an important detail that needs to be included as part of a serviceable usage. When the element of intent is focused upon, it becomes apparent that euthanasia is a species of the class homicide. A third party, the euthaniser, undertakes the final act of intentionally killing another person. Second, the description also fails to adequately account for the importance of including in a serviceable definition the use of an omission as the preferred means of intentional killing.

The definition of euthanasia offered by Tom Beauchamp and Arnold Davidson is a major improvement on the Oxford definition. Their definition expresses much of the non-arbitrariness, clarity and discrimination needed in order not to confuse the action-classification of euthanasia with other kinds of action. Beauchamp and Davidson define an action as one of euthanasia:

> ... if and only if: A's death is intended by at least one other human being, B, where B is either the cause of death or a causally relevant feature ... (whether by action or omission) ... [and] there is sufficient evidence for B to believe that A is acutely suffering ... [and] B's primary reason for intending A's death is the cessation of A's (actual or predicted) ... suffering.[21]

Serviceable as the definition of Beauchamp and Davidson is, however, their definition still needs further comment regarding the use of two qualifier sets used in the bioethical literature: (a) 'voluntary,' 'non-voluntary,' and 'involuntary'; and (b) 'active' and 'passive.'

Use of the term 'voluntary euthanasia' is somewhat odd at face value since the qualifier refers not to voluntariness on the part of the euthaniser but to the request of the candidate being euthanised. In addition the term voluntary is being loosely used, for more than the merely voluntary is being supposed, namely, informed consent. Absence of coercion does not begin to capture the need for patients to be properly informed about the nature and significance of the choice they are considering. Nevertheless, what the qualifier is drawing attention to is the cooperative nature of the final act of killing with the express will of the suicide, so we can step over this obstacle and continue to use the qualifier 'voluntary' providing it is borne in mind that what is being signified is the element of consent and not just the absence of coercion.

Given that an occurrence of euthanasia is voluntary, such an occurrence can be said to entail both an act of intentional self-killing on the part of the suicide and an act of intentional killing on the part of the euthaniser. An act of voluntary euthanasia can be differentiated from an act of 'non-voluntary' or 'involuntary' euthanasia. Non-voluntary euthanasia would entail the intentional killing of a person not capable of granting his or her consent. Involuntary euthanasia would entail the intentional killing of a person who expressly withheld his or her consent.

The 'active' and 'passive' qualifiers are also commonly used in the bioethical literature. When we often think of 'classic' cases of euthanasia or suicide, we usually think of 'active' killing—a physician who intentionally injects a lethal dose of drugs into the vein of a patient in order to kill him or her; a suicide who intentionally takes a lethal dose of drugs in order to kill himself or herself. The phrase 'active euthanasia,' then, invokes the idea of creating a new lethal chain of causation in order to kill. 'Passive' euthanasia, on the other hand, is often associated with either the non-provision or withdrawal of medical treatment (or some combination), resulting in death. Since passive euthanasia is not 'active killing' in the above classic sense, 'passive euthanasia' is often not thought to be as ethically problematic. The problem with the 'passive' qualifier, however, is that it, at times, appears to 'insulate' treatment decisions from important questions of intention that shape the moral quality of a treatment decision. It is entirely possible for a third party to intend to kill 'passively' by withholding or withdrawing treatment as the adopted means for ending pain and suffering. A physician (whether or not acting in consort with the patient, with a surrogate decision maker or both), can withdraw or withhold treatment with the specific intention that the patient be killed as a means to an end.

The moral quality of a choice to withhold or withdraw treatment cannot turn on a mere appeal to 'passivity' but must be critically assessed *viz.* the intentions of the parties involved. What needs to be questioned from the outset is the perception that a physician simply cannot be held morally responsible for killing a patient by an intentional omission not to treat—especially where patient consent is operative—for he or she is not held to be 'actively' hastening a patient's death in the classic manner described above.

1.4 Subsequent Arrangement of the Book

Having undertaken preliminary analysis over the scope and meaning of 'natural law ethics,' and also 'suicide,' 'assisted suicide,' and 'euthanasia,' I will now conclude this initial chapter with a brief account of the subsequent chapter by chapter arrangement of the book.

In Chapter 2, 'Justifications for Suicide, Assisted Suicide and Euthanasia,' I review the major ideas that have come to the fore in shaping the push for the moral and political acceptability of some forms of suicide, assisted suicide and euthanasia. Particular ideas focused upon include: (i) the value and status of human life, especially the quality of personal life instead of mere biological life; (ii) self-determination and the value of personal autonomy; (iii) the rejection of concrete moral absolutes; (iv) the rejection of double effect reasoning; and (v) the rejection of perfectionist appeals to state authority to enforce morals legislation.

In Chapter 3, 'A Revised Natural Law Ethics,' I explicate the foundations justifying my revised non-natural approach to natural law ethics. I explain my pluralistic account of the primary goods of persons and identify practical requirements for choosing reasonably. My revised natural law approach then forms the basis for subsequent applied ethical analysis.

Chapter 4, 'The Good of Human Life,' argues that this good generates both positive and negative demands. I then argue that respect for and non-violation of that primary good generates a concrete moral absolute never to intentionally kill an innocent person, whether as an end or as a means to an end. I then proceed to explain and defend (i) an analysis of innocence, (ii) the use of double effect reasoning and (iii) the use of the action and omission distinction.

In Chapter 5, 'Suicide, Assisted Suicide and Voluntary Euthanasia,' the ethics of consensual death are examined. I contest the coherence of the notion that a person can be 'better off dead.' I then tackle the case for consensual death by (a) challenging the use of quality-of-life criteria to assess the worth of human life and (b) by critiquing appeals made to personal autonomy in order to justify a single or cooperative decision to terminate the very being of a person.

Chapter 6, 'Non-voluntary and Involuntary Euthanasia,' defends the basic notion that all individualized human beings are persons. I argue that those who are 'higher brain' dead are still persons and may not be intentionally killed. I examine the ethics of withholding and withdrawing treatment from anencephalic infants and PVS patients and conclude that some but not all cases of withholding and withdrawing care are being informed by an illicit intention to kill and constitute cases of non-voluntary euthanasia.

In Chapter 7, 'State Intervention and the Common Good,' I proceed with a critical assessment of the arguments of anti-perfectionists that it is not the business of the state to enforce upon its citizens deep or substantive conceptions of what constitutes the good. The chapter also assesses the case for liberal perfectionism centered on the good of personal autonomy. I go on to argue that a natural law conception of the person in society, cenetred on the common good, provides a solid framework for assessing both the justification for, as well as limits on, the use of the state power to legally enforce certain (appropriately qualified) moral standards. The concluding part examines the relevance of prudential slippery slope reasoning to the contemporary debate over the legalization of assisted suicide and voluntary euthanasia.

Notes

1 A phrase first coined, I think, by the late Peter Geach.
2 See Michael B. Crowe (1977), for a well written historical account of the different kinds of natural law theory. Also useful is Pauline Westerman (1998).
3 Kant's maxim is discussed, amongst others, by W. D. Ross (1930), p. 5.
4 See John Rawls (1993).
5 See Mark C. Murphy (2001), pp. 64–94, for an extended discussion of both subjectivism and objectivism. On scepticism see Renford Bamborough (1981).
6 See Robert P. George (1989).
7 On the different forms of perfectionism operative in politics see Douglas B. Rasmussen and Douglas J. Den Uyl (2005); Steven Wall (1998).
8 See George (1993), ch. 1.
9 Some contemporary natural law accounts, while embracing a measure of diversity, continue to be too restrictive in their moral assessment of genuinely worthwhile forms of living. I have in mind public debate on the topic of homosexuality, where, I think, genuine goods advanced by committed homosexual partnerships have been unfairly characterized. For example, I disagree with John Finnis's analysis of the goods of marriage and family (1994) and (1997) because he fails to recognize the *pro bono* nature of certain committed homosexual partnerships.
10 The phrase 'pluralistic perfectionism' is coined by George (1993), chs 6 and 7.
11 See further Craig Paterson (2006).
12 See Joseph Kupfer (1990). Kupfer acknowledges the point that how an action is characterized will inevitably affect its moral evaluation. An implication of Kupfer's analysis is that definitions of suicide and the like cannot function in an entirely 'neutral' way. See also David Daube (1972).
13 See Alfred Alvarez (1972), p. 50, citing Sir Thomas Browne's *Religio Medici* (1635), London, *sect*. XLIV. On different Latin neologisms see Anton J. L. van Hooff (1990).
14 For an interesting examination of rhetoric and historical and contemporary usages see Suzanne Stern-Gillet (1987).
15 A significant usage that does not definitionally rule out the possibility of moral suicide is seen in the Roman Catholic tradition, whereby a distinction is made between cases of 'direct' and 'indirect' suicide. Only direct suicides are held to entail the illicit taking of innocent human life. See Robert Barry (1994), 91–163.
16 Émile Durkheim (1951), p. 44.
17 Richard B. Brandt (1980), pp. 117–18.
18 Tom L. Beauchamp (1986), p. 77.
19 Case discussed by Alan Donagan (1977), pp. 175–7.
20 On the notions of coercion and duress see Craig L. Carr (1991).
21 Tom L. Beauchamp and Arnold Davidson (1979), p. 304.

Chapter 2

Justifications for Suicide, Assisted Suicide and Euthanasia

2.1 Introduction

The purpose of this chapter is to present to the reader key arguments used to support, under certain circumstances, a moral and political right to some or all of the practices of suicide, assisted suicide and euthanasia. In order to examine a subject well, it is necessary to carefully consider the assumptions and strengths of opposing arguments. The key arguments used to support a right to intentionally kill with a view to ending pain and suffering, explained in this chapter, will then be systematically addressed and countered in subsequent chapters according to the moral and political norms established by my revised natural law ethics approach.

First, I look at the claim that traditional sanctity-of-life doctrine is based upon dodgy religious premises, premises that are unable to support the conclusions required of them. Moreover, even if some key religious premises were conceded for the purposes of argument, they are judged incapable of generating the sanctity-of-life conclusions required of them.

Second, I examine the argument that sanctity-of-life doctrine is inconsistent. Opponents argue that this perspective is inconsistent because it cannot justify intentional killing in cases of self-defence and capital punishment and yet deny the legitimacy of some other forms of intentional killing.

Third, the idea that the worth of human life is readily commensurable with other values or disvalues is considered. Life is regarded as a positive value as long as it can 'hold its own' against other competing considerations like the disvalue of human suffering. The value of human life, in the face of competing considerations, is said to diminish or wane in quality to the point that intending death becomes a rational choice-worthy option.

Fourth, I present arguments arising from the idea of self-determination or personal autonomy that are said to preclude intervention in the exercise of certain lethal choices by means of coercion due to the key significance of this foundational value for persons.

Fifth, alternative accounts of action theory, accounts that reject the principle of double effect, are examined. If that principle were unsustainable, then the maintenance of concrete moral absolutes (for example, it is always wrong to intentionally kill the innocent), would result in the imposition of impossibly rigorist demands, resulting in a *reductio ad absurdum*.

Sixth, I turn to an examination of anti-perfectionist accounts of state authority. Anti-perfectionism supports the idea of neutrality on the part of the state when faced with the challenge of credibly responding to competing theories of the good life. Central to the anti-perfectionist claim is the idea that whether a way of life (or conception of the good) is judged valuable or worthless, should never be a reason for the government to seek to promote or discourage it. Anti-perfectionism challenges the traditional role of the state as a legitimate enforcer of morals legislation.

2.2 Invalid Religious Arguments

A rhetorically influential line of attack on the notion that human life has inviolable dignity is to critique traditional sanctity-of-life doctrine as being essentially religious or pseudo-religious in nature. Since sanctity doctrine, critics argue, is religious or ultimately depends upon religious assumptions, it is not held capable of legitimately furnishing us with a set of public grounds for regulating human conduct. David Hume is the most significant historical progenitor of this line of critique. In Hume's essay *On Suicide*, he rejected the grip of superstition over the power of the human mind to deliberate about life and death questions.[1]

Hume contended that if determining the time of death were entirely up to God, for he alone is said to have dominion over our lives, then it would also be wrong to intervene and lengthen our lives, for example, by using medicine to thwart the progress of a naturally occurring disease. Both actions—the ending of life and the continuance of life—can be said to interfere with God's will. Since humanity interferes constantly with all manner of 'natural laws,' why should the question of life or death be viewed any differently? If there is a tendency in nature towards the preservation of life, this cannot dictate whether or not it is right or wrong to end life any more than it is right or wrong to interfere with any other 'natural occurrence' in the scheme of things.[2]

Other religiously inspired arguments opposing suicide fare no better.[3] When separated from a religious framework, why does the bare 'fact' that the soul is considered immortal render it immoral to hasten its departure from the body? Since the bodily habitation of the soul is considered a transitory state, why is it wrong to release the soul from the body under conditions where considerable burdens are imposed? Answers to such questions, in order to have content, depend on religious assumptions. Remove such content and the claimed 'fact' of immortality is rendered incapable of doing the argumentative work required of it one way or the other.[4]

Dan Brock and Helga Kuhse are two key contemporary thinkers who carry Hume's torch. Both reject appeals to the idea that human life is sacred in order to justify the inviolability of human life against all forms of self-killing. Life, both argue, as with any other presumptive value, is not a value that can be held up for 'reification' regardless of quality-of-life considerations. The idea that life is in any way sacred is also viewed in Humean terms as the product of religious superstition. Abolish the relevance of God-talk and you abolish the relevance of sanctity-of-life talk. 'Secular sanctity' is viewed as an oxymoron.[5]

The judgment—as to whether a life, in the face of intractable pain and suffering, is worth living—can and should be determined by the conscience of the individual patient and not by the imposition of blanket prohibitions inspired by religion. Choices should not be foreclosed in the negative by the invocation of religiously inspired doctrine that insists on regarding all 'innocent' human life as an inviolable good. Removed from the context of religion, other forms of killing become justifiable. Questions of suicide and assistance in suicide cannot be subjected to any sort of absolutist ban.[6]

2.3 Inconsistency in Killing

Margaret Battin, Helga Kuhse, Marvin Kohl, and others, argue that the Western sanctity-of-life tradition is flawed in terms of its internal consistency. That tradition, they argue, forbids the direct killing of 'the innocent,' yet nowhere is it satisfactorily stated what the 'quality of innocence' really is and how it can justify 'carve out' exceptions to a general prohibition on intentional killing.[7] Just why does 'non-innocent' human life cease to be sacred and inviolable?[8] The radical dignity of the human person is often stated as something that can never be alienated. Do those who are 'non-innocent' therefore lack this radical dignity? How is this ontological transformation achieved?

Two key areas of inconsistency in the sanctity-of-life tradition, critics claim, are capital punishment and killing in self-defence. The sanctity-of-life tradition has historically supported the right of the state to use lethal force in the execution of criminals.[9] The criminal is designated a 'moral' non-innocent. Yet, how does moral non-innocence on the part of the criminal destroy the essential humanity of the criminal such that the criminal's life becomes non-sacred? States usually have a variety of other means at their disposal to protect society from future bad acts and perhaps rehabilitate the criminal. Is capital punishment, then, not a case of justifying unnecessary intentional killing?[10]

Further, regarding intentional killing in self-defence, critics assert, why does moral non-innocence on the part of an aggressor mean that an aggressor's life ceases to have inviolable dignity and worth? Moreover, it is not even clear that intentional killing in self-defence is actually being limited only to cases where an aggressor can be designated a moral non-innocent, for intentional killing also seems to be justified in some cases where a lethal material risk is being posed to others without any moral fault on the part of the person who poses the risk (for example, those who are coercively conscripted as combatants into furthering a war they morally oppose). What then of claims that intentional killing is being limited only to the ranks of those who are morally non-innocent?

2.4 A Life Worth Living

Stripped of its quasi-religious context, and relying instead on a broad array of factors to determine life's relative value, how, opponents say, can it make sense to talk of human life as an intrinsic (*per se*) good that can never be intentionally acted against?

Challenges to a sanctity-of-life view of the good human life, of course, are not new and their historical roots can be traced back to ancient Stoic and Epicurean influences. For the Stoics, self-killing was justified, amongst other reasons, in order to offset the effects of pain, mutilation or incurable illness. For the Epicureans, suicide was thought desirable as a means of ending a painful existence that could no longer be endured.[11]

In contemporary consequentialist and mixed systems of reasoning, human life is also held not to be an intrinsic good that can never be intentionally acted against.[12] Life is regarded as a positive value as long as it can hold its own against other competing considerations like the disvalue of human suffering. Life can even be thought of as a weighty presumptive value since it underpins all of life's significant projects. When life manifests ever-increasing evils, however, life itself can cease to be a positive value that must override other competing values and can be intentionally ended.[13]

2.4a Utilitarianism

Utilitarianism is the main form of ethical theory that appeals to a thoroughgoing commensuration amongst different values in order to assess the rightness of an action. Actions or rules are to be assessed in terms of their ability to maximize utility and minimize disutility. The key thinker of classical utilitarianism was Jeremy Bentham. People seek pleasure and avoid pain. According to Bentham: 'Nature has placed mankind under the governance of two sovereign masters, *pain and pleasure*. It is for them alone to point out what we ought to do as well as what we shall do.'[14]

Bentham's view on the question of suicide was similar to the view of Hume—if life became too much of a burden, due to pain and suffering, it could be morally justifiable to intentionally seek to end it, the life having outlived its benefit or usefulness. Society's claim on the life of the individual loses its hold.[15] Bentham's work can be seen as a practical translation of the idea of utility into the governance of law. Contrary to the 'superstitions' of the age, Bentham thought that law should be based on the purely rational foundation of utility. He opposed laws that prohibited the practice of suicide, for such laws, he believed, were not conducive to the promotion of the greatest happiness for the greatest number of people.[16]

J. J. C. Smart, a contemporary act-utilitarian, argues that the rightness of an action can only be judged by an assessment of its consequences. There is an unmistakable classical ring to Smart's account. Right choices are those that have the best overall consequences. Wrong choices either do not pursue the best positive return of good over bad consequences or do not pursue the action with the least bad consequences. An act-utilitarian account of moral evaluation presupposes that the diverse consequences of a choice can be objectively commensurated by reference to a common scale of ranking.[17] For Smart, there are clear cases where the positive consequences of continuing to live will be outweighed by the negative consequences associated with continuing to live. Intentional suicide, assisted suicide or voluntary euthanasia, then, can all be justified by an act-utilitarian assessment of consequences.

Peter Singer is one of the best known advocates of contemporary preference-utilitarianism.[18] Preference or desire utilitarianism is a variant of classical utilitarianism. The preference utilitarian defines utility in terms of maximizing preference satisfaction.[19] Preference utilitarianism directs us to maximize the satisfaction of existing preferences. Singer holds that an impartial consideration of interests (the preferences of all) means that we are obliged to 'choose the course of action which has the best consequences, on balance, for all affected.'[20]

Singer argues against the claim that human life can be said to have any inherent non-instrumental value, for an assessment of persons' preferences cannot begin to support the rigidity of such a moral determination. Instead, Singer focuses on the notion of quality-of-life preferences in order to inform the shape of life and death decision making. An impartial consideration of quality-of-life preferences, for Singer, will justify the practices of suicide, assisted suicide, voluntary euthanasia, and in some cases, non-voluntary euthanasia (for example, some severely disabled infants).[21]

2.4b Mixed Systems

Deontological systems with a 'consequentialist twist' also admit of balancing or weighing different forms of basic value. Given compelling 'weight,' the good of human life can be intentionally acted against. Take, for example, the work of Tom Beauchamp and James Childress, influential authors of a leading textbook in the field of bioethics.[22] Principles of conventional morality, they argue, like the principle that prohibits the intentional killing of the innocent, are considered generally binding. Exceptions arise, however, in which the force of other values can outweigh the value of adhering to such a prohibition.[23] The basic approach adopted by Beauchamp and Childress draws heavily on the work of W. D. Ross.[24]

Ross addressed the problem of value commensuration within the deontological tradition by incorporating the call of duty within a framework of *prima facie* obligation. In any concrete situation rules based on duties can conflict. When faced with such a conflict the agent has to decide which duty has priority. While, on the face of it, to act against a duty is always *prima facie* wrong, the weight of one duty may be able to override another duty. The weighing of duties cannot take place in a vacuum divorced from consequences. The pull of consequences must be addressed when discerning which competing *prima facie* duty will prevail in any given case.[25]

Ross's basic method for resolving conflicts amongst duties has been influential. It is near orthodoxy in contemporary deontological circles that 'tragedy,' 'disaster' or 'escape' clause overrides are an essential part of the fabric of any practical morality. There can be no concrete moral absolutes, regardless of consequences, that always and everywhere unconditionally bind. As Charles Fried points out, in regular circumstances the norm prohibiting murder excludes the killing of an innocent person; the norm against torture prohibits the torture of an innocent person, and so on. Within the boundaries of regular situations deontological rules of morality are maintained. These regular boundaries, however, break down when confronted by the prospect of tragedy, justifying a resort to irregular consequentialist derived norms.[26]

A further example of Ross's influence can be seen in the deontological approach taken by Bernard Gert, Charles Culver and Danner Clouser.[27] They argue that common morality can apprehend the reasonableness of a general rule that prohibits 'unjustified killing.' What constitutes unjustified killing? An act of unjustified killing is an act of killing that lacks a compelling justification for the act. For instance, the burdens of pain and suffering can place the terminally ill patient in a tragic situation sufficiently compelling in weight to turn an act of unjustified killing into an act of justified killing. Unjustified killing can become justified killing when tragic situations are factored in to the moral assessment of an action. While Gert, Culver and Clouser are aware that there are going to be practical difficulties encountered in satisfactorily balancing the interests of patients who opt for suicide with the need to protect other patients from the burden of unjust pressure to commit suicide, they nevertheless argue that competent patients, can, in principle, intentionally choose to end their lives by means of suicide or assisted suicide.[28]

2.4c Quality-of-Life Assessment

Quality-of-life talk was traditionally used to assess environmental conditions that either improved or impaired the quality of peoples' lives. Social reformers also used this traditional concept to talk about the standard of living of underprivileged groups. In the wake of contemporary movements, however, this traditional quality-of-life framework has been significantly altered. Instead of measuring factors that improve or impair quality-of-life, the notion has increasingly come to signify a means for assessing the very worth of peoples' lives.[29]

Jonathan Glover, James Rachels and Peter Singer, for example, all argue for a significant distinction between 'being alive' (a life of little or no worth) and 'having a life' (a life worth living). The first, being alive, is merely the last vestiges, the near cadaver, of biological function, and the second, having a life, is an expression of worthwhile biographical characteristics. Having a life equals personal life. This is what we really value, not mere biological life. It is this complex of psychological and emotional features that makes a life worth living, not simply being alive or barely alive. For competent patients, at least, the weighing of different considerations impacting quality-of-life is left to be determined (within broad margins) by individual patients themselves. For non-competent or incompetent patients, negative quality thresholds are effectively established for 'having a life' instead of being 'merely alive,' thresholds that justify, in some circumstances, resort to non-voluntary euthanasia.[30]

Helga Kuhse, a former colleague of Singer, is also forthright in her rejection of the sanctity-of-life tradition. In determining whether a life is worth living, for Kuhse, our attention should focus upon the preferences and dispositions of patients. For competent patients, broad ranging quality-of-life assessment is to be undertaken as to whether or not there is significant quality-of-life worth maintaining. If not, then patients should be able to opt for assisted suicide or voluntary euthanasia whether by passive or active means. Different patients may well decide differently in their individual assessments. For non-competent or incompetent patients, Kuhse appeals to a form of 'minimum personhood' standard. A life falling below this minimum quality threshold is not considered to be worth living and can be intentionally ended via non-voluntary euthanasia.[31]

John Harris advances the argument that life can only be judged valuable if a person assessing his or her life is capable of determining it to be valuable.[32] Without any significant capacity to value, there can be no value. Moreover, a life is valuable precisely to the extent that a person actually values it.[33] It follows that the primary injustice that can befall a person is to deprive him or her of a life that he or she may think valuable. Suicide, assisted suicide and voluntary euthanasia can be justified on the ground that once competency has been established, the value of life, in large measure, is left up to individuals to weigh and determine for themselves.[34] In addition to consensual death, he holds it unproblematic to justify active non-voluntary euthanasia for those who will never acquire or who have irrecoverably lost the conscious capacity to value their lives.[35]

The idea of intentionally ending life due to quality-of-life assessment is not a feature unique to utilitarian thought. Some mixed deontological systems also adopt robust quality-of-life assessment as part of their justification for assisted suicide and euthanasia. Ronald Dworkin's mixed rights-based system, for example, links the value of human life to an interpretation of what constitutes a worthwhile life via the notion of investment.[36] Dworkin claims that there is a sense in which most people think that life is 'sacred.' When they say life is sacred, they mean that personal life, able to sustain critical interests, is inherently valuable. It is this sense of life that is sacred, not mere biological life that is no longer capable of sustaining personal creativity. A valuable life, therefore, requires more than natural investment. A valuable life requires creative personal investment. Our lives are judged valuable as long as we are able to maintain and appreciate the value of this creative investment. There is no intrinsic value to be had in bodily life, only in the conscious control of life through which individuals shape their lives. When the condition of the body no longer acts in the service of this creative life of authorship, it is reasonable to intentionally seek to end life.[37]

For Dworkin, then, the quality of a person's life is crucial to forming a judgment about whether or not a life is worth preserving. That decision, at least for competent patients (within the broad brush strokes of the idea of investment), will be determined by the judgment of individual patients. For non-competent or incompetent patients, life's value is to be assessed by something akin to the idea of a minimum investment standard. The fate of a patient suffering from, say, advanced senility, is to be determined by a third party judgment as to whether or not there is sufficient actual or prospective 'investment value' worth protecting.

2.5 Arguments from Self-Determination

The basic line of argument places great store on the recognition of a widespread right, on the part of individuals, to freedom from undue paternalistic interference, especially the imposition of coercive sanctions. If an individual demands a particular right and if the right primarily affects only himself or herself then what good reason can there be for denying the recognition of this right? Decisions made by individuals that shape the course of their lives should be respected as long as they do not significantly threaten, injure or harm others. The popular influence of J. S. Mill's historical work *On Liberty* looms large here.[38]

While John Stuart Mill rejected Bentham's narrow hedonistic account of value, and opted for a eudemonistic account, he nevertheless embraced an essential pillar of Bentham's moral and political philosophy—evaluation of human actions ought to be judged according to whether or not they promoted the greatest happiness for the greatest number. Mill, however, in contrast to Bentham, was aware of the difficulty of pursuing this principle when confronting the reality of choosing amongst many different possible courses of action. Mill's solution was to focus upon the promotion of individual liberty and freedom from external constraint as the best general mechanism for increasing the overall promotion of human happiness in society. For Mill, liberty enhanced '... the permanent interests of man as a progressive being' and therefore promoted the general end of human happiness for the many.[39]

Mill's defence of liberty of action is reflected in his 'harm principle.' As he expressed it, '... the only purpose for which power can be rightfully exercised over any member of a civilised community, against his will, is to prevent harm to others. *His own good, either physical or moral is not sufficient warrant.*'[40] In terms of Mill's formulation of the harm principle, only the restraint of significant other regarding harm could justify the imposition of legal coercion on adults. The spread of human happiness in society, for Mill, is increased by the recognition of this key principle.[41]

While Mill never directly argued the point that a regulated scheme of assisted suicide or voluntary euthanasia could be permitted by the state, others in the contemporary era have advocated these ideas on the basis of his thought. Once it is admitted that there is a general liberty right to live or die as one wishes (providing one does not significantly and directly harm another individual and provided that the choice is rationally and voluntarily undertaken), it is but a short step to justify the provision of assistance in suicide or voluntary euthanasia by third parties.

Contemporary supporters of assisted suicide and voluntary euthanasia generally hold that the Millsian inspired right to self-determination is the single most important right in ethics and law and that in any conflict between this right and other rights, the right of self-determination ought to prevail. The right to self-determination is especially held to apply within the context of medical decision making. The manner, timing and circumstances of a person's death are held deeply intimate to a person's conception of what constitutes his or her well-being.[42] By unduly restricting choice concerning the manner, timing and circumstances of death, the state is said to impose paternalistic restraint by coercion, depriving people of a profound sense of their own self-worth.[43]

2.5a Rights of Ownership

A popular claim made in favor of a right to self-determination is based on the concept of ownership. If I have a right of dominion over my property, including disposal and destruction, the right of dominion can be extended to cover body parts and ultimately life itself. Self-ownership is a concept invoked to justify the freedom of the individual from the dominion of others. In a free society, the argument goes, you own your life, and your only obligation is to respect the legitimate rights of others. Everyone is entitled to be treated as the sole owner of his or her own life. Accordingly, people who choose to commit suicide (and grant permission to others to lend assistance) are within their rights to do so as long as they are being exercised without significantly jeopardizing the proprietary rights of others.[44]

John Locke is the historical figure whose influence has help shaped the language of Western property rights. For Locke, all human ownership derived from the property possessed by individuals in their own persons. Individual ownership of the body entailed ownership of all those things that were the product of the body's labor. Locke, however, did not support a right to die via suicide, for Locke held that since human beings were made by God, God's property rights could not be infringed. It was left to subsequent followers to derive a right to die from his concept of ownership.[45]

Locke's influence over property theory is keenly felt in libertarian circles. Robert Nozick, while rejecting Locke's religious argument against suicide, appropriates his theory of property, arguing that a right of full-blown self-ownership is vital if we are to protect people from the burdensome demands of state demagoguery (the secular equivalent of divine tyranny). The full-blown idea that people own themselves, their lives and their bodies, gains gusto from the fact that the idea strongly opposes dominion at the hands of God or other people. As Nozick points out, if we are not under God's dominion, and we are not slaves to be placed under the ownership of others, it follows that we must own ourselves—our labors, our skills, our bodies, and our lives.[46]

Jan Narveson, another libertarian thinker, argues that because people have the general right to do as they wish with their property, it follows that they have a right, in principle, to destroy their lives. What was once regarded as God's prerogative— the power to destroy life—is now deemed a prerogative right vested in the sovereign ownership of the individual. Moreover, because there is a right to suicide, there is no reason why assisted suicide or voluntary euthanasia cannot also legitimate practices, for property rights include the ability to transfer such permissions to others.[47]

2.5b Equal Concern and Respect

Ronald Dworkin has championed the claim that a right to make momentous personal decisions, free from coercive interference, is derived from the notion of equality of persons. In failing to respect another person's conception of what constitutes the good life, we devalue that person as a true equal. As Dworkin states in *Taking Right Seriously*, 'Government must not only treat people with concern and respect, but with *equal concern and respect*. ... It must not constrain liberty on the ground that one citizen's conception of the good life is nobler or superior to another's.'[48]

By depriving people of the opportunity to determine and act upon what life and death ultimately mean to them, we disrespect their worth. The freedom of persons to determine their own answers to questions of profound meaning is so fundamental to their sense of self and well-being, that invasive interference with this sphere of freedom is an affront to the basic dignity that ought to prevail between persons. Self-determination is regarded as a trump right that must be allowed to prevail. To do otherwise is to inform people, in the final analysis, that their most profound beliefs about themselves are ultimately either base or degrading.[49]

Since the societal enforcement of a particular conception of death, including its manner and timing, requires people to accept a conception they may deeply reject, such coercion effectively forces people to abandon their own sense of value and self-worth. For Dworkin, only choices that would deny other people a right to equal concern and treatment could plausibly offer grounds for imposing societal restrictions upon the exercise of individual liberty.[50]

In *Life's Dominion*, Dworkin directly applies his conception of equal concern and treatment to the assisted suicide debate. A right to equal concern and respect requires that we accept the right of others, in some circumstances, to end their lives intentionally. Life is a narrative, a novel, in which a person is the primary author or lead character. No person wants to 'die out of character' and lose control over the writing of the last chapter, thus '... making someone die in a way that others approve, but he believes a horrifying contradiction of his life, is a devastating, odious form of tyranny.'[51]

For Dworkin, recognition of a right to suicide and assisted suicide would give patients a basic entitlement to defend their own critical interests in the face of an overly paternalistic medical establishment committed to the relentless extension of life. Recognition of this right would represent a significant effort to empower patients with some measure of control over external forces that all too often fail to respect their profound choices over life and death questions.[52]

2.5c Idea of Personal Autonomy

The idea of personal autonomy is also central to many pro-choice accounts calling for a moral and legal right to suicide, assisted suicide and voluntary euthanasia.[53] Autonomy over a person's conception of life, supporters argue, can extend to the manner and timing of death since such an exercise in self-determination is considered to be deeply expressive of a person's core values.[54]

Joel Feinberg has advanced one of the most comprehensive accounts of the personal autonomous self. He lists the qualities that inhere in an autonomous life; qualities such as authenticity, integrity and distinct self-identity. These qualities provide a kind of overview of the self in whom these qualities inhere. The autonomous self, for Feinberg, strives to maintain self-direction in a world where external factors impinge on personal deliberations.[55]

In discussing the extent to which autonomous persons are self-created, Feinberg acknowledges social influences that help to form character and parental influences that help implant the potential for authenticity. Feinberg states that the 'moral independence' that characterizes autonomy should not be read to require non-commitment to the demands of others. In important ways, though, these provisions form the exceptions rather than the general rule. In terms of the characteristics that distinguish autonomous persons, most highlight forms of self-directedness and distinguish self-directedness from the condition of being subject to the controlling influence of others. The truly autonomous person forges his or her own tastes, opinions and values. In order to genuinely respect persons as autonomous persons, we must recognize that they are able to direct their own lives and actions in accordance with their own plans, projects and personal commitments.[56]

For Feinberg, an autonomous person can reach a choice consonant with self to be free from the burdens of life providing that the choice is genuinely an expression of the self and not the result of other factors that can radically impinge upon and distort considered judgment. Feinberg thinks that a request for assistance in suicide, for example, can be justified as long as a suitable framework is in place to ensure that the choices made by persons are genuinely reflective of their settled and abiding dispositions and are not generated by undue external or internal influences (family pressure; mental illness, etc.).[57]

In *Harm to Self*, Feinberg rejects the paternalistic idea that the state or other individuals can legitimately interfere with the mainly self-regarding interests of autonomous persons. The paternalist, by unjustly interfering with crucial self-determining choices—choices that do not significantly affect or harm the legitimate interests of others—denies them their due and treats them as subordinate beings lacking in true capacity for self-directedness. Feinberg draws on an analogy with state sovereignty to support this line of reasoning.[58] As it is part of the constitution of the nation-state to protect the state from border infringements that undermine sovereignty, so it is part of the constitution of a person to protect his or her 'personal sovereignty' from such unwelcome infringements. As Feinberg states, 'Sovereignty is an all or nothing concept: one is entitled to absolute control of whatever is within one's domain however trivial it may be.'[59]

Along with Joel Feinberg, David A. J. Richards is another liberal thinker who champions the idea of personal autonomy. Self-determination is characterized by the significant capacity persons have for personal autonomy. The moral freedom of people to shape their lives for themselves, without being subject to undue external control, is held central to the idea of respect for persons. In order to genuinely respect persons, we need to recognize an extensive autonomy derived right to choose how to live (and die). In a fashion similar to Feinberg, Richards reasons that if the value of personal autonomy is critical for self identity—of who and what we are—this core value justifies the creation of a strong negative liberty right plus a strong duty not to coerce or force others into accepting choices that are profoundly at odds with their deep sense of self identity.[60]

Richards believes that his account of personal autonomy is derived from the legacy of Immanuel Kant, not J. S. Mill, as first appearances might suggest. Kant significantly advanced the idea of the self-legislating person, even if he was far too restrictive in his attempt to characterize autonomy of deliberation and choice in purely rational terms. For Richards, underlying desires and preferences heavily shape authentic self-determining acts of willing and choosing. Contemporary personal autonomy opens up the self-governing will to a broader array of different influences, enabling persons to creatively shape and fashion their own significant ends in life.[61]

Richards ties his understanding of personal autonomy to the language of rights by stating that the core value of personal autonomy and respect for that core value constitutes the stuff of moral rights. In consequence, the only restrictions that can be placed on our actions are (a) those that manifest a lack of autonomous decision making capacity and entail significant harm or (b) directly and significantly interfere with the rights of others to make self-determining choices. By appealing to an extensive right of non-interference, Richards argues that a variety of traditional moral offences, including suicide, assisted suicide and voluntary euthanasia, should have immunity from state censure.[62]

2.5d Rationality of Intentional Suicide

The concept of personal autonomy, supporters argue, must entail the freedom to make profound constitutive choices over life and death. In order to make such a momentous self-determining decision, however, it is important to ensure that individuals have sufficient levels of awareness and control to make such an irrevocable choice. Providing individuals have (i) a demonstrable capacity to deliberate and (ii) a certain reflective independence of mind—their ultimate choices over life—within a framework of appropriate safeguards—should be respected.

'Rational' suicide as opposed to 'non-rational' or 'irrational' suicide is worked out within an instrumentalist means-ends framework for understanding rationality. 'Instrumentalism' is roughly the idea that we act rationality when we intelligently pursue our underlying ends, whatever they happen to be. Reason with a capital 'R' does not supply 'fixed ends' for us. Instead, ends are supplied by the constitutive nature of our personal desires and dispositions. Thus, If X happens to be a patient's end and Y is than most efficient and effective means for the patient to pursue X, the patient should be able to opt for Y in order to pursue X. If a patient expresses a persistent plan for self-initiated death (Y) in order to end pain and suffering (X), and is able to effectively justify that plan in the light of alternative options, suicide (Y) can be viewed as a rational means for the patient to pursue his or her end (X).[63] While caution is required in case the autonomous nature of a momentous choice is seriously compromised, for example, by depression or undue family pressure, such impediments, in many cases, will not be serious enough to invalidate the autonomous nature of a choice to commit suicide.

Margaret Battin and James Margolis, amongst others, advocate an instrumentalist approach to the rationality of suicide and assisted suicide. Battin claims that an act of suicide or assisted suicide would be rational if the suicide candidate is able to articulate a consistent worldview and is also able to articulate rational information for and against a choice to commit suicide. Providing a person can articulate these factors, and the nature of the effects that an act of suicide would have, the person has a rationally informed basis to justify suicide and to seek support from others.[64] Margolis argues that suicide can be thought of as a rational means if it is understood to be the only realistic way of enabling patients to attain settled and articulated goals. Such a form of rationality does not presuppose that patients need be in 'perfect sound mind' but that they are competent enough to grasp and explain how it is that suicide is the most efficient and effective means for them to pursue their settled and articulated goals.[65]

2.6 Rejection of Double Effect Reasoning

Ethicists in the natural law tradition often appeal to double effect reasoning in order to resolve conflict situations entailed by a clash between exceptionless moral obligations.[66] The use of double effect reasoning is especially prevalent in analysis concerning the good of human life where pursuit of one instance of that good can come into conflict with other instances of that good or with other goods. In double effect reasoning, focus is placed on the intention informing the objective of the action hence the traditional prohibition on killing is interpreted to mean no 'intentional' killing of the innocent.[67] If double effect reasoning were rejected, it would catch sanctity-of-life doctrine in the twin horns of a dilemma. Either it would need to adopt an overly rigorist approach to morality that would render sanctity-of-life doctrine impractical—no foreseeable harming of the good of life full-stop—or it would need to abandon its position on concrete moral absolutes in favour of an ethical approach that, ultimately at least, would permit the consequentialist weighing of goods in order to determine the morality of an action.[68]

2.6a Double Effect Criteria

The starting point for a discussion of double effect reasoning is often traced to Aquinas's discussion of self-defence in his *Summa theologiae*.[69] Aquinas's analysis of self-defence seems to be the first explicit discussion of double effect reasoning. In his 'two effect' analysis, Aquinas stated that it was not licit to intend to kill an aggressor. Nevertheless, while it was not licit to intentionally kill, it was licit to use lethal force to repel the aggressor's attack if the intention was not to cause the aggressor's death but simply to use proportionate force to repel the attack.[70] The modern form of the principle, as it has been refined over the years, can be stated in terms of the following necessary and sufficient criteria:

(1) the objective of the action must be morally good or indifferent in itself;
(2) the bad effect(s), though foreseeable, cannot be intended;
(3) the bad effect(s) cannot be the antecedent causal means used to achieve the good effect(s)—the good effect(s) must either causally precede or be collateral with the bad effect(s);
(4) a serious reason must exist in order to permit the causation of the foreseeable bad effect(s).[71]

Because all the criteria are deemed *necessary and sufficient* in order to justify the toleration of bad effects resulting from an action, a defect in any one of them is said to render a proposed action defective and immoral.

As the first criterion of double effect makes clear, double effect reasoning cannot be appealed to in order to justify an action that intentionally contravenes an express prohibition of the kind—'it is always wrong to intend to do X whether as a means to some further end or as an end in itself.' Thus, the intentional killing of an innocent person is said to function as an exceptionless negative prohibition, since the intended object of the action (the killing of an innocent person) is always considered wrong no matter how laudable the end or tragic the circumstances.

The second criterion is thought to express a morally relevant distinction centered on the direction of an agent's intention and the significance of that intention for determining the goodness of the action (for evil cannot be intentionally willed that good may come). The bad effect cannot be intended but can only be permitted or tolerated. If the bad effect is really intended (even along with the good effects) then this cancels out any claim to be intentionally acting only for the sake of the good.

The third criterion requires that an agent cannot seek to bring about the good effect via the antecedent causality of the bad effect. To do so would be to say that an agent can intentionally will the causation of evil in the word prior to the onset of any good effect. Good intentions are not permitted to ignore the order of causal change in the physical world.

The fourth criterion expresses the requirement that the causation of a non-intended concomitant or postcedent bad effect is not merely a neutral or irrelevant consideration to the moral assessment of an action. Responsibility does not end once the good intention of an action has been established and the order of causality is satisfied. The good effect must be sufficiently grave in reason to justify the non-intentional concomitant or postcedent causation of the bad effect(s). Lacking a sufficiently grave reason, an action may be immoral because it causes harm in the world without sufficient justification.

2.6b No Concrete Moral Absolutes

Many contemporary ethicists reject the notion that there can be concrete exceptionless moral norms that always prohibit the performance of certain types of action. The first major line of attack on double effect reasoning, therefore, is the consequentialist or mixed-system turn of denying that there can ever be concrete moral absolutes in the first place. Double effect reasoning is considered to be the unique Byzantine creation of a system of morality hedged in by rigid and inflexible moral norms of its own devising. Abolish these prohibitions and the need for double effect reasoning is removed.[72] Consequentialist systems oppose concrete moral absolutes and defend intentional killing on the basis that such killing, in some circumstances, can maximize the overall balance of good over bad consequences in the world.[73] Jonathan Glover, for example, rejects concrete moral absolutes by attacking the avoidable inhumane results, he believes, strict adherence to them would generate. For Glover, if a bystander were to answer a man's plea to shoot him and save him from the agony of his dying while trapped in the cab of a burning lorry, it would surely be right to shoot him thus breaking the concrete moral absolute against the intentional killing of the innocent.[74] To oppose such an act of killing, for Glover, would be to defend 'moral fanaticism' resulting in the needless suffering of a person for the sake of maintaining the harsh purity of an exceptionless rule.[75]

Deontological opponents of concrete moral absolutes argue that there can, all things being equal, be a strong presumption against permitting the intentional killing of the innocent. It is, however, a presumption that can be overridden given 'compelling justification,' for example, the enduring request of a competent patient to end a life of intolerable pain and suffering.[76] Defence of concrete moral absolutes, for contemporary deontologists, then, is also considered to be an unwarranted form of moral rigorism that is 'beyond the pale.'

2.6c Erroneous Act Characterization

Another attack on double effect reasoning is to challenge its basic method for analyzing the moral character of a human action. Jeremy Bentham was the historical progenitor of this line of critique.[77] For Bentham, only a hedonistic assessment of the various outcomes of an action could provide a true basis for judging the rightness or wrongness of an action. The analysis of intention was irrelevant to the objective task of weighing up the overall result of an action's positive and negative consequences. It makes no difference as to whether or not an action is said to fall under any traditionally prohibited 'kind of action.' The balance of consequences, the overall state-of-affairs produced by an action, for Bentham, was '… the right and proper, and the only right and proper and universally desirable end of human action.'[78]

James Rachels further advances Bentham's basic argument as to how the moral character of an action should be examined. We should not conflate the rightness or wrongness of actions with the goodness or badness of agents. An agent can be said to have different subjective intentions (good or bad) while the external 'signs' of an action remain exactly the same. For Rachels, the rightness or wrongness of a human action does not dependent upon how its good or bad effects are dispositionally 'embraced' by the agent. Rather, we need to address the character of rightness solely in terms of an action's extrinsic consequences.[79] Judgments of rightness and wrongness refer to the observable assessment of an action's effects in the world. Judgments of goodness and badness refer to the interior character of the agent. A good person can act wrongly out of ignorance and a bad person can act rightly if the right action coincides with his or her bad ends. The criteria of double effect reasoning, then, are said to commingle questions of rightness with goodness resulting in an inappropriate appeal to rectitude of intention while attempting to establish objective criteria for determining the rightness of actions.[80]

Jonathan Bennett further advances Bentham's basic objection to traditional moral analysis by rejecting the very meaningfulness of the common distinction drawn between an 'action' and its resultant 'consequences.' Doing X with the resultant consequence Y can be re-described as a case of doing Y. For example 'shooting a man with resultant fatality' can be re-described as 'killing Robert.'[81] What then the claim of traditional action analysis that 'action kinds' can be meaningfully distinguished from their resultant consequences? Since there is so much capacity for an 'accordion-like' re-description of an action—the potential for elision between the 'object' of an action and its resultant 'consequences'—Bennett maintains that traditional action analysis should be abandoned. Instead, ascriptions of responsibility should focus on how well people use their powers of agency to bring about change in the world by rationally comparing and choosing (planning) between different future states-of-affairs.[82]

2.6d Intention and Foresight

Glanville Williams, John Mackie and Alan Donagan, amongst others, reject the relevance of the intention/foresight distinction as a valid ground for limiting liability for bad effects. It appears absurd to say that an agent can knowingly use a means to an end that will almost (even) certainly result in death but not be said to intend that effect.[83] Examples of intention being 'narrowed' or 'stretched' so as to justify crucial moral differences are cited in order to discredit the distinction between intention and foresight. Consider, for example, the case of a fat man stuck in a mouth of a cave trapping his fellow explorers inside. The water level in the cave is quickly rising. A handy stick of dynamite is placed at the mouth of the cave and set alight. The mouth of the cave is opened and the fat man is blown to smithereens. Can defenders of the distinction really claim that the bad of the fat man's death was foreseen (even certainly) but was not intended for all that was intended was to clear the mouth of the cave?[84]

The validity of the distinction is dissolved in the minds of critics by arguing that a person reasonably intends all the consequences that predictably flow from an action. It is only in the area of uncertainty, where consequences are unforeseen or hazy, that it becomes possible to say that an effect was not intended due to lack of knowledge. Reasonably foreseeable side-effects are intended consequences. The agent is said to intend all that can reasonably be expected to flow from the action itself. Thus, if an agent performs an action with the intention of bringing about B, and it is reasonable to assume that B implies C...F, then, in order to act logically, the agent must intend both B and C...F.[85] Consider a medical example to illustrate the point. Physician X is faced with a dying patient whose cancer is quite advanced. The physician administers ever increasing doses of morphine to the patient in order to ease pain. She knows that in giving large doses of morphine to the patient, death may follow due to respiratory depression (B implies C). The physician is said to intend all the consequences that foreseeably flow from her repeated actions; both (B) the relief of pain and (C) the hastening of death.

2.6e Causal Ordering

A further critique of double effect reasoning is directed at the third criterion concerning sequences of causality. According to double effect reasoning, the bad effects of an action cannot causally precede the good effects. Thus <action> → <bad effects> → <good effects> is a prohibited causal chain. Only <action> → <good effects> → <bad effects> or <action> → <concomitant g/b effects> are permitted causal chains.[86] Yet, critics assert, why does the precise internal causal ordering of the good and bad effects of an action really matter? For the critic of causal ordering, what really matters is the overall sum of the effects generated by a course of action, not the precise internal ordering of causal patterns. Thus <action> → <bad effect> → <good effect> is as valid a pattern of causal ordering as the other two.[87]

Consider an example. A craniotomy (crushing of the skull) is performed on a foetus in order to preserve the life of the mother. The good effect of saving the mother's life (removing the obstruction) and the bad effect for the foetus (death due to skull crushing) could be viewed as 'concomitant' effects. [88] For the critic, however, what is of real significance, regardless of whether or not the two effects are causally concomitant, is the overall balance of good and bad effects that will result—the saving of one life (mother) where two lives would otherwise perish (mother and foetus). The critic of double effect reasoning thus challenges the moral relevance of causal ordering. It matters not whether B precedes G, G precedes B or G and B occur concomitantly if both B and G are foreseeable and predictable effects. All reasonably expected effects are treated in the same way—<action> → <all effects>—when determining the moral rightness of a plan of action.[89]

2.6f Veiled Consequentialism

A criticism of the fourth criterion of double effect is that it is actually consequentialist in outlook. Is the fourth criterion not really one of weighing different good and bad effects in order to reach a judgment that, on balance, more good that evil will occur? If the good consequences of an action must be proportionate with the bad consequences, is it not the case that good and bad effects are being weighed up and balanced? Peter Singer, for example, strongly voices this objection to double effect reasoning. For Singer, consequentialist reasoning is used in double effect to determine the weighing of different consequences. The preceding three criteria are said to be a distraction from an appeal to consequentialism in the last criterion.[90] An action can be considered right or wrong depending on the state-of-affairs it would likely produce. When all is said and done, double effect reasoning turns out to be heavily dependent on this key consequentialist requirement.

2.6g Acts and Omissions

A final distinction intimately linked to discussion of double effect is the distinction drawn between action (doing) and omission (allowing to happen; refraining). Michael Tooley, Judith Lichtenberg, and James Rachels, amongst others, argue for the moral irrelevancy of the distinction. A popular misconception prevalent in contemporary bioethics discourse, they argue, is the belief that truly culpable killing requires the performance of a positive act. Once we admit that intentional killing can also be performed by omission, however, then symmetry can be said to prevail between the two. Symmetry runs both ways. If it is widely regarded as legitimate to intentionally kill by omission, in some contexts, it can also be licit to intentionally kill by positive action.[91]

The standard approach to rejecting the moral relevance of the distinction is to posit two parallel cases that are deemed to be equivalent thus refuting any moral distinction between the two cases in terms of action or omission. Consider first Tooley's parallel cases. Two sons seek to inherit a substantial sum of money from their wealthy father. They both decide, independently of each other, to bring about his death by poisoning their father's favourite tipple—whisky. As one son is adding poison to the whisky decanter, the other observes and does nothing further. He allows his father to drink the whisky without intervention. Tooley concludes that both cases are, as far as common understanding goes, morally equivalent. Whether by action or omission both sons intended to kill their father for personal benefit.[92]

Positing her own two cases, Lichtenberg also contends that there is no significant moral distinction to be drawn between an action and an omission. A boat fully equipped with resources lands on a desert island where a man has been stranded for a few days. There are no significant resources on the desert island and the man is sure to die if not helped. In the first case a sailor refuses to render assistance to the stranded man in the form of provisions or a passage to safety. In the second case there is no omission but a positive act. The sailor decides to shoot and kill the man. Lichtenberg concludes that both cases are morally equivalent to each other. The stranded man is as surely killed by the decision of the sailor in the first case as he is by the sailor in the second case.[93]

Critics thus conclude that equivalence runs throughout the distinction between action and omission as nothing of real moral import can ever turn upon it. To talk of actions and omissions as if they were capable of grounding a distinction between 'killing' on the one hand and mere 'letting die' on the other is rejected as being little more than the product of confused thinking. Such confusion merely serves to detract from a proper consideration of the real determinants of moral responsibility—how we use our powers of agency, whether by action or omission, to influence different possible outcomes for the better.

2.7 Politics, Anti-Perfectionism and Neutrality

Critics of traditional sanctity-of-life doctrine direct their attention to what they see as unwarranted and continuing attempts to impose divine imperatives or thick partisan doctrine on secular political society. Such criticism has not gone unnoticed among natural lawyers. Louis Dupré, a Thomist, agues that suspicion of natural law reasoning is not difficult to understand when deeply controversial negative moral norms, for example, the 'illicitness' of artificial contraception, are paraded under the banner of natural law but seem to be held only by deeply conservative Catholics.[94]

In order to prevent the political sphere from being held hostage to such deeply contestable views of the good life, views that 'evangelically' seek to control and govern the actions of all persons—believers and non-believers, adherents and non-adherents, insiders and outsiders—the political sphere, at least, it is argued, must insulate itself from such deeply contested sources of 'right reason.' It is not the legitimate business of government in liberal society to try and make people live valuable lives or inculcate lofty ideals as determined by partisan doctrine whether based on religion or on some comprehensive metaphysical view of the nature of human beings. Neutrality of justification is required. Neutrality of justification implies that grounds for imposing restrictions and burdens on the actions of persons must not involve reference to comprehensive visions of the good life. To find valid sources of political justification, we must instead focus on the non-partisan idea of a limited kind of public rationality that alone is judged suitable for coordinating political life together in democratic society. It is illegitimate for the majority, by appealing to comprehensive doctrine, to require dissenters to accept their comprehensive view of the good.

By imposing such limitations on forms of reasoning appropriate for political dialogue, many of the major political implications of natural law theory, flowing from its moral conclusions, are held to lack legitimate political warrant. The state cannot legitimately require people to obey laws based on such a deeply contested theory of the good. Legitimacy of authority requires the establishment of 'thin rationality,' a shared underpinning that all persons—when acting politically out of concern for fair treatment—can be called upon to support.

In taking up the question of the use of reason in the political sphere, I will proceed to illustrate the kinds of way in which appeals to limited 'public reason' are being used to shape discussion over legitimate state authority by drawing on the work of two contemporary liberal theorists—John Rawls and Ronald Dworkin—and one political libertarian—H. Tristam Engelhardt, Jr.

2.7a Rawls and Public Reason

In his first significant work, *A Theory of Justice*, Rawls's major aim was to derive neutral or impartial premises upon which contemporary political society could be founded.[95] Rawls's approach was to adopt a form of contractarian pact that sought to resolve conflicts between the key values of liberty and equality. Rawls argued for an 'original position' in which individuals would be placed under a 'veil of ignorance' so that they would be unaware as to their specific interests.[96] Individuals in this original state would be instrumentally rational, free and self-interested. Principles selected in the original position, due to procedural fairness, would then be neutral in relation to various available comprehensive views and conceptions of the good.

For Rawls, two principles of political justice would emerge from the original position. First, each person would have the most extensive liberty compatible with similar liberty for others (liberty principle). Second, social and economic inequalities would be ordered so that they would be to the advantage of everyone and be attached to positions open to all (difference principle).[97] These principles would be ranked lexically so that liberty could only be restricted for the sake of liberty, and liberty concerns would need to be met first prior to addressing social and economic inequalities.

In his later work, *Political Liberalism*, Rawls sought to overcome what he judged to be certain controversial doctrinal assumptions that compromised the structure of his initial project.[98] In *Political Liberalism*, Rawls instead sought to hold on to the key tenet of neutrality yet place it on a footing that would require no 'doctrinal grounding' in 'comprehensive liberalism.'[99] Rawls now argues for a revised conception of political justice—a revision that draws upon the twin accessible principles of 'legitimacy' and 'reciprocity.'[100] The principle of legitimacy holds that '... our exercise of political power is fully proper only when exercised in accordance with a constitution the essentials of which all citizens as free and equal may reasonably be expected to endorse in the light of principles and ideals acceptable to their common human reason.'[101] The principle of reciprocity requires that persons, in interacting with others, limit justification of their positions to an appropriate framework of common shared understanding. For Rawls, terms of cooperation amongst citizens would be fair if publicly accessible reasons are offered for engagement. If reasons are to be classified as publicly accessible they cannot depend on an appeal to substantive doctrine. Citizens must not appeal to thick religious or philosophical doctrines but to a political conception of justice that is understandable and defensible apart from any particular comprehensive doctrine. Rawls's standards of legitimacy and reciprocity are judged fair because all comprehensive viewpoints can grasp that respect for citizens is properly exercised only by offering people from diverse viewpoints accessible reasons to guide and shape political action.[102] As Rawls states, concerning the content of basic standards of political justice, we can only appeal to '... presently accepted general beliefs and forms of reasoning found in common sense, and the methods and conclusions of science when these are not controversial.'[103]

Rawls's central project, then, is to demonstrate that public reason is necessarily heavily restricted in scope. Appeals to substantive doctrine, moving beyond the limits of the publicly reasonable, are illegitimate because they fail to respect the 'fact of reasonable pluralism.'[104] The need for accessibility excludes claims from private sources of knowledge as well as claims that are decidedly metaphysical in nature. All persons, believers and non-believers alike, must be treated in a manner compatible with an appeal to the limited scope of public reason.[105]

By constructively engaging in the challenge of dealing with our political problems in a publicly reasonable manner, Rawls thinks we can develop 'circles of overlapping consensus' that can form a cohesive enough social glue sufficient to hold diverse societal viewpoints together. Since policy is erected on the foundation of public reason, people are respected in their ability to forge patterns of consensus concerning assisted suicide and euthanasia and many other areas of disagreement.[106] For Rawls, appeals to traditional sanctity-of-life doctrine could not form the basis for publicly reasonable discourse over life and death questions. Legislation banning assisted suicide and euthanasia informed by comprehensive doctrine would not satisfy the requirements of public reasonableness. People who hold alternative comprehensive views could not be fairly expected to endorse it. Thick doctrine, if used as a source of political justification, would not satisfy the rules of engagement governing respectful dialogue with other citizens.[107]

2.7b Dworkin and the Politically Reasonable

For Dworkin, the basis for politically reasonable discourse is the notion of equal concern and respect. Viewpoints that seek to discount the fact of reasonable disagreement over deeply contestable questions, for example, the status and significance of human life, fail to treat their fellow citizens with equal concern and respect. Citizens should accept a form of political discourse that moderates and restricts their power to enforce their own views over the good life, otherwise, standing in opposition to the fact of reasonable disagreement, they would unreasonably be imposing their viewpoints on their fellow citizens.[108]

Dworkin defends the liberal view that the state ought to be neutral with regard to an assessment of different incompatible ways of life. When faced with the reality of deep disagreement, the notion of equal concern and respect strongly points towards the empowerment of individual decision making. In *Life's Dominion*, Dworkin contends that certain key life issues are essentially governed by incompatible doctrines and that answers to such questions cannot be determined by resort to coercive state power. Failure to respect neutrality would result in the unfair privileging of one group's view of the good at the expense of violating another group's entitlement to equality of treatment and worth.[109] Dworkin examines two key areas of value conflict—abortion and euthanasia—believing that deep principled disagreement over the value of life plus respect for liberty of conscience, empowers individuals to make their own choices. The meaning of the value of life is such a deeply contestable topic, open to many divergent viewpoints—viewpoints that can express sophisticated defences—that it is unreasonable for one viewpoint to seek to impose its account over all other viewpoints.[110] For Dworkin, as with Rawls, the fact of pluralism requires the suspension of seeking to impose thick fundamental viewpoints. Instead, it directs attention to finding common political principles—i.e. freedom to act on the dictates of one's own conscience—principles that are broad enough to encourage different groups to live together respectfully and fairly as they face up to the reality of public life together under conditions of pluralism.

It is interesting to note that both Rawls and Dworkin were co-authors (with four others) of a *Philosophers' Brief* on the topic of assisted suicide written in 1997.[111] In that *Brief*, there is a clear emphasis, in the face of competing theories about the value and meaning of life, that it would be politically unreasonable for the state to privilege one account of the meaning and purpose of life over another. By prohibiting the option for assisted suicide, for example, it is claimed that the state adopts a sectarian viewpoint and denies the legitimacy of other deeply held viewpoints concerning the value and meaning of life. Such a sectarian display would fall afoul of the basic requirement that the state should treat all its citizens with equal concern and respect. The solution, within boundaries, is to facilitate self-determination over the question of the manner and timing of death.

2.7c Engelhardt and Procedural Rationality

Rawls and Dworkin are not alone in their scepticism concerning a sense of thick rationality by which to morally underpin our shared political life together. Engelhardt is similarly convinced that there is no light to be cast on the question of a common thick source of rationality. His claims for public life, however, are decidedly more minimalist than Rawls's and Dworkin's. Engelhardt would hold that their notions of public reason are still too contentful in seeking to provide a common source of justification for the construction of a valid political framework.[112]

Engelhardt, in common with Rawls and Dworkin, points to the problems faced by any of the existing moral theories and traditions to come up with rationally compelling grounds for adopting their substantive viewpoints in contemporary pluralistic society. If ever there were a golden age of robust shared standards, for example, the age of Christian hegemony, it has long gone. These approaches can provide a common frame of reference only for those who accept their assumptions, for instance, Christian or Muslim faith communities that recognize the authority and binding nature of the *Bible* or the *Koran*. Since these thick sources of normative appeal are not shared by others, however, they can have no public status and thus no public warrant.[113]

In the face of intractable moral disagreement between individuals, Engelhardt proposes a retreat to an entirely contentless procedural platform, a minimalist version of social contract theory that can inform minimal standards of political cooperation. Since there is no substantive conception of the good upon which to model the state, it must be replaced by an entirely artificial procedural construct. This construct is necessarily a limited one in which 'moral strangers' can work to agree upon minimal obligations. He adopts a kind of 'state of nature' approach in which the 'principle of permission' becomes operative. Permission is a brute fact of political life and does not depend on any substantive or thick conception of autonomy to justify its relevance.[114]

On Engelhardt's account, 'moral strangers' would jealously guard against the imposition of substantive values, for example, a hegemonic sense of the meaning of life itself and thus control over an individual's self-regarding death. Laws banning assisted suicide and euthanasia would not be legitimate for such laws would not be consented to by those who share profoundly different viewpoints over the meaning and significance of life. For Engelhardt, the operative condition of permission legitimates and underpins the entire political enterprise. Without consent there is no legitimacy to state action.[115] Since individuals would jealously guard power to determine for themselves what the value of life means to them, power to restrict would not be transferred to the comprehensive control of the state. By stressing the principle of permission in the face of incompatible diversity, Engelhardt's construct seeks to provide a key justification for limiting the authority of the state to impose a contestable view of the good life. The principle of permission is permissive in allowing consenting people to perform a wide array of actions (providing they are not directly harmful to the legitimate interests of others who have not consented), but also restrictive in that it does not allow the imposition of thick theories upon those who do not consent to them.[116]

2.7d Political Implications for Natural Law

In the thought of Rawls, Dworkin and Engelhardt, despite divergences of approach, we can nevertheless observe the presence of common anti-perfectionist ideas used to construct a 'neutral vision of the state' that opposes the privileging of one theory of the good life over other competing theories of the good life. All oppose appeals to any thick or substantive vision of the good as the basis for informing shared political life together. In the face of moral disagreement, all resort to the adoption of 'thin' forms of reasoning; forms of reasoning alone judged suitable for the task of determining the basic rules of political engagement independent of any substantive theory about the good.[117] All reach the conclusion that forms of reasoning suitable for political engagement cannot reasonably justify a state policy opposed, in principle, to the legality of assisted suicide or voluntary euthanasia, for such a 'perfectionist viewpoint,' under conditions of accessible shared rationality, would lack public legitimacy.

For Rawls, Dworkin and Engelhardt, the case for neutrality, built on the advocacy of accessible forms of political reason, establishes some pretty blunt conclusions for the continuing relevancy of thick natural law reasoning to public life.[118] Since natural law is held to be comprehensive doctrinal reasoning about human goods and the ends of worthwhile action, such reasoning simply cannot meet the publicly accessible conditions required for the respectful coordination of public life together. Because natural law is held to invoke controversial comprehensive doctrine about the ends of human well-being, it cannot, without resort to illegitimacy, ground the basis for determining what the content of public policy over hotly contested issues like assisted suicide or voluntary euthanasia ought to be.

Notes

1 David Hume (1998). The essay was first published in 1783.
2 Hume (1998).
3 See Hume (1998) for his essay *Of the Immortality of the Soul*. The essay was also published in 1783. For a contemporary assessment of arguments over the natural immortality of the soul see Don T. Asselin (1995), pp. 17–27.
4 Hume (1998). See also Tom L. Beauchamp (1976), R. G. Frey (1999) and Margret P. Battin (1998) and (2005). On the Roman Catholic Church's traditional teaching see Niceto Blázquez (1985) and Robert Barry (1994).
5 Dan W. Brock (1986), (1993) and (1998); Helga Kuhse (1987) and (1998); James Rachels (1986). See also Peter Singer's opposition to sanctity–of–life doctrine in Singer's (2002) collection edited by Kuhse.
6 Brock (1986) and (1993); Kuhse (1987).
7 See for example Battin (1998), pp. 114–30, 212–15; Marvin Kohl (1974), pp. 3–38; Glanville Williams (1968), 311–28; Kuhse (1987), 311–28; R. A. Duff (1973), pp. 16–19.
8 Kohl (1974), pp. 28–31. See also David Wasserman (1987) .
9 Aquinas, for example, sought to justify capital punishment by arguing that the criminal becomes lower than a beast and could be killed, for 'By sinning man departs from the order of reason, and consequently falls away from the dignity of his manhood ...' See his *Summa Theologiae*, II–11, q. 64, a. 2, ad 3.
10 See Philip E. Devine (2000a) for a discussion of the sanctity-of-life tradition and the topic of capital punishment.
11 On the Stoics and the Epicureans see Ron M. Brown (2001), pp. 21–48; Paul Carrick (2001), pp. 147–72; Anton J. L. Van Hooff (1990).
12 As G. E. M. Anscombe (1958) noted, these are the dominant contemporary forms of ethical theory. 'Mixed system' deontologists often permit the non-consensual intentional killing of the innocent in extraordinary circumstances and therefore do not 'escape' from the 'logic of consequentialism' in those extraordinary situations. See discussion in *sect.* 4.7.
13 Brock (1986).
14 Jeremy Bentham (1979), p. 33. Original emphasis.
15 The comparison with Hume is made by James Rachels (1986), p. 19. See also Mary P. Mack (1963), pp. 112–13, 213.
16 Mack (1963), pp. 112–13. See also James E. Crimmins (1990), pp. 76, 258. Bentham has a strong disregard for natural law and natural rights approaches to legislation, regarding them as 'nonsense on stilts.' See Ross Harrison (1983), pp. 77–8.

17 J. J. C. Smart (1973), pp. 1–25. See also D. W. Hodgson (1967), ch. 2.

18 See Singer (1993), (1994) and (1998).

19 Matti Häyry (1994), pp. 63–6.

20 Singer (1993), p. 12.

21 Singer (1993), ch. 1. See also (1994), chs 4 and 6; Kuhse and Singer (1985).

22 Tom L. Beauchamp and James F. Childress (1994).

23 Beauchamp and Childress (1994), pp. 219–38.

24 W. D. Ross (1930) and (1939).

25 Ross (1939), pp. 40–42, 316–25. See also Jonathan Dancy (1993), pp. 219–29.

26 Charles Fried (1978), pp. 7–28.

27 Bernard Gert, Charles Culver and K. Danner Clouser (1997), pp. 15–50.

28 Gert, Culver and Clouser (1997), pp. 279–306.

29 Hadley Arkes (1997), pp. 421–33. See also the essays in James J. Walter and Thomas A. Shannon, eds (1990).

30 See Jonathan Glover (1977), pp. 51–3, 158–62, 192–4; Rachels (1986), pp. 60–77; Singer (1993), ch.7.

31 Kuhse (1987), pp. 198–220.

32 John Harris (1985), pp. 64–86, 87–110. See also Harris (1997).

33 As Harris states (1997), p. 11, '… the value of our lives is the value we give to our lives.'

34 Harris, (1985), pp. 64–86.

35 Since they are 'non-persons'—incapable of valuing their lives—the active as well as passive killing of profoundly damaged newborns and PVS patients can be countenanced. As Harris (1997), p. 9 states, '… death does not deprive them of anything they can value. If they cannot wish to live, they cannot have that wish frustrated by being killed.'

36 Ronald Dworkin (1993), pp. 68–101.

37 Dworkin (1993), pp. 199–213.

38 David A. J. Richards (1981), (1982) and (1986).

39 John Stuart Mill (1962).

40 Mill (1962), p. 135. My emphasis.

41 On self–regarding actions in Mill see C. L. Ten (1968), pp. 29–37 and (1980), ch. 7. See also some of the essays in Gerald Dworkin, ed. (1997).

42 Brock (1993), p. 206.

43 Harris (1997), p. 11, 'The point of autonomy , the point of choosing and having the freedom to choose between competing conceptions of how, and indeed why, to live, is simply that it is only thus that our lives become in any real sense our own.'

44 See Roger F. Friedman (1995).

45 Gary D. Glenn (1984).

46 Robert Nozick (1974), pp. 171–2.

47 See Jan Narveson (1983), pp. 240–53 and (1999), chs 2 and 3.

48 Ronald Dworkin (1977), pp. 272–3. My emphasis.

49 Dworkin (1985), pp. 190–91, 205–6, 364–7.

50 Dworkin (1996), pp. 130–46.

51 Dworkin (1993), p. 217.

52 Dworkin (1993), pp. 119–30, 190–95.

53 See, for example, discussions by Janet E. Smith (1997), pp. 182–95 and Ian N. Olver (2002), ch. 4.

54 Richards (1981), pp. 3–20 and (1982), pp. 59–62.

55 Joel Feinberg (1986), pp. 27–51 and (1989), pp. 27–49. See also (1992), pp. 260–82.

56 Feinberg (1989), pp. 27–53.

57 See Feinberg (1978).

58 Feinberg (1986), pp. 52–7.

59 Feinberg (1986), p. 55.

60 Richards (1981), (1982) and (1986).

61 Richards (1981), pp. 10–11. See also (1987).

62 Richards (1982), pp. 174–7 and (1981), pp. 11–17.

63 Richard B. Brandt (1980), 117–32. The rationality of suicide approach finds historical justification in the thought of David Hume. Hume was opposed to the idea that reason could objectively discover or establish the normative ends of all worthwhile human action. There are no reason-ordained ultimate ends. His instrumental account of practical reason—reasoning about human action—held that the sole function of reason is to serve our constitutive passions (desires) whatever they happen to be. The essential thrust of the Humean model of practical reason—contrasted with Aristotelian and Kantian models of practical reason—is that our final desires and preferences cannot be judged 'contrary to reason.' Categories of rational and irrational apply only to the election of means whereby we seek to pursue our ends.

64 Battin (1998), pp. 132–53 and (2005), pp. 17–46.

65 James Margolis (1975), pp. 24–8. See also James L. Werth (1999).

66 See Joseph Boyle (1998), pp. 72–9.

67 For discussion of double effect and the killing of the innocent see Boyle (1989). See also Suzane M. Uniacke (1984), pp. 188–218 and (1994), ch. 4.

68 Charles Fried points out that rigorism leads to the evils of non-action or contradiction. See (1978), pp. 15–16. Fried endorses a consequentialist override clause in disaster situations. See also Peter Byrne (1990), pp. 131–60.

69 *Summa theologiae* II–II, q. 64, a. 7. Actually, implicit appeal to double effect reasoning goes back much further than Aquinas. Socrates' analysis, in *The Phaedo*, of his decision to impose the Athenian death penalty upon himself by taking hemlock may be interpreted as implied case of double effect reasoning. Augustine's analysis of martyrdom also makes implied use of double effect reasoning when assessing the legitimacy of self-sacrifice. On some of the history of double effect reasoning see Anthony J. P. Kenny (1973) and (2001) and Thomas A. Cavanaugh (2006), ch. 1.

70 On the use of double effect by Aquinas see Alfred Wilder (1995), pp. 571–80 and Kenny (2001), ch. 4.

71 The precise wordings used here are adapted from various contemporary discussions of the principle.

72 For example R. G. Frey (1975); Shelly Kagan (1991), ch. 4; Alison McIntyre (2001). Warren S. Quinn (1989b) takes the position that double effect reasoning also applies to non-absolutist moral systems. Determining whether or not a harm was deliberately intended, irrespective of moral absolutes, can be a matter of significant moral concern.

73 For example Kai Nielsen (1990), pp. 128–62.

74 Glover (1977), p. 90, mentioning a case first posed by H. L. A. Hart.

75 Glover (1977), pp. 86–91, on double effect. See also Nielsen (1990), pp. 113–27.

76 See for example Howard Brody (1992) and (1993). For Brody, the intentional killing of a terminally ill person who endures a life of intractable pain and suffering would be a compelling circumstance for resort to voluntary euthanasia.

77 Gerald J. Postema (1986), pp. 308–13.

78 Bentham (1979), p. 33.

79 See also R. E. Bales (1971).

80 Rachels (1986), pp. 92–6. See also (1975) and (1993).

81 Jonathan Bennett (1968).

82 See Bennett (1968), (1981) and (1995).
83 Glanville Williams (1968), pp. 286–90; Alan Donagan, (1977), pp. 163–4 ; J. L. Mackie (1977), pp. 160–68.
84 See Philippa Foot (1978), p. 21.
85 Roderick Chisholm (1970), pp. 636–40.
86 Alison McIntyre (2001) clearly acknowledges causal sequencing as an important integral condition of double effect reasoning.
87 Bennett (1995), ch. 11, regards causal ordering within an action as being irrelevant to moral analysis.
88 Joseph Boyle (1977), pp. 303–18. A similar conceptual example is the proposed performance of an operation to separate conjoined twins. See Benedict Guevin (2001).
89 Mackie (1977), pp. 160–68; Rachels (1986), pp. 92–6; Harris (1985), pp. 43–5. See also Justin Oakley and Dan Cocking (1994), pp. 201–16.
90 Singer (1993), pp. 209–12.
91 Michael Tooley (1994), pp. 103–11 and (1995), pp. 305–22; Judith Lichtenberg (1982), pp. 19–36; Rachels (1986), chs 7 and 8.
92 Tooley (1994).
93 Lichtenberg (1982).
94 Louis Dupré (1988), pp. 241–4.
95 John Rawls (1971), pp. 11–17.
96 Rawls (1971), pp. 17–22.
97 Rawls (1971), pp. 60–65.
98 Rawls (1985).
99 Rawls (1996), pp. 191–4.
100 Rawls (1996), pp. xliv–xlvi.
101 Rawls (1996), p. 137.
102 Rawls (1996), pp. 15–22.
103 Rawls (1996), p. 224.
104 Rawls (1996), p. 24.
105 See Rawls's chapter on public reason (1996), pp. 212–54.
106 See Rawls (1996), pp. 133–72.
107 For discussion of Rawls's more recent work see Chandran Kukathas, ed. (2003).
108 See Ronald Dworkin (1977), pp. 272–3; (1985), pp. 190–91, 205–6, 364–7; (1996), pp. 10–36.
109 On Dworkin and neutrality see Jan Narveson and Susan Dimock (2000), pp. 41–58.
110 On death and dying see Dworkin (1993), ch. 7.
111 Dworkin *et al.* (1997), pp. 41–7.
112 H. Tristram Engelhardt (1996), pp. 11–17. See also discussion of Engelhardt's work by Brendan Minogue, Gabriel Palmer-Fernandez and James E. Reagan (1997).
113 Engelhardt (1996), pp. 40–64.
114 Engelhardt (1996), pp. 103–21.
115 Englehardt (1997), pp. 101–8.
116 Engelhardt (1996), pp. 68–74.
117 Although, as I have recognized when discussing Engelhardt (*sect.* 2.7c), not all accounts of public rationality are viewed as being equally 'thin' in terms of their basic assumptions.
118 As well as other 'communitarian' forms of comprehensive reasoning.

Chapter 3

A Revised Natural Law Ethics

3.1 Introduction

Having reached this point in the book, the reader may well think there is a strong case to answer concerning the moral and legal permissibility of assisted suicide and at least some forms of euthanasia. Some of the arguments laid out in the previous chapter are very strongly crafted. Moral debate would not run so deep or generate such public interest if there were broad agreement on the moral standing of these practices or if the arguments in favor of permissibility patently lacked merit. As strong as the cumulative case might seem, however, I'm sure that the reader is well aware that I would not be writing on the topic of assisted suicide and euthanasia from a natural law ethics perspective if I thought that these practices were morally or politically justifiable. A supporter of the parliamentary debating tradition, I sought to present to the reader the main opposing arguments first before turning to the major task of explaining and defending, in the light of these arguments, my own revised natural law approach to the ethics of intentional killing. The scope of the task is such that it necessary for me to break down my natural law responses into several more manageable components. In this chapter I will develop the general rudiments of my revised approach to natural law ethics. Chapter 4 then proceeds to examine in detail the status and significance of the primary good of human life, exploring its implications for a consistent ethic of killing. The following chapters—Chapters 5 and 6—apply natural law reasoning to a detailed examination of the moral status of suicide, assisted suicide and different forms of euthanasia. Finally, Chapter 7 turns to the political and legal sphere and seeks to counter arguments designed to 'neuter' the contribution of natural law reasoning to public policy formation in secular pluralistic society.

3.2 Secular not Supernatural

One of the biggest credibility burdens facing natural law ethics is the need to address the widespread conviction that natural law ethics is essentially a 'creature' of religion, that despite claims to be grounded in natural reason alone, it is, in fact, 'supernaturally' grounded. This widespread assumption is fueled by (i) the fact that the largest institutional defender of natural law ethics has been and continues to be the Roman Catholic Church; (ii) the fact that most authors who write about natural law ethics just happen to be Catholic.

In response, let me caution the reader to be wary of the all too human propensity to dismiss arguments because of their past or present associations. Certainly it is understandable that suspicions are aroused. But suspicion alone *is not* conclusive argument. It is invalid to infer: (a) that because some arguments A, B, C ... advanced by a religious body turn out to be based on religious assumptions that *all* arguments advanced by that body must be similarly compromised; or (b) that any independent reappraisal of A, B, C ... based on *secular reason alone* is not possible.

The task, then, is to work out and distinguish which arguments are based on independent secular grounds from arguments that either explicitly or implicitly trade on the supernatural in order to have normative content. By engaging in a fresh revision of natural law ethics, I hope to be able to convince the reader that not all forms of natural law are 'irredeemably religious' in nature and hence 'beyond the pale' for 'non-believing secularists.'[1]

Two historically influential religiously inspired arguments that can be set aside from further consideration are (a) the 'condition of the soul' argument and (b) the 'dominion of life' argument. Both arguments are Platonic in origin.[2]

The 'condition of the soul' argument is really based on premises supplied from faith not reason. First, there are no plausible metaphysical arguments offered that can successfully demonstrate how it is that a truly 'personal' soul can survive the destruction of the body and yet maintain continuity with the person that was.[3] Second, even if we were to concede for the purpose of argument that we have a personal immortal soul, this 'ontological fact' alone cannot justify the prohibition on suicide supported by subsequent natural law tradition. Just how do we get from the very idea that the personal soul is immortal to a resolute declaration that the 'spiritual' condition of the soul cannot be improved by releasing the soul from conditions of pain and suffering? Why can it not be argued that a bodily life of misery and pain instrumentally impairs rather than improves the spiritual condition of the soul? Much more needs to be assumed *on other than philosophical grounds* in order to inject appeals to personal immortality with such normative content. Claims concerning the condition of the soul really turn on religious not philosophical assumptions, whether supplied in Plato's case by Pythagorean Mysticism combined with Greek pietism or in the case of Christian thinkers by faith in the God of Abraham and Isaac.[4]

The argument from dominion is no more successful that the first argument. First there are profound problems with ontological arguments that seek to demonstrate the existence of a God endowed with the traditional attributes of omnipotence, omniscience, omnipresence, and beneficence. Second, even assuming that that some of the philosophical proofs offered for the existence of God were found to be convincing, how does this help the case regarding what is and is not held to be compatible with God's will regarding stewardship of his creation? Why must suicide necessarily be held incompatible with due respect for his dominion over human life? Could he not use suicide as his instrument for releasing people from their terrible burdens of pain and suffering? As with the condition of the soul argument, the dominion argument, in order to have normative content, relies and trades upon privileged faith-based content. Remove the legitimacy of such appeals, however, and the dominion argument, as with the condition of the soul argument, is not capable of functioning as a genuine secular ground for opposing the intentional ending of human life via suicide.

3.3 Non-natural not Natural

A key area in which my account of natural law is undoubtedly revisionist concerns its negative assessment of ethical naturalism as a viable meta-ethical foundation—the belief that ethical norms can be accounted for in entirely non-moral terms; that ethical properties can be reduced to a fact-based analysis of natural properties.[5]

One of the curiosities of intellectual thought is the ability we have to benefit from the thought of different thinkers and traditions, opening ourselves up to being 'persuaded' by the rational power of their ideas and arguments. Curiously, I wonder how it is that post-modernist thinkers reject the idea that human discourse lacks any power to rationally persuade, while they simultaneously devote pages of text to the task of seeking to convince opponents of the veracity of their own positions. Jumping over the 'post-modernist paradox,' we can see in the thought of David Hume an excellent example of a thinker who, notwithstanding his own decidedly sceptical tendencies, nevertheless advanced belief in the power of argument to rationally influence people across different traditions of intellectual inquiry. In 3.2 above, I have already made use of Humean inspired 'trans-historical' and 'trans-cultural' arguments against opposition to suicide in order to question the secular legitimacy of 'supernatural law ethics.' Now, I turn to make use of another Humean inspired line of argument that takes to task a significant meta-ethical feature of 'traditional' natural law theory—the 'is/ought' problem also known as the 'fact/value' distinction.

In the first book of his *Treatise of Human Nature*, Hume described the distinction between 'is' and 'ought' and the logical non-derivability of the latter from the former. Hume's central point was that if you want to give a valid argument for a normative conclusion you will need to start, at the very outset, with a normative premise. Thus, from non-normative premises (about what 'is'), we cannot derive a normative conclusion (about what 'ought-to-be' or conversely about what 'ought-not-to-be').[6] The central thrust of Hume's objection to naturalistic appeals can be best explained by means of an example. Imagine that you are trying to prove the status of an ethical proposition:

(a) *I ought to do X.*
   Imagine also that you are a traditional natural lawyer.
   The premise by which you seek to derive (a) is:
(b) *My natural inclinations tell me to pursue X.*
   Yet (a) does not follow from (b).
   To make a valid inference an extra premise must be added:
(c) *My natural inclinations tell me to pursue X therefore I ought to pursue X.*

The problem with the leap from (b) to (a) is that a moral norm cannot be derived unless moral norms are already included (c) as part of the premises of the argument. The conclusion of a valid syllogism cannot contain terms that do not appear in the premises. A proposition involving an 'ought' cannot be deduced from premises that are, so to speak, 'ought-less.' We cannot derive (a) from (b) unless we explicitly introduce the (c) premise which begs the 'is-ought' problem.[7]

Further development of this line of objection directed at naturalistic ethics was advanced by G. E. Moore. Moore contended that adherence to ethical naturalism wrongly sought to reduce the normative to the non-normative thereby rejecting the genuinely distinctive character of autonomous ethical inquiry. In *Principia Ethica*, by means of his 'open-question argument,' Moore argued that reductionism was untenable because it entailed an illicit attempt to 'explain away' the distinctive nature of 'goodness' by asserting that 'X is good' means that 'X is equivalent to natural property Y.'[8] Take any naturalistic definition of an ethical term (good is defined as X, Y, Z, where X, Y, Z are desires, inclinations or any other natural property). It is always an intelligible and open question to ask: 'you define X, Y, Z as good (or bad) but is X, Y, Z good (or bad)'? If good really meant X, Y, Z as a natural property, as naturalism claims, then this should not be a meaningfully open question to subsequently pose. Instead, it should be an unintelligible or closed question.

Suppose 'X is bad' stands for 'X frustrates or thwarts a natural inclination,' as in traditional natural law, it is an entirely reasonable (open) question to ask: 'X (suicide) frustrates or thwarts our natural inclination towards Y (preserving life), but is it bad'? The question cannot be closed by making further appeals to the natural properties of human nature. To say that X is bad because 'X helps realise the natural ends of human nature' merely invites the inquirer to pose the further question: 'why is it bad to act against the natural ends of human nature'?

The way to more fully appreciate the import of Moore's open-question argument is to consider our ordinary use of language. Moore is not simply referring to the fact that a naturalistic answer to the question is deemed open only in the sense that posing the further question is logically possible. The frame of reference for Moore's open-question argument is not merely the realm of the possible but the plausible. The idea of openness relates to the *plausible openness* of a naturalistic account of good framed as an ordinary language question—of how ordinary people in their linguistic discourse use and understand the concept of good and its cognates.[9] Moore's open-question argument holds naturalistic argumentation to account at the bar of ordinary language usage. We can understand all the natural properties of a thing but still plausibly question the transition made from the non-normative to the normative. Ordinary people, in their modes of speaking, can and do understand the point that normative propositions have a truly unique status unlike anything else, a status that cannot be accounted for or otherwise explained away by attempting to reduce the non-natural to the natural. Because ordinary people in their linguistic usages do not find the very idea of distinctive moral properties 'beyond the pale,' they are, in consequence, much more receptive to the idea that 'good' has a unique status that cannot be absorbed or otherwise reduced to description expressed in purely natural terms.[10]

Thomistic natural law thinkers like Heinrich Rommen, Jacques Maritain, Henry Veatch, and Ralph McInerny, amongst others, all seek to derive or deduce moral norms from factual-descriptive interpretations of human nature. They argue that practical reasoning (*ratio practica*)—reasoning about what ought-to-be-done by the agent—necessarily hinges on 'theoretical' or 'speculative' reasoning—reasoning about the 'is' of human nature. Normative succedents are, so to speak, derived from a factual study of descriptive antecedents.[11]

Rommen, Maritain, Veatch, and McInerny all argue that Thomas Aquinas's first principle of practical reason—'*bonum est faciendum et prosequendum et malum vitandum*' ('good is to be done and pursued and evil avoided')—is really a moral command incumbent on agents to pursue and promote the given trajectories or functions of human nature. The starting points of practical reason are normative conclusions already deduced from prior speculative inquiry. Justification of the 'ought' and therefore of ethics resides in the general pursuit of naturally given ends. Acts in conformity with natural human ends, as apprehended by theoretical reason, are judged morally good, and acts not in conformity with natural ends are judged morally bad.

These Thomistic approaches to meta-ethics are naturalistic in structure, not because they somehow embody fundamentally flawed interpretations of Aquinas's moral thought, as some interpreters allege, but because Aquinas's thought, in faithful Aristotelian fashion, also displays a strong commitment to ethical naturalism in the form of seeking to derive or deduce moral oughts from a study of the *inclinationes naturales* of human nature.[12]

Having first established the importance of apprehending the ordering of an inclination towards its natural end, Aquinas proceeds to argue that these inclinations are normative for us, are good, because the ends they fulfill are judged by reason to be properly natural. Understand the built-in purposes of human nature and you understand the normative force of these inclinations. It is thus wrong, for example, to intentionally end human life because the natural inclination to preserve life *qua* natural ought not to be thwarted or interfered with. Suicide is wrong because it is held to be 'unnatural' to act against the naturally apprehended inclination to preserve human life.[13] Aquinas also invokes the charge of '*vitia contra naturam*' ('contrary to nature') as a means of arguing against the licitness of certain sexual practices— masturbation, sodomy, etc.[14] Aquinas's contrary to nature argument is functionalist because it is based on the supposition that it is illicit to interfere with the ordering of a natural inclination towards its given end. If intentional actions involving the sexual organs accord with natural teleology they are judged fitting and virtuous, if not, they are judged unfitting and vicious. Similarly, if intentional actions help promote and preserve human life they are judged fitting and virtuous, if not, they are judged unfitting and vicious. Grasp the natural ordering of a given inclination and actions that intentionally promote its natural ordering are good and actions that intentionally thwart its natural ordering are bad.

Thomists typically respond to the charge of 'naturalistic fallacy' in three general ways. One response is to deny the existence of the fallacy in the first place. The fallacy is itself fallacious. Acceptance of the fallacy is a sign of the extent to which epistemological scepticism, following Hume, has gravely distorted the landscape of modern and contemporary ethical theory. Ralph McInerny, for example, calls the 'the alleged naturalistic fallacy' the stuff of 'nonsense.'[15] Another line of response is to argue that since facts must be related to norms, for the two do not belong to separate parallel universes, the naturalistic fallacy must be ill conceived. A third line of response accepts the validity of the naturalistic fallacy insofar as 'a good X is said to be defined in terms of X possessing natural property Y'—type A naturalism—but rejects the applicability of the fallacy to claims that 'a good X and natural property

Y just are one and the same thing'—type B naturalism. Since good is not being defined in terms of the possession of natural properties, the charge of engaging in reductionism does not apply to type B naturalism.[16]

The first line of response is inadequate for it often amounts to little more than an *ad hominem* dismissal of an argument because of its source, Hume, the *bête noire* of Thomism, falsely assuming that because Hume was an epistemological sceptic all arguments advanced by him must somehow necessitate acceptance of his far reaching scepticism. On the contrary, support for the naturalistic fallacy is not synonymous with support for ethical scepticism, for naturalism, crucially, is not the only basis we have for objectively seeking to ground objective sources of normativity. Acceptance of the naturalistic fallacy, then, does not equate to cognitive defeat at the hands of subjectivism or emotivism.

The second line of response has more bite to it, for it forces the supporter of the naturalistic fallacy to address how facts are related to norms (in a non-haphazard and orderly fashion). Yet, upon further investigation it too will be found wanting. Grounding norms are related to natural facts but not by way of attempting to deduce or derive the former from the latter. First, facts furnish us with the data of possibility (or impossibility). As Immanuel Kant said, 'ought implies can.' With life we have the possibility of experiencing; with sight we have the possibility of viewing many different visual sensations, and so on. Without the facts of nature, we cannot pursue health, knowledge, play, beauty, and so on. No supporter of the naturalistic fallacy, therefore, need be committed to the untenable position that facts are 'ethically irrelevant.' If facts create the wings of possibility, they also burn away the wings of possibility. Because I am not a 'little god' I do not have super-human powers. Because I cannot be in two places at the same time, I cannot simultaneously bathe and study in the library, and so on.

Facts are also indispensable for fleshing out the demands of established normative premises, for example, normative premises derived from prior normative premises ultimately traceable back to the primary fonts of morality—underived normative starting points. Granted, for the purpose of argument, that there is a normative duty not to intentionally kill another human being, it is a crucially relevant fact that X is indeed a living human being and not a cat or a mouse. Granted further that there is a 'good Samaritan' obligation to help rescue a drowning human being, I am, unless there is an acceptable excuse, bound to render assistance. Here it is ethically relevant to know whether I knew that a fellow human being was drowning and that I had the physical capacity to be able to render effective assistance in circumstances that would not have gravely imperilled my own life.

Supporters of the naturalistic fallacy, then, are not committed to some kind of Spinozan 'parallelism' of building and defending an impossible wall of separation between the world of facts and the world of norms, for, as we have seen, facts implicate norms and norms implicate facts in many ethically relevant and complex ways. What this analysis crucially does not support, however, is the claim that grounding norms can be derived, inferred or otherwise deduced from prior theoretical inquiry into the structures of human nature. The idea that there is a built-in normative structure to natural properties only appears plausible, I think, because it trades on a misleading understanding of the relationship between 'nature' and 'reason.' Nature sets limits upon what is possible for human beings to value as 'goods for us.' Beyond this parameter-setting, however, practical rationality has the crucial task of working out and establishing what constitutes worthwhile goods for human beings to pursue and promote. When emphasis is placed upon the role of practical rationality in the genesis of normativity, attention rightly shifts from the 'natural' to the 'practically reasonable.'[17] Thus, whether an inclination is determined to be good for us or not cannot be established by an appeal to the supposed ontological 'naturalness' of the inclination viewed within a schema of natural ends. Instead, the goodness of an inclination, if good it is, must be established by direct normative insight.

The third line of criticism purports to by-pass the naturalistic fallacy by rejecting the applicability of the fallacy to its brand of naturalism. Anthony Lisska in his *Aquinas's Theory of Natural Law*, for example, argues that nature has a built in normative teleology. Nature is composed of natural kinds. A natural kind has a characteristic set of dispositional properties. These properties are not static but dynamic. They are ordered towards the actualization of ends. Once we grasp the dynamic nature of this unfolding, we will understand that it is fitting for any natural kind to realize its essential nature. Since human beings are natural kinds with dispositional properties, we understand the normative directedness of human nature by understanding these dynamic properties. Lisska develops an interpretation of human 'essence' as a set of dispositional properties, properties that are dynamically ordered towards the final cause of human flourishing. 'End' and 'good,' for Lisska, are entirely substitutable terms. A Good X is not defined in terms of its possession of natural property Y. Instead X and Y are merely different labels accounting for the same dynamic phenomenon.[18]

Does this argument really side-step the naturalistic fallacy by outflanking the force of Moore's open-question argument? I think not. The assertion that 'good' is a 'natural end' and vice versa is not an analytic statement in the manner 'a bachelor is an unmarried man.' 'Bachelor' contains the meaning 'unmarried man' in a way that 'end' does not, of necessity, convey the meaning of 'good.' If it is not an analytic proposition, it is a synthetic proposition. Yet, as a synthetic proposition, its status is plausibly questionable. The difficulty arises because good as normative cannot be explained away by claiming that 'X is good' states nothing more than 'X is a natural human disposition' or something like it. If the only argument to overcome the naturalistic fallacy is the claim that 'goods are ends and ends are goods,' we can plausibly doubt that the good being referenced is fully expressive of the concept of normative good as understood in ordinary language usage. Ordinary people, without contrivance or artificiality, can plausibly assert: 'how do we know that the end being realised by dispositional property X is in itself good?' or 'you say that X is dynamic and not static but how does that tell us that X is really a good for us?' These remain full-blown open questions, the product of an influential argument that continues to haunt the precincts of naturalism. Simply because a disposition is said to be dynamic and not static, and good is treated as being identical with these dynamic trajectories, *pace* Lisska, does not ultimately make type B naturalism any less problematic as a naturalistic claim.[19]

3.4 Whose Practical Rationality?

Traditional natural law thinking, heavily influenced by Aristotle and Aquinas, adopts a view of practical reason which states that deliberation with a view to action is fundamentally not deliberation about what the basic ends of human action are but about how we pursue these ends by deliberation over means. Practical reason takes the goods supplied to it by theoretical reason as 'givens.' A structural order of entailment exists between the two forms of reason. Ends worthy of pursuit are presented to practical reason by way of conclusion from prior theoretical inquiry. Practical rationality thus has no role to play in determining whether or not an end has the status of a genuine good. For Aquinas, like Aristotle, our understanding of what is good is structurally dependent on our speculative understanding of the functions of human nature.[20]

Proponents of this view of practical rationality argue that to claim otherwise is to fall into the trap of believing that the ultimate ends of action are chosen by the agent. As objects of choice they can be accepted or rejected according to subjective will.[21] Reject the idea that the ends of human flourishing are fixed by direct reference to the inclinations of human nature and we are faced with the prospect of abandoning our ability to establish an objective framework for determining the existence of authentic human goods. Hume abolished theoretical reason's ability to determine rational ends for human action thus turning ethics into a study of passions served by an 'if-then' instrumentalist account of practical reason. On this view, an attack on the ability of theoretical reason to determine what the ultimate ends of worthwhile action are, leads precipitously to a sceptical view of reason's formative role in ethics.[22]

Fortunately the defender of objectivity in ethics need not be forced into the false dilemma of either jettisoning opposition to ethical naturalism or of renouncing belief in the ultimate power of reason to determine basic sources of normativity for us. There is a third way. This third way accepts that objectivity in ethics is based on a different understanding of the role that practical reason plays in the ethical enterprise. We do not need to accept the Humean view that the ultimate purposes informing human action are non-rational desires, nor need we accept the view that only theoretical reason can play an establishing role in determining the sources of normative value. Instead, sources of normativity are generated and moderated by a revised understanding of practical rationality. Practical rationality itself (a) directly grasp the goods that persons spontaneously seek to pursue and promote as the intelligible starting points for human well-being, and (b) generates requirements governing the way reasonable choices can be made concerning how we respond to and cultivate these goods in our own lives and in the lives of others.[23]

3.5 The First Principle of Practical Rationality

All purposeful action, whether or not it is morally good or bad, engages our pursuit of goods. Pre-moral goods are appealing possibilities that motivate us to act. By engaging in purposeful action we are already participating in the appeal of an array of goods in our lives. To act practically is to pursue via action some goal judged worth pursuing. Our capacity for practical reason initially directs us to 'pursue good and avoid what is bad.' Goods, pre-morally understood, are simply pursued with a view to expanding or promoting some aspect of our general sense of well-being. For example, by pursuing different opportunities for knowledge in our lives, we are implicitly accepting that knowledge is good for us and ignorance is bad. By having and cultivating friendships we are implicitly accepting that friendship is good for us and to be deprived of friendship is bad. We eat and drink in order to maintain the good of our health and we avoid disease because it bad for our health. Countless other examples can be cited. Good or bad (evil) are both intelligible pre-moral realities.[24] Because practical rationality directs all purposeful action, and all purposeful action is undertaken for the sake of something good, we are now in a position to present to the reader a first principle of practical rationality: *Good is-to-be done and pursued and bad is-to-be avoided.*

This formulation of a first principle of practical rationality is none other than Aquinas's formulation.[25] His formulation, removed from the context of deduction from prior speculative inquiry or direct inference from the facts of nature, is an accurate expression of a first principle.[26] The principle is general in scope because it informs purposeful action in general. Before we can deliberate ethically we experience the evaluative pull of an array of goods in our lives and we also experience deprivations that are bad for us—disease, thwarted friendship, death of a family member, and so on. If the first principle of practical rationality were a moral principle and not a pre-moral principle, as some state, it could not convincingly claim to be the first principle of all practical rationality, for it could not then be presupposed in all acts of practical reason whether moral or not.[27] Good without specific moral content simply refers to our actual pursuit of whatever we understand to be worthwhile. In a manner analogous to the way in which the first principle of theoretical reason—the principle of non-contradiction—'the same thing cannot be affirmed and denied at the same time'—informs theoretical reasoning in general so the first principle of practical rationality informs practical reasoning in general—'act with a view to a purpose and avoid senseless action.'[28]

How do we come to grasp the truth of this ultimate first principle of practical rationality? The principle cannot be established by theoretical inquiry, by inference from nature or by referring back to some yet more fundamental principle of practical rationality. Instead, the principle is constituted and grasped by direct unmediated rational insight. The principle is self-evident in status.[29] The self-evidence of the principle does not mean that the principle is 'instantly obvious' such that no one would dream of denying it. Instead, self-evidence refers to a particular mode of knowing. Self-evident propositions—acts of rational insight—cannot be deduced or inferred from anything else.[30] Their truth status is directly cognized. While subsequent analysis can help support and clarify our understanding of a self-evident principle's scope and implications, the directive but not-yet-moral intelligibility of the first principle is not established other than by this mode of knowing.

The first principle of practical rationality directs us to pursue good in general and avoid bad in general. The first principle, however, is not the only principle of practical rationality to be directly grasped by rational insight. Further 'specificatory principles' are also grasped by direct rational insight. While everyday experience of ourselves and the world around us is undoubtedly required if we are to begin to grasp and then pursue the intelligible content of these further specificatory principles—'primary goods of persons'—nevertheless the starting points of our normative experience, at first pre-reflexively encountered, then mingled with reflective awareness, cannot be directly inferred from any non-normative structure. Instead, grasped by direct rational insight, these further specificatory principles 'flesh out' the generality of the first principle—'good is-to-be done and pursued and bad is-to-be avoided'—by identifying what the primary goods of persons are to be pursued and promoted.[31] Thus, we seek to determine with reference to the following formula what these 'specificatory X's are: *Good (primary good X) is-to-be done and pursued and bad (harm or damage to X) is-to-be avoided.*

3.6 The Primary Goods of Persons

While we pursue a variety of different goods in our lives, only primary goods, due to their ultimate non-derived appeal, are directly grasped as initial specifications of the first principle of practical rationality. The grounding purposes for which we act cannot form an infinite chain. Some goods must stand as being non-derivatively good—that is as 'goods in themselves.' All other goods—instrumental, auxiliary or facilitative—while they are intelligible goods worth pursuing, are not pursued quite for their own sake but are pursued for the sake of some other fundamental non-derived goods of persons. These non-primary or secondary goods are valuable to us insofar as they help us pursue and promote the primary ingredients that make up a fulfilling life. Secondary goods, unlike primary goods, are derived goods. Primary goods alone, then, unlike secondary goods, are the very purposes or goals in life that ultimately inform and shape the content of all worthwhile human action.

What then are the primary goods of persons? They can be summarily listed as: life and health; knowledge, truth and contemplation; practical rationality; family and friendship; work and play; beauty.[32] Together, they constitute the irreducible primary ingredients of a humanly fulfilling life.[33] Given their status, I will proceed to *briefly* describe and discuss each of these primary goods before turning to consider other goods that are secondary in nature. Dialectical argument, since it is based on theoretical reason, not practical reason, cannot function as direct justification for the normative standing of these primary goods. Since the initial normative pull of a primary good is directly grasped, dialectical argument can only provide *indirect support* for the standing and significance of these goods. Dialectical argument can, however, help flesh out the scope and significance of implicitly grasped normative starting points, thereby helping to shore up the full normative import of these specificatory principles with a view to action.[34] When considering each primary good, I will offer dialectical reasons for inclusion (X is a primary good) in order to counter arguments that would seek to reject any genuine primary good as a primary good of persons. Later, I will move to consider reasons for exclusion (X is not a primary good) in order to tackle the elevation and treatment of some secondary goods as though they were truly primary goods of persons.[35]

3.6a Human Life and Health

Life, including health, is a primary good of persons. The good of life encompasses our bodily existence as psychosomatic beings. The good of life certainly has an instrumental dimension to it, for we need to be alive in order to pursue any other primary (or secondary) good. Life is thus a grounding good because it sustains all of our choices and actions.[36] Yet, while life is instrumentally valuable to us as we pursue other goods, it is also intrinsically valuable. Something X has intrinsic value to the extent that the value of X is due to what X fundamentally is, apart from X's relations to other things. Are our bodies only relationally and derivatively valuable to the extent that they are able to service our conscious pursuit of other human goods?

Contrary to many dualistic views that have influenced Western culture over the years, it is, I think, ontologically flawed to hold a view of the person that the 'human body' is (i) ultimately some kind of disposable container temporarily inhabited by an immortal soul or (ii) some kind of non-personal biological entity created purely for the sake of servicing conscious existence.[37] Unsound dualisms, because they distort our reflective understanding, make it more difficult to appreciate the basic awareness we have that the human life *qua* human life is directly encountered by us as a unitary good. Bodies are not 'prisons of the immortal soul' nor are they 'mere biological equipment.' Bodies are intrinsically and not merely extrinsically valuable to us because they are seamlessly integral to the very reality of who and what we are as persons. A body is not something 'sub-personal' to 'personal life' as if X (consciousness life) can be radically juxtaposed with Y (bodily life) such that X can be held intrinsically valuable to us but not Y. Both X and Y are fully integral to our personal beingness.[38]

Of course, I do not seek to resolve many questions pertaining to status and significance of this primary good here. My purpose, at this point, is simply to relay to the reader the general contours of my thought. Since the status and significance of this good is of fundamental concern to the ethics of assisted suicide and euthanasia, it will receive detailed analysis in subsequent chapters (especially Chapters 4–6).

3.6b Knowledge, Truth and Contemplation

The object of knowledge is truth. To know is to comprehend something truthful about ourselves and the world around us. Intellect is the mental capacity we have for truth discovery. None of us can live well or fulfill ourselves if we live in widespread ignorance. To pursue truth and acquire understanding, whether of basic facts or abstract propositions, is a highly significant good of persons. No one can look after his or her life and health if he or she lacks a basic knowledge of safety hazards; no one can relax if he or she is ignorant of the ways and means of relaxation, and so on. Thus, in general, we can say that knowledge is good and ignorance is bad. Of course, the extent and kind of knowledge pursued will vary markedly from person to person reflecting wide differences in personal situations. The nuclear scientist and the traffic warden have different frames of reference. What is generally true, however, is that all persons, whatever their situation, need to acquire varied knowledge of many things in order to successfully pursue all manner of goals and projects.[39]

It is sometimes said that acquisition of knowledge may be good but can also be bad because acquired knowledge can serve evil purposes, ergo, knowledge cannot be viewed as an unqualified good of persons. This, however, would be an incorrect conclusion to draw. Knowledge can be acquired for bad purposes but it is not knowledge in itself that is bad. Rather, it is the uses to which it is put, or the manner in which it is acquired, that are bad. We can acquire knowledge of the plans of a building in order to ensure that a building is safe and secure or acquire the same knowledge in order to rob and destroy its inhabitants. We can gain knowledge of drugs in order to treat illnesses but that knowledge can also be directed to the goal of quickly killing people with little or no pain. That knowledge can become entangled with evil, then, is not a convincing argument for rejecting the view that knowledge *per se* is a primary human good of persons.

Knowledge is capable of being intrinsically valued for its own sake and not for the sake of any other extrinsic reason. The pursuit of knowledge, in order to achieve other ends, is certainly a common reason to acquire knowledge, but if it were 'merely' an instrumental good (pursuit of X in order to achieve Y), no matter how useful, it could hardly qualify as a primary good (pursuit of X for the sake of X), for primary goods furnish us with ultimate reasons for action. A primary good is a good capable of being valued and respected for its own sake *even as it might also* serve instrumental purposes in our pursuit of other important goods.[40]

By 'contemplation,' I do not mean to presume that the object of our thought is necessarily the God of Christianity or any other religion. Rather, the good being referenced here is the general good of considering how we orientate and position ourselves with regard to some ultimate questions of existence and being. Why does anything exist? Is all existence material? Are we spiritual beings? Is there life after death? Does the universe have an ultimate cause? Contemplating and reflecting on such questions in our lives, even if they are not thought answerable or are thought answerable in different ways, are inspired by the appeal of ultimate knowledge. This holds true regardless of whether we would classify ourselves as atheists, agnostics or theists. It is fundamentally good for us to ponder for ourselves such deep and profound questions and how we might seek to answer them.[41]

3.6c Practical Rationality

Practical rationality or reason (*ratio practica*) itself is a primary good of persons. Through reason we pursue understanding and praxis. Intellect directed towards understanding is a primary good. So also is intellect directed towards the pursuit of rational action in our lives. Certainly we pursue the good of practical rationality in order to identify and develop plans for the pursuit and promotion of other primary and secondary goods in our lives. The good of practical rationality, however, is also intrinsically good even as it constitutes and facilitates our pursuit of other goods. It is more than 'merely' instrumentally good for us to be rationally directed and motivated in our deliberations with a view to action.[42] The good of practical rationality is often overlooked as a primary good because it seems so 'ubiquitous' to purposeful choosing and acting in general. It is, however, entirely possible to participate in some goods in pointless or senseless ways. Since we insightfully grasp that it is generally good for us to choose and act intelligibly not unintelligibly, it is reasonable to accord to practical reason the status of primary good.[43] The strength of the 'call to intelligibility-in-general' we experience—rather than to the content of any specific action or plan—endows the good of practical rationality with such an ultimate and non-instrumental dimension. Only by appreciating this dimension to practical rationality can we adequately account for the 'pull of the normative' we experience to 'be reasonable' beyond considerations of instrumentality alone.

Further, it is an apparent paradox only to think that practical rationality cannot encompass both (a) the mode of knowing for establishing what the primary goods of persons are (direct rational insight) and also (b) constitute the very vehicle whereby practical rationality itself is held to be a primary good of persons. There simply is no logical barrier to a kind of 'self-grasping' by practical rationality regarding its own status as a primary good.

Clearly, what I have just said about practical rationality only refers to its general significance as a primary good. Detail concerning the criteria for intelligible and purposeful deliberation is needed if this good is going to be formative in directing our choices and actions. Further 'sub-principles' or 'requirements' of practical rationality supply the substantive content of this good. These requirements of practical rationality will be addressed in a later section of this chapter (see s. 3.9).

3.6d Family and Friendship

Family life is also a primary good. While the familial good certainly overlaps with the primary good of friendship, its appeal is distinct enough for it to be regarded as a distinct good.[44] The familial good, underscored as it is by particular bonds of belonging, attachment and affection, undoubtedly facilitates many of the instrumental needs that persons have. Family members 'help each other out' in many ways that would seem strange to us unless we viewed these actions under the aegis of loving familial ties—spouses, parents and children, and siblings. Again, however, as with the good of knowledge (and all primary goods), the good of family does not merely function as an instrumental good. It is also an intrinsic good. A direct appeal to the 'good of the family' or a familial sub-good like the 'good of the marriage' or the 'good of parenthood' in and of itself can provide us with an intelligible ultimate reason for action. Family members, for example, often make sacrifices for the sake of their family. If Joe said he performed action X for the 'sake of his family,' such an explanation can stand as a primary reason for action. As a primary reason for action, the action cannot be rendered more fully intelligible by locating a deeper explanatory reason informing his action beyond the appeal of the family good.

By family I do not intend to be narrow or restrictive in specifying what constitutes a family and what does not constitute a family. Traditional natural law theory, due to the influence of religious faith, has unfortunately adopted an overly restrictive view of marriage and family life. A secular reason-based understanding of the 'blessings' of family life is more open and expansive. The nuclear family is a family but so too is the extended family encountered in many non-Western societies. Marriage and birth are traditional ways of constituting membership in a family but membership can also be constituted in other ways, for example, adoption. The idea of adoption need not be narrowly viewed but can apply to the informal or formal adoption of a person (whether child or adult) into family membership. Communities of religious, for example, function as surrogate families and are constituted by adoption. The traditional marital relationship between husband and wife is a familial good but so too can spouses of the same sex participate in this familial good.

Persons who do not participate in the good of family, for whatever reason— death, divorce, separation, estrangement, etc.—experience deprivations in their lives because they are not able to actively participate in the special ties of familial belonging and attachment that contribute to our general sense of well-being. An expansive understanding of family life, however, should help us see that it is possible to instantiate the good of family life in a variety of non-traditional ways; alternative ways that help us to overcome obstacles that might otherwise stand in the way of pursuing this good in our lives.

Friendship is another primary ingredient of a humanly fulfilling life that overlaps with the good of family. A world populated only by strangers would be burdensome indeed. Friends render assistance and support to each other. We need friends if we are to be instrumentally helped in our pursuit of varied goals and projects. Friendship, however, is not just a mere 'utility pact.'[45] X can use Y for instrumental purposes and Y can similarly use X for instrumental purposes but that does not constitute genuine friendship. A genuine friend truly acts for the sake of the other in ways we could not expect from those who do not share mutual bonds of fellowship, kindness, trust, and care. If friendship were merely an instrumental good it would hardly make sense to say that we acted quite for the sake of friendship and not for any other primary reason. Yet, since it does make sense to say that we can act for the sake of friendship as a fully intelligible end in itself, and not for some other overarching reason or explanation, a utility view of friendship cannot do justice to the normative appeal of this good in our lives.

Since the good of friendship is an interpersonal shared good, it also follows that friendship, in a broader less intense sense, is also the good of acting for the sake of community.[46] Community is best understood as a more encompassing form of friendship, ranging from, say, the mutual care and concern of neighbors to the wider good of civic friendship. A community shares common ends and its members cooperate with one another in pursuing these ends for the sake of enriching the entire community. Members of a community (contrasted with purely instrumentalist forms of association), cooperate and help each other in ways that intelligibly make sense only when we understand that they are acting for the sake of a 'common good,' a shared participatory good that cannot be adequately reduced to accounts of that good framed according to interests of personal advantage or even 'joint self-interest.'[47]

3.6e Work and Play

Both work and play are primary goods of persons.[48] The reader may well wonder why work is listed as a primary good. Many will ask how it can be intrinsically good to slog away at an unrewarding job in return for a meager pay packet. Some jobs are degrading to the esteem of persons and others are tantamount to forced labor. The answer to those doubts is to be found in distinguishing between jobs that offer little or no opportunity to authentically instantiate the good of work and those that do offer such opportunities. Jobs that are mind drudging, lack stimulation and lack any scope for creativity may be regarded as a means only to the pursuit of other ends. Just as acquaintances and associates, no matter how long we have known them, do not become friends without genuine bonds of friendship, so too jobs do not instantiate the intrinsic good of work unless they inherently contribute to our creative ability to fulfill ourselves as persons.[49]

As work is a primary good, so too is play. Clearly the two goods can seamlessly overlap in many ways. Many hobbies, for example, can be aspects of both work and play. We seek many and varied opportunities for play and recreation as a means of relaxation and renewal yet we also purse and promote instantiations of this good for no other primary reason than an intrinsic sense of satisfaction and contentment that the good of play provides to us.

3.6f Beauty

Aesthetic experience is also a primary good of persons because it is a good capable of being valued for its own sake and not for any other ultimate reason. Instantiations of beauty can be created or occur naturally in the world. We can appreciate a sense of beauty in the tangible or the intangible. We can find intrinsic sources of beauty in both the seemingly mundane and the extraordinary.

The wonder and awe we experience when we encounter beauty cannot be reduced to the experience we have of any other good even though many instantiations of beauty are often commingled with instantiations of other primary goods. A person who visits an art museum, gazes at a sunset or contemplates a sense of mathematical harmony, is engaging in the pursuit of beautiful experiences that are intelligible to us quite for their own sake.

Instances of beauty are not fully intelligible to us simply because they are sources of pleasure. Beauty is not an instrumental good that is to be pursued simply for the sake of pleasure. This would be to put the proverbial cart before the horse—a derivative good (pleasure) before a non-derivative good (beauty). Instead, we can best account for the feelings of pleasure we often experience in a beautiful encounter by regarding them as a closely related 'by-product good' that may be experienced as we pursue appealing instances of beauty and appealing instances of other primary and secondary goods (further on pleasure see s. 3.7b).[50]

3.7 Non-Primary or Secondary Goods

Non-primary or secondary goods are goods that are not capable of being grasped as fully intelligible ends of action to be pursued quite for their own sake. They have a non-intrinsic status. They do not furnish us with ultimate reasons for action. Secondary goods can be instrumental—pursue X for the sake of Y—even where Y is some further instrumental good as long as we reach a terminus that is non-instrumental—or they can be by-product goods—where X accompanies Y but is not intrinsic to Y. They can be material or non-material. In all cases their value as a good is ultimately derived from their relationship to primary goods. Secondary goods are authentically valued to the extent that the ends or purposes they support are themselves held valuable. This division between primary and secondary is a division of considerable practical import because, in part, it structures how it is we can reasonably seek to resolve clashes between goods when the goods in question are not equal in their category status.

3.7a Material Goods and Power

Money surely has instrumental value for us. Many of the things we seek to purchase are themselves material things—food, shelter, medical care, transport, clothing, etc.—things that are indeed valuable to us but valuable to the extent that they help us pursue or promote some further good in life. An instrumental good can be a means to promote some other instrumental good or it can directly facilitate our pursuit of a primary good. Ultimately, however, we do not value material goods in and of themselves. Instead, we value the facilitative contribution they directly or indirectly make to our pursuit of primary goods. There is surely something odd about a person who treats the excessive accumulation of material goods—the miser, the hoarder, the obsessive shopper— beyond any reasonable claim of need—as if material goods were a pseudo form of primary good.[51] To say that material goods are secondary goods, is not to deny that these goods are very important to our ability to flourish as persons. The wasting away of a person due to starvation and malnourishment is a terrible evil. A displaced person without shelter suffers many serious deprivations. Material goods are important conditions that support us in our quest to live a flourishing life. Important as they are, however, objectively we value them as a means only in-so-far as they contribute to our teleological pursuit of non-derived primary goods.

Without any power we are powerless to act. Some degree of power, then, an ability to control our actions and influence the course of events, is an important precondition of human agency. Yet, is pursuit of power truly intelligible to us because it is pursued quite for its own sake as an end in itself (an intrinsic good) or is our pursuit of power really intelligible to us because we pursue it as a means of realizing some other instrumental or intrinsic good in our lives? The appeal of power can best be accounted for by regarding it as an instrumental good not a primary good.[52] We value power to the extent that it facilitates our pursuit of other goods that are ultimately capable of constituting ends-in-themselves. Power certainly has positive value to persons but power has value because it can be utilized as a means of achieving X, Y, Z. Certainly we abhor, for example, the deprivation of power experienced by persons under slavery. Deprivation in power is assuredly evil for those so deprived, for they are stultified in their ability to make important life determinations for themselves. Still, we should accurately represent such power deprivation as instrumental and not intrinsic. It is sometimes good and not bad to impose deliberate restrictions on the power of persons to act. Intentional deprivations of power can be instrumentally good, for example, as in the case of punishment meted out to offenders against the order of justice.

3.7b Pleasure and Pain

Pleasure may roughly be described as either a 'physical sensation' or as a 'state of consciousness.' When we start to reflect on the question of how we directly pursue the good of pleasure as if it were a fully intelligible *end in itself*, however, we start to confront the reality that pleasure is ultimately derived from our pursuit of some other purpose that brings pleasure. Whether pleasure is a physical sensation or a state of consciousness, we have no ability to directly pursue pleasure as such. Even self-professed hedonists cannot pursue pleasure as such but must pursue certain kinds of activity that give them pleasure. Pleasure, therefore, is a kind of by-product good, a derivative good that can accompany our performance of certain kinds of activity in life.[53]

When we reflect on the good of pleasure, we start to see why it cannot be regarded as a non-derived primary good. Take, for example, the activity of drinking a fine glass of wine. The taste and aroma of the wine contribute to the good of relaxation, of play, of knowledge regarding the properties of the wine, and so on. We may indeed experience pleasure as an accompaniment to our pursuit of some intelligible activity like drinking a fine glass of wine, but it cannot function as a fully intelligible reason for acting just in itself when pleasure is severed from the activity it accompanies. Often we talk of our pursuit of pleasure as a kind of shorthand to describe positive feelings that result from the performance of an activity we value. When the performance of the activity is subject to further scrutiny, however, we can begin to comprehend that it is not pleasure as such that we ultimately value in our performance of the activity but rather the felicitous properties of the activity itself, often (but not necessarily) accompanied by the by-product of pleasure. We ultimately derive pleasure from an activity because of the properties of the activity itself and not because pleasure is capable of being directly pursued as an ultimate end quite for its own sake.[54]

Pursuit of pleasure, when thought of as an end in itself, is also destructive of any deeper sense of what constitutes the integral well-being of persons, for an appeal to the inherent goodness of hedonistic pleasure, can, in principle, be used to justify the intrinsic worthwhileness of any possible objective for action, as long as it is held to be pleasurable enough. Is it intrinsically good to seek pleasure by torturing a child, for example, or to derive pleasure from the act of killing another person? The defender of pleasure as an intrinsic good may state that it is not the pursuit of pleasure that is bad but the negative effects surrounding the pursuit of pleasure, in these sorts of circumstances, which makes its pursuit instrumentally bad.[55]

In response, I would argue that pleasure is a conditional good only, the conditionality of its goodness being contingent on the content of the activity from which pleasure is being derived. This kind of conditional portrayal, I think, better accounts for our intuitive sense that terribly destructive and harmful pleasures are not intrinsic goods because of the negative content of the activity that is evoking the pleasure. It is intuitively more intelligible to describe the pleasure derived from a torturing or killing activity as a 'bad pleasure' or 'bogus good,' rather than attempt to claim that despite the bad effects of the torturing or killing activity, at least it generated some intrinsic good for the torturer or killer. Pleasure, to the extent that it is good, is best understood as a by-product good, a good not sought as an end in itself but as a welcomed non-intrinsic benefit accompanying our pursuit of some other good.[56]

If pleasure is not a primary good is the 'absence of pain' a primary good of persons? No one can doubt the debilitating impact that severe pain can have on our ability to flourish well in life. The continuing experience of pain is a severe deprivation to both our physical and mental health. Certainly we seek to avoid such pain in our lives. Personally and collectively we invest a great deal of time and energy in treating and avoiding such pain. We seek to avoid pain in order to promote the good of health as well as our ability to actively participate in other primary (and secondary) goods that are impacted by debilitating pain.[57] When pain impacts our ability to maintain the good of health, it becomes a derivatively evil phenomenon. I say 'derivatively evil' phenomenon, not in order to trivialize the horrors of pain in our lives, but to recognize that absence of pain intelligibly matters to us because it impacts our ability to benefit from the good of health as well as other primary and instrumental goods.

If severe pain is a derivative evil for us, the experience of pain can sometimes fulfill a positive role in our lives. Consider here, the value of pain we experience when our hand touches something very hot. This experience of pain is instrumentally good not bad because it acts as a warning signal to avoid greater potential damage to the tissue of our hand. Without the phenomenon of pain we would not be promptly alerted to take avoidance measures. When functioning in such an instrumentally good way, pain is efficacious as a means of protecting the intrinsic good of our health.

While severe pain is a gravely debilitating experience for persons, it is not the only grave evil that can affect our lives. Pain is best regarded as a species of the genus 'suffering.' Suffering can be brought about by a deprivation in our ability to pursue any significant good in life. We need only reflect a little on the loss we experience, for example, in bereavement or abandonment to appreciate that severe pain is one of many other grave evils that can afflict us as persons.[58]

3.7c Personal Autonomy

Is personal autonomy a primary good of persons? Is it a non-derivative intrinsic good? Conditions such as competence to act and ability to choose among options are important preconditions for self-directing action. A life lacking competency or deprived of liberty to make important constitutive choices is seriously diminished. We thus value these important prerequisites of our agency. As a precondition for self-directing action, however, I fail to see why these conditions have intrinsic value when viewed *quite apart* from the very nature of actual choices made and actions undertaken. It is, I think, counter-intuitive to think that we can truly value such preconditions as having intrinsic non-derivative value when we divorce them from the very content of the choices and actions they enable.[59] Why is a person's autonomy to be regarded as intrinsically good when he or she uses that preconditional autonomy to gravely injure another person or to execute a profoundly self-destructive choice? If autonomy is equally present in the making of worthwhile choices and the making of profoundly harmful and destructive choices, then we are right to question the claim that autonomy, valued just for its own sake, is a primary good of persons.[60] When viewed as a preconditional necessity for the exercise of constitutive choice and action, autonomy is, of itself, not intrinsically valuable but is, rather, instrumentally valuable to the extent that it facilitates and supports our pursuit of worthwhile objectives. The goodness of an autonomous choice or action will, crucially, hinge on the pursuit of the objective to which autonomy is directed.

Autonomy can be said to afford us with an operational sphere of freedom to make constitutive choices regarding ourselves—what we stand for and what we will become—but the underlying value of that freedom is ultimately dependent on the content of the constitutive choices we make. A plurality of authentic goods affords many opportunities to make countless worthwhile choices as we fashion our own unique life narrative. The diversity of worthwhile content is immense. That enabling freedom could not exist if it did not also enable the making of bad choices made in pursuit of bad overarching projects. For the sake of empowering a broad array of worthwhile diversity, then, we also, so to speak, derivatively empower the bad. We should not conclude from this, however, that autonomously made choices, irrespective of content, simply as such, actually manifest intrinsic goodness.

As with my brief discussion of the good of life above, this is but a partial treatment of the good of autonomy. I wanted to summarily mark for the reader at this stage of my analysis why personal autonomy in not included in the list of primary goods of persons. More, of course, will need to be said. I will take up the subject again in Chapter 5 (see s. 5.6) when countering autonomy-based objections to restrictions on suicide, assisted suicide and voluntary euthanasia.

3.8 Pluralism and Normative Theory

The primary goods of persons, as we have seen (see s. 3.6) are irreducibly plural in nature. We speak of primary goods not the primary good. Practical rationality cannot objectively establish the truth of the proposition that primary good X is inherently more valuable than primary good Y, or Y is inherently more valuable than Z, or even that X and Y are of the same value. There is no objective scale that could begin to underwrite and validate such commensurations. Two or more goods are only objectively commensurable if there is a common standard for measuring or ranking the diverse qualities and pulls of each good.[61] How, for example, do we *objectively rank or prioritize* a satisfying cycle ride in the park (instantiation of the primary good of play) with having an enjoyable conversation with friends (instantiation of the primary good of friendship)?

The central problem with cardinal or ordinal schemes of value is that they inevitably impose denominators or rankings between primary goods that fail to capture the diverse richness of these goods in our lives. Of course, we do make practical choices that shape the goods we pursue and promote—priorities are established. Acting in concert with others, pooled community priorities are also established. Yet, here, we are crucially referring to the shaping of commitments and priorities framed according to the prior application of the requirements of practical rationality (see s. 6.9), for example, the requirement to respect and not violate the unique normative demands generated by each of the different primary goods or the requirement not to treat a secondary good as if it were a primary good of persons.

Since there is an irreducible diversity of primary goods, goods that give us very different kinds of reason to act, then monism—the view that there is one overarching supreme good to be promoted or greater overall good to be maximized—cannot be sustained. If there were only one supreme good or standard, then our reasons for pursuing primary goods would only really make intelligible sense to us in so far as they promoted some singular teleological reason to act. Yet goods like truth, beauty and friendship are irreducibly and intelligibly worthy of pursuit quite for their own sake, apart from any reference to some supreme overarching good or product maximizing standard.[62]

A fully pluralist understanding of the status of primary goods stands in contrast to both (a) Aristotelian-Thomistic and (b) utilitarian teleology. Both are monistic approaches to the good. For Aristotle and Aquinas there is an overarching supreme good or ultimate end (*finis ultimus*) to which all things aim. Reference to a supreme good is said to provide the intelligible means for ordering our pursuit of all other non-ultimate goods relative to our pursuit of the ultimate good. Goods are judged relationally worthwhile to the extent that they promote this ultimate end for humanity.[63] Primary goods thus effectively become secondary goods in the service of the primary ultimate good. For the utilitarian, whether a classic pleasure/pain reductionist in the mould of Jeremy Bentham or a modern preference satisfier in the mould of R. M. Hare, it is claimed that commensurations between goods can be objectively established via reference to a common standard.[64] Both monistic approaches to the good, despite deep structural differences between their respective systems, cannot be reconciled with the reality of pluralism over primary goods.

3.8a Aristotelian-Thomistic Teleology

Thomists contend that there can be no unity in any natural end for humanity if there are several primary goods that can be said to function as sovereign ends. Without an overarching unifying principle, we do not have a teleology but rather the 'incoherence' of several teleologies—a 'polyteleologism.'[65] Now, the challenge of coherently choosing and deliberating over a plurality of primary goods is certainly pressing. We will certainly need to explain how choices can be successfully coordinated and regulated—avoiding hopeless eventism or radical indeterminacy—without presupposing any singular unity of purposefulness. Yet, in rising to meet this challenge, we should not reject the practical understanding we already have of just why we value the diverse and different appeal of primary goods in our lives. It is important to realize that there simply is no requirement of practical rationality that compels us to conclude that there must be a single unifying end lurking behind our pursuit of primary goods in order to render our practical pursuit of these goods properly intelligible to us.[66] Primary goods are what they intelligibly are—non-derived irreducible goods ultimately informing all worthwhile choice and action—nothing more and nothing less. Thomists cannot insist, from the insightful experiences we have of these irreducibly different primary goods, that it is *necessary for us* to posit the existence of an overarching supreme good in order to 'complete' the picture we have of pluralism.[67]

3.8b Utilitarian Teleology

Utilitarian projects adhere to a maximizing conception of the good. Comparing different states-of-affairs, agents have to be able to work out which of these different states will produce the most optimific (or least pessimific) outcome.[68] First, there is good reason to reject the proposal that hedonism can provide us with anything like an underlying good to which all of our actions are ultimately directed towards. How, for example, does an agent impartially rank and compare the pleasure derived from a profound aesthetic encounter with the pleasure derived from understanding a complex passage of literature? How many hedons is X objectively worth compared to Y? The cardinal call to maximize pleasure and minimize pain does not begin to account for the deep seated reasons we have to value our pursuit and promotion of irreducibly diverse goods in our lives. Hedonistic reductionism erroneously supposes that we cannot seek to engage in the pursuit of some experiences because they are found intrinsically rewarding to us, quite for their own sake, rewards that cannot be reduced to the lure of pleasure or the aversion of pain.[69]

Preference utilitarians attempt to provide an objective measure of comparison by developing the idea of maximizing preferences. Individuals can rank their own subjective preferences and those of others and arrive at a standard for maximizing outcomes. Subjective preferences can be inter-personally ranked, for example, according to the criteria of strength of intensity and length of duration.[70]

Taking subjective preferences as the object for comparison, however, leads to the twin horns of a dilemma that preference utilitarianism cannot satisfactorily resolve. If only mere intensity and duration of preferences matters, then we are forced to adopt a radically egalitarian approach to the inclusion of all preferences in our rankings. Some people have intense preferences for sadistic pleasure, torture or racism. Are these preferences to be weighed equally in calculating the most optimific outcome? If intensity and duration of preferences alone counts, we are faced with the highly counter-intuitive insistence that we cannot, prior to ranking, exclude any preference from our assessment, for all preferences must be treated equally. If the preference utilitarian insists on the inclusion of all preferences, then he or she is forced to treat highly destructive and harmful preferences on an equal par with preferences that seem inherently worthier. Any view of the good which insists that the pleasure derived by the child torturer is to be included in a 'maximizing mix' is operating with a fundamentally flawed conception of value.[71]

The other horn of the dilemma is encountered when trying to stipulate that preferences can be divided into 'rational' and 'irrational' preferences, so that only rational preferences are included in the rankings and irrational preferences are excluded. What is the source for such exclusionary stipulations? Utilitarianism adopts a monistic approach to the good. Utility is defined in terms of preference satisfaction. If other robust evaluative considerations determine what is good, then the central rationale of preference utilitarianism is itself gravely undermined.

If preference utilitarians adopt an essentially Humean view of practical rationality whereby ends equate to subjective wants or preferences, then the preferences of a committed and enthusiastic torturer cannot be dismissed from the ball-park of consideration. If a robust view of practical rationality is taken, a view that includes evaluative considerations that assess the very content of preferences for potential inclusion or exclusion, these non-utilitarian requirements for reasonable choice and action are expanded at the direct cost of undermining why we should be intelligibly committed to the subjective satisfaction of preferences as a good making standard in the first place.[72]

If utilitarianism is, in my view, fatally challenged in its many attempts to provide a common monistic standard by which to commensurate very different values, its 'maximizing' rationality is also flawed as an approach to making value judgments. If we adhere to the demand of utilitarianism for outcome maximization, and attempt to follow this requirement in directing all of our actions, it would place crippling demands on our integrity as persons.[73] Crucial to our sense of integrity, is a deep seated need we have for narrative structure in life that prevents our life becoming essentially one of shear eventism whereby we experience life as a string of disparate maximizing episodes.[74] In order to have a sense of unity in our lives we must be committed to ground projects. These projects help shape our dispositions and frame our choices. Unless they are treated with commitment and deference on our part, they will be undermined or thwarted, either by our own acts of utility maximization or by the maximizing acts of others.[75]

Consider the case of Joe. Joe is a junior faculty member and hopes to have a future career as an academic. It is a strongly held commitment on his part. It necessarily leads to a certain partiality in the shaping of his present and future choices. Joe's pursuit of his goal has continuity with the past in the form of many years of study and reflection. It promises to have continuity with the future if he diligently pursues his teaching and research. Imagine, however, the existence of a 'rebel angel' always looking over Joe's shoulder and exhorting him to maximize outcomes in each of his actions. The goodness or badness of an action is always to be judged with reference to the rebel angel's demands. Such scrutiny would radically undermine his integrity as a person because it would constantly question whether his work commitments were optimific. The unity in his working life would be nothing more than a specious form of unity that would amount to satisfying the calls of this rebel angel. The demands imposed by the rebel angel are clearly analogous to the kinds of demand that would be imposed on us if we were to attempt to make our decisions in conformity with utilitarianism's key requirement to maximize.

Some consequentialist thinkers respond to this outcome maximization problem by proposing a rule of practical rationality that an agent is not always required to choose the optimific option but may always do so. Such a rule is said to create an agent-centered prerogative, granting the agent a power of veto over always having to maximize outcomes.[76] On the face of it, the creation of an agent-centered prerogative may appear to be a plausible solution. A prerogative is recognized that grants relief from the scrutinizing gaze of the rebel angel, thereby restoring some control to the agent. There is, however, a key reason for doubting that the creation of such a prerogative is going to be strong enough to adequately preserve our sense of integrity.[77] It leaves the following central problem unaddressed. Suppose a research body were to offer Joe a year long research grant. Joe was promised support because it was judged by the body to be the best outcome at the time it was promised. Imagine, though, that James, a brighter and more resourceful scholar came along with a more promising project. Could the body be justified in breaking its promise to Joe and favor James's research instead? After all, agents are always entitled (but not required) to act optimifically. External assurances undertaken by one party to another are also extremely important to our deep seated sense of integrity—a life that is not rendered eventistic or episodic by the maximizing deeds of others. Critical ground projects, then, would still be placed on far too fragile and precarious a footing.[78]

3.9 Key Requirements of Practical Rationality

As I have stated previously (see s. 3.6c), practical rationality is itself a primary good of persons. Practical rationality requires us to pursue goods and avoid evils. All the primary goods constitute ultimate reasons to act. They are not components of a hierarchy of goodness culminating in the pursuit of a supreme good, for they are all final ends in themselves. As sources of ultimate goodness they are irreducibly diverse. Nor are they units of pleasure or preference that can be ranked and weighed as part of a relentless quest to maximize outcomes. Because each primary good is irreducible, non-derivative and incommensurably diverse, each different and distinct primary good generates its own unique demands that shape the ways in which we can hope to make and execute practically reasonable choices in our lives.

How then can we choose reasonably when making choices that engage and impact these primary goods? Reflection on the first principle of practical rationality, allied to our normative grasp and experience of primary goods, gives rise to further specifications of the first principle of practical rationality that flesh out what the good of practical rationality itself requires of us by way of choice formation. These specifications of the first principle constitute the requirements of practical rationality, requirements that crucially frame how we can deliberate reasonably with a view to purposeful action.

It is by following the critical guidance of the requirements of practical rationality that we transition from the directive 'is-to-be' of practical rationality to the specifically moral domain of the 'ought-to-be.' We make the transition from pre-moral normative directivity to normative prescriptivity in ethics by following and applying, in full, all of the applicable requirements of practical rationality. Failure to follow all of the applicable requirements is to be committed to making and executing a practically unreasonable (that is, less than fully reasonable) choice.[79] Morally good choices are informed by and adhere to all the relevant sub-principles or requirements of the first principle of practical rationality. Morally bad choices fail to respect the requirements of practical rationality when deliberating with a view to action.

3.9a Underlying Status of a Good

Primary goods should not be treated as if they were secondary goods and vice versa. Primary goods are primary goods. Secondary goods are secondary goods. In doing and pursuing what is good, we are required to accord to each good its objective status. It is practically unreasonable to upgrade or downgrade the categorical status of a good. The status of a good of persons is reason-based and is not merely a matter for subjective attitude or opinion. We should make due efforts to ensure that we do not mistake a pseudo-good for a primary good or confer on a secondary derived good the status of primary good. We are required to ensure that primary goods are not downgraded and treated as if they were only means-end instrumentalities.[80]

3.9b Control of Practical Rationality

It is practically unreasonable to ignore the positive or negative demands exerted by a primary good due to the influence of sub-rational motivations. Practical rationality is required to exercise direct governance over all sub-rational motivations to act. It is not unreasonable to be motivated by sub-rational desires and wants provided that we are not led astray to choose and act in ways that are incompatible with all the key requirements of practical rationality. Wants, desires and emotions must ultimately be subject to the scrutinizing and revising jurisdiction of practical rationality itself.[81]

3.9c Life as a Structured Narrative

An episodic life, one lacking a structured sense of ongoing narrative, is not practically reasonable. In order to lead any kind of fulfilling life, we cannot abandon the integrating requirement to develop and cultivate narrative structure in our lives. Consider the case of Jane. Jane eschews commitment to narrative structure. She recognizes the discrete value of different primary goods but pursues them as isolates in a shopping list of goods. Today she plays tennis. Tomorrow she collects, polishes and trades seashells. The day after she reads a book on fishing. Another day, another good. She simply thinks that she can engage the primary goods in her life by lurking eventistically from discrete engagement to discrete engagement. There is no deeper sense of integrating connectivity. Her life lacks a progressive sense of narrative structure than can only be achieved by being committed to the furtherance and cultivation of rational ground projects. Without such commitments, Jane cannot begin to explore the bounty of primary goods in her life, for she has unreasonably opted to respond to the diverse appeal of these goods in shallow and superficial ways.[82]

If it is unreasonable to eschew commitments to ground projects, it is also unreasonable to be fanatical in our reification of any particular ground project such that its frustration or failure is thought to rob our lives of any further purposeful meaning. Often events outwith our control can seriously compromise our ability to pursue a ground project. Death, unrequited love, redundancy, bad health, etc. Practically reasonable commitment, however, does not equate to zealous attachment. The failure of a ground project, no matter how significant the project, should not ultimately devastate our very ability to 'pick up the pieces' and redirect ourselves, either by reinvigorating our commitments to other existing ground projects or by developing and cultivating new ones.[83]

3.9d Constrained Partiality

Primary goods are not merely 'goods for me' but 'goods for us.' They are the primary goods of all persons. While we have certain partialities towards our own projects and interests, we are nevertheless required to accord to other people opportunities to find fulfillment in life. Reasonable self-concern (constrained partiality) does not equate to a charter for selfishness (unconstrained partiality). The 'Golden Rule,' formulated as—'treat others only in ways that you are willing to be treated in the same situation'—places important limitations on a person's ability to develop and cultivate their own priorities in life to the detriment of others. To meet the requirement of the Golden Rule, we are required to discern what impact our choice to act or to refrain from acting might have on the lives of others. Reflectively and imaginatively, we need to consider ourselves in the place of others, as being on the receiving end of the choice, and ask: are we fairly scrutinizing the impact that our choice may have upon the reasonably formed commitments and priorities of others?[84]

3.9e Respect for Primary Goods

In deliberating with a view to action, practical rationality requires that we pursue and respect primary goods and do not violate them.[85] We are required to pursue and engage primary goods in our lives. We are not unreasonably required to pursue every good to the maxim extent possible. Maximization is a strategy that would radically attack the varying importance we attach to diverse goods *viz.* our differing projects and commitments in life. To have a narrative is to cultivate certain priorities in our lives and this leads to certain partialities. If we were to try and maximize our pursuit of every primary good, we would quickly start to see the fabric of our commitments tear apart. By being maximally stretched in every direction, we would cease to be able to pursue our projects and commitments in ways that are inherently fulfilling to us. Properly understood, maximization strategies undermine rather than promote different worthwhile ways of living.[86]

Instead of maximization, we are required to actively cultivate the pursuit of at least some of the different primary goods in our lives. Some goods will be pursued more actively than others, depending on our stage of life, our ground projects, our dispositions, and so on. Released from the daunting specter of maximization, we are rationally empowered to make different levels of responses to different primary goods according to the unfolding nature of our personal commitments and priorities.[87] A musical vocation, for example, is not inherently better than a vocation as a hermit. Yet, both vocations are commitments that will, in part, shape the way in which the primary goods are pursued. Hermits will pursuit some goods more fully than musicians and other goods less so. Hermits may place more of a stress on the good of contemplation and less stress on active companionship with others. Musicians may place more priority on the goods of friendship and play. Engagement and pursuit, not maximization, then, leaves ample scope for the reasonable cultivation and promotion of different priorities in life.

If we have considerable freedom of scope to pursue different primary goods with differing levels of engagement, we are nevertheless always required to accord due respect to the minimal demands exerted by any of the primary goods. Minimal demands are very often negative or they may, more rarely, be positive. Negatively we disrespect a primary good, when, contrary to its own discernable normative demands, we do not actively refrain from performing certain kinds of action that would, by intention or by negligence, harm or attack the minimal level of due commitment owed to the primary good in question. Positively we disrespect the discernable demands of a primary good when we fail to perform actions that are minimally required of us.[88]

A hermit, for example, by physically removing himself from the company of others, can respect (and thus not violate) the minimal demands generated by the good of friendship by not deliberately renouncing or despising the genuine significance of that good as a primary good of persons. The musician can respect and not violate the good of contemplation as long as the musician does not renounce or denigrate the significance of that good as a primary good of persons and refrains from attacking reasonable instantiations of that good in the lives of others.

Both the hermit and the musician can respect the minimal positive demands of the good of human life, circumstances permitting, by taking active steps to maintain their health by eating and exercise. Each different primary good, then, discernibly generates its own minimal levels of demand. The violation of a good's minimal demands, whether negative or positive, will always result in an unreasonable choice to disrespect the proper standing and significance of a primary good *qua* primary good.

3.9f Discernment of Normative Demands

In order to decide between different courses of action that may negatively impact one or more instances of different primary goods, the different demands of the different goods in play must be carefully discerned.[89] Consider, for example, a seeming conflict between the primary good of human life and the primary good of knowledge. A captain of a Nazi U-boat has boarded your vessel and commands you (the captain of the other vessel) to tell him whether or not there are any Jews on board. What do you do? Does the primary good of knowledge 'override' or 'outweigh' the good of human life or vice versa? The response *viz.* due respect for discernable demands, however, is not that weight of good A 'outweighs' the weight of good B or vice versa. Discerning the demands of very different goods is a different kind of process from consequentialist-based reckonings that seek to establish the greater comparative worth of one good against the other.[90] Rather, the discernment answer emphasizes that due and proper commitment to the primary good of knowledge does not impose upon any of us the key negative demand that communicative truth may never be intentionally acted against where one party to a communication has no reasonable basis for requiring truthful communication from the other party. The good of human life, on the other hand, is just the sort of intrinsic good that does positively demand from us that we should come to the aid of innocents, especially when life and limb are being threatened, where it is both practicable to do so and where the lives of other innocents would not be unfairly jeopardized.

In the case of the command from the Nazi U-boat captain, then, a careful discernment of the different negative and positive demands of the different goods in play would permit the telling of an untruth in order that the Nazi U-boat captain may be deceived.[91] It is important to realize that there is, here, no 'justified violation' of one good by another being proposed, for no violation of a primary good can ever be reconciled with the requirements of practical rationality (see s. 3.9e). Instead, the respective levels of commitment demanded from us by each of the two different primary goods discernibly differ, rendering it permissible, in the circumstances, to tell an untruth to the Nazi U-boat captain.

Notes

1   For discussion of different types of natural law theory see Kevin Wm. Wildes (2006), pp. 29–37.
2   Plato's Socrates in the *Phaedo* advanced the argument that the condition of the immortal human soul cannot be improved by seeking to destroy the body, for the body is a necessary instrument for improving the condition of the soul. Second, Plato advanced the notion that bodily life is not the possession of the person. As dependent beings, we have been placed in our bodies by the gods and we are not free to abandon this station. See Plato (1997), 61d–62d.
3   Only the 'miraculous' could account for such a phenomenon.
4   On Plato see Michael L. Morgan (1992), pp. 227–47. On Christianity see John Hicks (1994), chs 9–12.
5   On some of the key distinctions between metaethical naturalism and non-naturalism see Roger Crisp (1996), pp. 113–29.
6   Hume (2000), III, 1, i.
7   See further Craig Paterson (2006), pp. 301–4.
8   See Moore (2002), p. 68. For general commentary on Moore's non-naturalism see Alexander Miller (2003), pp. 10–25.
9   Stephen W. Ball (1988), pp. 197–213.
10 See further Terence Horgan and Mark Timmons (1990–91), pp. 447–65 and (1992), pp. 153–75.
11 Heinrich Rommen (1947); Jacques Maritain (1951); Henry B. Veatch (1971) and (1990); Ralph McInerny (1997) and (1992).
12 See for example Patrick Lee (1997), who, I think, unsuccessfully tries to reconstruct Aquinas as an ethical non-naturalist. On Aquinas and the *inclinationes naturales* see Paterson (2006).
13 *Summa Theoligicae* II–II q. 64, a. 5.
14 *Summa Theoligicae* II–II q. 154, a. 11.
15 Ralph McInerny (1992), p. 194.
16 See Antony J. Lisska (1996).
17 See Gómez-Lobo (1985), pp. 232–49.
18 Lisska (1996), pp. 195–201.
19 For more on the metaethical defence of non–naturalism see Russ Shafer-Landau (2006), pp. 209–32.

20 See Paterson (2006).

21 See for example, McInerny (1992) and (1997).

22 Thus falling into the hands of scepticism and subjectivity à la Mackie (1977), pp. 15–49.

23 A general positioning of practical reason that admittedly has a something of a 'Kantian twist.' Here I have been influenced by Roger J. Sullivan's (1989) account of Kant as something of a natural law theorist. Sullivan interprets Kant's account of practical reason as being teleological. See esp. his chs 6 and 13. See also J. B. Schneewind (1991).

24 See John Finnis (1980), pp. 100–103 and (1983), pp. 10–19.

25 *Summa Theoligicae* I, II q. 94, a. 2.

26 See Martin Rhonheimer (2000), pp. 31–2 for an endorsement of Aquinas's principle as an underived first principle of practical rationality. See also Alfonso Gómez-Lobo (2002), ch. 1. See further Alan Donagan (1969), pp. 325–39 for a proto-Kantian interpretation of Aquinas's teleology of practical reason.

27 Russell Hittinger (1987), for example, insists that the first principle of practical reason is a full-blown moral principle. Perhaps it was for Aquinas. This, however, is further reason to argue for needed revisions in Aquinas's own account of practical reason.

28 See Rhonheimer (2000), pp. 22–31.

29 An excellent review of self-evidence is given by Philip Stratton-Lake (2002), esp. pp. 18–23. See also Robert Audi (1996), pp. 101–36. Crucially, it is essential to differentiate between implicitly grasping the truth of a self-evident proposition and being reflexively aware that the truth of a proposition is actually self-evident in status.

30 Clearly this discussion of self-evidence owes much to the broad intuitionist tradition of British ethics during the first half of the twentieth century, especially G. E. Moore and W. D. Ross. See Karen Jones (2005), pp. 70–73.

31 On self-evidence as 'rational insight' see Finnis (1980), pp. 32–3, 64–9, 73–5. On his interpretation of self-evidence in Aquinas see (1998), pp. 86–94. Lloyd L. Weinreb (1987), pp. 109–13 and Russell Hittinger (1987), pp. 44–5 both mistakenly view claims to self-evidence as being a resort to 'personal fiat' masquerading as objectivity. The conception of self-evidence is not, as it were, an empirical statement of the actual acceptance of practical truths by those who have capacity to know, whether philosophers or field labourers. Rather, it is an assertion of the capacity, in principle, to so know. Several reasons can account for this fissure between capacity to know and acceptance, for example, prior cultural or intellectual commitments already made that color our reflective awareness of the sources of normativity. Talk of barriers to acceptance may sound somewhat 'strident' to the reader, but it is really no more strident that the claims of other objectivists, who, in seeking to avoid the Scylla of relativism and the Charybdis of subjectivism, assert (a) that moral truth must be assessable to human reason while (b) accounting for the fact that many people, often very intelligent, do not share and indeed positively reject their account of moral truth.

32 G. E. Moore's list of intrinsic goods consisted of only friendship and aesthetic experience (hence the quip that the good life for Moore consisted of gazing at objects of art in the company of friends!). Other, more adequate and expansive lists are: John Finnis (1980)— life; knowledge; play; aesthetic experience; friendship; religion; practical reasonableness. David S. Oderberg (2000a)—life; knowledge; friendship; work and play; the appreciation of beauty; religious belief and practice. T. D. J. Chappell (1998)—life; truth, and the knowledge of the truth; friendship; aesthetic value; physical and mental health and harmony; pleasure and the avoidance of pain; reason; rationality and reasonableness; the natural world; people; fairness; achievements; the contemplation of God (if God exists). Philip Devine(2000b)—life and health; procreation; friendship; knowledge; aesthetic experience; play; autonomy; harmony with ultimate power. My own list overlaps in many

ways with these listings. However, I do not regard the good of religion as a separate good. Ultimate questions of meaning and explanation are components of the goods of knowledge and of beauty. All maintain that life and heath are primary goods of persons. I disagree with Chappell's inclusion of pleasure and pain avoidance as primary goods—see s. 3.7b. I also disagree with Devine that autonomy can rightly be classified as a primary good of persons—see s. 3.7c.

33 The *summum bonum* is replaced by several irreducibly basic goods.

34 On the use of dialectical argument see Robert P. George (1999), pp. 31–82.

35 I use further dialectical arguments in subsequent chapters to help defend and shore up (i) the use of double effect reasoning; (ii) a conception of material innocence; (iii) the action and omission distinction; (iv) the notion that death is a primal evil for all persons; (v) a traditional definition of death; and (vi) the key idea that all individuated human beings, however profoundly damaged, are indeed persons *not* non-persons.

36 On life as a basic grounding good see Oderberg (2000a), pp. 138–43. On the intrinsic and instrumental distinction see Mark C. Murphy (2001), pp. 101–5.

37 On dualism see Patrick Lee (1998), pp. 135–51; See also David Braine's seminal critique of dualism (1993).

38 We can intelligibly grasp (despite the currency of some popular euphemisms) that profoundly damaged human beings are still essentially persons and not non-persons. See s. 6.3.

39 See Finnis (1980), pp. 59–79; Murphy (2001), pp. 106–8; Oderberg (2000a), pp. 41–2 and (2000c), 519–21; Gómez-Lobo (2002), pp. 21–3.

40 Murphy (2001), pp. 106–8.

41 Contra Hittinger (1987), p. 148 and Oderberg (2000a), p. 44, for example, I think that religious questions about the purpose of existence and life are generally subsumable under the good of knowledge and also of aesthetic experience. There is no separate primary good of religion.

42 See Finnis (1980), pp. 88, 100–103 and (1983), pp. 1–15; Chappell (1998), p. 39. See also Rhonheimer, (2000), pp. 58–61.

43 Murphy (2001), pp. 114–18 calls practical reason the good of excellence in agency.

44 See Gómez-Lobo (2002), pp. 13–16 for the separation of family and friendship.

45 The *locus classicus* for friendship as an intrinsic good is Aristotle's *Nicomachean Ethics*. At 1156b10–11, 1157b3, he tells us that a true friend loves his friend for what he is and not for pleasure or utility and he cares for his friend for the sake of the friend. The good of friendship is one of G. E. Moore's two intrinsic goods. See Moore (2002), pp.188–9.

46 On the civic form of friendship in Aristotle see Suzanne Stern-Gillett (1995), pp. 148–69.

47 Murphy (2001), pp. 126–31; Devine (2000), pp. 72–3; Oderberg (2000a), pp. 42–3; Finnis (1980), pp. 141–8.

48 Murphy (2001), pp. 111–14; Oderberg (2000a), p. 43; Gómez-Lobo (2002), pp. 17–18.

49 Finnis (1980), p. 87 (on play but not work); Murphy (2001), pp. 111–14; Oderberg (2000a), p. 43; Gómez-Lobo (2002), pp. 17–18.

50 On beauty or aesthetic experience see, for example, Moore (2002), pp. 188–9; Finnis (1980), pp. 87–8; Murphy (2001), pp. 9–11.

51 See Chappell (1998), pp. 40–41.

52 See Chappell (1998), pp. 40–41.

53 Murphy (2001), pp. 96–100.

54 See Oderberg (2004a), pp. 129–32. Oderberg penetratingly responds to Chappell (1998), p. 38 who claims that pleasure is a fully intelligible and irreducibly basic reason for action quite on its own account.

55 See, for example, Dan W. Brock, (1984), pp. 83–106.
56 Oderberg (2004a), pp. 129–32.
57 Murphy (2001), pp. 96–100.
58 Gómez-Lobo (2002), pp. 34–5.
59 See Roger J. Sullivan's (1989) account of Kantian autonomy at p. 47. Sullivan stresses that for Kant, autonomy refers to our ability and responsibility as rational persons to know what morality requires of us and to act in accord with truly objective moral principles.
60 Joseph Raz (1986), defends an account of personal autonomy as an intrinsic good. Devine (2000b), 73–4 also states that autonomy is an intrinsic good. See also Douglas B Rasmussen and Douglas J Den Uyl (1991). I think, however, that it is only really moral autonomy to authentically deliberate and organize a life narrative under the aegis of practical rationality itself that can be properly said to have an intrinsically good dimension. As Hittinger puts it (1993), p. 83, referring to Rasmussen and Uyl on liberty of choice: 'A prospective agent who grasps that a particular good or end is basic to his perfection, but who has given no consideration to the rectitude of the means to be chosen, is not yet engaged in practical reasoning.' See 5.6a.
61 See Joseph Raz (1986), pp. 322–4 for a discussion of incommensurable options.
62 See Chappell (2001a) and (2001b).
63 See Douglas B. Rasmussen (1999), pp. 1–43 for an unconvincing discussion of nesting 'final' ends within the pursuit of one ultimate primary end.
64 On Peter Singer see Stephen buckle (2005), pp. 175–94 and on R. M. Hare see Tom Carson (1993), 305–31. See also introductory discussion of different kinds of proposed methods to commensurate values in Ruth Chang (1997), pp. 1–38.
65 Ashley uses the phrase 'polyteleologism'—Benedict M. Ashley (1994).
66 On ethical pluralism versus monism see Robert Gay (1985), pp. 250–62 and Chappell (1998), pp. 13–21.
67 Moreover, the Aristotelian-Thomistic project, in my view, illicitly attempts to commit what has become known as the 'quantifier shift fallacy.' There is a shift in the scope of the quantifier from the plural to the singular. It is basically unsound to argue that since all action aims at some good, there is a good, the Good, at which all things aim. It is as unsound as arguing that 'since all roads lead somewhere, there is an ultimate destination to which all roads lead.' See, for example, Michael Pakaluk (2005), p. 49.
68 D. W. Hodgson (1967), ch. 2.
69 See Alistair MacIntyre (1981), pp. 62–6, 70–1.
70 On preferences see Amartya Sen and Bernard Williams (1982), pp. 1–22 and Jon Elster (1982), pp. 219–38 in the same collection. See also Christoph Fehige and Ulla Wessels (1998), pp. xx–xliii.
71 On immoral preferences see John C. Harsanyi (1988), pp. 89–99. See also Anne MacLean (1993), pp. 162–86; Tom Carson (1986) and (1993).
72 See Bernard Williams (1985), pp. 83–4, 87–8, 89–91. See also Thomas Nagel (1986), pp. 15–16. Individuals commend their judgments to others, but not for the reason that it will maximize preferences in the fashion stated by Hare. Rather, individuals commend a certain form of action rather than another because it is a worthwhile account of what seems good and worthwhile in a given situation. Despite all the attempts of utilitarians to find the single font of morality based on a common denominator, their attempts have proved unconvincing. Either the source of the value is not univocal, as is the case with happiness; is univocal but too base as in the case of hedonism; or we accept preferences as a source of value but are forced to engage in commensurations based on preferences that no individual could weigh and accept in the impartial terms that utilitarianism requires.

73 See Bernard Williams (1973), pp. 108–18. See also Edward Harcourt (1998), pp. 189–98.
74 On eventism see Anselm W. Müller (1977), pp. 115–32
75 Geoffrey Scarre (1996), chs VII–VIII.
76 Samuel Scheffler (1994), pp. 1–12, 19–32.
77 Scarre (1996), ch. VIII.
78 Harcourt (1998), pp. 189–98. Scheffler (1994), ch. 4, searches for but alas cannot locate within the structure of consequentialism itself a viable basis for defending the importance of agent-centered restrictions. Agent-centered restrictions go beyond agent-centered prerogatives and can justify obligatory prohibitions on the execution of certain action kinds even if they are held to be outcome maximizing.
79 On the transition from pre-moral to moral see Robert P. George (1999), pp. 49–53 and Finnis (1980), pp. 100–103, 126–7.
80 See Murphy (2001), pp. 198–201.
81 On practical reason's civil rule over the emotions see Finnis's analysis of Aquinas (1998), pp. 72–8.
82 Narrative structures are at the center of T. D. J. Chappell's pluralistic conception of how we pursue diverse primary goods in our lives. See Chappell (1998), ch. 6.
83 On avoiding extremes of under-commitment and over-commitment to projects and plans see Murphy (2001), pp. 246–52; Finnis (1980), pp. 109–10.
84 On the Golden Rule see Finnis (1980), pp. 106–9 and Alan Donagan (1977), pp, 57–66.
85 For Chappell (2004), p. 102, natural law ethics 'does not require the agent to take a maximizing attitude to any of the goods that confront him.' Instead, goods must be promoted and respected but not violated.
86 See Chappell (2003), pp. 161–77 and (2004), pp. 102–26.
87 See Chappell (2003), pp. 161–77 and (2004), pp. 102–26.
88 Chappell (1998), pp. 84–92 uses the language of respecting and not violating the 'demands of goods' and I adopt this language for subsequent use in the book.
89 Emphasis upon insightful discernment of the key demands generated by different primary goods is essential if we are to (a) defend the unique and diverse appeal of different primary goods and (b) not fall into creating a position whereby an appeal to incommensurability is used to try and warrant an overly extended criteria of practical reason—essentially the position adopted by John Finnis—that it is always and everywhere wrong to choose to intentionally attack, harm, destroy, thwart or otherwise impede any primary good or any instantiation of any primary good (1980), pp. 118–24. For a critique of Finnis's strict interpretation of incommensurability and its implications for practical deliberation see Russell Pannier (1987), pp. 427–39. On incommensurability and choice see further Andrew F. Reeve, (1997), pp. 545–52.
90 See Chappell (1998), pp. 84–92 on the different kinds of demands that can be generated by the unique pull of different intrinsic goods.
91 Other options would, of course, also be in play—refusal to speak, equivocation, dissimulation, etc.

Chapter 4

The Good of Human Life

4.1 Introduction

All of the primary goods discussed in the previous chapter constitute the basic ingredients for a fulfilling life. Each good enriches our lives in countless ways and there are countless fulfilling lives to live. Each good presents to us many attractive possibilities for choice with a view to action. Crucially, the primary status of a good cannot be grasped by any form of naturalism that purports to derive norms from some more foundational descriptive premise. It is not, therefore, possible to prove the normative status of the good of human life, say, by means of a traditional scholastic syllogism, where the goodness of human life is included as the second premise of an argument—P1, persons tend [incline] to preserve their lives; P2, human life is good; C, persons, therefore, ought to preserve their lives. The normative status of the good of human life in P2 cannot be deduced from the factual foundation stated in P1. Primary goods are, nevertheless, objectively grounded normative sources for they are not the mere product of subjective opinion or convention. The objective normative appeal of a primary good is directly grasped by practical rational insight.[1]

As a primary good of persons, capable of being valued for its own sake, and not merely instrumentally (as a facilitative means to some further goal or end), human life is an intelligible good whose goodness is not deduced or derived from the goodness of other goods and whose goodness is not reducible to any other good. By insightfully grasping that human life is a primary good for us, we are also able to appreciate that human life *qua* human life is an intrinsic good for all persons. Due to the operation of practical rationality, itself a primary good, a good that specifies the requirements directing all practically reasonable choice, it is not practically reasonable to (1) deny to human life its intrinsically valuable standing or (2) disrespect or violate any of its key normative demands. A deliberative choice made to treat human life as if it were a non-intrinsic good of only instrumental worth would be a choice to unreasonably (wrongly) discount its objective worth as a primary good (see s. 3.9a). It is wrong (practically unreasonable) to devalue the good of human life by regarding it as a pure instrumentality. In making a choice to disrespect or violate any of the key normative demands generated by the good of human life, the agent is making a wrongful choice to set aside or disregard a key requirement of practical rationality (see s. 3.9e). A morally right choice needs to adhere to all of the applicable requirements of practical rationality if a choice is to pass muster in the reasonableness stakes. Of course human life does have an instrumental dimension that constitutes part of its make-up, since it is a good that is utilized in the pursuance of all other goods. In seeking to utilize it instrumentally, however, it ought to be respected and not violated in and through its own proper status as the very kind of intrinsic good it is.[2] A decision to set aside or ignore a requirement of practical rationality is wrongful because we are opting to direct our actions in a less than fully reasonable way. Right choices adhere to all of the applicable requirements of practical rationality and wrong choices fail to adhere to all of the applicable requirements.

4.2 Action Types

As we saw in Chapter 2 (see ss. 2.4a; 2.6c), full-blown consequentialists typically deny that there is any defining structure to an action such that we can meaningfully talk of morally wrong 'types' or 'species' of action that ought never to be performed—murder, rape, torture, etc. As argued by Jonathan Bennett, it is said not to be possible to 'isolate' the specific elements of an action from questions of consequence. The structural evaluation of an action cannot be viewed in this delimited way. The proximate or immediate objective of an action, due to the operation of what is called the 'accordion effect,' is capable of being re-described in many different ways. Accordingly, the action-consequence distinction is considered too subjective and malleable to do any substantive work required of it. The moral assessment of an action, it is argued, is best performed in terms of comparisons between states-of-affairs. Different possible states-of-affairs are compared and a plan is formed to bring about the best state-of-affairs via the implementation of a series of performances. Right actions are those whose product will likely generate the best balance of good over evil effects.

We have already seen in the previous chapter (see s. 3.8b) that different possible maximization strategies proposed by utilitarian thinkers are unsound in their underpinnings. Maximization is a flawed approach to normative guidance because it (1) unreasonably attempts to comprehensively aggregate very different kinds of good, and (2) it fails to take our important sense of personal agency seriously, limiting how we can reasonably pursue and promote very different goods in our lives. To this list, we can add a third shortcoming of consequentialism, (3) a levelling approach to action appraisal that illicitly seeks to set aside the moral significance of different structural elements of an action—(a) means, (b) end and (c) circumstances—in an attempt to justify an overall 'state of affairs' approach to moral assessment.

I do not wish to deny that terms used to describe an action can sometimes be elided into terms that can re-describe the consequences of an action and vice versa. Performing action X with the resultant consequence Y can often be re-described as simply performing Y. Multiple descriptions are possible. Not all descriptions, however, best capture or bring into focus the *morally significant* aspects of an action.[3] Killing (performing X) in order to permanently end pain (consequence Y) can be re-described as permanently ending pain (performing Y). Such a re-description, although possible, is inadequate for the purpose of ethical analysis. Instead of expressing the underlying structure of an action, such re-description conceals from view the relationship between the proximate and further objective of an action.[4] Certain types or species of action—rape, torture, murder, etc.—are of such normative significance to us as persons—because they gravely impact important constitutive goods—that we cannot, without deep distortion, elide their moral description into re-descriptions centered on the assessment of further objectives or consequences.[5] Intentionally killing an innocent woman (proximate objective) with the beneficial effect that several other innocent lives could be saved (further objective and resultant consequence) cannot adequately be re-described as the 'execution of a life saving plan,' for this kind of re-description disingenuously attempts to conceal from us *intuitively significant moral matter*—that the woman was innocent, that she had not consented to her being killed, that she was being killed as the means to procure a benefit for others, and so on.

Placing to one side whether or not it is ever licit to intentionally kill an innocent person, it is *crucially relevant moral matter* to understand that an innocent woman is being intentionally killed (proximate objective) as the adoptive means used to pursue the saving of several lives (further objective and resultant consequence). Acceptance of this kind of leveling description is, I think, a sign that an ethical system is prepared to countenance *concealment by misdescription* in order to insulate itself from the observation that what is really being justified here is the commission of an evil (the killing of an innocent woman) in order that good may come of it (the saving of several other innocent lives).[6]

As agents, we are concerned to assess the structural make-up of morally significant actions and are not content to rest with the description of an action that is focused only on its further objective or consequences. Thus, if it were intended to kill an innocent as the proximate means-objective for the procurement of beneficial consequences, this structural connectivity must be brought to light in any adequate account of the action. It is true that there may be many instances in which elision between an action and its consequences is of little import. Often we are indifferent with regard to means and such elision is common and harmless. It does not matter if I boiled the water for a cup of tea in an electric kettle or used a pan on a gas stove top. 'Boiled water' will suffice. Such elision will not suffice, however, when it comes to tokens or instances of action types that have a grave impact upon important goods. In such cases we demand to know more about the structural make-up of the action, especially the reasons (if any) that could permit A doing X for the sake of Y.[7]

Many areas of human endeavor make use of action types to direct activity—law, sports, games, medicine, sciences, etc. Can we imagine a sport that does not designate action types that are compatible with the rules of a sport from action types that are not compatible with those rules, for example, punching an opposing football player in the stomach in order to gain control of the ball? Can we imagine the functioning of law in society without being able to specify that instances of certain kinds of action are violations of the law, for example, parking a vehicle in an area prohibited to vehicular traffic? Why should ethics be inherently different with regard to the need for action types? Action types, as with any other area of human endeavor, are also indispensable to our analysis of ethical conduct. It is no 'accident' that we have developed action types around forms of human conduct that seek to disrespect or violate primary goods and important secondary goods that facilitate our pursuit of primary goods.[8]

4.3 Elements of an Action

The intended objective of an action, as we have seen (see s. 4.2), can be proximate or more distant (further/remote). Very often proximate objectives are action types selected as an intended means. A further objective, for the sake of which a means is adopted, is often termed the end of an action. Using scholastic terms, the 'what' element—the proximate objective to be performed as a intentional means to some further end—is designated the *finis operis* ('end of the work') and the 'why' element—the further objective for the sake of which the *finis operis* is chosen to be performed—is designated the *finis operantis* ('end of the worker [or agent]').[9] The third circumstantial element informing an action pertains to such questions as how? where? when? who?, etc.[10] Thus, taking a rest or going for a walk, for example, may be a good, bad or neutral action, depending on the circumstances.

Such is the importance of these three elements to the moral quality of an action, that any substantial defect in the elemental structure of an action—a bad end, a bad means or bad circumstances—vitiates the *integral rightfulness of an action*.[11] Aquinas succinctly expressed this requirement for right action as *bonum ex integra causa; malum ex quocumque defectu* ('for something to be good, it must be good in every respect; for badness, one defect suffices').[12] A bad end deprives an action of a key source of its goodness, as does the intentional election of a bad means to pursue an otherwise worthwhile end, as does the presence of bad circumstances that would render its performance unfair. Actions are wrong to the extent that they are lacking in any critical component needed for their moral integrity and fulfillment. These three morally relevant conditions, taken together, determine whether actions are actually right or wrong.[13]

Consider the following two examples. First, a man who gives a female work colleague a gift in order to deceive her into thinking that he personally cares for her but really despises her, is not performing a morally right action, notwithstanding the appeal to consequences that (i) the gift makes her feel good about herself and (ii) she is unlikely to discover the deceptive motive informing the action. The motive (intended end) crucially matters to the rightness of the action. An intended bad end can render an action wrong that might otherwise be right. Second, a woman cares for a male work colleague and does not want to hurt his feelings. She lies to him in order to spare his feelings when he asks her how his work reputation is viewed by other colleagues. Notwithstanding the good motive she has, she is performing a wrongful action because he has a communicative right to a truthful answer. She elects to execute a bad intended means in order to bring about a good consequence. A bad means-to-an-end can render an action wrong in spite of a good intentional end.

As we can see from the above examples, intentions pertaining to ends and means, contra consequentialism, are not incidental to moral assessment but are, rather, positioned at the very heart of moral assessment. The assessment of rightful action cannot be severed from an assessment of the good, bad or neutral intentions that inform the make-up of an action. Intentions critically matter to us because they emanate from and shape the center of our lives as persons. By the content of our intentions, we reveal the kinds of action that we are willing to perform and reveal the sort of person we are (or are prepared to become).[14] Only an ethics that unreasonably discounts the importance of a person's integral character to moral assessment—his or her dispositions, ground projects and commitments, and the negative intransitive effects that bad intentional choices inevitably have on character—could minimize the critical relevance of intentions over ends and means to the moral assessment of right action.

4.4 Normative Demands

When people think of a natural law approach to ethics, they usually think of absolutist prohibitions that ban all instances of certain action types—intentional instances of lying, masturbation, contraception, homosexual acts, killing of the innocent, etc.—regardless of the end or consequences for the sake of which the action is performed. These absolutist prohibitions are concrete and not merely general exhortations to maximize good and minimize evil or to commit no unjust actions or to commit no wrongs. Formal moral absolutes are not considered controversial whereas 'concrete' moral absolutes are.[15] I accept the practical reality of concrete moral absolutes as an indispensable feature of the normative landscape. Concrete moral absolutism, as I understand it, is the notion that the licitness or illicitness of an action is to be morally assessed according to the 'type of action' that it is. If a type of action is wrong then it is wrong to intentionally perform any instance of that action type. Where I significantly differ from traditional accounts of natural law theory, however, is (a) over the ways in which certain forms of intentional behavior—for example, all contraceptive or homosexual acts—have been subjected to unwarranted blanket prohibitions, not, I think, on the basis of unassisted natural reason but on the basis of 'supernatural overspill';[16] and (b) over the ways in which some moral norms and action types are best framed with regard to scope and content, thus challenging, for example, the blanket prohibition that all actions intended to harm any primary good as a means to an end must always be subject to negative prohibition.[17]

Lest the tenor of my immediate comments be misunderstood, let me make it clear that I do seek to articulate and defend the practical rationality of some concrete moral absolutes regarding the good of human life and health that are quite traditionally framed: 'it is always and everywhere wrong to intentionally kill an innocent person, regardless of any further appeal to end or consequences'; 'it is always and everywhere wrong to intentionally torture an innocent person ... '; 'it is always and everywhere wrong to intentionally rape a person ... '. My list is not intended to be exhaustive but illustrative of the kinds of exceptionless norms that, I think, due appreciation for the good of human life demands from us.

Since concrete moral absolutes are usually framed in terms of negative prohibitions—'do not perform action X'—and not positively 'you are required to perform action X'—I will first turn to examine the topic of life's positive demands. After discussing positive demands I will turn to consider the scope and content of life's negative demands.[18]

4.4a Positive Demands of Life and Health

Different positive demands are generated by different primary goods, for as we have seen, each primary good is unique and distinct in its appeal (see s. 3.6). The normative demands of the good of beauty differ from the normative demands generated by the good of knowledge, and so on. Some goods demand more ongoing attention and consideration from us than others. However, depending on the shape of our life's narrative structure and ground projects, we will respond to and engage with some goods more fully than others. We may set aside more time for work than play; we may place more emphasis on the good of friendship than the pursuit of beauty; we may stress the good of family life more than work, and so on. In pursuing goods, then, we will positively engage with some goods more fully than others.

The good of human life itself is also pursuable, according to circumstances, by different levels of positive engagement. The depth of its positive demands will vary. An athlete is likely to more intensively pursue the good of health than a sedentary arm chair philosopher; a woman with a terminal illness may decide to more intensively pursue her artistic endeavors instead of opting to put them to one side in order to prolong her life span; a patient may decide to forgo a treatment that may reduce pain levels but may shorten his life because he values all the time he has to be with his family; a patient in order to maintain peace of mind, having accepted the nearness of her death, may forgo the mental and physical burden required to eat and drink, thus slightly advancing the moment of her death, and so on.

All these above examples indicate that life (or indeed any other primary good) is not a good that positively demands from us a strategy of response such that life is treated as if it were a dominant or superior good to all the others (see s. 3.9).The goodness of life does not positively demand from us single minded devotion to its promotion regardless of any other rational commitments we might have to pursue and engage other primary goods (and derivatively, secondary goods). Instead, life demands from us levels of commitment directed towards its maintenance and furtherance that are in broad accord with a reasonable life narrative and ground projects (see s. 3.9c).

Responding positively to the demands of health requires due attentiveness to the needs of health maintenance. We should, for example, within the constraints of knowledge, as well as material provision, and other factors, try to eat well and exercise. If we fall ill, and cannot treat the source of illness or disease on our own, and if we have ready access to available health care provision, we should make a reasonable attempt to avail ourselves of it. We should also be attentive to the health maintenance needs of others, especially to those for whom we have special responsibility—spouses, children, dependants, etc. Again, I realize that the circumstantial conditions that affect our ability to pursue and maintain our own health and the health of others will vary considerably from society to society and person to person. Yet, notwithstanding such societal and personal variations, we should, where reasonably practical, be attendant to, and care for, our own health and the health of others.[19]

As well as being positively required to have regard for the maintenance of our own life and health, we ought to attend fairly to the impact that our actions and omissions may have on the life and health of others (see s. 3.9d). A key obligation to act with regard to the life and safety of another would be to come to the assistance of another placed in a life threatening or hazardous situation—a 'ready rescue' obligation.[20] Consider the case of Joe and an elderly lady who has fallen in the middle of a busy road and who cannot move. Joe has observed her fall and her apparent state of incapacity. Joe is able bodied and could, without any physical difficulty, assist the elderly lady to the safety of the pavement. There is no traffic currently approaching that section of the road and he would not be placing his life in jeopardy. Given such circumstances, Joe, out of fairness to the elderly lady, has a positive ethical obligation to render her assistance. Responding to the positive demands of the good of life and health, in such circumstances, requires action not culpable omission. Failure on his part to render such positive assistance, in the circumstances, would be practically unreasonable and hence wrongful. If Joe were not able bodied or could not come to the elderly lady's assistance without jeopardizing his own life, these material circumstances would affect the moral quality of his omission. Where we have the ready means to act to avert death or serious injury, and where due regard for our own life and substantive health is not threatened, we cannot idly stand by and watch an elderly lady get run over by a car, any more than we idly stand by and watch a helpless baby drown in a pool of water, watch a blind man walk over the edge of a cliff, or fail to warn work colleagues of a safety equipment failure that poses a serious risk to life and limb.

4.4b Negative Demands of Life and Health

The level of positive demand generated by the good of life and health will vary according to our reasonable commitments and priorities. In addition to positive demands, the good of life and health also generates negative demands that we desist or refrain from acting in certain ways that, without compelling reason, damage, attack, or destroy—that is disrespect or violate—the intrinsic good of our own life and health or the life and health of others (see s. 3.9e).[21]

Since health is of value to us intrinsically, for its own sake, and not just because of the grounding role it plays in supporting countless worthwhile projects and activities in life, it is practically unreasonable and hence wrongful to intentionally harm or damage our own health or the health of others without compelling reason.[22] The general norm guiding our concerns here can be stated as 'do not intentionally inflict a significant harm upon yourself or others unless there is a compelling reason to do so.' Some examples will help flesh out the scope and extent of this negative norm.

Consider, first, the case of a man trapped on an exposed mountainside, his hand having been caught and unable to be pulled free. Time passes. If he cannot free himself he is likely to die, due to exposure, before he is rescued. He is able to reach an item of equipment that could act as a primitive saw. Is he prohibited from intentionally sawing off his hand, thus harming himself, in order to free himself from his entrapment and hopefully find medical assistance? No. Given such circumstances, he is neither prohibited nor required to do so. An action can be classified as 'supererogatory' if it goes above and beyond any necessitating requirement to act.[23] Many of us, when faced with such a predicament, would not be able to bring ourselves to perform such an action. It is, however, legitimate for him to intentionally sever a part of his body in order to preserve his whole, namely, his continuing to be.[24] This is a 'compelling reason' so to act. Acting to preserve life itself or some fundamental aspect of our health might permit us to undertake an action that would otherwise be an instance of 'mutilation,' 'maiming,' or 'disfigurement'—an intentional action that would damage our body or the body of another, resulting in permanent loss or impairment of functioning, without compelling reason. The demands of the intrinsic good of life and health do not require of us, always and everywhere, regardless of reason, that we always refrain from performing actions that would intentionally damage our own bodies or the bodies of others. Here, there is no conception of a 'justifiable mutilation,' of justifiably disrespecting or violating what would otherwise be a binding prohibition 'not to intentionally damage our bodies or the bodies of others *full-stop*,' for no such negative demand is required by practical reason. It is mistaken to think that due respect for the intrinsically valuable good of life and health requires a blanket prohibition on all forms of intentionally damaging action *full-stop*, for life and health, nor indeed any other primary good, imposes upon us such a broad prohibition of this kind.

Is the notion of 'compelling reason' so malleable that practically any putative reason can be said to be 'reason enough' to perform an intentionally damaging action? No. It would, for example, be wrong to intentionally harm the intrinsic good of our health by using destructive substances primarily aimed at the pursuit of drug induced pleasure. Pleasure, as we have seen, is not a primary good of persons and there is thus a disordered set of commitments and priorities in operation (see s. 3.7b). It is practically unreasonable to treat a secondary or derived good as if it were a primary good of persons (see s. 3.9a). The kind of drug use typical of heroin addicts cannot be viewed as a compelling reason to harm the good of health and it therefore constitutes a violation of the moral norm prohibiting the infliction of significant intentional harm without compelling reason.

As it would be wrong to intentionally take heroin in order to pursue drug induced pleasure, so it would be wrong to inflict permanent damage or substantive irreparable loss upon ourselves or others, say, as a means of artistic expression or in order to pursue a combat sport. It is not, for example, practically reasonable to cut off an ear or a finger for the sake of artistic expression. While the pursuit of beauty is a primary good of persons, it is *simply not the kind of good* that would ever demand from us the intentional severance of an otherwise healthy limb in order to make an artistic statement (see s. 3.6f). The respective demands placed upon us by goods of health and beauty are not being adequately addressed. Notwithstanding assertions to the contrary—by artists who think that such intentional self-harm betokens the depth of their commitment to the good of art—willingness to execute such an action is a clear sign that personal commitments and priorities have not been rationally formed.[25]

What of the sport of boxing? Is pursuit of the intrinsic good of play not a compelling reason to intentionally inflict bodily injury with a view to demonstrating sporting prowess (see s. 3.6e)? Although the distinction is a finer one than in the previous two examples, I would argue that commitment to the good of sport as instantiated in boxing cannot be reconciled with the mutual infliction of bodily blows of such duration and severity that a substantial risk of permanent damage to health or even death may occur.[26] The good of demonstrating sporting prowess does not positively demand from us the running of any such a risk. Boxing matches, at least those of a sporting kind, are voluntary undertaken. The fact that the risk is voluntary in nature is itself a sign that running the gauntlet of such a risk is practically unreasonable. The skill demonstrated in, for example, bare knuckle boxing is not a compelling reason to accept the risk of permanent damage to oneself or another. (Reference to knuckle boxing is not a mere red herring, as the popular newspapers, of late, distressingly chronicle.) Nor, I think, does professional boxing pass muster either in the reasonableness stakes because protective head gear is not worn (it is prohibited) and the wearing of such protective headgear does not (save a 'knockout' blow) significantly impair the display of sporting prowess. Is not sporting prowess, after all, the central point of the sport? Amateur boxing, however, where the wearing of protective head gear is required (minimizing the risk of serious injury), alone seems respectful enough of the scope of the negative norm not to intentionally inflict significant harm.

Moving on, a change in status, for example, becoming a spouse or a parent—due to the assumption of new responsibilities to love, support and nurture others—requires that we practically address what revised demands might exist for us.[27] Relationships can certainly condition the standing of a reason to act. Thus, a bread winner may conscientiously decide to take a job potentially hazardous to his or her health for the sake of providing his or her family with food, shelter and clothing where no other job is in prospect. This toleration of hazardous risk, however, is significantly different from an unreflective choice made by a spouse or parent, say, to continue to pursue a dangerous recreational sport as if he or she were still single and unattached. By becoming a spouse or a parent or both, the good of family life demands more from us by way of commitment (see s. 3.6d). Failure to carefully reassess priorities in the light of changing commitments is practically unreasonable and hence wrongful.

4.5 Negative Demands and Concrete Moral Absolutes

All forms of intentional harm, as we have seen, do not fall under the scope of a blanket negative prohibition (see s. 4.4b). If there is a compelling reason to permit an intentional harm, then the action is not morally wrong. There is, however, a crucial negative demand that the primary good of human life does unconditionally imposes upon us: 'it is always and everywhere wrong, [without compelling reason], to intentionally kill an innocent person.' Innocent human life, whether in our own person or the person of another, can never, without compelling reason, be intentionally destroyed. Since, however, practical reason, *viz.* its grasp of each primary good and the unique demands generated by each good, will, in the case of human life, admit of no truly 'compelling reason' to ever intentionally destroy an innocent person, any action that intentionally kills an innocent person can never rightfully be chosen with a view to action. Due respect for human life imposes upon us the key negative demand that it is always and everywhere wrong to intentionally kill an innocent person *tout de suite*. Minimal respectful commitment towards the good of human life demands from us that we do not intentionally kill the innocent. Since there is never a 'compelling reason' to intentionally kill an innocent person—the bracketed qualification above [without compelling reason] can be omitted from the wording of the negative norm, generating a concrete moral absolute.[28]

Unlike the primary goods of beauty, work or play—where the goods, *crucially*, do not demand from us that we always refrain from all intentional acts of destruction—for compelling reasons can sometimes be admitted—practical rationality's due regard for innocent human life, rejects all attempts to 'justify' the intentional killing of an innocent as a means of promoting some further end or consequence.[29] 'Murder' is a moral action type that, I think, approximately captures this sense of no intentional killing of the innocent.[30] 'Culpable homicide' is a more general moral action type that approximately seems to captures our sense of (i) the intentional killing of an innocent in circumstances of diminished responsibility; (ii) the non-intentional but otherwise culpable killing of an innocent; (iii) the blameworthy intentional or non-intentional killing of a non-innocent.[31]

4.5a Intentional Killing

Why only the 'intentional killing' of the 'innocent' in the wording of the concrete moral absolute? By 'intentional killing,' I do not mean to convey to the reader the potentially misleading notion that only actions of intentional killing can ever be held to be actions of wrongful killing. We can assuredly be held accountable for culpable non-intentional killings that are negligent or reckless in nature.[32] Stating that a killing is non-intentional, therefore, should not be thought of as equivalent to the claim that a person can never be held morally blameworthy for an action of non-intentional killing. Yet, the kind of moral responsibility we bear for what we specifically intend as a means to an end or as an end in itself is significantly different in quality from the kind of moral responsibility we bear for the non-intentional circumstantial side-effects of an action. Further explanation of the relevance of the 'intentional killing' qualifier must await a defence of double effect reasoning (see s. 4.6a). I will now turn to explore what the second qualifier 'innocent' is meant to convey concerning scope of coverage.

4.5b Innocence

As we saw in Chapter 2 (see s. 2.3) on the 'Inconsistency of Killing,' 'innocent' is not a word that has a univocal sense of meaning. Roughly, 'innocent' can be used in two appreciably different senses. It can be used to denote immunity from killing regarding (i) the 'moral innocent'—a person who has either not culpably perpetrated or is not culpably threatening to perpetrate an immediate deadly or gravely injurious act of aggression towards others, and (ii) the 'material innocent'—a person whom—regardless of culpability, is posing no immediate deadly or gravely injurious threat towards others.[33]

Given problems with its use, some have called for its abandonment and have resorted to the characterization of all killing in terms of 'justified killing' and 'unjustified killing.' Killing, in general, can be justified according to a consideration of many variable factors—risk of threat, consent, extreme circumstances, overall outcomes, etc. Innocence is held to be too problematic a term to do the major work required of it in a moral analysis of killing. Since we cannot prohibit all intentional killing of persons *full-stop*, for that would be too rigorist a negative norm, we ought, instead, to embrace the notion of justified killing.[34]

While I agree that a prohibition on all intentional killing of persons would be an overly rigorist formulation of a negative moral norm, I do not concur with their reasons for such rejection. My reason for rejection is that the negative normative demands generated by the good of human life itself, and due respect for them, simply do not evoke such a prohibition. Due respect for the good of human life does not require that we always and everywhere refrain from all acts of intentional killing. Support for rigorism (apart from divine will-based arguments) is generated by the contention of some natural law thinkers that (i) since all human life is held to be intrinsically valuable, (ii) it follows that no person can ever be intentionally killed, for it is always wrong to intentionally destroy what is held to be intrinsically valuable.[35] Yet, this conclusion does not follow. Is it always wrong to intentionally destroy a priceless wooden sculpture where the wood is urgently required for a fire in order to generate life-saving heat? Is it always wrong to intentionally terminate a game of golf in order to address some other pressing vital need? It is not the intrinsic or non-intrinsic status of a primary good that determines whether or not an instantiation of a good may ever be intentionally destroyed, but rather the very nature of the demands exerted upon us by the particular good or goods in question. Not all acts of intentional destruction are necessarily disrespectful of our minimal commitments towards primary goods. While different primary goods bring to bear different demands, and thus different thresholds for violation—some more vigorous than others—*no primary good ever demands that we always and everywhere refrain from intentionally destroying all possible instantiations of it.*[36]

Difficulties with the term 'innocent' should not drive us into the creation of an overly rigorist concrete absolute that is untenably framed according to a division between intrinsic and non-intrinsic value, for it is not practically unreasonable to maintain that (i) X's life is intrinsically valuable, and (ii) it is not always and everywhere wrong to intentionally kill X. The latter may, *but need not* be disrespectful towards the demands of human life. If the Scylla of unwarranted rigorism is to be avoided, we should also avoid the Charybdis of laxism—of thinking that an act of intentional killing—where a person is the subject-bearer of its 'innocent' normative protections—can truly be reconciled with due respect for the primary good of human life.[37]

Assessing the scope of the qualifier 'innocent'—who is protected and who is not always protected against intentional killing—is, I think, best served by appropriating both the notion of 'moral innocence' and the notion of 'material innocence' into a matrix of responsibility in order to see what kinds of intentional killing may be permitted in the paradigmatic case of self-defence:

(a) Moral Innocent + Material Innocent—(i) If a woman is morally innocent and (ii) if she poses no immediate material (deadly or gravely injurious physical) threat to others, (iii) she is immune from any act of intentional killing.
(b) Moral Non-innocent + Material Innocent—(i) If a man is morally non-innocent but (ii) is materially innocent, for example, having been apprehended

and placed in custody so that he poses no immediate material (deadly or gravely injurious physical) threat to others, (iii) he is immune from any act of intentional killing.

(c) Moral Non-innocent + Material non-innocent—(i) If a woman is morally non-innocent and (ii) she continues to pose an immediate material (deadly or gravely injurious physical) threat to others, (iii) she is not immune from any act of intentional killing and (iv) may not licitly resist the self-defence efforts of her victim(s).

(d) Moral innocent + Material non-innocent—(i) If a man is morally innocent and (ii) if he yet poses an immediate material (deadly or gravely injurious physical) threat to others, (iii) he is not immune from any act of intentional killing but may nevertheless, due to his moral innocence, (iv) resist the self-defence efforts of his material victim(s).

In this matrix, the life of a person is always held inviolable unless the person, either now or prospectively, is posing a deadly or gravely injurious threat to others. Actions that seek to repel or stop such threats may be classified as actions of self-defence.[38] This, I think, is the normative reach of what human life negatively demands from us by way of protecting persons from intentional acts of killing. In order to protect our own life or the lives of others, we may intentionally use appropriate harmful or even lethal force to thwart the execution of a destructive threat for which we ourselves (or those we are protecting) *are not culpably responsible*.

Trying to tackle some of the confusion surrounding the intentional killing of the innocent requires that we do not jettison either facet of innocence but rather appropriately combine and align them. By use of such a matrix, we can rationally avoid the distorting problems associated with exclusive emphasis on either form of innocence.[39] Exclusive emphasis on moral innocence alone does not adequately address the following kinds of case: the deranged killer or the innocent projectile. In deranged killer examples, a person is placed in circumstances where he or she poses a serious life threat to others through no personal fault. Often they are insane or have been unwittingly placed under the influence of a psychotic drug. In innocent projectile cases, the body of a morally innocent person is involuntarily used as a weapon to severely injure or kill another. In both sets of case, I would argue, notwithstanding moral innocence, the causal threat to self-preservation is such that respect for intrinsic human life does not demand from us that we must absolutely set aside any resort to intentional killing.

Exclusive emphasis on material innocence, however, can blind us to the following kind of case: unjust defender. Imagine the scenario in which a policeman is shooting at perpetrators who are attempting to escape from a bank robbery in which customers are being killed. They are cornered yet they refuse to surrender and lay down their weapons. They continue to fire for they argue that they are defending themselves against the fire of material non-innocents! If material innocence were all that mattered, and not moral culpability for placing themselves in such a predicament in the first place, they would, in such circumstances, be able to claim the permissibility of self-defence. Surely this is wrong.

By combining both kinds of innocence in a matrix of responsibility, then, we are better able to appreciate the scope of the negative norm regulating the intentional use of lethal force. Certain cases fall outside the scope of permissible self-defence. If a person is a material innocent, it is never licit to intentionally kill him or her.[40]

What of the case of capital punishment, a practice historically defended as part of the natural law tradition? Is such killing licit? While the detained murderer, for example, is morally non-innocent, he or she is usually posing no immediate material (deadly or gravely injurious physical) threat to others. Prisons exist to prevent killers from posing a serious continuing risk to the community. The intentional killing of the moral non-innocent but material innocent is never licit. Such intentional killing cannot be reconciled with due respect for the good of human life unless, of course, circumstances dictate that a killer is realistically posing an immediate threat to others (for example, via a breakout from prison or in a marginal community where little or no prison provision exists to protect the community).[41]

4.6 Killing and Double Effect Reasoning

In Chapter 2, s. 2.6, we explained the thoughts behind a variety of attacks on the use of double effect reasoning to resolve conflicts between actions that entail the causation of both good and evil. While the intentional killing of an innocent is never morally right, I believe that certain non-intentional effects resulting in the death of an innocent are nevertheless permissible because of the significance of the element of intention to the moral anatomy of an action.[42] Without double effect reasoning we would be forced into either: (i) an untenable rigorism that would demand extensive non-action, for example, no action that could foreseeably result in the death of an innocent or (ii) we would be forced into renouncing the very notion of concrete moral absolutes.[43] We are, however, not faced with the prospect of having to select either option and can defend the critical relevance of double effect reasoning to moral analysis. Since I have already argued for the moral intelligibility of the act-consequence distinction (see s. 4.2), the reality of moral action types or species of action (see ss. 4.2; 4.3), and the reality of having a good (or at least neutral) objective pertaining to both the means and the end of an action (see s. 4.3), I will take it that the first criterion of double effect reasoning—that the objective of the action must be morally good or indifferent in itself—passes muster in the reasonableness stakes. I now turn to defend the reasonableness of the other three criteria of double effect reasoning—intention/foresight; causal ordering; proportionate reason.

4.6a Intention and Foresight

Turning to examine the second criterion of double effect reasoning—that bad effect(s), though foreseeable, cannot be intended—we saw in s. 2.6d that the relevancy of this criterion was rejected on the basis that it was dependent on an invalid epistemological division between the notion of intention and the notion of foresight. Critics argue that we intend all the effects of an action that we reasonably foresee will happen as a result of its performance. If Y and Z are foreseeable consequences of action X then we intend all the effects whether good or bad because they are foreseeable.

Before proceeding to defend this criterion of double effect, it is necessary to start with an admission. Some authors who have defended the validity of the intention/ foresight distinction do seem to offer justification for the distinction as if it were based on some form of epistemological underpinning. As G. E. M. Anscombe has stated, resort to double effect reasoning lacks credibility when the effects of an action are thought certain, or virtually certain, to the knowledge of the agent. For Anscombe, only less than certain effects could hope to fall within the purview of the non-intentional.[44]

Now, I accept Anscombe's basic point that if an effect is virtually certain or certain to happen, we cannot reasonably sustain a distinction between the intentional and the foreseeable on epistemic grounds. For Anscombe and others, the case of the fat man caught in the opening of a cave is a key case (see s. 2.6d). We cannot claim on pure epistemic grounds that the death of the fat man (bad effect) was certainly foreseeable and yet not intended. Rather than adopt a more circumscribed scope for intention, tethered to conditions of uncertainty, as Anscombe does, justifying the intention/foresight distinction only where the causation of a bad effect is less than certain, I would instead argue that an epistemological underpinning is not the correct basis for arguing for the validity of the intention/foresight distinction. The crucial distinction is *volitional* not epistemic.[45]

The validity of the intention/foresight distinction rests on the anatomy of the will. The volitional nature of intention is supported by our use of ordinary language.[46] For example, it is raining outside and I have a hole in my shoe. My foot gets wet as a result. Whilst I knew that my foot would get wet while I walked several hundred yards from the classroom to my car, it is plainly odd to say that I intended that my foot would get wet even though I knew with near certainty that my foot would get wet. Intention is differentiated from foresight. Consider further the following ordinary language example. A boy suffers from Tourette's syndrome. Demonstrating bravery, he is invited to give an address to his school assembly on the nature of the affliction. Some members of the audience will inevitably be offended by his involuntary use of colorful language. Others will inevitably snigger. Yet, it would be strange indeed to say that the boy intended to cause offence or intended to cause the sniggering, even though some such effects were near certain to happen.[47] Ordinary language use suggests that those who dismiss the intention/foresight distinction altogether, or those who reject it on epistemic grounds in cases where an action's effects are near certain, are not adequately addressing the real basis for validating the meaningfulness of the distinction.

An action engages not only our faculty of knowledge but also our faculty of willing.[48] To intend the perpetration of an evil as an end in itself most deeply embraces the will's commitment towards evil. It is, after all, for the sake of pursuing an end that we will a chosen means. To intentionally will the perpetration of an evil as the means to an end, even for the sake of pursuing a good end, still closely entangles the set of the will in deep existential commitment towards evildoing. Unlike willing evil as an end or evil as a chosen means, it is only by permitting evil effects lying outside the immediate means-end trajectory of the will that it becomes possible to talk of 'tolerating' or 'accepting' the negative (even certain) 'side-effects' of an action. Only here, where an effect is not being specifically targeted as end or as a chosen means to an end, can there be said to be sufficient detachment between the targeting of the will and the production of bad effects in order to tolerate their non-intended causation.[49]

By intention we thus refer to the targeted willing of the end and the targeted willing of a chosen means adopted to pursue the end of an action. Intentions crucially shape our actions with respect to what it is we are proposing to do and why we are proposing to do it. The importance of volition cannot be ignored as the will is a faculty of the mind that acts as a mediator between our faculty of knowledge and our other mental faculties to produce action.[50] It does not follow, therefore, that having knowledge of near certain effects can justify the rejection of the intention/foresight distinction, for the validity of the distinction is based on the entanglement of the will with evil as an end or as a means to an end and not the degree of certainty of foreseeable knowledge. To the extent that critics of intention/foresight have concentrated on epistemic grounds for setting aside or truncating appeal to double effect reasoning, they are, I think, off target.

To reinforce the importance of viewing what we specifically intend as the targeted willing of ends and means, consider some examples. A man is escaping from a looming natural disaster and decides to seize hold of an elderly lady's car. He threatens her nearby daughter with torture if she does not hand over the keys to her car. Here, a good or neutral effect is being directly willed as the targeted end of the action (escape from the path of a natural disaster) but bad effects (threats of torture and coercive intimidation) are being directly willed as the causal means used to procure the good effect. Because bad effects are being specifically willed as the direct causal means for bringing about the good effect, it is unreasonable to argue that the man did not intend these bad effects.

Consider further the case of an ambulance driver who comes to the assistance of ill people and takes them to hospital. She switches on the vehicle's siren in order to warn other motorists of the ambulance's presence on the road so that they can pull off to one side. Switching on the siren has the good effect of helping to clear traffic ahead but also the bad effect of slowing it down. By her action, of turning on the siren, she wills the good effect of clearing the traffic in order to facilitate the journey to hospital. She does not necessarily will the near certain bad effect of slowing down traffic on the road.

Returning to the example of the fat man caught in the mouth of a cave (see s. 2.6d), I think that such an action, of setting off an explosion near the fat man, resulting in his death, could be permitted as a non-intended though certainly foreseeable side-effect of an action to open up the mouth of the cave for escape purposes (although, given what I have said on material innocence (see s. 4.5b) , such action could, perhaps, also be defended on the ground that the fat man is a 'material non-innocent' since he, in the circumstances, is posing a non-culpable but grave threat to the lives of others). The death of the fat man need not, strictly speaking, form a necessary part of the willed means-end enterprise. The bad effect need not be viewed as the directly willed causal effect by means of which the good effect is procured. In this case, I think, the good effect could be directly targeted as a means to an end without also directly willing the concomitant causation of the foreseeably certain bad effect.

There remains one further point to be considered here, namely, James Rachels's argument concerning the viability of distinguishing between extrinsically identical acts and interior dispositions of the will (see s. 2.6d). Underlying Rachels's critique is basically the attitude that an agent possesses an array of mental states and those states can simply be manipulated by an instant change of thought pattern. Intentions are indeed forms of mental state, but they are not mere states of mind that can be 'selected' or 'de-selected' at the drop of a penny.[51] The very nature of an extensional action, from the beginning, and during its performance, depends upon the means-end enterprise that is being willed. Intention does not amount to 'fixing' our vision on the good effects of an action and then simply 'keeping our minds' off the bad effects. Real as opposed to token intentions are not so fleeting or malleable. Contra Rachels, we are often well aware of what the willed targets of our own actions are, and often, indeed, we can also reasonably infer what are the willed targets of another person's actions.[52] We can scrutinize and assess the intentions of others by looking at all the available evidence; by asking a series of pertinent questions concerning the observed action and its circumstances: What did the agent do to minimize or lessen the side-effects of his or her action? Was a less damaging solution available? Did the agent take other counter steps available to help offset the causation of the bad effects? What causal pattern did the good and bad effects follow?

While I would agree with Rachels that we are indeed blind with respect to any superhuman ability to directly view the heart of another person, he significantly overlooks the question of evidential inference as to a person's actual intentions. For example, if a man physically tortures a young child with a view to intimidating others for information, we can, I think, get a pretty good handle on his intentions. Even assuming that the end for the sake of which the torture is being performed is a good one, the mere performance of this action type informs us of the presence of a bad intention with respect to means. The child is a helpless victim. There is no question as to the child's material innocence. The child is protected by a concrete moral absolute that utterly prohibits the intentional torture of the innocent. Torture, a bad causal antecedent, is being utilized in order to procure the resulting good effect. Here, we do not need any superhuman ability to gaze into the hearts of others in order to understand and denounce the willed action of the torturer.[53]

4.6b Causal Ordering

The third criterion of double effect reasoning—that the bad effect(s) of an action cannot be the antecedent causal means used to achieve the good effect(s)—the good effect(s) must either causally precede or be collateral with the bad effect(s)—is designed to place limits on what can be claimed in the name of intention with reference to the order of physical causality. Critics charge this criterion with irrelevancy as to the moral assessment of an action for what really matters is an overall assessment of an action's good and bad effects, not causal sequencing (see s. 2.6e).

In reply, we first need to be aware that whether or not a bad effect is intended is a key criterion for determining the moral quality of an action (see s. 4.6a). Second, in order to form and shape our intentions adequately—especially with regard to intending a bad effect as the causal means for bringing about a good effect—we need to sincerely reckon with the order of physical (but *not* temporal) causality by which we seek to extensionally influence and shape the physical world.[54]

The order of causality places tangible side-constraints on the formation of our intentions with a view to action. It is important that intentions should not be viewed as ghostly 'free floating' entities able to attach themselves to 'effects' in the blink of an eye, but rather should be viewed as being closely tethered to the causal sequencing of actions and their producible effects. Well formed intentions simply cannot fly in the face of the causal understanding we have of the world. If the good effect of an action is truly intended, but not the bad effect, then, *as a necessary but not sufficient marker of our volitional probity*, the good effect of the action should be causally prior to (or at the very least be concomitantly simultaneous with) the causation of the bad effect.[55]

Causal changes in the word that proceed from our actions, particularly those that bring about the death, so to speak, 'cry out' for explanation. They demand: why should X not be held responsible for bringing about, via his or her agency, a bad causal change? Two patterns of causal ordering alone seem to be reconcilable with (although no pattern *guarantees*) the possession of a well formed will regarding the physical causation of good and evil in the world—(i) <action> → <good effects> → <bad effects> or (ii) <action> → <concomitant g/b effects>.[56]

Such is the relevance of these two causal patterns—of not first doing (causing) evil in order that good may come—if the causal sequencing of good and evil cannot be reconciled with either pattern, then the action should not be performed because it suffers from a structural defect. An otherwise good resultant effect will suffer moral vitiation by virtue of its positioning in a wrongful causal chain—<action> → <bad effects> → <good effects>. Whilst a well formed intention cannot be reconciled with disregard for an acceptable pattern of causation, it does not follow that a bad intention can never utilize an otherwise acceptable chain of causality in order to advance wrongdoing.

Consider now the craniotomy case mentioned in Chapter 2 (see s. 2.6e). Again, as with the case of the fat man stuck in the mouth of the cave (see s. 4.6a), it is possible that this case could be resolved by an appeal to the material non-innocence of the foetus (see s. 4.5b).[57] Assuming, however, that the foetus is always a material innocent and thus immune from intentional killing, is the chain of causal ordering really irrelevant as to the moral quality of the action being undertaken by the surgeon? I think not.[58] If, as I have argued, the manner and order in which a cause is brought about, and not simply the 'brute fact' of a causal happening, is relevant to the moral structure of an action, then the surgeon can only proceed if he or she has due regard for the chain of causation brought about by his or her action.[59] In my assessment, the certain death of the foetus (the effect of having its cranium constricted) is causally concomitant with the good effect of unblocking the mother's uterus. The two effects (one good and one bad) simultaneously flow from the same causal antecedent— <action> → <concomitant g/b effects>. The death of the foetus is not the bad causal antecedent used to procure the good effect of removing the blockage. On causal grounds, then, the action of the surgeon need not be thought impermissible. Such causal ordering could be reconciled with a good will on the part of the surgeon to target only the good effect of his action.[60]

4.6c Responsibility for Side-Effects

The last criterion of double effect reasoning—that a serious proportionate reason must exist in order to permit the causation of the foreseeable bad effect(s)—is criticized by Peter Singer on the ground that it is a thinly disguised attempt to smuggle in consequentialist methodology by the 'back door' (see s. 2.6f). A more detailed examination of the fourth criterion, however, reveals the crucially limited and qualified ways in which the consequences of an action are held relevant to moral decision making; a relevance that makes no attempt to pretend that the real diversity of goods involved can be reduced to the ready reckoning of outcomes informed by grand schemes of cardinal or ordinal ranking. Instead, what the fourth criterion appeals to is the idea that all pertinent requirements of practical reason be brought to bear as we seek to justify and place limits on our responsibility for the causation of bad side-effects in the world (see s. 3.9). The fourth criterion represents an attempt to summarily capture the obligations we have not to act unfairly—whether negligently, recklessly or with undue bias—towards the reasonably apprehended goods of self and/or others (obligations that may be general in scope or may be limited, say, to the obligations of a particular profession, role or position of assumed responsibility). The fact that a bad effect is said to be brought about as a foreseen but non-intended side-effect of an action, does not, of itself, show that it is permissible to cause the bad side-effect. This is a common but mistaken criticism often versed against double effect reasoning.[61]

The non-intentional killing of a person, for example, always requires a compelling reason to tolerate its causation. Consider a driver who speeds along a city road at 120 mph. She seeks to experience the thrill of fast driving. The car strikes a pedestrian crossing the road. The pedestrian is killed. She pleads in her defence that she did not intend to kill anyone. This may well be true. Foresight is not equivalent to intention (see s. 4.6a). The range of moral responsibility, however, extends beyond the intentional to encompass the culpability we bear for our negligent or reckless actions. There is a death caused by the action of the driver. She had the power to substantially decrease the risk of death by driving carefully at moderate speed. The thrill of fast driving cannot stand in any fair correspondence to the risk posed to human life. Because it was foreseeable that such an event could occur, notwithstanding a lack of intent to kill, the driver's conduct is seriously blameworthy. A culpable state of mind is wider than the matter of intent and blameworthiness rightly attaches to human conduct of a negligent or reckless nature.[62]

The following are some non-exhaustive examples of general obligations that delimit our scope for tolerating the causation of bad side-effects for the sake of the good. These obligations function as agent-centered side-constraints. First, if an agent is going to cause a serious bad side-effect, there needs to be a serious reason to permit its causation. A trivial or minor reason will not suffice. It would not be permissible to chop off a patient's hand in order to treat an irritating tingling sensation of the fingertips. It would not be permissible to tolerate the risk of killing a person by carelessly shooting in a public wood for the sake of target practice. It would not be permissible to subject a patient to a significant grave health risk in order to incrementally advance our knowledge of cosmetic treatments. Second, if a non-intended bad effect would most likely (or even certainly) happen anyway, in the proximate course of events, the case for permission becomes stronger. Thus, a parent could reasonably throw a child out of the window of a burning building, risking the child's death, if the only other alternative is for the child to be burned alive. Third, if opportunity allows for the causation of a bad side-effect that is clearly less grave, then the lesser bad effect should be chosen instead of the graver bad effect.[63]

Analyzing this third side constraint further, consider the case of the trolley problem first introduced by Philippa Foot.[64] A trolley is running out of control as the brakes have failed. In the trolley's way are five persons tied to the track. If a switch is flipped the trolley can be diverted down another track. Unfortunately there is also a single person who is also tied to that track. If the driver were to refrain from acting, five would die and if he diverted the trolley one would die. Should the driver flip the switch and divert the trolley? If it is the case that five strangers will surely die instead of one, all other considerations being approximately equal, then the lesser effect, out of fairness, should be chosen.[65] Here is an example where there is (i) a good object (the saving of five innocent lives); (ii) where the bad effect (the death of one innocent) need not be intended as the means of saving the lives of the others; and (iii) where the good effect is at least causally concomitant with the bad.

Respect for the good of human life requires that we never intentionally kill an innocent person as the causal means for bringing about the sought good effect. If this categorical negative demand cannot be adhered to then we can never proceed with the execution of our action. Innocent human life is protected by an inviolable sphere of protection against intentional destruction. Due respect for the good of human life, however, also requires that where human life is risked, even certainly, as a non-intended side-effect of an action, we apply *all relevant requirements of practical rationality* to assess and limit the impact of our action. One such requirement is Golden Rule fairness. Treat others as we ourselves, in the same circumstances, would reasonably expect to be treated (see s. 3.9d). The Golden Rule is an applicable standard of practical rationality for fairly assessing the impact that non-intended side-effects may have on the vital goods of others. Here, I think, Golden Rule fairness supports an obligation to positively rescue the five and sacrifice the one. If the driver were one of the five, what would he think of a proposal to sacrifice himself and four others rather than one? Could he fairly ignore the combined 'pull' of five claims in relation to the claim of one? If he were the one, would he think it fair to demand that his life be preserved, regardless of numbers, by insisting upon the non-intentional sacrifice of the five? If numbers never ever mattered then each person that was added to 1 as in 1+1n would always be treated, to all intents and purposes, as an 'irrelevance' to ethical decision making.[66] Considerations of fairness, I think, go beyond the level of optional permissibility (choice as to whether to save one or five) or letting the tossing of a coin decide, requiring instead that the driver flip the switch in order to divert the track.[67]

Note how this case differs from a variation of the trolley problem advanced by Judith Jarvis Thomson. The trolley is out of control and is rapidly advancing towards five innocents. The trolley will pass under a bridge. A heavy weight dropped on the track in front of the trolley would stop it moving. A bystander is on the bridge. There is also a very fat man on the bridge peering over the side. Could the bystander push the fat man over the bridge onto the tracks, thereby causing his death but saving five other innocent lives?[68] The answer is no. In this case, unlike the original trolley problem, the bystander would be intending the death of the fat man as the causal means used to procure the good effect. Here, we are not permitted to make a numerical assessment as between lives saved and lives sacrificed, for the death of the fat man in this case, unlike the cave explorer example (see s. 4.4a), crosses a forbidden threshold demanded by the primary good of human life—no intentional killing of the innocent *full-stop*. No 'compelling' reason can justify the intentional killing of an innocent whether as an end or as a means. Commitment towards respecting the good of life minimally demands that we always adhere to this concrete moral absolute. The question of assessing numerical instances quite ceases to have contextual bearing. The action is already inherently defective (see s. 4.3). Whether we willingly intend evil or whether we permit but do not intend evil, is a moral distinction of crucial and not mere 'token' relevance to the moral quality of an action. A bad intention can never be redeemed by an appeal to the overall balance of good over bad effects. The unfair acceptance of bad side-effects can vitiate the moral standing of an action but the promotion of good resultant consequences can never rectify the defect of a bad intention.

By examining all requirements limiting the scope we have for tolerating the causation of bad side-effects, the kinds of assessment being proposed here, in consideration of the fourth criterion of double effect, do not begin to serve the needs of any full-blown consequentialist methodology. The final criterion is largely informed by a consideration of agent-centered side-constraints and makes no pretence to being an adequate, complete or otherwise self standing and sufficient standard for determining what moral responsibilities we have for causing evil in the world.

4.6d Actions and Omissions

Another distinction of relevance to moral analysis is the action/omission distinction. As we saw in Chapter 2, Michael Tooley, Judith Lichtenberg, James Rachels, and others, argue that if we can establish examples of moral equivalence or symmetry as between actions and omissions, such a distinction will be irrelevant to moral decision making. They seek to argue that it makes no difference whether or not an agent brought about an effect by action or an omission, as long as the effect falls within an agent's general sphere of control (see s. 2.6g).

A major problem with the rejection of the action/omission distinction is that its rejection would demand far too much from us in terms of moral responsibility for the production of 'states-of-affairs' in the world. Any omission to act would be equally as culpable as any action to extensionally cause an effect in the world. Recall, again, the problem of the rebel angel always instructing us to maximize consequences (see s. 3.8b). If we are always as blameworthy for our omissions as we are for our actions, our distinctive sense of agency would be subjected to an invidious sense of always being held hostage to the eventistic maximization of consequences. If it was within the control of my agency to intentionally kill one person and thereby save the life of two or three others, then my decision to omit such action would always place responsibility for the unnecessary deaths squarely on my exercise of agency. By thus failing always to maximize consequences in my omissions as well as my actions, I would be acting immorally.

Given the scope of what we would be equally responsible for in the world, our personal commitments and priorities in life would be seriously imperilled. If we are not going to surrender our reasonable life projects and commitments to the relentlessly oppressive demands of consequentialist maximization, then, I think, we need to accept the relevance of the action/omission distinction as one of several important distinctions (action/consequences; moral absolutes; positive and negative duties; innocence; intentions; side-effects ...), that are indispensable aspects of moral analysis—aspects that challenge the underlying consequentialist assumption that the overall balance of states-of-affairs in the world is all that crucially matters to questions of moral assessment.

If the distinction between an action/omission is to have any moral relevance, there needs to be a relevant criterion of difference between them that matters as to the moral quality of a choice. There is. An omission, strictly speaking, is not an action. It is a non-action; a non-doing; a causal refraining or abstention. An action is a causal doing.[69] Admittedly, we are at the intuitive bedrock of ethics, but, I think, we do grasp, *all things being equal,* that it is worse to extensionally cause a bad effect in the world than it is to causally abstain thus allowing a bad effect to happen or to continue to happen. Intuitively, it is worse to cause the slander of a colleague rather than omit to correct a slander not of one's own making; it is worse to push an adversary over a precipice than it is to omit an intervention to stop the adversary from inadvertently walking over it; it is worse to send starving children poisonous food than it is to omit sending them any food, and so on.[70] These examples invoke our moral sense that actions which causally extend from our agency into the world can be worse than the corresponding omissions that seem to shadow those actions.[71] All things being equal, a 'causing will' is more closely associated with the existential presence of evil in the word than a 'refraining will.'[72] The 'all things being equal' clause is crucially important, for I am not claiming that omissions are always permissible or that omissions can never be held deeply reprehensible. They assuredly can.[73] Rather, what I am claiming is that the responsibility we bear for our omissions will be judged by a different standard of moral assessment—a failure, either intentional or non-intentional, to causally act where there was a positive obligation to so act; whereas actions are assessed according to whether there was a failure, either intentional or non-intentional, to refrain from causation where there was a negative obligation to so refrain.[74]

As T. D. J. Chappell notes, actions demand explanation as to why we should not be held accountable for bringing about the causation of a bad effect in the world. There is a presumption of responsibility. Omissions, on the other hand, demand explanation as to why we should be held accountable for a causal abstention to prevent a bad effect in the world. There is a presumption of non-responsibility. The discharge of these respective burdens of proof will, other things being equal, implicate an action more than a corresponding omission.[75]

We often seek to ascribe 'causal efficacy' to omissions because we believe that unless omissions are somehow regarded as causes we cannot hold persons responsible for them. But this line of argument is mistaken. We can assuredly hold people accountable for their intentional or otherwise culpable failures without having to regard them as causes.[76]

Because responsibility for omissions potentially casts a much wider net of restrictive entanglement over our choices than responsibility for actions, and there is a difference between actions and omissions that has moral import—the intensity and depth of our commitment to the production of evil as between a 'causing will' and a 'refraining will'—we can hardly expect all correspondences between actions and omissions to be symmetrical. If we are to assign responsibility for an omission, due to a failure to act, it will depend (i) on what the extent of the positive obligation to act was, especially the presence of any special assumptions of responsibility; (b) whether the failure to act was intentional or non-intentional; and (c) if non-intentional, whether the failure to act nevertheless in some relevant way negligent or reckless.[77]

I turn now to briefly address the two sets of cases proposed by Tooley and Lichtenberg (see s. 2.6g) as examples of moral equivalence. Do they really render redundant the moral significance of the distinction drawn between actions and omissions? I think not. Turning first to consider Tooley's two cases, one son stands as a murderer (intent plus actualized—attempted and completed—execution) and the other as having a will to murder (intent minus actualized execution) aligned to a subsequent intentional failure to rescue. We should not automatically assume, just because the second son's behavior is very wicked, that it is just the very same thing as murder (intent to kill plus actualized execution). The second son's intentional failure to act did not actually cause the death of his father even although he would have executed and completed the same kind of lethal causal chain if the other brother had not beaten him to it. The actualization of an action brings forth bad effects (the death of the father) that, until the execution of the action, remain potential. Murderous intentions, prior to execution, assuredly have deep bad effects on the character of the agent. Such effects, however, are further hardened and deepened by the execution plus completion of an action. The second son is, admittedly, only marginally less culpable than the first son, but here, 'marginally less' will do *pace* Tooley in order to distinguish the two sons from being held in a complete state of moral equivalence.

Consider now Lichtenberg's two cases (see s. 2.6g). In the first case a sailor fails to give a stranded man either provisions or a passage to safety. He dies. In the second case the sailor intentionally kills the stranded man by shooting him in the head. Here, I would submit that a will that intentionally causes evil as a means is implicated more deeply in the production of evil in the world than a will that intentionally refrains from action thereby failing to prevent an evil. All things being equal, it is worse to intentionally will the causation of evil than it is to intentionally refrain from the prevention or continuance of an independently existing evil. Of course, if an agent was originally responsible for bringing about the pre-existing pattern of causation, then a subsequent refraining must be viewed in such a context.

Since the sailor in the first case omitted to rescue a person he had a positive obligation, in the circumstances, to rescue, such an omission would be culpable (see s. 4.4a). The omission is more culpable because it is intentional rather than non-intentionally negligent or reckless. We need to bear in mind, however, had the sailor never existed or had the sailor never landed on the island, that the stranded man would still have died. The conduct of the sailor, in the second case, is graver, for he, via his extensional agency, intentionally created a new lethal causal chain by choosing to shoot the stranded man in the head. Again, the margin of difference between the two cases may seem slender, for the sailor's conduct in the first case is also wicked, but even a slender distinction in very tough cases is matter enough to support the general claim that we need not be driven into accepting the case for complete moral equivalence as between actions and their shadowing omissions.

4.7 Disaster Escape Clauses

Opponents of concrete moral absolutes often challenge their validity on grounds of religious dependency. All talk of the 'sanctity' or 'sacredness' of innocent human life, for example, is said to bespeak of religious underpinnings. By now it should be apparent why, I think, the general idea of that tradition—respect for the inviolable dignity of innocent human life—is supported by secular-based natural law reasoning. Religious concepts and phrases, due to supernatural association, have not been invoked. Still, critics say, only a 'zealot' or 'fanatic' could defend the existence of a concrete moral absolute when faced with the prospect of impending disaster. Surely, support for concrete absolutes must have religious underpinnings after all, for only a believer in God and divine providence could defend the existence of a concrete moral absolute when faced with a choice that would otherwise result in disastrous consequences.[78]

In contemporary deontology, it is common to hold that moral norms can never be absolute. All obligations, in the final analysis, are said to be conditional or imperfect. For many contemporary deontologists, the underlying appeal of consequentialism is that an otherwise exceptionless negative moral norm, like the intentional killing of the innocent, can be overridden or trumped in at least some hard cases. In order to accommodate this appeal into their systems, many contemporary deontologists bolt on to their systems a 'consequentialist proviso' as a safety-valve feature. Due to a trade off between adherence to a negative norm and the production of unacceptable outcomes, these qualifications are often termed 'disaster overrides' or 'escape clauses.' As examples, consider the stances taken by Charles Fried, Thomas Nagel, Tom Beauchamp and James Childress, and Robert Nozick.[79] While their deontological systems differ from one another in many key respects, they all ultimately agree that deontological approaches to ethical deliberation are concerned with regular boundary setting. Within regular boundaries, rules of morality set limits on what constitutes the respectful treatment of persons. A critical mass of irregular bad consequences can arise, however, sufficiently 'heavy in weight' to jettison the bindingness of regular obligations.

There are, unsurprisingly, differences among deontologists as to where thresholds between the regular and the irregular are drawn. For Fried, limits can only be breached by disaster or tragedy.[80] For Nozick, rights can be only encroached by catastrophic situations where the costs of not violating those rights would be substantial.[81] For Nagel, absolutes can be overridden by overpowering weight.[82] For Beauchamp and Childress, a cumulative mass of consequences can justify the abandonment of regular limits.[83] Nevertheless, for all these thinkers, there are said to be hard cases that render untenable adherence to otherwise binding norms.

What is curious to observe here, however, is the blatant shift that takes place between the governing standards of reason held applicable in regular circumstances and the standards of reason held applicable in irregular circumstances.[84] The shift is tantamount to saying that deontological requirements for action govern regular situations, but, cross a threshold, and consequentialist-based considerations govern morality. Reason-based norms, applicable in normal circumstances, become 'transmuted' into reasoning by sheer appeal to consequentialist weight when confronted by the irregular. As Anthony Ellis has convincingly argued, however, how do you begin to objectively and impartially 'trade off' the weight of bad consequences versus the wrongness of violating deontological obligations framed according to qualitative notions of innocence, intention, action/omission, etc.? Deontology and consequentialism have fundamentally different conceptions about the basic structure of moral thinking.[85]

Attempts to bolt a threshold proviso onto a deontological system, thereby instructing agents to disregard the regular logic of deontological requirements under weight of consequences, alas, cannot be achieved without resort to arbitrary stipulation. If the threshold at which it is justifiable to intentionally kill innocents is held to be 'catastrophe,' 'disaster' or 'tragedy,' how can it be argued that any of these thresholds is any more or less arbitrary than the other? If we stipulate a number of one hundred lives saved in order to justify the intentional killing of one innocent, then why not ninety nine ... until we reach the number two? The arbitrariness of any threshold—below which the lives of innocents are protected, and above which they are not protected—is jarring. The common retort that we can talk of heaps of consequences without specifying the exact size of the heap, thereby avoiding questions of exact numbers, simply will not pass muster, for we are still crucially faced with arbitrary stipulations as to general size of the heap. Why should one vague heap like notion be insisted upon rather than another? Why is catastrophe held to be the threshold and not tragedy? How can it be right to intentionally kill an innocent for the sake of saving thousands of lives but not hundreds of lives?[86]

Proviso deontologists want to oppose the logic of consequentialism in regular circumstances and hold it illicit to intentionally kill one innocent for the sake of saving two lives, yet, having set aside principle, they can offer no convincing reason to insist upon any given threshold below which regular deontological morality applies and beyond which irregular consequentialist morality applies.

Deontological systems, of course, beyond adherence to core deontological requirements, can consider the moral relevance of consequences. As I have argued above (see s. 4.6c), the fourth criterion of double effect reasoning is a relevant example of reckoning with numbers, whereby we must fairly attend to the non-intended collateral fall out that may ensue from the execution of an otherwise permissible action. Proviso deontologists, however, cannot reasonably maintain, without resort to arbitrary stipulation, that the *intrinsic wrongness of an action*, as determined by non-consequentialist fonts, can be overridden, set aside or trumped by an appeal to consequences.

Still, proviso deontologists say, is the defender of concrete moral absolutes committed to maintaining their non-violation at just any price? The aim of this question is to suggest that a person who fails to breach a concrete moral absolute is somehow morally responsible for an ensuing evil that could have been prevented. If B fails to torture an innocent C in order that the whereabouts of D can be determined, where D is threatening to execute action X, resulting in hideous consequences, then B is somehow 'co-responsible' for D's evil action. Since it was within the control of B to torture C and thus obtain information as to the whereabouts of D, B could have prevented the execution of action X but failed to do so.[87]

This kind of objection to concrete moral absolutes, whilst familiar, is mistaken, because it is based on a critical misunderstanding about the moral responsibility we bear for the presence of evil effects in the world.[88] B does not assume responsibility for the causal actions of D unless there was a culpable failure on the part of B to discharge a binding moral obligation. Torturing an innocent person is simply not a binding moral obligation. An immoral means used in pursuit of an otherwise worthwhile end, is never a moral option, for the intentional willing of a good end cannot justify the intentional willing of an immoral means. A wrongful action simply cannot be 'transmuted' into a rightful action by appealing to the 'bloody' awfulness of the consequences. If hideous consequences result, we should clearly apportion moral responsibility to D and to anyone who knowingly and willfully supported D in his plan to execute action X. The extent of B's moral responsibility is to use *all moral means* at his or her disposal to stop D executing action X. Our basic sense of moral responsibility for patterns of causation in the world, a sense that proviso deontologists accept in regular circumstances, is yet another casualty of an attempt to jettison fundamental non-consequentialist notions when vague and arbitrary thresholds are said to have been crossed.

Notes

1   For more on the irreducible nature of normative starting points in the natural law ethics tradition see Joseph Boyle (1992), pp. 3–30.
2   For further clarification surrounding instrumental uses of the good of human life compatible with respect for the good see Joseph Boyle (1989), pp. 221–50.
3   See Alvin I. Goldman (1970), pp. 20–48.
4   See the work on acts by Eric D'Arcy (1963), pp. 18–28.
5   See Ruth Maclin (1967), pp. 72–80; D'Arcy (1963), pp. 18–28.
6   On appropriate description being essential to acting well see Anselm W. Müller (2004), pp. 18–26. On the intentional killing of an innocent as an illicit means to an end see John Zeis (2005), pp. 133–4.
7   G. E. M. Anscombe (1963), stresses that our intentions are explanatory of our conduct. Thus what is intended is determined by which of our beliefs provide us with reasons for acting.
8   D'Arcy (1963), pp. 18–28.
9   Alfred Wilder (1995), pp. 577–8.
10   G. E. M. Anscombe (1963), pp. 37–40 gives us a more sophisticated modern analytic account of the traditional *tres fontes moralitatis* 'three sources of morality.'

11 On contemporary use of the three fonts or 'determinants' see, for example, David S. Oderberg (2000a), pp. 105–10. The importance of the 'triple font theory' to action analysis is also ably defended by Surendra Arjoon (2007), pp. 395–410. The general structural meaningfulness of this action schema is, I think, supported by our pre-reflective intuitions. As practical reason deliberates over choice with a view to action it assesses (a) whether the intentional end of an action is good (reasonable), bad (unreasonable) or indifferent (neutral), (b) whether the intended means proposed as the vehicle for pursuing the end is good (reasonable), bad (unreasonable) or indifferent (neutral), and (c) whether the circumstances of the action with a view to its performance are good (reasonable), bad (unreasonable) or indifferent (neutral).

12 *Summa Theologiae*, I–II, q. 18, aa. 2–4.

13 See Daniel Westberg (2002), pp. 90–102; Martin Rhonheimer (2000), pp. 430–37.

14 John Finnis (1987a), pp. 159–75.

15 Joseph Boyle (1998), pp. 72–9; Nicholas Denyer (1997), pp. 39–57; Philip Devine (2000), pp. 115–32.

16 G. E. M. Anscombe (1981) and (2005) and Peter Geach (1977) have traditionally defended a wide range of concrete moral absolutes—contraception; sodomy; abortion; lying; killing of non-combatants, etc. Geach is more explicit that Anscombe in his explicit appeals to religious justification. See also William E. May (1989).

17 See John Finnis's defence of moral absolutes in his (1991a) text.

18 Positive and negative demands reflect to some extent Philippa Foot's (1978) distinction between positive and negative duties. Negative duties are not to injure a person whereas positive duties are to benefit a person. Where I clearly differ from Foot is over concrete moral absolutes and the need for double effect reasoning.

19 On the good of health and its importance for well-being see Patricia Donohue-White and Kateryna F. Cuddeback (2002), pp. 165–96; also Joseph Seifert (2002), pp. 109–45.

20 For discussion on the scope of a duty to rescue see A D. Woozley (1983), pp. 1273–3000; Violetta Igneski (2006), pp. 439–66; Alan Gerwith (1978), pp. 217–29.

21 A compelling reason, in a given situation, for not X-ing is one which, when introduced into our process of ethical discernment, directs us to the conclusion to not X rather than X.

22 By 'compelling reason,' I further mean reasons that so shape and condition the normative 'pushes and pulls' of a good, that the good does not rule out *tout de suite* the intentional performance of certain actions. Reasons A…D may so impact the normative demands generated by a good that they permit or more rarely require actions (or omissions) that should not otherwise be performed. The devil is, of course, always in the details: what compelling reasons?; impacting which goods?; to what extent?

23 See Gregory Mellema (1991), 1–12 and Julia Driver (1992), pp. 286–95.

24 This is often referred to as the 'principle of totality.' A subordinate bodily part may be intentionally sacrificed for the sake of preserving the whole body. The principle as a reason for action applies to the individual only. It does not justify treating individuals as if they were subordinate parts of a societal body. See David S. Oderberg (2000a), pp. 78–81.

25 Since there is no compelling reason to permit such an act of intentional self-harm, the action is rightly regarded as falling under the action type of mutilation.

26 On the ethics of boxing see Angela Schneider and Robert Butcher (2001), pp. 357–69.

27 The language of legal scholarship speaks of 'assumption of responsibility' and 'duty of care.' For a good collection exploring the complexities of family ties and special obligations see Laurence D. Houlgate (1999).

28 The extent of the concrete norm extends only to innocent life. On the scope of qualifier 'innocent,' see s. 4.5. My defence of the concrete absolute extending only to innocent life contrasts with Germain Grisez who seeks to include all intentional killing of human life *full-stop* under the aegis of a concrete moral absolute. See Grisez (1970), pp. 64–96. See also discussion in Gerard V. Bradley (1998), pp. 155–73.

29 Contrast my position here with that of John Finnis (1991a), pp. 54–7.

30 Anscombe defined murder (1970), p. 45 as: '... the deliberate killing of the innocent, whether for its own sake or as a means to some further end.'

31 My action type definitions are not precise legal terms although they do substantively overlap with criminal concerns. See discussion of definitions in Philip Devine (1978), pp. 15–17.

32 See Finnis (1991b), pp. 32–64 and (1995), pp. 229–48.

33 For discussion of material and moral innocence and self-defence see Leonard Geddes (1973), pp. 93–7; R. A. Duff (1973), pp. 16–19; Susan Levine (1984), pp. 69–78; Michael Clark (2000), pp. 45–55.

34 See, for example, John Harris (1985), pp. 64–77; Marvin Kohl (1974); Helga Kuhse (1987); Peter Singer (1993) and (1994).

35 John Finnis and Germain Grisez are two defenders of this position. Also Mark C. Murphy (2001), pp. 101–5, 204–7 and Robert P. George (1999), pp. 92–101.

36 The demands of a good, however, may create 'spheres of inviolability' that delineate certain classes or categories of instantiation that are protected without exception.

37 On the variable justifications for self-defence and appeals to innocence in the natural law tradition see Suzanne M. Uniacke (1994), pp. 57–91.

38 Judith Jarvis Thompson endorses such an approach to self-defence. See Thompson (1991), pp. 283–310.

39 I have tried to combine both positions in my matrix by drawing on discussions of deranged killers, innocent projectiles, unjust defenders, etc. in Jeff McMahan (1994), pp. 252–90; Levine (1984), pp. 69–78; Clark (2000), pp. 45–55. Also Jefferie G. Murphy (1973), pp. 527–50.

40 A fleeing murderer takes hold of a female pedestrian as a human shield. The pedestrian is a material innocent. Although she may causally contribute to the insulation of a murderer from a bullet, it would be wrong to intentionally kill her as she is not posing an immediate threat to the life of anyone. Her life is protected from any intentional act of killing. Consider further cases in which innocents are killed in order to coerce a perpetrator to hand over valuable information to the authorities. A terrorist has planted a bomb and his five children are taken hostage. One child is killed and one will be killed every fifteen minutes the terrorist does not notify the authorities of the whereabouts of the bomb. The children are material innocents. They do not directly contribute to their father's evildoing. They are not posing an immediate grave threat to anyone. They cannot be intentionally killed.

41 On capital punishment see Philip Devine (2000a). See also Gerard V. Bradley (1998).

42 J. L. A. Garcia (1995a), (1995b) and (1997).

43 Although double effect reasoning is clearly also of relevance in non-absolutist contexts. For non-absolutist use see Don Locke (1982), pp. 453–75.

44 G. E. M. Anscombe (1982), pp. 12–25.

45 On intention as willed commitment not intellectual apprehension see Thomas A. Cavanaugh (1996), (1997), (1998a), and (2006). For Aquinas, of all three acts of the will—(*voluntas, fruitio, intentio*)—what is intended most fully engages the commitment of the acting person. See John Finnis (1987a), pp. 159–75.

46 And also assumed in common morality. See Mark P. Aulisio (1995) and (1996).

47 An example adapted from the stuttering case in Joseph M. Boyle and Thomas D. Sullivan (1977), pp. 357–60.

48 On the significance of rehabilitating the language of the will for an analysis of action see W. F. Hardie (1971), pp. 193–206. For the significance of different levels of engagement in different acts of willing see Cavanaugh (2006), ch. 3 and J. L. A. Garcia (1991).

49 See Cavanaugh (1996), (1997), (1998a), and (2006). See also Garcia (1990) and (1991).

50 Cavanaugh (2006), ch. 4. On Aquinas's relationships between different faculties of the mind see also Martin Rhonheimer (2000), ch. 10 and Finnis (1998), pp. 62–71 on *ratio* and *voluntas*.

51 See Odeberg (2000a), pp. 105–10. Also see Cavanaugh (1997), pp. 243–53 and (1999), pp. 181–5.

52 As Chappell states (2002), p. 226: 'Rachels' talk of purifying the intention is (as Rachels explains) an allusion to Pascal's satire on abuses of PDE, in the *Provincial Letters*. Pascal said that these abuses took it that all you had to do to avoid blame was learn to be careful where you pointed your internal acts of intending. PDE itself should not be equated with these abuses of PDE. Intending is not an internal act, a little speech that you make to yourself before acting; it is for instance possible to be *mistaken* in your beliefs about what you intend. Intending is rather *a set of the whole agent.*' Chappell's emphasis.

53 For contemporary discussion on absolutist prohibitions and the use of torture see Christopher W. Tindale (2005), pp. 209–22.

54 Jonathan Glover (1977) p. 89 asks: 'Is it closeness in time? If so, having someone poisoned in order to prevent them catching and killing me will turn out not to be forbidden if the poison used is very slow acting. If it is some other form of closeness, how is it specified and what degree of it is required?' Non-temporal causal sequencing helps address these kinds of question.

55 See, for example, Oderberg (2000a), pp. 91–3 who also defends causal ordering.

56 The language of the bad effect following 'immediately' from the intended good is sometimes used. For example in the formulation of the doctrine used by J. P. Gury in his *Compendium Theolgiae Moralis*. Language can mislead. Also Jeff Jordan (1990), p. 213: '… the intended good effect is causally separate from the unintended harmful effect.' What this really means is that both the good and bad effects must *at least* concomitantly flow from <A> as in <G/B> *not* <B> causing <G>.

57 Alan Donagan (1977) pp. 81–3, 168–71 would take such an approach to the status of the foetus. For discussion of Donagan's position see Terrence Reynolds (1985), pp. 866–73.

58 By training, physicians are deeply concerned with patterns of causation.

59 On the closely related case of separating conjoined twins see John Zeis (2005), pp. 133–5. Contrast Helen Watt (2001), 237–45.

60 Compare Stephen Theron (1984), 67–83 and Steven L. Brock (1998), pp. 204–5.

61 Asserted by Michael J. Coughlan (1990), pp. 55–61 and pointed out by G. E. M. Anscombe (1990), p. 62. Also Donagan (1977), p. 164 '… the doctrine underlying all forms of the theory of double effect is that what lies outside the scope of a man's intentions in acting does not belong to his action, and so is not subject to moral judgement.'

62 By not fairly scrutinizing the potential effects of her action, the driver assumed responsibility for her state of recklessness. There was a disregard for the safety of others, a general obligation incumbent on motorists. The side-effect is manifestly unfair. To classify a deadly effect as a side-effect, therefore, clearly does not entail the false conclusion that a side-effect is automatically allowable, since it was not intended, for human life should not be unfairly exposed to negligent or reckless risks. On the question of fairness in tolerating side-effects see further John Finnis (1991b) and (1995).

63 Germain Grisez (1978) discusses many ways in which the seemingly consequentialist or proportionalist concerns of the fourth criterion of double effect are not in fact compatible with full blown consequentialist methodology.

64 First introduced by Philippa Foot (1978).

65 J. J. Thompson (1985), pp. 1395–415 argues for permissibility of choice only. John Taurek (1977), pp. 293–316 would likely argue for the flipping of a fair coin as the method of judgment.

66 This, I take it, is the general import of Thomas M. Scanlon's (1998), ch. 5 contractualist concerns that if numbers are ignored, then additional persons are being treated as insignificant or irrelevant presences.

67 Rejecting both Thompson's and Turek's solutions. If added numbers never mattered in conflict situations, where *all other necessary moral requirements are met*, then a rescue team, for example, would never have good reason, were all lives cannot be saved, to save the lives of five innocent shipwrecked victims rather than the life of one innocent shipwrecked victim. Properly constrained and qualified, however, the pulls and pushes of different numerical instances of the same good can be discerned and can sometimes furnish us with a tipping reason to act one way rather than another. As Phillipa Foot points out (1978), p. 24: 'We are about to give a patient who needs it to save his life a massive dose of a certain drug in short supply. There arrive, however, five other patients each of whom could be saved by one-fifth of that dose. We say with regret that we cannot spare our whole supply of the drug for a single patient, just as we should say that we could not spare the whole resources of a ward for one dangerously ill individual when ambulances arrive bringing in victims of a multiple crash. *We feel bound to let one man die rather than many if that is our only choice*.' My emphasis.

68 Thompson (1985), p. 1403. For more discussion of different variations on the trolley cases and how they are, in general, actually supportive of double effect reasoning see Michael J. Costa (1986) and (1987).

69 For Warren S. Quinn (1989a), the distinction turns on action versus inaction—for example, pushing a person's head under the water versus refraining from throwing the person a life jacket.

70 These examples are taken from Philip Devine (1978), pp. 6–33 and Foot (1978), pp. 25–7.

71 G. E. M. Anscombe argues that if letting die (omission) is always as bad as killing (action) then simply not killing should always be as good as actually saving a life! We would then be moral heroes simply by getting through the day without actually killing anyone. For Anscombe, only where we have a positive duty to save must we causally intervene and not let a person die. To fail to save a life, where there is a positive duty, however, would be culpable by omission. Discussed in Jenny Teichman (1996), pp. 80–81. See also Anscombe (1994), pp. 219–24.

72 The deepest level of intense engagement with evil is by intentional causation and the least degree of intensity of engagement is via non-intentional but negligent refraining.

73 Daniel Dinello (1971), 84–6; Richard S. Trammell (1979), pp. 251–62; Joseph Boyle (1977b), pp. 433–52. Contrast Graham Oddie (1997), pp. 267–87 who argues that killing and letting die have the very same moral status.

74 On actions and omissions and the different reach of positive and negative duties see Foot (1978) and (1984); Quinn (1989a), pp. 287–312; Trammell (1975), pp. 131–7; Oderberg (2000), pp. 127–37.

75 Chappell (2002), pp. 219–20.

76 Chappell (2002), pp. 215–22.

77 Positive demands governing failures to act are always framed less precisely and are more conditional with regard to the nature of specific causal performances. An exceptionless positive demand requiring that we always intentionally promote the good of human life wherever there was opportunity to do so—apart from driving us mad—would be honored more in the breach than the observance. We could not but constantly fail to meet the unreasonable scope of such a positive demand. Fortunately, due regard for the good of human life imposes upon us no such overly rigorist positive demand. Negative demands, on the other hand—requiring that we always refrain from culpably causing certain kinds of harmful effects—can always be adhered to and usually leave open options as to the performance of alternative actions.

78 Kai Nielsen (1990), ch. 6.

79 Charles Fried (1978); Thomas Nagel (1979); Tom Beauchamp and James Childress (1994); Robert Nozick (1974); Ronald Dworkin (1977).

80 Fried (1978), pp. 10–18. Thus, for Fried, we cannot in such circumstances assert the Stoic view *fiat justitia, ruat coelum*—('let justice be done though the heavens may fall'). As Fried at p. 10 states: 'we can imagine extreme cases where killing an innocent person may save a whole nation. In such cases it seems fanatical to maintain the absoluteness of the judgment … even then it would be a non sequitur to argue (as consequentialists are fond of doing) that this proves judgments of right and wrong are always a matter of degree ... I believe, on the contrary, that the concept of the catastrophic is a distinct concept just because it identifies the extreme situations in which the usual categories of judgment (including the category of right and wrong) no longer apply.'

81 Nozick (1974), p. 30, 'The question of whether these side constraints are absolute, or whether they may be violated in order to avoid catastrophic moral horror, and if the latter, what the resulting structure might look like, is one I hope largely to avoid.' Avoid it, however, he cannot.

82 Nagel (1979), p. 56, 'While not every conflict between absolutism and utilitarianism creates an insoluble dilemma, and while it seems to me certainly right to adhere to absolutist restrictions unless the utilitarian considerations favoring violation are overpoweringly weighty and extremely certain—nevertheless, when that special condition is met, it may become impossible to adhere to an absolutist position.'

83 Beauchamp and Childress (1994), pp. 32–6, 99–106.

84 See Nancy A. Davis (1993), pp. 205, 215–16. She argues that the attempt to stipulate thresholds undermines the logic of deontological morality.

85 The 'wrongness of actions' *à la* deontology and the 'badness of consequences' *à la* consequentialism cannot be reconciled with each other, for their respective logics are very different. See Anthony Ellis (1992), pp. 855–75.

86 Ellis (1992) and Larry Alexander (2000), pp. 893–912.

87 See Chappell (1998), pp. 96–9.

88 For Anscombe (1970), it is always possible to obey a concrete moral absolute never to commit murder. Even if our refusal to murder results in murders committed by others, *we are not responsible for letting murders happen* by omitting to murder.

Chapter 5

Suicide, Assisted Suicide and Voluntary Euthanasia

5.1 Introduction

When we now turn to discern how general moral norms relate to the specific practices of suicide and euthanasia, we should bear in mind the relevance of a distinction drawn by proponents between a procured death that has been expressly chosen and consented to by the beneficiary and a procured death that has not been consented to by the beneficiary, either because consent has been expressly withheld or because the beneficiary lacks the mental capacity to grant or withhold consent. Since the presence or absence of consent is considered to be an important distinction shaping the licitness of different forms of procured death, I will first, in this chapter, tackle the topic of suicide and euthanasia for the sake of relieving pain and suffering where the factor of consent is held to be operational. In the next chapter, Chapter 6, I will turn to address the topic of intentionally procuring death where the factor of consent is not present.

5.2 Species of Homicide

Defenders of suicide and assisted suicide sometimes claim that such practices cannot fall under the purview of general norms concerning the ethics of killing, articulated in Chapter 4, because suicide is simply not a species of the genus 'homicide.' Homicide requires the killing of one person by another person, ergo, suicide and even assisted suicide cannot be held to be species of homicide. The suicide, without assistance, intentionally procures his or her own death, not the death of another (see s. 1.3a). The suicide assister does not perform the final act of killing, thus assisting with a suicide, due to the limited role the assister plays in the suicide, cannot turn assisted suicide into a species of homicide either.[1]

Contrary to this narrowness of definition, I see no reason to exclude self-procured death from being considered a species of homicide.[2] The killing of a person is surely entailed (as to 'persons' see s. 6.3). A wider, more plausible, definition simply requires the killing of a person *simpliciter*, making no difference to such a definition as to whether or not the killing was self-executed or was performed by another person. The role of others in the procurement of a killing is a relevant factor with regard to the classification of different species of homicide, not the genus. The focus on killing ought to result in the classification of suicide as a species of homicide, thus falling under the scope of the negative and positive moral norms applicable to homicide generally.

Even assuming, for the sake of argument, that we were to follow the narrower definition of homicide—that suicide cannot be classified as a species of homicide—the assister in suicide cannot reasonably escape from the reach of moral norms applicable to homicide, for the kinds of cooperation typically rendered by an assister in a suicide amount to acting in joint consort with the will of the suicide in order to procure his or her death (see s. 1.3b).[3] There is a common shared enterprise. The action of an assister, say, of placing a lethal dose of pills within reach of or in the hand of a suicide, typically denotes a willed intent on the part of the third party assister that the suicide should be killed. The will of the assister is intimately and strategically connected to the execution of a shared causal chain leading up to the performance of the final act. If the suicide were incapable of reaching for the lethal pills, would the assister not instead place the drugs in the suicide's hand or mouth? If the suicide could not execute the final act, would the assister not be prepared to execute the last act in such a common enterprise? Given the degree of joint cooperation that is usually associated with a pact for assisted suicide, there is no significant moral difference to be drawn between such a pact and a pact for voluntary euthanasia where the final act is performed by a third party. Voluntary euthanasia is certainly a species of homicide—of what is sometimes termed 'consensual homicide'—for a third party, acting as part of a joint enterprise, executes a lethal causal chain that is intended to procure the death of the beneficiary (see s. 1.3c).

Since suicide, assisted suicide and voluntary euthanasia are all species of the genus homicide—according to the wider definition of homicide—they all fall under the scope of a concrete moral absolute prohibiting the intentional killing of an innocent person, regardless of any further appeal to end or consequences (see s. 4.5). Due respect for the primary good of human life minimally demands that we always refrain from actions intent on killing an innocent person. Proponents of assisted suicide and voluntary euthanasia argue that such an exceptionless prohibition must be flawed in scope because the twin operational factors of (i) consent by the beneficiary and (ii) killing in order to end pain and suffering, render an otherwise wrongful action of intentional killing morally permissible (see ss. 2.5; 2.4). Respect for the autonomy of an individual, combined with intolerable burdens of pain and suffering, are said to override or trump the force of any negative obligation to refrain from actions specifically intended to terminate life.

In order to challenge the case for permissibility, I seek to explain just why it is unreasonable to conclude that a person—by trading in the burdens of pain and suffering (diminished quality-of-life) for non-existence—can be said to be 'better off dead'; and (ii) explain why it is unreasonable to conclude that consent is a right-making condition that can render the intentional killing of an innocent permissible. If it is unreasonable to trade off the burdens of pain and suffering with non-existence, and if certain harmful actions cannot reasonably be consented to, then the moral case for permissibility cannot be sustained.

5.3 Better Off Dead?

Supporters of suicide, assisted suicide and voluntary euthanasia claim it makes sense to say that a person can be 'better off dead' instead of continuing to live a life of 'severely diminished quality.' Such value judgments, it is said, are comparatively sound. Yet, how is it possible for a person to 'benefit' from his or her death? Does death not destroy the person's existence? How can the beneficiary, the self, be said to benefit if the self is rendered non-existent?

One of the commonest lines of argument advanced here is termed the 'deprivation account' of death. Key exponents include Thomas Nagel, Harry Silverstein and Fred Feldman.[4] The general argument states that since a person can be posthumously harmed by his or her future loss (depriving him or her of a worthwhile future that would have existed had he or she continued to live), a person can also be posthumously benefited by his or her future gain (the ending of a burdensome existence that would have continued if he or she had gone on living). For example, suppose Charles Dickens's life would have included more literary achievement if he had lived for a few more years. Because literary achievement is a good, Dickens can be said to have had a less good life overall than he would have had if he had lived longer. Living a less good life is a loss to the person. By excluding those future possible achievements, then, Dickens's death can be said to be a loss to him, for it prevented a life that would have been better off than it was. Trading on this parallel of posthumous loss, it is argued that death can be a benefit by comparing future possible lives. Suppose a person's life would go on to contain severe pain and suffering. That person would be better off having a shorter life than having a life of prolonged misery. Since living a better life is a benefit, and the better life is provided by the shorter life, it follows that the shorter life is a benefit. By ending prospective pain and suffering then, a person's death is said to be a genuine benefit to him or her, since it prevents a worse prospective life being lived than need be.[5]

By engaging in comparisons of future projections, the conclusion is reached that death is only an evil for a person if the future lost is one that offers better prospects than a shorter life. Death is typically conceived of as the destruction of the self; the non-existence of the self; the non-state of non-being.[6] A person can be 'better off dead,' it seems, even though death means that the beneficiary is no longer in existence to experience it. How can we respond to this account that death is a benefit to a person where future life prospects are grim? Can it truly be a rational act for a person, when faced with bleak prospects, to intentionally choose the destruction of self over the continuation of self? Are persons who make and act upon such comparative assessments objectively justified in opting for a shorter life?

Whilst I would certainly agree that a life that is less burdened by pain and suffering is, all things being equal, a benefit, and the contrary less so, it does not follow from this that 'posthumous losses or gains' can underwrite a decision to opt for death. A person simply cannot be harmed or benefited when they cease to exist, for there is no *ontological existent* to be harmed or benefited.[7] To assign a meaningful benefit or loss to a person requires the continuing existence—the beingness—of the person.[8] The real evil inflicted upon a person by death is to terminate the very existence of the person, rendering a person a non-existent.[9] It is this radical ontological change from personal existence to non-existence that crucially explains why it is that death *per se* is considered to be a primal evil for persons.[10]

When we assert that a person is harmed or benefitted by some state, this requires that there is actually a person in existence who is capable of being the bearer of the value or disvalue. If it is good to be without pain and suffering, as indeed it generally is, this presupposes the existence of a person in order to instantiate that good (any good). If a person can be 'better off dead,' then the continued existence of the person must somehow continue after death. Yet, no one on the basis of natural reason alone can justifiably claim that death can allow for the continuation of the person *qua* person.[11] The person, as we know it, ceases to exist. To realize goods and to minimize evils requires the presence of that single constant, a living human existent, whose continuing life can make sense of such value statements. It is therefore improper to leap from (i) the evaluation of means to lessen or minimize the evils of suffering and pain to reach the conclusion that (ii) existential destruction can, in any real sense, make a person 'better off.'[12] All we can reasonably do is seek to benefit persons—by promoting goods and avoiding evils—in their present lives, as best we can, via a humanitarian framework of care and support.[13]

Talk of 'posthumous harms and benefits' can best be accounted for in other ways.[14] Consider, for example, the concerns people often have over their funeral arrangements and the disposal of their bodily remains. If a person's wishes are willfully disrespected after death, can he or she be said to have been personally harmed? I think not. It is the 'legacy' of the former person that is being harmed by the willed disrespect of others, not the person who was but now no longer is. Similarly, the legacy of a former person is benefitted by due respect shown towards the wishes of the person who was but now no longer is. Persons, while alive, often seek to protect their legacy after they die because they realize that their legacy, unlike their personal existence, can endure after they are dead.[15]

5.4 Quality-of-Life

The notion of 'quality-of-life' was traditionally used to measure environmental conditions that either improved or impaired the quality of a person's life. Social reformers used this traditional concept to increase standard of living by improving working conditions, health care, education, and other living conditions.[16] In the wake of contemporary movements, however, the notion of quality-of-life has significantly altered.[17] Now, rather than measuring conditions that improve life, the notion of quality-of-life has increasingly come to signify the very worth of a person's life.[18] Jonathan Glover, James Rachels, Helga Kuhse, John Harris, and Peter Singer, all make a distinction between 'having a life' and 'having a worthwhile life' (see s. 2.4c). For competent persons, at least, providing some rather vague and indeterminate threshold of pain and suffering has been crossed, the worthwhileness of a person's life will be subjectively determined by a quality-of-life self-assessment exercise. If the pain and suffering burdens are judged too great, then self-assessment can readily result in a decision to intentionally end life.

Individuals should be free to decide, based on their evaluation of goods and bads, whether the continuing burdens of life are worthwhile putting up with or not. Suicide, assisted suicide and voluntary euthanasia can therefore be justified on the ground that once the competent nature of the person making the decision has been established, and some loose form of pain and suffering line has been crossed, persons are free to determine for themselves as to whether or not their lives are worthwhile continuing with or not.

Now, no reasonable person would say that a life of less complete, less perfect, human well-being is better than a life of more complete, more prefect, human well-being. In that sense there can be said to be more 'quality,' a greater instantiation of different goods, in the former than the latter. But it is an improper move to go from our sense of well-being and its diminishment to reach the conclusion that life itself is not worth living, for there is quite simply no 'threshold' that can be crossed, such that a diminishment in well-being ceases to instantiate any inherent good genuinely worthwhile preserving.[19] Whilst the use of language can certainly be ambiguous— especially the phrase 'quality-of-life'—leading us to think that we can indeed rationally trade the 'overall value of life' against the 'non-existence of death' (see s. 5.3), we should nevertheless be critical of any attempt to extrapolate from: (i) 'doing X is a valuable part of B's life and B's life is diminished by not being able to do X' to (ii) 'B's very life is no longer worth living because B can no longer do X' or from (iii) 'B's life is burdened by the effects of illness combined with treatment' to (iv) 'B's very life ceases to be worthwhile because of the burdens of illness combined with treatment.' The correct locus of evaluation to be focused upon in medical contexts, contra Ronald Dworkin, Helga Kuhse and John Harris, should be whether a proposed treatment for a patient is worthwhile or not, not whether a patient's very life, in and of itself, is worthwhile or not.[20] Quality-of-life concerns should always be focused on the ways and means in which humanitarian resources can be deployed to improve the health of patients and should not be conflated with attempts to assess the overall 'benefits of living' versus the 'benefits of death' as if the two can really be rationally weighed and compared to one another.

Let me be quite clear that I am not seeking to trivialize in any way the burdens on life imposed by illness, pain and suffering. Medical reports are full of heart rendering accounts of the pain and suffering endured by patients in the course of their illnesses. A burdened life is assuredly deprived in its full pursuit of well-being. Such burdens, very understandably, often seem to overwhelm the capacity of patients to cope with them. Yet, notwithstanding the heavy toll those burdens inflict on patients, the only reasonable way to respond to those burdens is to do all we can to cure or diminish the pain and suffering of patients *as best we can*. We constantly need to remind ourselves that a life that is severely diminished in 'quality' is still capable of realizing and participating in an wide array of primary and secondary human goods—friendship, family, beauty, truth, etc.[21]

The primary responsibility for making critical health care decisions, at least for competent patients, rests with patients. Physicians are present to inform and counsel patients concerning their health condition and what the burdens and benefits of different treatment options are. Patients are usually best placed to discern, given relevant information from physicians, what impact the benefits and burdens of a proposed treatment will have on their ability to pursue different goods in life. That patient discernment should focus on evaluating the benefits and burdens of proposed treatment options, however, is not tantamount to endorsing the idea advocated by Singer, Harris and Kuhse that we can truly judge the very worth of our own lives. Patient assessment should be structured around the extent to which a treatment can improve or diminish a patient's reasonable commitments to pursue different goods in life.[22] It should not be focused on misguided attempts to discern whether life 'overall' can be judged worthwhile living or not. Given the diversity of choices and ways of life that are reconcilable with a pluralistic conception of the good, patients will often have considerable leeway to decide on whether or not a treatment or discontinuation of treatment, in their circumstances, is the best course to take. Yet, leeway does not endorse license, and there are moral requirements placed on decisions made by patients to refuse or demand the discontinuance of treatments.[23]

The non-consequentialist framework being defended here, one that defends the intrinsic good of human life, should be differentiated from *naïve vitalism*, the view that life, is a 'super good' that must be preserved at all costs.[24] The good of life, whilst a primary good, is not the supreme good. We are required to respect both its negative and positive demands (see s. 4.4). The good of life does not demand from us that we 'strive officiously to stay alive' regardless of the other deep seated commitments we might have.[25] As a patient carefully discerns the benefits and burdens of treatment or withdrawal of treatment, he or she is obligated to respect human life (i) by not intentionally seeking to destroy their innocent life, and (ii) by not treating their life as if it were a subordinate non-primary good of mere instrumental worth (see s. 3.6a).

Without offering any exclusive listing of factors, Germain Grisez and Joseph Boyle helpfully list several factors that would offer reasonable grounds for justifying the non-provision or withdrawal of a medical treatment: a risky or experimental treatment; no reasonable hope of benefit; medical futility; avoidance of significant pain or trauma associated with treatment; the impact of a treatment on a patient's participation in valued activities or experiences; irreconcilable conflicts with deep-seated moral or religious commitments; treatment that is psychologically repugnant; burdensome toll on family members or finances.[26]

Consider the case of Jennifer. Jennifer has been a long distance runner for many years. She is deeply committed to long distance running. The active pursuit of this sport matters a great deal to her. It occupies much of her spare time. She is single and has no dependants. Her life is largely structured around the pursuit of this sport. Gangrene has been diagnosed in her left leg. If the leg is not removed she will likely die due to septic poisoning. Discerning the burdens and benefits of treatment is going to be complex. If her leg is removed she will likely live. Surgery does offer a reasonable hope of benefit. It is not medically futile. The amputation, however, will cause pain and trauma. She will be unable to pursue long distance running. She finds the prospect of having a leg amputated psychologically repugnant. Here, notwithstanding the benefits of extending her life, and her participation in other goods by having extended life, the proposed treatment is morally permissible but not obligatory. In fairly discerning the benefits and burdens of the proposed treatment, Jennifer may determine, (i) without intending to die, and (ii) without treating life as if it were a mere instrumental good, that the burdens of treatment are too onerous for her to bear.

Contrast Jennifer's case with Tom's case. Tom is married and has three young children. He has developed a severe case of diabetes. His doctor informs him that if he does not regularly monitor and regulate his sugar levels, by injecting insulin, he will imperil his life and health. He can afford the medication. Tom, however, has an aversion to needles. Is it reasonable for Tom, in the circumstances, to refuse the benefits of treatment due to needle aversion? Such an aversion cannot stand in any fair correspondence to (i) the good of his life and health and (ii) the responsibilities he has towards his family. The benefits of treatment would be unfairly set aside if Tom were to refuse treatment due to a minor psychological burden that can, given effort and help, be overcome.

Frameworks for decision making can, of course, be abused. Considerable leeway is given to patients to make benefit and burden determinations. Patients must ask themselves, however, if they are acting in good faith when discerning the burdens and benefits associated with the refusal or withdrawal of treatments. Do they intend only to avoid the burdens of the treatment or do they really intend that the burden be used as a vehicle to justify an intentional decision to end a life judged 'unworthy'?[27]

When considering the public policy realm, there are significant reasons as to why wide discretion is granted to competent patients to discern burdens and benefits for themselves. It is a 'brute fact' that intervention over treatment decisions would be visited with all manner of difficulty, not least the concern that a successful treatment usually requires the active cooperation of the patient. The problems caused by enforcing treatments against the will of a patient would be immense. Negative effects on the morale of patients, their families and the medical professions would be considerable. One only has to mention 'force feeding' a person against his or her will to envision some of the traumatic means that may have to be resorted to. For the sake of avoiding the many negative effects of forced intervention, then, the general decision not to overrule a patient's intent to end life by refusing or withdrawing treatment, other than by means of persuasion, cannot be prevented. Such a policy, however, does not amount to any endorsement of suicide, assisted suicide or voluntary euthanasia by the 'back door,' for (a) patients can often refuse treatments the result in death without any culpable (intentional or negligent) failure to act, (b) physicians and nurses can cooperate in the non-provision or withdrawal of treatment without having homicidal intent, and (c) intentional wrongs are being tolerated only as a side-effect of seeking to protect and not undermine other important goods at stake.

5.5 Killing and Letting Die

It is sometimes argued by proponents of assisted suicide and active voluntary euthanasia, that since life is not always preserved either by not providing or by discontinuing treatments—when it could still have been preserved—'killing' is really being morally and legally sanctioned.[28] Why, then, can the other methods for killing patients not also be permitted? Such a straightforward equivalencing under 'killing,' however, is highly misleading for it concentrates only on the fact that death is brought about by some action or omission to act, or some combination, without addressing vitally important questions pertaining to intention/foresight (see s. 4.6a), action and omission (see s. 4.6d), responsibility for side-effects (see s. 4.6c), and the reach of prior obligations incumbent on both patients and physicians to act or refrain from acting (see s. 4.4).

Consider the following case. A patient is dependent on a ventilator due to an underlying condition that cannot be cured. She would not be able to breath without the assistance of the ventilator. She finds being hooked up to the ventilator increasingly burdensome. After careful deliberation, she finally decides that the ventilator treatment should be discontinued. Acting on the patient's instruction, the ventilator is withdrawn by her physician. She dies a few minutes later. Do the patient and the physician in this case stand in the same relation to the causation of death as a patient and physician who embark upon a joint enterprise to kill by withdrawing the ventilator with the specific intent that the patient be killed?

There are negative demands generated by the good of life to refrain from intentionally killing an innocent person. Patients and physicians are never permitted to intentionally kill. This obligation is exceptionless. Patients and physicians are also subjected to positive demands generated by the good of human life and health. Unlike a negative absolute, however, positive demands are not exceptionless in nature. We are not required to preserve our lives in existence regardless of the impact treatments may have on our ability to pursue other goods and commitments. Providing a patient and physician do not intend to cause death by withdrawing the ventilator, and both the benefits as well as the burdens of treatment have been carefully scrutinized, there need be no breach of an existing negative or positive obligation generated by due regard for the good of human life. But for the withdrawal of the ventilator, the patient would have continued to live. Yet, the responsibility we have for causation in the world is not governed by the fact of causation viewed as an isolate but rather is conditioned by the blameless or culpable manner by which causal change, or for an omission, failure to generate causal change, is shaped by our intentions (see s. 4.6b). Neither the patient nor the physician need have intended the causation of death. The patient may reasonably foresee the near certainty of her death as a known side-effect and yet not intend her death. The physician need only seek to comply with the patient's wishes *viz*. her assessment of the burdens and benefits of treatment. The physician can also foresee the near certainty of death as a side-effect of the action (withdrawal of ventilation) and subsequent omission to act (not restarting ventilation) and yet not intend death. The good effect for the patient, the cessation of a burdensome treatment, is concomitant with the causation of the bad effect. Analysis of culpability is, alas, severely distorted when intention is held equivalent to foresight and the naked fact of causation is viewed in isolation from the scope of intention informing the moral quality of an action.[29]

If the patient or physician intended the death of the patient, then the death would be morally wrong. The action would have a different moral status. The action may be legally permissible due to the difficulty of determining intent where the extrinsic appearances of an action do not significantly differ, but operational questions informing legal permissibility clearly do not justify the conclusion that the action is morally permissible.[30] Such a conclusion would be quite incompatible with an intention-sensitive ethics. Intending death by withdrawing life support is a case of 'killing,' of passive voluntary euthanasia. Intending only to be shorn of the burdens of treatment resulting in the causation of death as a side-effect is a case of 'letting die.'[31]

Consider now a second case. In order to hasten the death of a patient, for the withdrawal of a treatment may take several days to kill, the patient is injected with a lethal dose of drugs. The patient has consented to the lethal injection. The patient dies minutes later. Here, there is the execution of an action intended to result in the death of the patient. Causation of this kind is specifically intended to kill the patient.[32] The bad effect of death is the intended means used to bring an end to a patient's pain and suffering. Unlike cases of not providing or withdrawing treatments, where there need not be an intention to kill, here, there can be no permissible room. The patient is being intentionally injected with a lethal substance in order to kill. This is a clear case of active voluntary euthanasia not 'letting die.'

If not all actions resulting in death are morally equivalent, not all omissions resulting in death are equivalent either. Consider the following two cases. In the first case a forty-year-old AIDS patient refuses to undergo a treatment of antibiotics to combat pneumonia because of the further burden of adding this treatment on top of many other treatments he has received. He accepts that he may likely die as a result of the omission not to treat the pneumonia but is reconciled to that prospect. In the second case a forty-year-old patient refuses to undergo a treatment of antibiotics to combat pneumonia because his life is not going well. His girlfriend has left him. His prospects for material enrichment seem dim. While there is an excellent chance that his pneumonia will be cured and will not reoccur, and he has no other major health concerns, he refuses the treatment because it provides him with an opportunity to end his 'unworthy' life without the additional resolve and steps needed to actively commit suicide.

In the first case there is no intentional failure to act concerning the positive obligation to preserve life. By his omission, the AIDS patient need only intend that the additional burden of receiving a further kind of treatment be avoided. Foreseeing and accepting the onset of a bad happening is not the moral equivalent of intending the bad happening. There is no intentional or negligent failure to act on his part. In the second case, however, there is an intentional failure to act. His underlying intent in refusing treatment is not directed at an assessment of the different burdens and benefits of antibiotic treatment versus non-treatment, but is being used as a pretext to end his life because he judges that his life is not worth living.[33] Such an intentional omission to act *viz.* the positive obligation to preserve life would be morally wrongful. It would be a case of 'self-killing.' Yet, wrongful as his failure to act is, all things considered, his conduct would, I think, be graver still if he were to intentionally will and execute a new lethal chain of causation and actively kill himself by deliberately ingesting a lethal dose of pills (see s. 4.6d).

5.6 Intentional Killing and Personal Autonomy

Defenders of a right to suicide, assisted suicide and voluntary euthanasia (or to some but not all of these practices) argue that such a right exists when certain factors pertaining to motive and consent are held operative. Suicide, for example, is considered permissible when a soldier is captured by the enemy and he kills himself in order to prevent disclosure of vital information under torture. Suicide is also considered permissible when a patient kills herself in order to prevent the continuation of levels of pain and suffering that can no longer be tolerated by the patient. Given a significant motive, competent persons can grant themselves permission to take their own lives. When relevant, given consent, a third party can also assist or execute the final act of killing. In short, voluntary and knowing consent + significant purpose = permissibility (see s. 2.5c).

In this section, I am concerned to argue, notwithstanding appeals to motive, that personal autonomy, the value underlying the idea of consent, cannot rightfully be invoked in order to justify the decision of a person to self-kill or to justify the decision of a third party to help kill another person.

5.6a Personal Autonomy and Moral Autonomy

As we explained in Chapter 2 (see s. 2.5c), D. A. J. Richards is a contemporary philosopher who claims to derive a robust notion of personal autonomy from the moral philosophy of Immanuel Kant. Due to Kant's 'rational biases,' however, Richards sought to 'update' Kant's notion of autonomy. The ends of action are decidedly more fluid and open in texture than Kant had realized. Reason does not so constrain and limit the exercise of self-constituting personal choices in the way that Kant thought. Instead, reason's role in moral deliberation is decidedly more limited in scope, being largely restricted to: (i) an evaluation of the ways in which our pursuit of immediate goals may impact our pursuit of deeper 'nested' ends; (ii) an evaluation of the effectiveness and efficiency of different available means as we pursue our ends; (iii) an evaluation of the harms that our actions and omissions may have on the interests of others.

Does Richards, however, really offer us an interpretation of personal autonomy that, so updated, can be described as being authentically Kantian? I think not.[34] The view of autonomy adopted by Richards seeks to radically downplay the ability of rationality to morally regulate the substantive content of a willed choice. For Richards, personal choices, within broad limits, should be respected simply because they reflect the constitutive values of a person, not because these constitutive values must first pass muster according to any overreaching sense of what rationality with a capital 'R' is said to require of us. Richards's notion of personal autonomy really owes a great deal more to the liberty tradition of J. S. Mill that it does to Kant's central concern with reason guided 'moral autonomy.'[35]

This distinction between Millsian inspired 'personal autonomy'—the right to self-determination—and Kantian 'moral autonomy'—the will subject to the dictates of reason—is important to the framing of contemporary debate and is not a mere historical aside.[36] Talk of 'moral autonomy' gives the opponent of full-blown personal autonomy a label for referring to a cluster of important pre-conditions needed in order to pursue different kinds of goods in life—the integrity of agency; freedom to cultivate and develop worthwhile life projects and commitments; significant discretion to order priorities in a life narrative—whilst being able to differentiate these important conditions from broader self-determination claims made by personal autonomy supporters.[37] Under the aegis of moral autonomy, for example, I can partially agree with Joel Feinberg's articulation of many important conditions required for the making of an autonomous choice, and can agree with him that that there is an important sense in which persons are at least (part) authors of their lives, without conceding that an autonomous choice can be said to truly command respect unless the very content of the autonomously made choice is actually good or at least indifferent (see s. 2.c). Autonomous choices matter to us because it is through our choices that we are able to reflectively take responsibility for and promote our well-being as persons (and that of those around us). The conditions needed to exercise autonomous choice in general, bring with them responsibility for making not just any choice, but choices that actually promote rather than undermine our reasonable pursuit of primary goods (see s. 3.9).

By my use of the term 'moral autonomy' rather than 'personal autonomy,' then, I intend to signify the importance of autonomous conditions for deliberation and action, whilst holding: (i) the fact that a person has a deep commitment towards a personal choice cannot be sufficient to demand from us anything more than presumptive respect; (ii) the content of a personal choice, in order to be worthy of respect, must actually be good or indifferent; (iii) good or indifferent content can only be determined by a prior account of the good, not independently of it; (iv) an objective account of the good exists; (v) this objective account generates negative and positive obligations that shape the moral content of our choices.

5.6b Supreme Value of Personal Autonomy

Now, no defender of personal autonomy, despite the rhetoric sometimes used, can seriously wish to defend the proposition that all autonomously made choices, regardless of content, are morally permissible choices. The mere fact that choice Y is a deeply held reflective conviction of person X is not sufficient to justify the permissibility of Y. If autonomous choice alone were sufficient to justify X's choice to Y, autonomy would amount to little other than advocacy of unrestrained license. Since unrestrained license is not a serious option, we must grapple with the question of what moral side-constraints exist that place limits on the exercise of autonomous choice. If we wish to say that the content of a choice can render an autonomous choice wrongful, then the content of a choice needs to be assessed according to an objective account of what constitutes a wrongful autonomous choice.[38]

A common way of proceeding to limit the exercise of unrestrained autonomy is to appeal to an apparently neutral principle like J. S. Mill's harm principle.[39] Such a principle, it is said, can justify the creation of some moral side-constraints that permit the restriction of certain autonomous choices for the sake of harm prevention. Such a side-constraint, supporters claim, is held to be defensible without seeking to privilege any particular substantive conception of the good life. Mill's harm principle broadly states that a person's freedom to act can only be restricted if a choice harms another person. Self regarding harm cannot be subject to the overreaching paternalistic control of others. Persons are free to forge their own diverse paths and choices in life as long as they do not inflict significant harm other people.[40]

Such a principle, however, is far from being simple or straightforward and cannot be said to be neutral *vis-à-vis* competing conceptions of the good life. What constitutes harm? Why can there be no obligations to self that regulate self-regarding harms? Can consent nullify or absolve the infliction of harm? These are important questions that inevitably trade upon express or implied theories of the good, and cannot be articulated independently of them. Any non-formal or substantive conception of harm requires that harms be defined according to some kind of pre-existing standard for judging whether or not a choice to Y constitutes a harmful choice.[41]

If harms are to be identified according to an implicit or express theory of goodness, the critical question becomes which theory of goodness? Advancing autonomy of choice on the grounds of complete scepticism over what constitutes the worthwhile ends of action will not do, for if certain choices are truly being ruled out as being wrongful because they are harmful, this can only be because of an appeal to an underlying theory of goodness as to why certain autonomous choices are truly deemed harmful in the first place.

Libertarian defenders of personal autonomy make a strong appeal to the positive value of consent itself as the key ground for determining whether or not a choice to Y actually constitutes a harm or not. If an individual grants consent, then no moral harm will result. All harms are 'putative' only. If B grants consent to self-impose harm Y, then no moral harm will result. If B and C mutually consent to B imposing harm Y on C, then no moral harm will result.[42] If B and C mutually consent to the imposition of harm Y on each other, then no moral harm will result. Where valid consent is granted, therefore, there is said to be no resulting moral harm and hence no wrongdoing. Providing consent is of the genuinely autonomous sort, then, suicide pacts, assisted suicide, voluntary euthanasia, Russian roulette, duelling, dangerous fights, etc. are all said to become permissible non-culpable harms. For the libertarian defender of personal autonomy, the value of valid consent trumps other concerns. Consent, in short, makes right.[43]

Other non-libertarian defenders of the value of personal autonomy reject the ready libertarian equation of autonomy with the present exercise of consent. The future autonomy interests of persons may be at stake. Do we really seek to argue that no moral harm is being perpetrated when a man consensually risks his future autonomy in a game of Russian roulette for the sake of high stakes gambling pleasure? That a drug addict may damage her future exercise of autonomy for the sake of her present pleasure-seeking goals? These and similar examples are said to challenge the credibility of maintaining the libertarian view that present consent can always be regarded as the key right making condition of a choice. Consent can stand in conflict with the need to defend the ongoing prospective autonomy interests of self and others.[44]

Non-libertarian defenders of personal autonomy seek to avoid a universal 'consent makes right' reading of personal autonomy and seek some restrictions on the making of present autonomous choices for the sake of preserving the future value of autonomy. Protecting the future value of autonomy becomes a ground on which to justify the impermissibility of certain present choices. Mill himself encroached upon his own self/other regarding harm distinction when he claimed that it would be morally wrong for a man to freely renounce his future freedom by selling himself into slavery without violating due respect for that good.[45] Following Mill's example, non-libertarian defenders appeal to the idea of preserving the continuing autonomy of a person in order to justify restraints on the present exercise of certain choices. It is thus wrong to become a drug addict, or assist in such, thereby risking the curtailment of future autonomous choice for the drug addict. It is wrong to sell oneself into slavery, or to enslave another person, thereby radically limiting one's future potential to make autonomous choices. It is wrong to duel to the death, for each party to the duel destroys the future autonomy interests of the other.[46]

Certain actions, then, on account of preserving the ongoing autonomy of a person, are judged wrongful—slavery, duelling and drug addiction. Yet, if consent to a harm does not make a choice right, and due regard for the future significance of autonomy necessitates the wrongfulness of certain contentful choices, why is it that suicide, assisted suicide and voluntary euthanasia are not held similarly wrongful on the ground that the present exercise of autonomous choice is being illicitly used to justify the destruction of a person's future ability to make autonomous choices? Why is it that those choices to kill are accorded special treatment? Is it a mere question of timing as to the future length of a predicted autonomous time span before it can cease to be valued as an autonomous future worth preserving? If so, what prospective length of future autonomous choice can or cannot justify a present autonomous decision to terminate the future?

Here, the non-libertarian defender of personal autonomy is asserting that individuals faced with burdens of pain and suffering can determine for themselves whether their autonomous futures are actually worth preserving or not. A trade off between the future worth of autonomy and the continuing burdens of existence is being explicitly endorsed. Yet, if an autonomous choice to kill, in such circumstances, can be made, then why can individuals not decide for themselves whether to sell themselves into slavery? Could the burdens of present disvalues like hunger and poverty not be traded against the curtailment of future autonomous choice associated with such subjugation? Could the value of honor not be vindicated by a mutually agreed upon duel to the death whereby present challenges to honor can be traded against the risk of future destruction?[47]

The problem for the non-libertarian defender of personal autonomy is that the exception carved out for suicide and assisted suicide is *just the sort of unruly exception* that seriously undermines the notion that the preservation of future autonomy alone is being appealed to in order to justify the non-permissibility of some present choices but the permissibility of others. If personal assessment as to future life worth is permissible in the case of medically related pain and suffering, then why not in other cases where the condition of consent may apply? Why are medically related burdens being treated so specially?

Consider the case of Alice. Alice is 20 years of age. She suffers greatly from the unrequited love she has for Jim. She finds it hard to envisage a life worth living, for all the hopes she had for Jim loving her have been dashed. Jim has married another and left the country. Alice will not see Jim again. She seeks to end her life. Perhaps the non-libertarian may argue that, in time, Alice will come to value other things in life. She receives counseling. Yet, what if six months go by and she does not see much in her future worth valuing? Another six months go by. After a year, is it still impermissible for Alice to kill herself? Here, I think, the non-libertarian defender faces the twin horns of a dilemma. If the answer is yes, the non-libertarian defender is overriding Alice's reflective and abiding decision to trade off the burdens of her existential suffering against future prospects. The non-libertarian defender seems to be privileging certain categories of pain and suffering as permissible candidates for trade off where no principled grounds for such exception making really exist. If the answer is no, then the non-libertarian defender is practically embracing the voluntarist doctrine that 'consent makes right.' If Alice's action is morally permissible, then we are once again confronted with the prospect that all manner of subjective value judgments, no matter how destructive, become licit as long as the requirement of consent is met. If Alice can commit suicide or be assisted in committing suicide, then why should persons in general not be able to exercise their 'rights' to sell their organs on the open market, sell themselves into servitude, duel, mutilate themselves, and so on?

5.6c Moral Autonomy

In contrast to personal autonomy, moral autonomy stresses the importance of exercising autonomous conditions in the pursuit of morally worthwhile options. If a choice is to be judged morally worthwhile, it needs to be directed towards the pursuit of a moral end achieved via the election of a moral means. Value pluralism usually offers the individual a range of moral options and choices compatible with the objective standing of various primary goods and the demands generated by these goods. Autonomy is always bounded by the key requirements of practical rationality when deliberating over the worthwhile content of a choice. The objective requirements of morality need to be observed if a choice is to be deemed reasonable. The conditions of autonomy are only truly valuable to the extent that they are directed towards the making of good choices that in turn help with the formation of good character. If a life narrative is being populated by bad choices, then the capacity for autonomous choice is being critically misdirected and abused.

If we are to lead a morally responsible life, we must have a measure of freedom which brings with it the possibility of choosing wrongly. Without the possibility of choosing wrong, we cannot in any meaningful sense be said to make important constitutive choices about ourselves at all. Also, a will overcome by passion and compulsion would rob us of this necessary freedom. Autonomy, then, can be said to afford persons an operational sphere of freedom to make constitutive choices regarding themselves. This, however, does not equate to the proposition that autonomy, as such, can therefore claim to have the status of being a primary good of persons let alone a supreme good (see s. 3.7c). Rather, it justifies regarding the good of autonomy as a necessary prerequisite, a conditional possibility, for the facilitation of practically reasonable decision making with a view to executing good or at least indifferent actions. If an autonomous choice is morally permissible, it can only be because the content of the choice respects and does not violate any negative or positive demand generated by the primary goods of persons.

Given the legitimate plurality of lifestyles and life choices that are consistent with the open ideal of human well-being, countless autonomous choices are good and worthwhile. As such, they truly merit respect. The value pluralism defended in this book generates an immense array of worthwhile options for people to choose from. Given such diversity of worthwhile choice, it is important to be circumspect when deliberating over the moral standing of an autonomous choice. Still, an exercise of autonomy truly merits respect only when it is exercised in accordance with (or is at least compatible with) a framework of reason that recognizes the objective status and significance of different goods. For example, X's decision to assist Y commit suicide does not truly merit respect, nor does Y's own decision to commit suicide (the choice and *not* the person for the dignity of persons must always be respected), since their mutual agreement violates a concrete moral absolute that prohibits all intentional killing of the innocent. The appeal to the preconditional and facilitative good of autonomy simply cannot 'override,' 'trump' or otherwise 'set aside' the binding nature of this obligation. Authentic respect for the status and worth of human life cannot be reconciled with a will disposed towards the intentional or careless ending of innocent life whether of self or other.[48]

Autonomous choices, then, are always bounded by the positive and negative demands of primary goods. Everyone would like, where possible, a broader rather than a narrower field of choice made available to them. Yet, whether broader or narrower, we are constrained by the requirements of practical rationality to choose from among the different morally legitimate courses of action available. Even when there is a very narrow choice range left, even a single stark choice between a moral option and an immoral option, for example, to relieve pain by all humanitarian means possible versus intentional killing, moral autonomy requires that the only remaining moral option be chosen. If an autonomous choice disrespects or violates the key demands of primary goods, it cannot generate a claim to moral permissibility. This is especially so when a decision to act seeks to intentionally violate innocent human life or the dignity of persons, for example, a decision to duel to the death, to sell oneself into slavery, to self-mutilate, to commit suicide, or to assist in a suicide. Since the capacity of autonomy is being misused, the resulting choice can generate no moral claim to permissibility nor can the choice (again, the choice not the person) generate a 'moral right' to be respected by others.[49]

5.6d Compromised Autonomy

Many patients faced with the burdens of severe pain and suffering entertain suicidal thoughts due to the influence of severe depression or other forms of psychological disturbance. The degree to which pain, feelings of worthlessness, guilt, and isolation may radically compromise deliberative choice, are all too easily underestimated.[50] This is evidenced by the fact that when these kinds of problems are addressed and substantially ameliorated, often in a hospice environment, most patients do not in fact seek to kill themselves or seek the aid of others in doing so.[51] Requests for suicide, assisted suicide and voluntary euthanasia are usually not the requests of the defiant autonomous will, in the face of adversity, as assisted suicide proponents would lead us to believe. Rather, they are all too often pleas for help, for love and commitment, on the part of others.[52] The true object of our concern, as with any medical and humanitarian problem, ought to be the minimization or amelioration of burdens that afflict patients, creating suitable care environments in which to achieve this. Creative endeavors, utilized on behalf of suffering patients, ought to be precisely directed at the relief of burdens, not at the intentional killing of patients whose autonomy capacities are very often under considerable strain and who may be understandably lured by the seemingly attractive but wrongful solution to end those burdens via suicide, assisted suicide and voluntary euthanasia.[53]

5.6e Self-Ownership and Property Rights

A related argument mustered in support of a personal autonomy right to self-determination trades on the ideas of ownership and property in order to justify a decision to commit suicide, to assist in a suicide or to commit voluntary euthanasia. Crucially, the kind of right claimed is the right to self-determine how 'owned property' can be treated and disposed of. Since property owners have a right to decide how property is treated and disposed of, and since 'the self' owns the attributes and assets that constitute 'the self,' the self must determine how the self is treated and disposed of. As long as owners do not violate the rights of other owners, individuals possess the right to decide for themselves how their assets, including their lives, can be treated and disposed of (see s. 2.5a).[54]

It should be observed that the very notion of 'self' owning the 'self' is deeply suspect. The idea that people own themselves gains some negative plausibility from the fact that a well known religious claim faces obvious objections. I am referring to the religious claim that persons cannot be said to own their lives because they are deemed to be the property of God. Since it is not a reasonable secular argument to hold that persons are owned by God, and since persons do not belong to any other entity or thing, it is said to follow that persons must own themselves. Yet, that conclusion does not necessarily follow.[55]

The concept of ownership implies that the thing owned can be meaningfully distinguished from the person owning the thing. As Kant recognized, thing and person are not one and the same. Yet, how can a person's corporeal existence X be meaningfully separated from the existent person Y, such that Y can be said to own X? The separation of X and Y is a metaphorical not a real separation. Since X and Y are really existentially inseparable, Y cannot literally be held to own X.[56]

If corporeal existence cannot be separated from the idea of self, life itself cannot be separated from the idea of self either. In order for something to be my property, it must be capable of being separated from me and thus be capable of being transferred to another—I can own a book, the fruits of my labor, a piece of land, even my severed body parts—all can be transferred to others—but I cannot literally own my life for life is not some kind of property attribute that can be existentially separated from my essential self.[57]

Perhaps it might be argued that peculiar talk of 'self' owning 'self' can be set aside if it is interpreted to mean that a person owns his or her 'body.' Here, however, we must question the intelligibility of seeking to differentiate 'body' from 'person' such that a body can be considered to be a mere physical thing that is the property of some sort of 'inner' being. The personal 'I' and the embodied 'I' are one and the same thing.[58] Certainly we can talk of persons having rights and duties with regard to the control of their bodies. Persons can authorize the removal of a diseased limb, a burst appendix, they can consent to physical intimacy, remove and donate body parts, and so on. Yet, none of these issues necessitates acceptance of the idea that persons literally have ownership over their bodies.[59] Metaphors again are apt to mislead. When I speak of 'my life' and 'my body,' I am conveniently addressing both personal identity and control questions. Pressed further, however, the usefulness of these metaphors starts to fall apart. I can surely refer to 'my consciousness,' 'my thoughts,' 'my mother,' and 'my friend Joe' without implying the conclusion that I actually have ownership of my thoughts, my mother or my friend![60]

The concept of self-ownership, whereby a person has property over his or her own person, also gives rise to structural problems of property alienation. To characterize a right as inalienable is usually to claim that the consent of the right-holder is held insufficient to (i) destroy the right or (ii) transfer it to another. Now, defenders of the concept of self-ownership often argue that property can be alienated by destruction in the case of suicide yet cannot be alienated in the case of slavery. Why should the concept of self-ownership permit only the former case of 'alienation by destruction' but not the latter case of 'alienation by transfer'? Perhaps it might be argued that while people own themselves, they can never alienate their perpetual right to self-ownership and this right cannot be transferred to another. If so this restriction on ownership should surely also apply to perpetual alienation via the destruction of self. Assuming, I hope, we do not really think that person X can own person Y, is there any good reason to suppose that X's self-ownership confers on X a right of alienation by destruction?

Self-ownership is actually invoked as a uniquely framed class of ownership quite unlike any other class of ownership. The concept of ownership usually conveys rights of acquisition, transfer and disposal.[61] In the case of self-ownership, however, it is said that the perpetual right of continuing self-ownership (i.e. voluntary slavery) cannot be alienated by consensual transfer.[62] This qualifying exception, however, opens up a range of moral concerns that can further serve to restrain exercisable property rights by people over their lives. If such a moral restriction on the general right of property transfer can be reconciled with the notion of self-ownership, then I fail to see why other important restrictions cannot also be imposed on the concept of self-ownership, most crucially that self-ownership cannot be alienated by intentional destruction.[63] Since life must be an indispensable part of the concept of self-ownership, there is no essential reason why the unique concept of self-ownership cannot be further qualified to embrace the inalienability of life itself by intentional destruction. Since a person cannot alienate his or her radical right to own himself or herself, a person should not be able to alienate his or her radical right to continue to own himself or herself by means of self-destruction.[64]

The language of rights claims whereby B asserts against B his or her right to X or not X, is admittedly rather odd. Negative and positive right claims are usually claims addressed to others to either act or refrain from acting. If B has an inalienable right to X then C has a correlative duty not to interfere with B's continuing right to X. It is strange, however, to speak of B violating his or her own right to life, for B is asserting against B, B's right that B not X. This awkwardness of resorting to a right claim asserted by the self against the self can be avoided by recognizing the existence of duties prior to rights, especially, here, an exceptionless duty not to intentionally kill an innocent person whether self or other.[65]

A moral duty is a broader concept than a right. Duties and rights are not always correlative. There are, for example, duties of beneficence and charity towards persons and animals that do not generate corresponding rights.[66] The notion of a duty gives rise to the possibility that there can be duties to self as well as others without generating the strangeness of appealing to self-asserting rights claims. Duties to self arise from the intelligibility of the self considered from an objective standpoint. Morality requires that we address the objective status and significance of goods of persons, not merely our own subjective dispositions as to their worth.

To illustrate the notion of duties to self, take the case of a person who persistently feels burdened by having to think and act with her present level of high intelligence. She now considers that she no longer values the intellectual capacity she has. It makes her miserable. She thinks that having the intellectual capability of a four-year-old would be preferable to her recurring state of unhappiness—a state that a battery of counselling sessions and drugs have not been able to successfully treat. She considers having a lobotomy—a less drastic solution than suicide. She positively seeks to have the surgery. If the surgery is not made available then she will opt for suicide. Is the surgery not then permissible? Surely not. The surgery is no more permissible than the option for suicide.[67] There is a moral duty incumbent on her—notwithstanding her own subjective assessment concerning the 'present worth' of her life—to respect the objective value of her intelligence.

5.7 Some Interesting Cases from the Literature

Given the moral reasoning defended in this book, I now seek to conclude this chapter with an examination of some interesting cases from the literature that further examine the moral boundaries of consent based suicide assisted suicide, and voluntary euthanasia.

5.7a Morphine Administration

Proponents of assisted suicide and voluntary euthanasia often point to the use of opioid analgesics that relieve pain but may cause respiratory depression resulting in death as cases of 'back door' voluntary euthanasia.[68] Since the effect of respiratory depression is an anticipated risk of high dose pain relief, and since the risk of the side-effect is a foreseeable consequence of the action, it is said to follow that the patient and physician are knowingly causing the death of the patient. If it is licit for a physician to facilitate the death of a patient in this manner, patients should be entitled to avail themselves of other methods for ending their lives.

This kind of argument, alas, may contribute to the fear of physicians and nurses that they may be willfully hastening the death of their patients if they aggressively treat the symptoms of pain with opioid analgesics. The temptation may be to under-treat rather than appropriately treat the pain symptoms of patients due to this ready equation of intent with foresight. The disservice rendered by such an analysis, however, will not do.[69] The distinction between what we specifically intend via our action and what we foresee (even certainly) as an effect of our action, is a real not token distinction (see s. 4.6a). The distinction is crucial to the accurate ethical analysis of a physician's moral responsibility for both the good and bad effects caused by his or her execution of an action. In the case of the administration of morphine to a patient, all that the physician or patient need intend is to provide humanitarian pain relief to the patient. In very severe cases this may even require that the patient be induced into unconsciousness. Respiratory depression is a serious risk. Yet, there need be no intentional willingness on the part of the physician or the patient that the patient be rendered dead as a result of providing humanitarian pain relief. Neither the certainty of an effect nor the relative gravity of an effect necessitates that an effect, as such, need be intended.

Of course the administration of drugs can be abused in order to intentionally kill patients. The effects of an illicit action may appear extrinsically similar to legitimate pain management. Some maladministration, inevitably, will need to be tolerated for the sake of preserving due scope for legitimate pain treatment. What is not morally similar, however, is the volitional state of a physician who intentionally kills his or her patient, albeit with consent, compared to a physician who intends only to treat, as best as he or she can, the pain symptoms of his or her patient.[70]

If a physician genuinely intends only the treatment of pain and not the intentional hastening of a patient's death, the resultant death, due to respiratory depression, will be a bad non-intended side-effect of a morally justifiable action. All of the criteria of double effect reasoning can be satisfied—(i) the objective of the action—the relief of pain—is good; (ii) the intention is only to relieve pain; (iii) the bad effect (death) is not the antecedent causal means for procuring the good effect (pain relief); (iv) serious reason exists to permit the foreseeable causation of the bad side-effect (see s. 4.6).

That death can be said to the non-intentional side-effect of a legitimate action to treat only the symptoms of pain can be further illustrated by means of a thought experiment. Imagine a situation in which additional medicine could be provided that would counteract the negative effects of the morphine and may actually increase a patient's life-span. A physician who truly wills only the good effect of pain relief could reasonably provide such additional treatment, since his or her intention is not to act against the good of human life. There would be no contradiction of the will in simultaneously adopting both courses of action. The same cannot be said of the physician whose intention is contra life since he or she cannot simultaneously, without contradiction, intentionally will both the hastening of death and the continuation of life.[71]

5.7b Burning Man

Consider now Jonathan Glover's burning lorry case (see s. 2.6b). A man is trapped in a burning lorry and is being burned alive. He screams in agony to be released from his torment. There is no prospect of rescue. He will be burned to death. Assuming we had a rifle handy, would it be licit to shoot the man in order to bring a speedy end to his pain and suffering? Whilst it would be wrong to follow Glover's advice and intentionally shoot the man in order to kill him, thereby ending his pain, for we cannot intentionally cause an antecedent bad effect (killing of an innocent) in order to procure a good effect (relieving pain), here, I would argue, another moral assessment resulting in the death of the burning man is possible. In shooting the burning man, the intention may not be to kill him in order to end the burden of pain and suffering. Instead, the specific intention may only be to render the man unconscious (impervious to the pain) via the only blunt and ready means available. The fact that death would almost certainly follow from the execution of an action is *not sufficient* to establish intent. Further, the intended state of unconsciousness, in order to relieve his pain and suffering, would be simultaneously concomitant with the causation of his death. Given (i) the man was going to die very shortly; (ii) the seriousness of the reason for tolerating the bad side-effect; and (iii) use of the only means available, as a very last resort, to render the man unconscious (lesser means, e.g. tranquilliser gun not being available), the death of the man, I think, could be judged a permissible non-intended side-effect of an intentional act of shooting in order to render him unconscious.[72]

It is important to bear in mind, just because a death is classified as a non-intended side-effect of an action, that such a classification does not somehow make the causation of death automatically permissible. Some non-intended side-effects may be wickedly reckless or irresponsible such that we rightly hold a person highly culpable for bringing them about. Still, we should not be forced into adopting the view that the death of an innocent person must, of necessity, be intended (even if it often or usually is) by virtue of (i) intimate causal concomitance between the good effect and the bad effect and (ii) the fatality of the bad effect.

Compare the burning man case to the following case. A man chops off his wife's head claiming that he only intended to stop her talking, not kill her.[73] This can scarcely be thought equivalent to the circumstances of the former case. Even if he really did not intend to kill her as the means of procuring the good effect of his action, his action would be wickedly reckless in nature, for the action would clearly not have been undertaken as a last resort. Walking away or removing himself from her presence would clearly have sufficed.[74] No reasonable understanding of the moral demands of fairness, in the circumstances, could have legitimized the execution of such a drastic solution. His reason for the action cannot stand in any fair correspondence to the evil effect brought about by the execution of his action.

5.7c Captain Oates

Another case commonly discussed in literature is the death of Captain Oates.[75] Captain Oates left the shelter of the Antarctic exploration camp and wandered out into bitterly cold weather. He could not survive long in those conditions. Was this a case of suicide, albeit one motivated by altruism? On the basis of the contextual evidence there is a case for arguing that the action of Oates need not be classified as a suicide. As I have argued, actions can be identical in extrinsic appearances and yet have a different moral character (see s. 4.6a). There is, I think, a reasonable description of his intentional action that need not be classified as a suicide. Oates could reasonably have intended the object of preserving the means of life support for other members of the exploration party in circumstances where his own ill health would have placed a greater burden on those resources. His objective need not have entailed the intentional destruction of his own life, but rather the toleration of that effect as a side-effect of his intentional object (preserving important life-sustaining supplies for the rest of the members of the party). It is important, again, not to confuse foreseeing a bad effect as being certain with the conclusion that it is necessarily intended. Corroboration of this is supplied by the order of his behavior. The action of placing himself outside the shelter and away from being 'rescued' by the other members of the party is antecedent to the bad effect of his death. The good effect precedes the bad.

Even if his death was not intended, however, did his action not entail an immoral risk to his own life? Here we should recognize another moral action type for acts of this nature—'reckless self-endangerment'—that would be morally wrong. Nevertheless, there is good reason to think that Oates's action would not fall under any such action type. He could point to the serious reason of furthering the chances of the survival of several others in order to permit the toleration of the non-intended bad effect. Further, given the context, it is not unreasonable to assume that the other members of the party would attempt to dissuade or even prevent him from embarking on such a course of action unless he departed from the shelter in the manner he did. His acceptance of the bad side-effect of his own death, then, need not fall under the action types of suicide or reckless self-endangerment.

5.7d Soldier and Hand Grenade

Consider the case of a female soldier who launches herself on top of a grenade in order to minimize an explosion that, left unmuffled, could reasonably be expected to have killed several of her nearby comrades.[76] Is this necessarily a case of intending suicide as a means of pursuing an altruistic motive? Here, I think, the object of the soldier's action could reasonably be described as one of protecting the lives of her fellow comrades. The soldier need only have specifically intended, in acting to minimize the blast by muffling it with her body, that the lives of others would be protected. Again, even if death were seen as being certain, this does not mean that the bad effect of the action was intended. Such an account can be supported by the causal sequencing of events. The bad effect of the soldier's death did not causally precede the good effect. Rather, the bad effect was concomitant with the good effect. Finally, there is good reason to think that the final criterion of double effect reasoning—proportionate reason—would permit the causation of the bad effect since the action was undertaken for a serious reason (the saving of several lives).

5.7e Soldier Under Torture

Some possible cases of suicide arise in war conditions where a soldier is captured behind enemy lines and is fearful of passing on critical intelligence information to the enemy under torture. Could a soldier who sought to take a lethal capsule, prepared for such an eventuality, justly intend to end her life for the sake of protecting the lives of others?[77] Given the prior preparation of the means used to rapidly bring about the onset of death, I find it impossible to argue that consumption of it would not constitute an act of intentional killing as the means used to avoid the bad effects of talking under torture. Such an action, informed by a *conditional intention* (to do X when and if Y), would fall afoul of double effect reasoning.[78]

Here, however, I think, the case can be handled by resort to the idea of material innocence. If a captured soldier, while under torture, earnestly thought that she could not resist the effects of the torture by resort to lesser means, for example, escape, non-communicativeness or dissimulation, she could appeal to the idea of material non-innocence to justify an intentional decision to self-kill. As I have already argued, it is not always and everywhere wrong to intentionally kill a material non-innocent (see s. 4.5b). It might seem somewhat at the margins, but I can see no barring reason why a soldier, in the circumstances, could not assess the mortal danger she poses to others, and, in consequence, intentionally self-minister lethal means in order to prevent others from being placed in severe danger. If I am entitled to intentionally shoot and kill a material non-innocent soldier who is about to divulge crucial military information to the enemy, no matter how unwilling the soldier was, then I see no reason why a soldier may not assess the level of material threat that she may pose to others. If a third party may assess and so act, I see no barring reason why a soldier cannot make that same judgment concerning herself and so permissibly aid the defence of others via the self-execution of a lethal act.

5.7f Judicial Self-Execution

Did Socrates commit suicide by the manner of his own death? Could his actual death not give witness to the notion, notwithstanding opposition to suicide in the *Phaedo*, that intentional self-killing, for the sake of an underlying motive, is justified? Such an interpretation is argued for by Roger G. Frey and Isidor F. Stone.[79] Both argue that by drinking the hemlock, thereby executing the death penalty decree of the Athenian court, Socrates necessarily intended his death. As such, his death must be classified as an intentional suicide.

Such analysis, notwithstanding its initial plausibility, given a more detailed understanding of the nature of his action in administering the poison to his body, can be subjected to plausible counter argument. It can be argued that he was intent on bearing witness to the importance of obedience to the law of the state for the sake of the common good. His end was therefore a good one. He would not flee and cause scandal. Second, it can be argued that the act of self-administering the poison, as a means to that end, need not be interpreted as an act of intentional self-killing. Certainly the act of self-administration was intended, but this need not automatically be thought of as equivalent to intentional self-killing by lethal means.[80] He could have intended only to perform the requirement of the law that he administer to himself the prescribed dose of poison. It is important to distinguish, as I have already stressed, questions of foreseeable knowledge from the scope of an agent's intent. Certainly Socrates had knowledge that the self-administration of the poison would most likely kill him. However, this is a different question from what he, strictly speaking, intended by his action. As such, it can be argued that his death need not have been intended and was a bad concomitant side-effect of the good objective of his action.

Notes

1 See Philip Devine (1978), pp.15–17, 180–84 and (1998), pp. 587–8.
2 Latin *homicidium*, *homo* (human being) + *caedere* (to cut; kill).
3 On the different kinds of cooperation in wrongdoing see David S. Oderberg (2004) pp. 203–27. The suicide assister, it seems, can be a 'coordinate agent' jointly sharing a wrongful intent but dividing up the responsibilities. The assister is at least a 'formal cooperator' for he or she supports the wrongful intent of the principal. According to Christopher Kaczor (2005), p. 88 'formal cooperation in evil might be defined as intentionally helping, encouraging advising, or in some way assisting another in doing wrong, and unlike material cooperation which can sometimes be justified, formal cooperation in the wrongdoing of another is always wrong.' See also Surendra Arjoon (2007), pp. 395–410.
4 Thomas Nagel (1986), pp. 9–18; Harry Silverstein (1980), pp. 401–24; Fred Feldman (1991), 205–27. The notion that the well-being of a person can return 'negative intrinsic value' is advanced in hedonistic terms by Fred Feldman (1995), pp. 567–85.
5 For a thorough analysis of deprivation and other accounts of death and the meaning of life see Jack Li (2002), pp. 43–65; Frances M. Kamm (1993), pp. 13–22. See also Thaddeus Metz (2001) and (2002).
6 See James M. Cameron (1994), pp. 30–42.
7 Even from a Christian perspective informed by Aquinas's philosophy, the human being, the self, ceases to exist, even though the soul may survive the destruction of the body. For detailed analysis of the soul as substantial form see David Braine (1993), 480–511.
8 John Donnelly (1978), pp. 96–100; J. L. A. Garcia (1993) and (1999). See also John M. Dolan (1999); Michael Wreen (1987) and (1996)—how can you fit non-existence into a value system that presupposes existence?
9 For Marcus Tullius Cicero, the evil of death is the very non-existence of the one who existed. See his first *Tusculan Disputation*, 1.13.
10 Ordinary language use can be confusing. On the one hand we say that the intentional killing of an old age pensioner who has only a few weeks to live is a homicidal act just as much as the intentional killing of a teenager with a promising future ahead. On the other, we often say that death X is more terrible than death Y because of the comparative loss of potential. The confusion can, however, be accounted for by saying that while all death is a *per se* evil for persons—the rendering of an existent, non-existent—the posthumous effects of different deaths upon the lives of existents, who survive them, will differ. Assuming that the pensioner and the teenager were both instantaneously killed and were unaware of their impending deaths, thus cancelling out any experienced harm of lost potential prior to death, only other persons are able to vicariously assign significance and meaning to the loss of potential.

11 For an Aquinian interpretation of substantial change resulting in the person ceasing to be brought on by death see Mary Rousseau (1979), pp. 581–602.

12 See, for example, Garcia (1993) and (1999). See also Jenny Teichman (1993), pp. 155–64.

13 Life's inherent value can never be computed such that it is deemed worthless or can return a negative score such that life—*pace* Feldman—can have 'negative intrinsic value.' Human life *qua* human life always has positive intrinsic value. The positive of human existence cannot be rationally traded in against the evil of death. What is crucially at stake here——and is dialectically supportive of the primary good of human life—is that death is a radical interference with the current life process of the very kind of being that we are. In consequence, death itself can be thought of as an incommensurable evil for all persons, notwithstanding the extent to which they are currently or prospectively capable of participating in a full array of the goods of life.

14 Ernest Partridge (1981), p. 248: 'After death, no events can alter a moment of a person's life. Nothing remains to be affected.' See also Oderberg (2000a), pp. 163–4.

15 See Joan C. Callahan (1987), pp. 341–52. Contrast Dorothy Grover (1989).

16 Hadley Arkes (1997), pp. 421–33. Peter Singer raised the need for jettisoning sanctity-of-life concerns in his (1983) article. On the branching out from social and environmental indicators see Greg Bognar (2005), pp. 561–80. On its multivarious meanings from Aristotle to preference satisfaction see Christpoher Megone (1994), pp. 28–41. On the controversial nature of quality-of-life judgments and the right to die see Matti Häyry (1991), pp. 97–116.

17 See Brian Johnstone (1985), pp. 258–70; P. Sundstrom (1995), pp. 35–8.

18 Ruut Veenhoven (2000), pp. 1–39, for example, proposes robust evaluative quality-of-life considerations centered on (i) livability of the environment, (ii) life-ability of the individual, (iii) external utility of life, and (iv) inner appreciation of life.

19 On literature that supports the inherent respect for human life notwithstanding deep affliction or debilitation see Lance Simmons, (1997), pp. 144–60; Richard Stith (2004), 165–84; William J. Zanardi (1998), pp. 151–68; Louis G. Lombardi (1983), pp. 257–70; Paul Ramsey (2002), pp. 113–64; Oderberg (2000b), pp. 66–71; T. D. J. Chappell (1998), pp. 129–34 and (1999), 530–36.

20 See John Keown (2002), pp. 39–51. See also J. L. A. Garcia (2007), pp. 7–24.

21 On continuing participation in the good of life for anencephalics and PVS patients see Chapter 6. See Daryll Pullman (2002), pp. 75–94 for an account of pain and suffering that expresses the radical dignity of a person's being.

22 As Edmund D. Pellegrino (2000), pp. 1065–7 argues, competent patients should make a decision to refuse life-saving or effective treatment using quality-of-life judgments only with the utmost care. There are clinical situations in which the burdens of treatment are so heavily fraught physically, psychologically and financially—and the benefits are remote enough—that refusal or withdrawal is justifiable.

23 See, for example, Pellegrino (1992), pp. 95–102; Robert A. Destro (1986), pp. 71–130; Simmons (1997), pp. 144–60. As Norman L. Geisler and J. P. Moreland (1990), p. 71 state, from a Kantian perspective, '… if persons have intrinsic value simply by being human and, thus, are ends in themselves, then active euthanasia inappropriately treats a person as a means to an end (a painless state of death). Not everything a person takes to be in his own best interests is morally acceptable. Similarly, not everything a person would wish to have done to him or her is morally appropriate. Quality-of-life judgments are often subjective and can be morally inappropriate.'

24 As Keown (2002) p. 39 states: 'Vitalism holds that human life is an absolute [the supreme] moral value. … Whether the life be that of a seriously disabled newborn baby or an elderly woman with advanced senile dementia, vitalism prohibits its shortening and requires its

preservation. Regardless of the pain, suffering or expense that life-prolonging treatment entails, it must be administered. In short, the vitalist school of thought *requires human life to be preserved at all costs.*' My emphasis.

25 'Thou shalt not kill; but need'st not strive/ Officiously to keep alive.' A line from A. H. Clough's satirical poem, *The Latest Decalogue.*

26 Germain Grisez and Joseph Boyle (1979), pp. 414–19.

27 See Luke Gormally, ed. (1994), pp. 61–6.

28 James Rachels (1975), pp. 78–80; Timothy E. Quill (1993), pp. 1039–40; Quill, R. Dresser and Dan W. Brock (1997), pp. 1768–71.

29 See Daniel P. Sulmasy and Edmund Pellegrino (1999), pp. 545–50.

30 On the legal position on killing versus letting die in the UK see John Keown (2005), pp. 393–402. In the US see Richard S. Kay (2006), pp. 693–716.

31 Also see Paterson (2000), pp. 25–44.

32 See Garcia (1997).

33 On differentiating terminal sedation as 'letting die' from euthanasia see Joseph Boyle (2004), pp. 5–60.

34 See Roger J. Sullivan's (1989) account of Kantian autonomy. Autonomy cannot be bended to Richards's interpretation without gravely distorting Kant's ethic.

35 On a comparison of Mill and Kant on autonomy see Onora O'Neill (2002), ch. 2. For more on the history of the idea of autonomy see J. B. Schneewind (1991).

36 On autonomy and reason see Ray Lanfear (1986), pp. 183–93.

37 Recognizing the distinction between moral autonomy and personal autonomy, Jeremy Waldron (2005), states, p. 307: 'A person is autonomous in the moral [Kantian] sense when he is not guided just by his own conception of happiness, but by a universalized concern for the ends of all rational persons.'

38 Janet E. Smith (1997), pp. 182–95.

39 Richards (1987).

40 Marina Oshana relies on the harm principle to articulate her notion of autonomy in practice. See (2003), pp. 99–126. Joel Feinberg relies on a modified harm principle to justify weak paternalism (1986) pp. 31–64.

41 See Nils Holtug (2002), pp. 357–89.

42 James Rachels (1986), pp. 181–2 argues that suicide is a self regarding action and so also is any action that is consensually entered into by individuals acting together.

43 Lance K. Stell (1979), pp. 7–26 for the permissibility of duelling and other dangerous pursuits. If consent is operative rights can be waived or alienated.

44 Examples of libertarian theorists are Robert Nozick (1974); John Hospers (1980); Jan Narveson (1983) and (2000); H. Tristam Engelhardt (1996).

45 See, for example, Gerald Dworkin (1972) and (2005).

46 J. S. Mill (1962), pp. 235–6: 'In this and most other civilized countries ... an engagement by which a person should sell himself, or allow himself to be sold, as a slave would be null and void, neither enforced by law nor by opinion. The ground for thus limiting his power of voluntarily disposing of his own lot in life is apparent, and is very dearly seen in this extreme case.' On commentary see C. L. Ten (1968), pp. 29–37 and (1980), ch. 7.

47 See Neil M. Gorsuch (2006), pp. 86–101—commenting on paternalism and the harm principle.

48 See Flint Schier (1993), pp. 1–18 for discussion of how persons may wish to trade off their autonomy in order to achieve other ends that they seek.

49 On a 'moral right to do wrong' see Russell Hittinger (1993), pp. 83–4; William A. Galston (1983), pp. 32–4. See also my discussion of Dworkin in Chapter 7 (s. 7.2c).

50 See for example E. H. Cassem, (1995), S2–S10 and R. G. Miller (1992), pp. 127–32.

51 For a view from hospice see Robert G. Twycross (1997), pp, 141–68. At p. 164, 'When everything is taken into account (physical, psychological social and spiritual), euthanasia is *not* the answer, either for the patient, the family, the professional careers or society.'
52 G. A. Sachs, *et al.* (1995), pp. 553–62; R. G. Miller (1992), pp. 127–32..
53 See Margaret Somerville (2001), pp. 173–232.
54 See Kevin W. Wildes (1998), pp. 143–57 who extends Engelhardt's libertarian position.
55 On Hume see R. G. Frey (1999), 336–51. See Dworkin (1993) for self-dominion.
56 See further Elizabeth A. Linehan (1984), pp. 107–8.
57 For a discussion of natural property right extensions to the idea of self-ownership see Douglas B. Rasmussen and Douglas J. Den Uyl (2005), ch. 9.
58 Joseph Boyle (2002), pp. 111–41.
59 Boyle (2002). For discussion of different ownership and property concepts and their implications for bioethics see Gideon Calder (2006), pp. 89–100; Courtney S. Campbell (1992), pp. 34–42. English law historically recognized no formal rights of ownership over the body or property in another's dead body. See Russell Scott (1981), ch. 1.
60 Teichman (1996), pp. 70–71; E. W. Kluge (1975), p. 119.
61 Terrance McConnell (1984), pp. 25–59 argues that a right to life cannot be alienated.
62 I think that Robert Nozick (1974) p. 58 is the only libertarian to argue for the possible alienation of ownership by voluntary slavery.
63 McConnell (1984); Randy E. Barnett, (1986), 179–202.
64 For interesting discussion concerning the inalienablility and the value of autonomy see Arthur Kuflik (1984), pp. 271–98.
65 For discussion concerning neglect for the concept of duty see Marcia Baron (1984).
66 In a theory where duty has primacy, respect for the inherent worth of persons and their dignity can ground constraints on freedom—duties to self; duties to others; duties to the community. On Kant's grounding of different categories of duties see Rodger J. Sullivan (1989). For an introduction to Kantian duties see Mark Timmons (2002), ch. 7.
67 Variation on an example from Linehan (1984), p. 110.
68 Timothy E. Quill, R. Dresser and Dan W. Brock (1997), pp. 1768–71.
69 Daniel P. Sulmasy and Edmund Pellegrino (1999), pp. 545–50; Sulmasy (1996), pp. 86–90; Sulmasy (2000), pp. 19–25.
70 Thomas Cavanaugh (1996), pp. 248–54; Joseph Boyle (2004), pp. 51–60. At p. 51, '… the intent of the physician prescribing the life-shortening analgesics is to control the suffering, *not to shorten life.*' My emphasis.
71 Such counter factual tests are not decisive as to scope of intent. They only offer helpful support. See Joseph Shaw (2006), pp. 201–4.
72 Contrast Alfonso Gómez-Lobo (2002), pp. 106–7.
73 R. A. Duff (1973), pp. 16–19; G. E. M. Anscombe (1982), p. 23: '"I am merely moving a knife through such-and-such a region of space" regardless of the fact that that space is manifestly occupied by a human neck ….'
74 Devine (1978), p. 118, '… a doctor who removes his patient's head in order to stop his migraine cannot claim that the patient's death is only an indirect result of his operation.'
75 See Suzanne Stern-Gillet (1987), pp. 60–70; James Rachels (1983), pp. 17–19; R. A. Duff (1976), 68–80.
76 See James G. Hanink (1975), pp. 147–51; Robert Martin (1980), pp. 48–68.
77 W. E. Tolhurst (1983), pp. 13–15.
78 On conditional and preparatory intentions see Finnis (1994), pp. 163–76.
79 R. G. Frey (1978), pp. 35–47; Isidor F. Stone (1988), pp. 194–5. See also R. A. Duff (1983), pp. 48–56.
80 Michael Smith (1980): pp. 253–4; Richard E. Walton (1980), pp. 287–99.

Chapter 6

Non-voluntary and Involuntary Euthanasia

6.1 Introduction

In this chapter, we turn to assess the ethics of intentionally procuring the death of persons who either (i) are not capable of granting or withholding consent from a third party to intentionally end their lives, either because they were never competent or have lost the capacity to make competent decisions for themselves, or (ii) have the capacity to consent but either do not grant or expressly withhold their consent to being intentionally killed.

6.2 Already Dead

If a person is classified as being dead, it follows that we can no longer be said to be killing him or her because it is not possible to kill the dead, only the living. Until forty years ago the twin functions of breathing and heartbeat were taken to signify the continued integrated life of a human being and their permanent cessation was taken to constitute human death.[1] If the heart could not pump blood round the body, the integrative loss of unity in the organism would quickly follow. If the lungs could not oxygenate the blood supply, the integrative loss of unity in the organism would quickly follow. Without cardiopulmonary function, then, the integrative functions of the body would irretrievably break down past the point of no return.[2] Once various medical committees determined that these functions could be artificially maintained or resuscitated but the whole-brain or the brain-stem could cease to function—the brain being designated the central integrating organ of the body—revised 'brain death' definitions of death were adopted in the UK (brain-stem death) and the US (whole-brain death).[3]

Both forms of brain death are predicated on the assumption that extensive critical damage to the brain results in the loss of integral functioning of the human organism. Brain-stem death advocates stress that extensive damage to the brain-stem, despite pockets of upper brain activity, entails that the key integrating functions of the brain for the human organism can no longer be performed. Whole-brain advocates stress that, due to lack of certain knowledge concerning interrelationships and interdependencies between different parts of the brain, all the main areas of the brain should cease to function before brain death is concluded.[4]

Debate exists among supporters of different criteria for brain death as well as those opposed to brain death criteria. Brain-stem death advocates are accused of being too prognosis orientated. Some integrated functions may be irreversibly and progressively impacted by brain-stem death, but until the whole-brain is actually irreversibly impacted, the patient is in the process of dying but is not yet dead. Brain-stem death advocates criticize whole-brain death advocates for not accepting that permanent non-consciousness combined with an inability to continue to maintain spontaneous breathing or heartbeat for any extended time is equivalent to the permanent loss of the brain's integrative functioning.[5] Other non-brain critics charge that the brain is not the indispensable integrating organ it was once thought to be since the body can act with extensive signs of integral functioning despite being declared brain dead. Only lack of respiration and circulation for a period of time can clinically indicate that a patient has reached a point disintegrative no return.[6]

Despite the divergence in the literature concerning the clinical criteria for determining the death of a patient, circulatory-respiratory advocates, brain-stem advocates and whole-brain advocates do not dispute that anencephalic infants and persistent vegetative state (PVS) patients are clearly living and are not dead. No brain-stem or whole-brain advocate argues that the traditional definition for death— the irreversible destruction of the integral functioning of the organism as a whole— need be questioned. The clinical criterion for brain death—whether whole-brain or brain-stem—is based on the claim that the brain has the function of organizing and integrating the human body as a whole. It is held that the hormonal, nervous and biochemical subsystems of the body are coordinated by the brain. The brain dead body is viewed as a set of fragmented subsystems. Even if this central claim is contested—that the brain is quite so crucial to general integrative functioning—as it is by circulatory-respiratory advocates—the central marking definition of death—the irreversible destruction of the integral functioning of the organism as a whole—is not being rejected by brain stem or whole brain advocates. Such is not the case, however, for 'higher-brain' death advocates.

In 1975, Robert Veatch proposed that the permanent loss of functioning of the higher-brain neo-cortex should be the criterion used for determining death since the neo-cortex is held to be essential for the exercise of consciousness.[7] Higher-brain advocates contend that human death cannot be adequately understood by assimilating it to death of the organism as a whole. Human death equals personal death. What we truly value is personal life not mere biological life.[8]

Such a higher-brain criterion for death clearly cannot be reconciled with the traditional biological definition of death. Death is clearly being redefined to mean the absence of certain present or future exercisable 'higher order' capacities, not the integral functioning of the organism as a whole. By referring to the neo-cortex as the area of the brain most associated with consciousness, thought and feeling, higher-brain advocates candidly declare anencephalic infants and PVS patients to be, in the words of H. Tristam Engelhardt, 'biologically living corpses.'[9]

Anencephaly is a condition in which an infant is born without a skull (cranium) and with a forebrain that is either absent or rudimentary. These infants can live, using the functioning of their brain stems, from a few hours to a few months.[10] PVS is a condition whereby neo-cortical functioning has been destroyed by disease or injury, so that the patient is in a chronic state of wakefulness without awareness. Since a PVS patient still has a functioning brain-stem, respiration, digestion, reflex responses, homeostatic mechanisms, and circulation usually take place spontaneously.[11]

Part of the momentum behind higher-brain advocacy is utilitarian in motivation. Anencephalic infants and PVS patients are excellent candidates for organ harvesting. If these patients could be declared dead, then their undamaged organs (due to continuing respiration and circulation) could readily be made available at an appropriate time for transplantation purposes.[12] By redefining death as 'death of the person,' not organic death, patients can still exhibit integrated functioning below the 'threshold needed for personhood' and still be declared dead. If they are dead, ergo, they are not being intentionally killed in order to harvest their organs, for they are already personally dead.

Here it is interesting to point out that Peter Singer, a key utilitarian defender of organ harvesting, regards the higher-brain approach to redefining human death as disingenuous and counterintuitive.[13] For Singer, higher-brain death advocacy is really a fiction created in order to justify the removal of organs from those who are really living (anencephalic infants and PVS patients) for the benefit of others. Higher-brain death is a means of getting around the current 'dead donor rule' which stipulates that vital organs may only be harvested from patients who are declared dead.[14] Anencephalic infants and PVS patients, for Singer, are not persons in any meaningful way, but loss of personhood and death *are not synonymous concepts*. If we really thought that higher-brain dead patients really were dead, then why could they not be cremated or buried whilst their lungs continue to breathe and their hearts continue to pump blood round their bodies?

Rather than disturb the deep-seated intuition that the meaningfulness of death should be related to the integral functioning of the human body as a whole, and not a conception of death that is non-biological, Singer argues that we should critically re-examine why it is thought wrong to harvest organs from those who are profoundly damaged but not yet dead in the first place.[15] Singer's thought, here, regarding a biological definition of death, is in general line with the thought of Charles Culver and Bernard Gert and also David Lamb. They argue that the concept of death is essentially a biological or organic concept. Death can only be applied to biological organisms and not to the functions associated with personhood, unless death of the person is understood to mean, in ordinary linguistic usage, the death of the biological organism known as a person.[16]

For Singer, the only honest course of action is to candidly admit to the intentional justified killing of a human being for the sake of the greater good of society. We should not disingenuously alter the definition of death in order to conceal what is really a justified act of killing. Biological death is being intentionally hastened in order to procure viable vital organs. Any good associated with their marginal continuing existence is outweighed by the good of procuring their organs in order to promote the life and health of others. Higher-brain death, then, is nothing but a mask to justify what is really an act of intentional justified killing.

Singer is not alone in drawing this conclusion. The neurologist Robert Truog has argued that perceptual difficulties associated with redefining death in terms of higher-brain in order to procure more organs for transplant, may best be overcome by viewing the procurement of organs from anencephalic infants or PVS patients as cases of justified killing similar to other cases of justified killing.[17] It is but a short step to argue that if the killing of anencephalics or PVS patients were somehow also a benefit for them—say, the ending of a pointless existence—then we would have an argument justifying non-voluntary euthanasia.

Now, I agree with Singer that a 'higher-brain' definition of death cannot be supported. Human beings, so to speak, 'die' once not twice. We do not first experience the significant death of the person followed by the second insignificant death of a biological human being. Our one literal non-metaphoric death should be defined as a biological phenomenon. Nevertheless, if anencephalic infants and PVS patients are not dead but are 'non-persons' because they are held to have lost the key attributes of personhood, can we not then, after all, intentionally kill these 'depersonalised human beings' in the circumstances advocated by Singer and Truog?

Given the arguments of Chapter 4, I have made clear my reasons for opposing all intentional killing of innocent persons—*full-stop*. The good of human life demands from all practically rational agents the inviolable protection of all material innocents. If a person is not a non-innocent, then he or she can never be intentionally killed. Respect for the primary good of human life is incompatible with all such actions. In Chapter 5, I argued that neither the consent of the patient, the condition of the patient, resource questions, nor the interests of third parities (or some combination thereof), can justify intentional killing. Throughout my arguments, however, I have talked consistently about the goods of persons; respect for the goods of persons; the inviolability of the life of innocent persons. Does this therefore mean that I subscribe to a significant moral distinction between 'persons' and 'human beings' such that the former are protected by these obligations while 'mere' human beings are not? Do I mean to signal that the exercisable loss of certain attributes effectively renders a person a non-person and thus a candidate for justified intentional killing? The short answer is no. In the next section, I will explain just why my use of the language of persons rather than human beings is entirely consistent with ordinary language use and tradition and does not signal any fundamental difference in status between persons and human beings such that we recognize fundamental duties and rights applicable to the former but not the latter.

6.3 Not All Humans Beings Are Persons

In Chapter 2 (s. 2.4), several challenges were posed regarding the status of the good of human life. Human life itself is often perceived only as an instrumental good at the service of the person. Opponents argue that mere human life is not a primary human good of persons. Human life, rather, is a necessary means utilized in the promotion of other worthwhile goods. When human life itself fails to live up to our expected functional requirements it can ultimately be dispensed with.

Lying behind those accounts of the worth of human life are appeals to various forms of threshold sufficiency criteria. These criteria are used to establish whether or not 'individual human beings' are able to qualify as 'human persons.'[18] On one side of the threshold there is held to be a human life worthy of being valued since it instantiates feature X or features X...Z. A human life with feature X or features

X...Z is alone considered worthwhile, since it instantiates that which is sufficient to attribute real value to human existence. There are effectively two primary categories concerning the status of human life: 'personal life' manifesting feature X or features X...Z and 'non-personal life' that is incapable or no longer capable of manifesting feature X or features X...Z. Human life is to be valued as long as it is capable of instantiating those feature(s) sufficient to constitute personal life. Mere non-personal life (not worth living and not worthy of full protection from intentional killing), is heavily contrasted with personal life (worth living and alone worthy of full protection from intentional killing).

Jonathan Glover, James Rachels, Ronald Dworkin, Peter Singer, Helga Kuhse, and John Harris, amongst others, all subscribe to the notion that what is really valued is not human biological life as such but personal life—life that is capable of manifesting—rationality, self-awareness, consciousness, and so on, or some composite thereof.[19] They identify certain attributes that alone are sufficient to warrant the classification of 'being a person.' The voice of John Locke can be seen to echo strongly in their threshold approaches, as he defined a person as 'a thinking intelligent being that has reason and reflection and can consider itself as itself, the same thinking thing, in different times and places; which it does only by consciousness.'[20] Locke built on Descartes 'cogito ergo sum'; 'I think, therefore I am,' a question concerning the metaphysics of human existence in general, adapting it to the metaphysics of personal identity to mean 'I think, therefore I am a person.'[21] Although Locke himself did not draw ethical conclusions regarding the status of individuals from his general metaphysical theory of personal identity, for both his Christianity and his natural rights theory granted traditional protections to all human beings, subsequent followers appropriated his definition to draw out ethical implications. Thus, if B cannot now think or never has been capable of thinking, B is no longer or never has been a person. Since only human beings who know they are persons really are persons, and only persons, as such, are bearers of rights, it follows that there are human beings who are not persons and do not have the rights of persons. Rights are not Lockean natural rights, nor are they even human rights. Rights are the unique preserve of persons.[22]

In the conclusions reached by the above-mentioned authors, all would argue that patients suffering from advanced forms of senility, the permanently comatose, as well as anencephalic infants, cannot be regarded as persons and cannot therefore be classified as being possessed of lives truly worth living. Only personal lives are worth living. Only persons have rights. Since they are not persons, they cannot be accorded the same protections that we ascribe to those we identify as persons. Without the ability to X...Z, there is no personhood, and without personhood there is no entitlement, in principle, to immunity from intentional killing.

The main problems with threshold theories of persons, in my view, are twofold. First, such thresholds suffer from arbitrariness associated with the selection of appropriate criteria and with specifying the appropriate level required for sufficient actualizable functioning. Second, they fail to acknowledge the significance of the argument that all individual human beings are already *radically and primarily actualized as persons* by virtue of their very class membership in a species that is characterized by rationality.[23]

6.3a Arbitrariness

Are the feature(s) defended by threshold supporters really arbitrary? In certain respects it may seem that they are not arbitrary since they seek to determine the attributes of being a person according to important ideas of rationality, consciousness, self-awareness, the capacity to feel pain, and so on. Yet, which general features should necessarily be included in the definition of person? To what extent or degree should a human being fulfill the selected feature or features so as to be considered a person?

Consider, for example, theories that specify several different features in order to be considered a person—for example, sentience; emotionality; reason; communication; self-awareness; moral agency.[24] Must all these features really be required in order for B to qualify as a person or is it the case that only some but not all of the features on the list are required? If the latter, what constitutes a *critical cluster* of features such that B can qualify as a person? If B had indications of any four out of the six features mentioned above, would that constitute a sufficient cluster for B to be regarded as a person? Why insist upon any four out of the six features anyway? What if B had only three out of the six features, would B be some sort of 'quasi-person' not quite a person and yet not quite a fully fledged non-person?[25]

Assuming that the stricter standard is applied and it is insisted upon that all six features (or some other number) are each required in order for B to be a person, what level or degree of each feature is required? What degree of self-awareness? What level of abstract thought? How much intentionality? Take, for example, self-awareness. What does it really mean to be self-aware? What is the minimum threshold whereby we can identify that B is somehow sufficiently self-aware or that B is not somehow sufficiently self-aware? Does B need to be able to use the personal pronoun? Does B need to be able to recognize her name? Does B need to be able to relay to others her awareness of her own likes and desires? What about a human being who has profound amnesia? B knows little about herself. B is conscious and grasps concepts but her self-identity is a shrouded mystery. Does her loss of memory mean that she, due to self-identity problems, lacks critical awareness of self?[26]

What of the level of functioning required for B to have abstract thoughts? Does B need to be able to communicate her grasp of concepts to others? Does B need to recognize concepts such as the 'self'? Do we grasp concepts prior to language development or do concepts depend on our ability to use language? If we follow widespread philosophical opinion—that the ability to form and grasp the significance of concepts presupposes the development of language—young children cannot be said to be persons, for their ability to understand language does not develop until approximately nine months plus. For some children, the development of language may take several years. Since rights are the rights of persons, then, children are not automatically members of the community of persons, for they must first satisfy some vague notion of what constitutes the required threshold for abstract thought.

What level of functioning is required for B to be rational? There are at least three basic types of rationality that we can speak of—instrumental means-end rationality; engagement with principles of valid reasoning; rational agency. Yet what level of manifestation do we require in order for B to count as a person? Is B a person if B can direct her thoughts to manipulate a spoon in order to eat some baby food? Must

B be able to articulate her means-end reasons for selecting the spoon? Must B be able to grasp the principles of effectiveness and efficiency with respect to means-ends relationships? Must B have and appreciate some consistent set of beliefs and preferences?[27]

Given the range of proposed features offered (some accounts specifying only one required feature while others specify two or more required features), combined with deep ambiguity over degrees or levels of functioning, it is hard to avoid the conclusion that the class of persons, in accordion-like fashion, can simply be expanded or retracted according to the will of the individual doing the personhood assessment.[28] Stipulative arbitrariness is permissible when determining whether or not, say, a motorized vehicle with three wheels can be classified as a car rather than a motorcycle. It is permissible to stipulate vague criteria for determining whether or not a painting can be included in an art exhibition. It is utterly unacceptable, however, when determining vitally important questions of whether or not 'different sorts' of human beings are fundamentally protected by important moral duties and rights.[29] Threshold definitions of persons seem so contrived precisely because they do resort to such arbitrary and vague stipulations when seeking to 'pick' and 'select' features and levels for determining the category of persons from the category of non-persons.

6.3b Radically Persons

I turn now to critique the claim that actual individual capacity to manifest a key feature or attribute is required in order for B to be categorized as a person. In non-philosophical usage, people in general do not make a distinction between 'person' and 'human being.' As Mary Midgley states, 'The question is quite a simple one; no tests are called for. The word "person" just means a human being.'[30] As G. E. M. Anscombe also states, '"The person" is a living human body.'[31] Basic widespread patterns of usage point not to an understanding of being a person as requiring individually actualizable 'self-awareness …X…Z.' Rather, being a person is treated synonymously with being a certain kind of being by virtue of his or her very membership in a distinct class of being. In ordinary, non-philosophical usage, 'Y is a human being,' and not, say, a horse, dog or cat, is interchangeable with 'Y is a person,' since 'Y is recognisably one of us' and 'not one of them.'[32]

This assertion, of an interchangeability between 'person' and 'human being,' is supported by the prevailing definitions offered by the *Oxford English Dictionary*, where the noun 'person' is viewed as referring to (i) an individual human being, and (ii) human beings distinguished from other things, especially lower animals.[33] It is, of course, right to be wary of dictionary definitions. They are clearly not definitive. Nevertheless, I think that patterns of usage witnessed by the *OED* help support the proposition that people generally do not use 'person' and 'human being' to refer to *basic differences in kind* between 'human persons' and 'human non-persons' such that the former are protected by negative prohibitions concerning killing while the latter are accorded no such protection.

Consider further a common reaction to patients suffering from advanced senility or PVS. Often we will say that such patients are in a profoundly damaged/

disabled state or that their quality-of-life is severely impaired. Often we will be deeply disturbed by the gap that exists between the condition of patients and their fullness of well-being. No one (except the insane or deeply disturbed) would want to be placed in such a condition. The fullness of human life is very imperfectly manifested. It simply does not follow, however, that we generally seek to infer from these debilitated states of being that patients suffering from them have quite ceased to be persons and have undergone such a *profound change in kind* that they are now correctly classified as 'non-persons.' Our ready ability to identify and show solidarity with 'human non-persons' in a way that we do not so readily identify with the debilitated condition of 'non-human non-persons' seems to offer additional testimony as to why we 'stubbornly' continue to view profoundly damaged human beings as persons *simpliciter.* Our ready ability to think of damaged persons as 'damaged persons' and not as 'damaged humans that have ceased to be persons,' helps make sense of the observation that people can and do seek to defend and promote profoundly impaired human life (i.e., when asked to explain actions such as continuing to feed severely demented patients), without seeking further explanation for protecting or preserving profoundly impaired lives beyond the intelligible appeal of human life itself as a primary good of persons. As a primary good, an indispensable constituent of our well-being as persons, human life is itself capable of providing us with an adequate explanation as to why continuing care and support actions for the profoundly damaged are truly intelligible to us—intelligible in ways that actions of this kind would lack real intelligibility if we were to view and treat profoundly damaged humans as mere non-persons.[34]

There is good philosophical reason to affirm that the pre-philosophical insights we have concerning the underlying and enduring meaning of 'person' as 'human being' are indeed sound. We can posit a credible account of what it is to be a person by appealing to the common nature all human beings have as members of the species *homo sapiens.* Appeal to individual membership in a class characterized by rationality helps account for just why we continue to show solidarity with and regard profoundly damaged members of our species as persons—not because of what threshold advocates would regard as understandable but misplaced sympathy or compassion towards the profoundly damaged—but because of what they *essentially are to us* as individual members of the human species.

Aquinas quoted and affirmed Boethius's definition of what it is to be a person: a person is 'an individual substance of a rational nature.'[35] The definition offered by Boethius is inherently more satisfactory than the definition offered by John Locke, for it is able to account for our understanding of what can be termed 'species belonging'—a belonging that points against the classification or treatment of profoundly damaged human beings as sub-personal entities (*semihominem*), whose lives are consequently judged to be of less worth than the lives of persons. Rather than focusing on the idea that the individual must be presently or prospectively rational (conscious, self-aware, etc.) in order to be thought of as a person, this definition points to a more fundamental understanding of what it is to be a person—a person is an individual who is a member of a class of being characterized by those attributes. Our species is a kind that is rational, self-aware, and so on. This holds true even if some members of that species are quite incapable of rational thought, lack self-awareness, and so on.[36]

Jenny Teichman supports this central line of argumentation when she states that 'the idea that a creature can have a rational nature without being rational ... does not appear to me to be any more intrinsically problematic than the idea that all cattle are mammals—even the bulls.'[37] Bulls are not capable of suckling calves but they are surely still mammals. Teichman challenges the idea that the way in which we classify our own kind ought to be treated any differently from the way we correctly classify other kinds. Does a dog cease to be classified as a dog when it has lost its ability to bark? Does a cat cease to be classified as a cat when it is blind and no longer has four legs? Is it not a blind cat with three legs? If not, then why should the very senile or the permanently comatose, even though they are deeply defective with respect to exercisable capacities for rational thought or self-awareness, be classified as non-persons?

We can credibly argue that 'non-persons' in a state of severe impairment are still fully members of the same species to which we all belong. The very senile or permanently comatose do not become members of a different species. Through their 'essential kind' they still 'speak to us' as members of the same species by virtue of having a common nature. As David Oderberg states, when Aristotle stated that we are by nature 'rational animals,' he was not referring merely to those fully functional members of the human species at the very height of their faculties. He was, rather, defining the essential nature of all members of the human species.[38] Thus, B is already primarily and radically actualized as a rational person by virtue of having an essential nature that is human. Why, then, should being profoundly damaged fundamentally detract from the moral status of certain individual human beings if they are, by virtue of their very nature, as fully human as the 'archetypal' members of our species? Such damage does not render them members of a different species, for differences between humans concerning levels of intelligence, levels of consciousness, levels of coherence in thoughts, etc. are, crucially, *questions of degree and not of kind*. A decline in or non-presence of a capacity does not bring about a substantial change in the essential nature of an individual human being. These changes in degree are all 'accidental' and not 'substantial.' Only biological death itself is capable of bringing about a substantial change in the very kind of thing that we essentially are. It is biological death that brings about a fundamental change in kind, for a corpse is no longer an individual with a human kind of nature. The loss of certain functional attributes *does not amount to a substantial change in kind*.[39]

6.3c Kantian Persons

It may be thought that the moral philosophy of Immanuel Kant can offer some support for the argument that since only rational beings can self-legislate morality, only those who have an exercisable capacity to rationally self-legislate can legitimately be classified as persons. No exercisable capacity, no strict rights of personhood. This is certainly a common contemporary interpretation of Kant.[40] The premium Kant placed upon the significance of rationality for the dignity of persons, however, is open to a different line of interpretation. When Kant held that persons have dignity by virtue of their rationality, this can be taken to mean that radical dignity is an attribute of 'humanity' generally. We should always treat 'humanity' whether in ourselves or in others as an end in itself and never merely as a means. To disrespect the inherent humanity of any individual is to act irrationally. It seems to me that if we were to deny to human beings their inherent humanity, that is, to fail to recognize ascribable moral claims solely by virtue of having a human nature, no matter how imperfect the individual manifestation, we would be dehumanizing them. Since dignity is a concept attached to the general idea of humanity, and all humans instantiate humanity, no matter how imperfect the instantiation, all humans possess a radical dignity attributable to their rational nature notwithstanding any actual inability on the part of B...D to exercise their rational nature.[41]

If the primary reason to intentionally kill B, a PVS patient, is to procure B's organs primarily in order to benefit others, B's inherent humanity is not being respected because B is being viewed and treated as something less than properly human, a denatured and dehumanized 'thing' with a 'price,' a mere instrumental means, and not as a subject of absolute regard. B's dignity should be respected and not violated—a radical dignity that is not 'granted' by the conferral of 'personhood status' only on those individuals who are presently (or prospectively) able to exercise rational moral agency.[42]

Under this Kantian interpretation, it is thus possible to argue that even though a human being may be severely demented and quite irrational, and thus incapable of adhering to the requirements of rational moral action, he or she remains a person and continues to be a subject worthy of continuing respect as a person. Respected, that is, *in spite of his or her present and prospective irrationality because of what he or she radically is*. There is no morphological change here from being a 'somebody' into being a 'something.' Since all human beings, regardless of whether or not they are able to exercise attributes X...Z, are persons, for they are not 'things,' all human beings should be treated with due regard for their fundamental dignity as persons.[43]

6.3d Protections for All Persons

By virtue of being a member of the species *homo sapiens*—a being with a rational nature—that status can indeed be said to be one of being a person *simpliciter*. All persons are subject to the same basic types of protection from intentional killing. It can, in consequence, never be morally justified to intentionally kill an innocent on the ground that an individual is judged to fall below some form of functional threshold required in order to 'qualify' as a person. A person does not cease to be until his or her integrated biological being ceases to be (see s. 6.2). We 'stubbornly' continue to hold onto this idea even though a person may not be able to consciously appreciate for himself or herself the continuing radical dignity of his or her personal existence.

By holding that all individual human beings are persons, we are far better able to account for the dignity protections we typically seek to accord to all members of our species. No one doubts, for example, that a day-old-human infant or the very senile may lack the actual capacities of, for example, a day-old-foal. Human infants and the very senile, in terms of mobility, awareness of environment, feeding ability, etc. are not very impressive in the exercisable functioning stakes. But surely this sort of comparison does not convince us that foals somehow have greater fundamental worth than human infants or the very senile.[44] If anencephalic infants or the very senile were, say, intentionally killed and sold for food, we would surely find such a practice deeply undignified and repugnant. This example may seem rather extreme to the reader, and yet, if the true worth of individual human beings, at the end of the day, were held to be ultimately and contingently dependent on having some ready prospect for individually exercising capacity X or capacities X...Z rather than their having 'radical dignity by virtue of their essential nature,' there should—apart from obvious health concerns or feelings of squeamishness or dealing with the reaction of relatives—be no deep moral problem with intentionally killing such profoundly damaged human beings in order to make use of their harvested dead flesh for the manufacture of consumer edibles.

6.4 Anencephalic Infants, PVS Patients, and Non-voluntary Euthanasia

Given my discussion of what it means to be a person above, it should be clear that anencephalic infants and PVS patients are persons because they are individual human beings and should be accorded all the rights and protections of persons. They are profoundly damaged persons. They are not non-persons. It is mistaken to think that these patients are already dead according to a misguided 'higher-brain' definition of death (see s. 6.2). They should not be treated as 'living cadavers' or as 'biological remnants' for organ harvesting purposes. They should not be treated as 'ready matter' for medical experimentation. As persons they have inherent worth and dignity that flows from their very humanity. Their radical worth and dignity as persons is not contingent upon their present or prospective ability to actually function with consciousness and awareness.[45]

Two key obligations we have regarding the primary good of human life, whether in ourselves or others, are (i) to respect the negative demand of the good of life not to intentionally kill the innocent, whether as an end or as a means to an end, and (ii) to respect the positive demand to generally promote and maintain life and health (see s. 4.4). We can violate the demands of these goods by procuring the death of a person intentionally or negligently. Intentional or negligent death can be procured by causal action, by omission, or by a combination of action and omission. It is always wrong to intentionally procure the death of an innocent person, regardless of motive, whether by action or omission (see s. 4.5).

As we have seen with the treatment and care decisions of competent persons in the previous chapter, they are accorded considerable leeway in making decisions about the impact of a proposed treatment or care regimen on their health. Competent persons are usually best placed to assess for themselves, with guidance and information, the potential burdens and benefits of a proposed treatment (see s. 5.4). Since anencephalic infants have never been and never will be competent to make heath care decisions for themselves, surrogate decision makers must assess treatment and care decisions in the light of how the benefits and burdens of a given treatment or care regimen will serve their best interests.[46] Since PVS patients were usually previously competent, their declared wishes, either by (i) prior written testimony (advanced directives) or by (ii) the substituted judgment of a family/friend surrogate decision maker, generally inform post-competent treatment decisions.[47] Where both (i) and (ii) are absent, either because there is no written evidence or because there is no one available to make decisions who is knowledgeable about a patient's values and commitments, the surrogate decision maker is required to make surrogate decisions according to what is in the best interests of the patient.[48]

6.4a Anencephalic Infants

It is sometimes argued that since anencephalic infants are not conscious and will never be conscious, they can have no critical interests worth preserving or defending.[49] Thus, it does not make sense to say that an anencephalic can really be benefitted or harmed by a decision to withhold or withdraw treatment because he or she does not and never will have any actual capacity to experience or be aware of benefits and burdens. This line of thought, however, is mistaken. Persons do not have to be consciously aware of a harm, either now or prospectively, in order to suffer from a harm. If I were grotesquely defamed behind my back to colleagues but never became aware of the defamation, I would still be harmed due to the defamation of my character in the eyes of others. If a person were to be sexually defiled in a comatose state, even though they would never become aware of the defilement, they would have been harmed. If a person was to be killed while sleeping, even though they would never become aware of the harm, they would be harmed by the very destruction of their life. It is not accurate, therefore, to hold that anencephalic infants do not have critical dignity and life interests that cannot be harmed.[50] The life of a person is a primary good (see s. 3.6a). Its status as a primary good of persons does not depend on its conscious appreciation in order for it to be an objective good of persons. Death, being rendered non-existent, is an objective evil for persons (see s. 5.3). Profoundly damaged persons, therefore, can be gravely harmed by an intentional decision to terminate their lives on the basis that their lives really are judged to be of no intrinsic worth.

Another line of argument concedes that while persons in such profoundly and irreversibly damaged states may be harmed, the continuation of life, in such circumstances, is held to be 'inherently undignified' and such indignity cannot be proportioned to any marginal benefit that may accrue from the maintenance of undignified existence.[51] Undignified existence is a grave injury to a person and can therefore justify a decision to release a person from that indignity by an intentional action or omission to procure death.[52]

The argument, that persons suffering from grave cognitive afflictions are leading inherently undignified lives, is also mistaken. It stems, in part, I think, from an illicit transfer from (a) assessing the benefits and burdens of proposed treatments and care regimens, and the impact they may have upon a patient, to (b) assessing the very worth of a person's life simply as such.[53] Yet, there is no good reason to think that being profoundly unconscious and unaware deprives persons of their radical dignity and worth. Innocent persons, even the most gravely damaged of them, always retain their radical human dignity and worth, notwithstanding the conditions that afflict them. Now, it is certainly possible to objectively talk of certain states or conditions as being 'undignified.' Slavery, for example, is a condition that is deeply incompatible with the radical dignity of persons. The enslaved are gravely wronged by their enslavement. It does not follow, however, that suffering from such a condition equates to the proposition that the very life of an enslaved person is not worthwhile. Suffering from an undignified condition, therefore, does not mean that those who suffer from an 'undignified condition' are 'inherently undignified.'[54]

When indignity judgments are made concerning medical conditions, we need to be acutely aware (i) that while medical conditions may be thought undignified, persons are never inherently undignified, and (ii) the immense scope there is for subjective projection from the competent onto the never-competent concerning perceptions of burden.[55] Take incontinence as an example. A person may regard the condition of incontinence as an affront to bodily self-control. He or she may suffer from the psychological stress of having to wear an adult nappy. He or she may therefore hold that it is personally undignified to be incontinent. Yet, while it is not good for persons to be incontinent, it does not follow that having loss of control over a malfunctioning bladder equates to having an 'inherently undignified existence.' Those born with the condition of incontinence may well view the experience of incontinence very differently from those who were formerly continent. Contrary to those who insist that certain losses of function must objectively lead to an inherent loss of dignity, then, I would argue that *any person with any grave impairment—* anencephaly; Down's syndrome; Tay Sak disease; cystic fibrosis; cleft palate, and so on—cannot be said to have an 'inherently undignified' existence.[56]

When thinking about the treatment decisions of never-competent persons—those who will never think for themselves regarding medical treatment questions—we must be acutely aware that subjective assessments of dignity *viz.* our own thoughts and values, may be illicitly transferred onto an assessment of others. The anencephalic infant, for example, can have no personal fears of being incontinent or of being bed ridden or of being the recipient of artificial hydration and nutrition. Unrestrained and unchecked, a surrogate's personal experience of quality-of-life issues, projected onto the patient, can gravely distort an assessment of the best interests of the never-competent. The potential hazards of benefit and burden assessment being implicitly or explicitly taken over by the personal values of the surrogate, whether religious or secular, are very real, and must constantly be borne in mind when striving to make best interest determinations for the never-competent.

Cases I bear in mind when thinking about wrongful non-treatment decisions for the never-competent are the US Baby Doe cases.[57] In the original case, a Down's syndrome newborn infant was denied critical but relatively uncomplicated life preserving surgery to unblock his oesophagus—a surgery with a predictably high successful outcome—on the ground that the life of the infant was held to be of little worth because he was not able to do as well and be as happy as a normal child. The decision not to treat in this case was tantamount to saying that the very life of the infant was of such low quality, of no intrinsic worth, that he was 'better off dead' (see s. 5.3). There was a judgment made that the impaired infant's life should be intentionally ended by an omission to treat.[58] The benefits of treatment here would have been considerable for Baby Doe. The treatment was not unduly risky, painful or overly intrusive compared to its promising therapeutic benefits. The decision not to treat, in this case, should be viewed as a case of non-voluntary passive euthanasia, for the omission to treat was intentionally taken with a view to hastening the death of the infant.[59]

It is sometimes argued that since maintaining the life of an anencephalic infant can be unduly (emotionally and financially) burdensome on all or some of the patient's parents and family, physicians, care givers, and society generally, any benefits of maintaining the life of an anencephalic must be outweighed by the burdens imposed on others.[60] This kind of argument, however, will not do. The appropriate standard of care for the never-competent is the best interests of the patient, not the best interests of the patient's family or society generally. The focus for medical decision making is centered on the patient. It is no justification to say that X's death can be procured because the value of X's life can somehow be directly 'traded off' against the burdens of caring for X. Third party burdens can never generate compelling reason to intentionally procure the death of a patient whether it be by action or by omission. While I do not in any way wish to trivialize the emotional burdens of care on the family or the financial costs of treatment and care that may result, for these burdens can be considerable, third party burdens can never, of themselves, justify a decision to intentionally end the life of any innocent person in order to emotionally and financially benefit others.[61]

The fact that parents may not be able to undertake the burden of caring for an anencephalic infant may be anticipated and eased, where possible, by the provision of appropriate support structures. I accept that the level of treatment and care will depend on the kinds of treatment and care options that may be available in a given society. Health resources in many societies may need to be rationed and apportioned between groups of patients and between different conditions and treatments. Not all that could be done—in an overall pool of patients and treatments—realistically can be done. Prior macro allocation decisions understandably condition the general level of treatment and care that can be given to anencephalic infants. Allocation decisions, however, when taken in good faith, need not be tainted by misguided worth of human life judgments—that anencephalics are already dead; are mere living corpses; are non-persons; are inherently undignified—thereby utterly discounting them from serious consideration as persons who are profoundly damaged but who nevertheless retain critical life, health and dignity interests that can be benefitted or harmed by the availability or non-availability of significant treatment and care options.

Consider, for example, the case of an anencephalic infant who is on a ventilator and develops a bacterial infection that could be rapidly treated with a course of antibiotics. The anencephalic is not dead or dying. Treatment and care are paid for by private health insurance. Given his or her condition, there is no pain or psychological aversion being experienced. The treatment of the infection is not fraught with risk. Nor is it very costly (although care structures are considerably more costly). A course of antibiotics is highly successful in clearing up such an infection which, if left unchecked, would be life imperilling. How can it be argued that the provision of such a treatment *qua* treatment is pointless or futile, where resources are available, unless it is really being argued that the treatment is futile because the very life of the infant is being judged pointless and futile? By concentrating on the 'worthwhileness of treatments,' not the 'worthwhileness of lives,' I think that a decision not to treat the anencephalic with the antibiotics, given the circumstances, would likely be informed by an illicit intention to hasten death because the life of the infant is held to be of little or no worth. Intentionally hastening the death of infants, whether by action or omission, can never be reconciled with acting in their best interests, no matter how profoundly damaged they happen to be.

Consider further the US case of baby K in 1993. An anencephalic infant experienced respiratory distress after birth and was given ventilation. The infant was subsequently discharged to the mother's care on the understanding that if the infant should have further distress the hospital would treat the distress with ventilation. Two months after discharge the baby went into respiratory distress and the infant was brought back to hospital. The hospital sought to discontinue its ongoing ventilator support on the ground that anencephaly was an incurable condition that could not be treated. Providing ventilation was 'medically futile' and not in the patient's best interests.[62]

My interest concerns the hospital's declared grounds for asserting that the treatment actively sought by the mother should not be provided. First, ventilation is futile in the sense that it cannot cure anencephaly. But this is hardly the purpose of ventilation. The purpose of ventilation is to assist with breathing and ventilation is not therefore futile with respect to breathing. Second, whilst the infant, with continuing treatment, would only have a short life span—perhaps a few weeks—irreversible illness is not the same thing as being in an imminent state of dying. Third, the infant would not be consciously experiencing any pain or distress. The argument that continuing with the treatment should be discontinued because it would be disproportionately burdensome on the infant and thus not in the infant's best interests does not apply in this case. Since (a) the treatment would be effective in maintaining the infant's life, and (b) life is a primary good, a primary good that the infant is still able to participate in, the hospital's case for not treating respiratory distress with ventilation is really being informed by an underlying value determination that the very life of Baby K was of such poor quality as to be not worth living.

6.4b PVS Patients

The decision to withdraw or withhold artificial hydration and feeding from PVS patients is another area of controversy. Withdrawing or withholding nutrition and fluids from PVS patients will invariably end their lives in a relatively short period of time.[63] An argument is advanced that since the provision of hydration and nutrition via tubes merely assists the ordinary processes of natural drinking and eating, these practices are not 'treatments' but ordinary everyday care and cannot 'usually' be withheld or withdrawn from PVS patients without intentionally seeking to procure their deaths.[64] The withdrawal of hydration and nutrition via tubes, where a PVS patient is not in the process of dying, therefore, is deemed to be a case of non-voluntary euthanasia.[65]

This line of reasoning—that it is usually wrong to withdraw or withhold hydration and nutrition from PVS patients who are not in the process of dying—is unsound for four reasons. I will proceed to make a summary statement of those reasons and then expand upon them. I seek to argue that it is permissible to withhold or withdraw hydration and nutrition from PVS patients where the prior will of the patient is known, either by advanced directive or by surrogate knowledge as to prior values and commitments. Absent evidence of prior values and commitments, however, I argue that artificial hydration and nutrition for PVS patients should be provided and maintained.

First, the provision of hydration and nutrition via the use of tubes is best regarded as a form of treatment and not simply the provision of 'mere everyday care.'[66] As such it should be subject to an assessment of the benefits and burdens of treatment. Second, the provision of such treatment may be considered intrusive and contrary to the reasonable values and commitments of competent patients, such that when they are no longer competent they can seek to have post-competent treatment decisions made in accordance with their preceding values and commitments. Third, the category of PVS patients whose values and commitments are known must be differentiated from treatment assessments for those whose values and commitments are unknown. Fourth, a decision to forego a treatment, made on the grounds of assessing burdens and benefits, need not be shaped by intent to procure death (although some decisions to withdraw or terminate hydration and nutrition undoubtedly are made on such a wrongful basis).

First, given that the reason for resorting to use of these tubes for PVS patients is an irreversible loss of function due to an underlying pathological condition that renders PVS patients unable to naturally imbibe water and food, it seems contrived to say that the substitution of natural bodily function by the insertion of either a gastronomy tube or a nasogastric tube is not some form of treatment remedy for a natural pathology. Is kidney dialysis—the cleaning of a patient's blood due to the non-functioning of the kidneys—not a form of treatment simply because the patient's blood is removed, cleaned and returned to his or her body via a tube? Are patients on mechanical ventilators not receiving treatment when a machine pumps a mixture of oxygen into their lungs via airways? Even if it seems more minor and less specialized than the provision of kidney dialysis or mechanical ventilation, this is not an adequate ground for seeking to designate tube-based hydration and nutrition as forms of 'non-treatment.' Even if tube-based hydration and nutrition can readily be performed in the home by family members, and does not require any high level of expertise, this only demonstrates that a treatment can be readily performed by carers generally. Non-health specialists can certainly provide treatment. Just because I have a cut on my skin and a friend treats it with ointment and a plaster does not make the intervention a non-treatment simply because my non-specialist friend is applying common first aid.

A common retort is that if hydration and nutrition via tubes are forms of treatment, then so too is using a straw or spoon to feed a patient who cannot hold a straw or use a spoon.[67] The essential point, however, I think, is that straws and spoons are implements that are used to support the natural imbibing function of a patient. Straws and spoons are not viewed as complete substitutes for natural imbibing. It is the purpose of tube-based hydration and nutrition, however, to completely by-pass such a breakdown in natural functioning. I can see no good reason, therefore, to insist upon the designation of hydration and nutrition provision via tubes as forms of 'non-treatment.'

Second, the benefits and burdens of any treatment need to be assessed in relation to the prior will of a formerly competent patient, if known. People are very concerned to control and influence what will happen to them if such a state of profound impairment should befall them. We can and do seek to honor and respect the prior known will of others. An obvious example would be to respect the burial wishes of a deceased (providing, of course, that those wishes were not too outlandish). There is nothing essentially odd or alien in the notion that surrogate decision making regarding the subsequent treatment of a person rendered incompetent can be informed by an the person's prior known values and commitments. If the will of a PVS patient, when competent, was made known in the past, either via a written form of testimony—an advanced directive—or by the testimony of those that knew the patient and his or her values and commitments well—then a decision to treat or not treat via tube hydration and nutrition can reasonably be informed by a treatment assessment based on those sources.[68]

People rightly seek to protect their future interests as persons even though they are no longer capable of being consciously aware of them. They may best safeguard those interests via written testimony and by nominating a knowledgeable surrogate. Still, the question arises, where patients are not actually in pain or suffering, but are no longer able to feed themselves, for example, certain dementia patients, should their present state be ignored if there is an advanced directive mandating no provision of hydration and nutrition?[69] The general answer, I think, should be a strong presumption in favor of adhering to the content of an advanced directive unless there is good evidence to indicate that an advanced directive was unreflectively adopted in haste or clearly stands at odds with known prior values and commitments. There ought to be a strong presumption in favor of adhering to the content of an advanced directive precisely because they are widely known to be important declarations that are not readily reversible once a person becomes incompetent.

How can the provision of hydration and nutrition be held 'burdensome' to the irretrievably unconscious and unaware? Surely PVS patients cannot experience pain or experience any psychological burden associated with being treated? If life is a benefit and there are no present burdens, how can hydration and nutrition be withheld or withdrawn?[70] Such an argument only holds water, however, if there is no reasoned basis for respecting the ongoing relevance of a patient's known values and commitments to subsequent surrogate treatment decisions.

Whilst I think it gravely mistaken to say that the provision of hydration and nutrition via tubes is somehow 'inherently undignified' (see s.4a), it is not unreasonable to accept that being the subject of such treatment can be held intrusive and undignified for a given patient. A surrogate decision maker, acting on prior testimony or knowledge, or some combination, may reasonably determine that being treated by tubes in order to receive hydration and nutrition, thus seeking to overcome the loss of natural functioning to imbibe and swallow, is an invasive treatment burden for that individual patient, thereby warranting a decision to withhold or withdraw. Simply because a person is no longer conscious and aware is not a good enough reason to discount the continuing relevance of his or her known values and commitments whilst competent to post-competency surrogate treatment decisions.

In addition to personal dignity concerns, it is also a valid concern for the competent to altruistically assess what the burdens of treatment and care might entail for others. It is not unreasonable for persons to determine that they may not wish to place their families in the position of carrying the extended emotional and financial burden of treating and caring for them. Note, however, I am talking only of a benefit and burden assessment that is voluntarily undertaken by patients while competent. Such altruism is, I think, permissible as a form of self-sacrifice, for the intention need only be to avoid the burdens associated with treatment and care, not the deliberate hastening of death. Altruistic self-sacrifice, however, cannot be required or insisted upon and it cannot be invoked where it is not supported by clear evidence as to the settled will of the patient when competent.[71]

In 2005 the Terri Schiavo case caused national controversy in the US. Since 1998 there had been many court hearings and appeals including in 2005 a rushed act of the US Congress, aimed at preventing the withdrawal of Terri's feeding tube. This was quickly blocked by the courts, and the tube was finally withdrawn in March 2005 leading to Terri's death a few days later. In 1990 she became PVS when she suffered extensive brain damage because her heart briefly stopped beating due to potassium deficiency caused by bulimia. There was no written directive. Terri's husband eventually sought to have the feeding tube removed in 1998, after some eight years and testified in court that she had intimated to him while she was competent that she did not want to be kept alive artificially in a profoundly damaged condition. While it is not my intention to analyze the legal situation in Florida or the US, and much turns on the actual credibility of the husband's testimony as to Terri's prior wishes and commitments (disputed by Terri's parents)—why, for example, did he wait some eight years before petitioning to have the feeding tube removed on the basis of this evidence?—I can see no justified moral ground, if the husband's testimony is held to be an honest account of Terri's values and commitments, for objecting to the withdrawal of Terri's tube feeding treatment. Such testimony, if credible, can I think be judged 'determinate enough' in scope and meaning to warrant a decision to withdraw the provision of continuing tube feeding treatment.[72]

Third, the position of a PVS patient whose values and commitments are unknown or indeterminate is substantially different from the position of a previously competent person whose values and commitments are known. Here, a surrogate cannot assume that it is permissible to withhold or withdraw hydration or nutrition on the basis of an appeal to prior values and commitments. Further, (i) neither the condition in itself nor (ii) the treatment itself can be viewed as being 'inherently undignified.' Nor can we impose on PVS patients a blanket decision that their lives ought to be sacrificed—for the sake of conserving resources—where financial resources for their continuing treatment and care are available and can be accessed (support from family members, public health service, private insurance, charity care or some combination thereof).

Sometimes proponents of withholding and withdrawal, where values and commitments are not known, make reference to surveys in order to justify a non-treatment decision, on the basis that this is what most people in such a predicament would likely have decided for themselves.[73] Yet, which categories of persons are pooled? How are the questions framed? If those who make advanced directives are pooled to see whether or not they favor artificial hydration and nutrition, are they not more likely to raise dignity concerns and burdens on others as justifying non-treatment compared to those without advanced directives? If we poll the population more generally, how do the factors of age, sex, creed, region, etc. inform the results? Absent the known values and commitments of an actual patient—especially when the benefit of treatment is the continuing maintenance of life—I see no compelling reason to accept as sufficient to withhold or withdraw hydration and nutrition the imposition of a 'constructive inference' that an individual PVS patient would have (i) deemed hydration and nutrition treatment an affront to his or her dignity or (ii) that he or she would have viewed himself or herself as an undue emotional and financial burden on others.

Given that the incompetent patient whose values and commitments are not known can continue to participate in the primary good of life, and given that constructive inferences are insufficient to determine that hydration and nutrition ought to be withheld or withdrawn, I see no compelling case, where medical and care resources can reasonably be accessed, to withhold or withdraw artificial hydration and nutrition for PVS patients who are not yet in the process of dying.[74] It is illicit to resort to inherent indignity or lack of worth appeals to justify the withholding or withdrawing of hydration and nutrition, for the decision to treat or not treat cannot be informed by such rationales without denying to them their full status as persons with all the moral rights of persons. All PVS patients have radical dignity and worth as persons and this crucial status simply cannot be ignored or sidestepped when determining vital treatment decisions.

Fourth, we are now in a position to clarify just why some decisions to withhold or withdraw hydration and nutrition, for those who are not in the process of dying, do not constitute cases of intentional or negligent killing. They are able to satisfy the criteria of double effect reasoning (see s. 4.6). Consider the case of Nigel. He is forty four-years-old and was diagnosed with PVS after a terrible mountaineering accident. He was fit and active all his life. He did not have an advanced directive but he had informed his wife, the surrogate decision maker, several times over the years that he would not want to be hooked up to tube feeding if profoundly and irreversibly impaired. Being fed from a tube, being regulated by others, and being subject to protracted dependency, would clash with his settled values and commitments. In such a case, there need be no intent, by withholding or withdrawing hydration and nutrition, that Nigel's death be willed as the adopted means of avoiding the burdens associated with treatment. All that need be intended by his surrogate and health workers is to respectfully honor the values and commitments of Nigel. The certainty of a bad effect (hastening Nigel's death) is not the equivalent of intending the effect. The good effect, based on an assessment of his prior known values and commitments, of not burdening Nigel with such treatment, is concomitant with the occurrence of the bad effect. The bad effect is not the causal antecedent of the good effect. Last, there is a sufficiently compelling reason to tolerate the bad effect that would inevitably result from a decision not to treat Nigel's inability to naturally imbibe and swallow with hydration and nutrition.

The case of Nigel can be contrasted with the case of Helen. Helen is a single woman in her fifties who has been placed in PVS as a result of a car accident. A surrogate decision maker has been appointed for her. There are no advanced directives. The appointed surrogate is not knowledgeable about her values and commitments. Helen has no close family or friends. Health resources are available for Helen's continuing treatment. Here, it would be wrong for the surrogate to determine that the benefit of continuing hydration and nutrition treatment—treatment that is effective in sustaining Helen's life—could be intentionally discontinued because Helen's life is judged not worth living. It is wrong to withdraw treatment that is otherwise effective in sustaining life on the ground that Helen's very life is itself pointless or futile. Given the surrogate's lack of knowledge as to Helen's prior values and commitments, the surrogate cannot rightfully determine (constructive inference from surveys *not* sufficing) that the provision and continuation of hydration and nutrition would be an undue burden on her. The criteria of double effect reasoning cannot be satisfied in this case. Helen's hydration and nutrition treatment should not be withdrawn.

6.5 Involuntary Euthanasia

Respect for the primary good of life demands that innocent life can never be intentionally taken. It is entirely possible for third parties, using unsound quality-of-life arguments, to seek to intentionally kill patients as a means of ending the 'burden of their continued existence.' Non-voluntary euthanasia entails the intentional killing of a person who has not expressly consented to the ending of his or her life. Involuntary euthanasia adds to the wrong of intentionally killing a patient, the further injury of consciously acting against the patient's will.

As with non-voluntary euthanasia, the intentional killing of a patient against his or her will may be achieved by action or omission or by some combination. The intentional decision to kill may be informed by the view that some people fail to appreciate that their lives are not worthwhile living and that death would be a benefit to them. People who are unable to accept or reconcile themselves with the benefit of death ought to be 'mercifully saved' from their own misguided assessments.[75] Alternatively, it may be argued that while death may not be a direct benefit to those who are killed, nevertheless, a person does not have a right to insist upon their continuing existence when they become undue emotional and financial burdens on others.[76]

Consider the case of Daphnia. She is a middle-aged burn victim from a gas explosion. She has no immediate family. It is touch and go as to whether the severity of Daphnia's extensive burns will mean that she will live for more than a few weeks. She is in constant pain. She is, however, lucid enough, despite the pain, to insist that her burns be treated and critical care continued. Is it reasonable to determine, against her will, that she is really mistaken in her judgment concerning the burdens and benefits of treatment and that she really would be be 'better off dead'? Surely not. To deny her treatment against her will—by substituting for her judgment the judgment of others that her life is not worth living—would add the harm of thwarting her will to the harm of intentionally seeking to end her life because her very life is being deemed unworthy. To deny potentially effective treatment positively sought by Daphnia, because third parties judge she would be better off dead, is a case of involuntary passive euthanasia.

Again, just because an omission to treat Daphnia is the vehicle used to intentionally procure death, does not mean that such an omission is not a grave moral wrong (see s. 4.6d). An intentional failure to treat in order to procure death by omission can be held the 'near' moral equivalent of actively killing Daphnia by intentionally injecting her with a lethal dose of drugs. Indeed, given that killing by means of a lethal causal agent would be quicker and more controllable, perhaps for the purpose of organ harvesting, supporters of involuntary euthanasia would likely support such an active causal method for ending Daphnia's life.

While I accept that for most practical purposes the public policy debates undertaken in the UK and USA, as well as other parts of Western Europe, are concerned primarily with assisted suicide, voluntary euthanasia and non-voluntary euthanasia, the moral arguments for killing, especially on act-consequentialist grounds do not end with a consideration of only the voluntary or non-voluntary. This is especially the case when the interests of third parties are focused upon and there is held to be no absolute side-constraint on the intentional killing of innocent persons. If we focus on consequences and not on due respect for the primary good of human life itself, we can end up with illicit attempts to directly 'trade off' the life of a critically ill person in order to advance benefits to others.

Consider the following hypothetical case. There are three sick persons in hospital awaiting liver transplants. Without transplants they will die. It so happens that an innocent person, Gordon, is also in hospital who is terminally ill but who will likely live for a number of weeks. Gordon is in considerable pain but he is adamant that he wishes to live out his remaining weeks. His liver tissue is compatible with the three patients needing transplants. His liver could be divided up amongst the three. It is unlikely that the three patients can be kept alive until Gordon has died from his underlying pathology. Does Gordon not realize that through his death he can save several lives? Does his autonomous decision to stay alive for a few more weeks, knowing that he can be of benefit to others, justify risking the lives of these other patients? So the logic of act-consequentialism proceeds. Would it not really be right to end Gordon's life, without his consent, and take his organs in order to promote the best overall consequences?

Given the use of act-consequentialist reasoning, the value of agent autonomy has no more right to be regarded as a 'sacred value' of moral thought any more than the intrinsic value of human life itself. An act or omission is obligatory for the act-consequentialist if the act or omission is held to be the best alternative outcome. Act-consequentialism, therefore, can be used as a framework to justify the involuntary killing of Gordon, possibly also for his own benefit (if only he would recognize it was in his own interest to die) and certainly for the benefit of others. The value of autonomy—the autonomous pursuit of goals by Gordon—is but one more consideration to be thrown into the melting pot of consequentialist calculation. If we thought it scandalous to kill people for the sake of procuring their organs—it might upset relatives as well as the public—the practice could be kept under wraps by not telling people what was really going on. Since there is but one ultimate moral aim for act-consequentialism—that outcomes be maximized—the logic of act-consequentialism is certainly capable of justifying involuntary euthanasia by action or by omission.

Notes

1   Michael Potts, Paul A. Byrne and Rihard G. Nilges (2000), pp. 1–20; D. Alan Shewmon (1985), pp. 24–80; Jason T. Eberl (2005), pp. 29–48.
2   Stuart J. Youngner and Robert M. Arnold (2001), pp. 527–37.
3   Youngner and Arnold (2001); B. Andrew Lustig (2001), pp. 447–5.
4   Youngner and Arnold (2001); Lustig (2001).
5   See David W. Evans (1988), pp. 139–58; Christopher Pallis (1999), pp. 93–100; David Albert Jones (2000), pp. 91–120; J. L. Bernat (1998), pp. 14–23; Courtney S. Campbell (2001), pp. 539–51.
6   For example, Shewmon (2001), pp. 457–78.
7   Veatch (1975), pp. 13–30 and (1993) p .21, 'The human is essentially the integration of the mind and body and the existence of one without the other is not sufficient to constitute a living human being.'
8   Michael B. Green and Daniel Wikler (1980), pp. 105–33. See further Jeff McMahan (1995), pp. 91–126 on questions of the difference surrounding higher-brain death and other brain death. McMahan argues for death of the organism and death of the person.
9   (1996), p. 248, 'Such bodies, since they are no longer the embodiment of persons or even a mind, would count, at least, in general secular terms, as biologically living corpses.'
10 Norman M. Ford (2002), pp. 86–7.
11 Gastone G. Celesia (1997), pp. 21–36.
12 Thus abandoning the 'dead donor rule.' See Veatch (2004), pp. 261–76. On the importance of respecting the dead donor rule, see James M. Dubois (2002), pp. 21–41.
13 See Singer (1994), ch. 3, esp. pp. 50–51.
14 Dubois (2002), pp. 21–41.
15 Singer (1994), ch. 3.
16 Charles M. Culver and Bernard Gert (1982), p. 183; David Lamb (1985), p. 93.
17 Robert D. Truog (1997), 160–69.
18 Michael Tooley (1987), p. 82, offers this ground for distinguishing persons from non-persons: 'An organism possesses a serious right to life only if it possesses the concept of self as a continuing subject of experiences and other mental states and believes that it is itself such a continuing entity.' Peter Singer (1993), p. 395, defines a person as having awareness of his or her existence and of having desires and plans for the future: 'There are many beings who are sentient and capable of experiencing pleasure and pain, but are not rational and self-conscious and so not persons ... Many nonhuman animals almost certainly fall into this category; so must newborn infants and some intellectually disabled humans.'
19 Jonathan Glover (1977), 51–3, 158–62, 192–4; James Rachels (1986), 26, 60–77; Peter Singer (1993), ch. 7; Ronald Dworkin (1993), pp. 68–101; Helga Kuhse (1987), pp. 198–220; John Harris (1985), chs 1 and 5.
20 John Locke (1961), p. 280.
21 See G. E. M. Anscombe (1975), pp. 45–65.
22 On rights simply by virtue of being human see Jenny Teichman (1985), p. 179.
23 See Christopher Kaczor (2005), pp. 41–66.

24 For example, Mary Anne Warren (1997), pp. 83–4, for a list of personhood criteria. David DeGrazia (2004), pp. 301–20 defends another 'cluster concept' approach to personhood.

25 See Kaczor (2006), pp. 41–66; William J. Zanardi (1998), pp. 151–68; Louis G. Lombardi (1983), pp. 257–70; T. D. J. Chappell (1997b), pp. 41–57.

26 On the difficulties of person and personhood in terms of definitions, lists and degrees of attributes see Kraczor (2006); Bert Gordijn (1999), pp. 347–59; Ludger Honnefelder (1996), pp. 139–60; Tom L. Beauchamp (2001), pp. 59–70; Edmund L. Erde (2001), pp. 71–90.

27 H. Tristam Engelhardt (1996), ch. 4 maintains that it is only developed rational agency that really counts in the personhood stakes and that foetuses, infants and the retarded are not persons (although we may still have duties towards them).

28 Beauchamp (2001); Edmund L. Erde (2001); Gordijn (1999).

29 Tony Lynch and David Wells (1998), pp. 151–64.

30 Mary Midgley (2003), p. 167. As she further notes in an earlier essay (1985), 'personhood' originally meant a 'mask' that was used during the performance of a play.

31 Anscombe (1975), p. 61.

32 See Patrick Lee (1998), pp. 135–51; Chappell (1997a), pp. 96–108; Michael Wreen (1986), pp. 23–8; Brian Scarlett (1997), pp. 77–95; Jenny Teichman (1996), pp. 29–36.

33 See discussion by Teichman (1985), pp. 175–85.

34 Joseph Boyle (1989), pp. 236–40; John Finnis (1993), pp. 329–37; Luke Gormally (1992), pp. 181–8.

35 '*Persona est naturae rationalis individua substantia.*'

36 Chappell (1997a), pp. 41–57 and (1997b), pp. 96–108; Lee (1998), pp. 135–51.

37 Teichman (1985), pp. 180–81.

38 See Oderberg (2000a), pp. 174–84, for a concise and well argued critique of 'personism.' See also Teichman (1992), pp. 26–9.

39 On death and substantial change see Mary Rousseau (1979), pp. 582–601; Jason T. Eberl (2005), pp. 29–48.

40 For varied discussion of Kant and the scope of 'respect for persons' see C . F. Cranor (1983), pp. 103–17; Stephen Darwall (1977), pp. 36–49; D. C. Hicks (1971), pp. 346–8. D. Klimchuk (2004), pp. 38–61; Lombardi, (1983), pp. 257–70.

41 See the analysis of respect for humanity by Richard Stith (2004), pp. 165–84.

42 Stith (2004), pp. 165–84.

43 This kind of Kantian view is expressed by Tony Lynch and David Wells (1998) who claim that all humans have dignity because, p. 156, '… it is plain humanity which counts (or should count) … not any quality or ability usually associated with humanity.' Lynch and Wells acknowledge that humanity is one of these 'primitive' but indispensable concepts necessary for the very underpinning of morality. At p. 162, 'Morally speaking, it is humanity that counts. … Any effort at reduction on this point means abandoning morality itself.'

44 On downgrading certain classes of person and on the question of solidarity with our own species see Philip E. Devine (1978), pp. 46–57.

45 Compare Erich H. Loewy and Roberta Lowey (2004), p. 231–2, who maintain that since anencephalics lacks 'primary worth,' they cannot be harmed or benefited.

46 See Richard W. Momeyer (1983), pp. 275–90, on best interests for never-competent patients.

47 Momeyer (1983). Also on the topic of decision making for PVS patients see Thomas A. Mappes (2003), pp. 119–39.

48 As a matter of morals. For a discussion of the legal position in the UK see J. K. Mason, Alexander McCall Smith and G. T. Laurie (2005), pp. 577–96. See also the comprehensive

statement of legal doctrine concerning the treatment of the incompetent and children by James Munby (2004), pp. 205–310. See also Ian Wall's discussion of competency (2004), pp. 39–50. For the US position see Barry L. Furrow *et al.* (2000), ch. 16.

49 See Peter Singer (2002), chs 13 and 16; Singer and Kuhse (1985); John Harris (1995) and (2001); Dan Brock (1986) and (1998).

50 Joseph Boyle (1997), pp. 194–7.

51 Norman L. Cantor (2005), pp. 26–32, 113–26. As Cantor states pp. 126–7: 'Intrinsic indignity as applied to a never competent person would be narrow. So far, only a few conditions—permanent unconsciousness, mental decline to a semiconscious state where the person can no longer recognize and relate to others, and serious irremediable—might be classified by reference to contemporary norms as an intrinsically undignified status. ... Admittedly, my approach to intrinsic indignity—making the removal of a permanently unconscious patient's life support mandatory (absent contrary preferences by a previously competent person)—is contrary to prevailing practice.' *Pace* Cantor, his concept of intrinsic is hardly 'narrow' in scope. Cantor's argument is yet another variation of injury of continuing existence rhetoric (also wrongful birth) that has emerged in the bioethical and legal literature.

52 Cantor (2005).

53 John Keown (2002), pp. 45–9, neatly describes the dynamic shift from quality-of-life with a small 'q' to Quality-of-life with a large 'Q.'

54 Leon Kass (2002), ch. 8.

55 On differences in perspective between those who competent and also the never-competent see John D. Arras (1984), pp. 29–31. See also D. Wilkinson (2006), pp. 454–9.

56 When detected, later term abortions are often performed. Foetuses, however, are prenatal persons and thus cannot be intentionally killed unless they can be viewed as material non-innocents in cases where the mother's life is at stake or where there is grave risk of severe damage to the mother's health. In the disturbing British case of *Jepson v. The Chief Constable of West Mercia Police Constabulary* (2003), a foetus was aborted at 24 weeks because ultrasound showed that the foetus had a cleft lip and palate.

57 For case reports and discussion see the collection by Gregory Pence (2004), ch. 9. The second case was Baby Jane Doe. She was born with spina bifida (an opening of the spine) and hydrocephalus (water on the brain). The parents were told that she would never experience joy or sorrow. The baby was not dying and surgical intervention was not futile because with surgery it was estimated that she could have lived for up to twenty years.

58 The term 'neonaticide' is sometimes used in this context.

59 D. Wilkinson (2006), pp. 454–9, discusses disability in the context of quality-of-life as a common ground for withholding treatment.

60 Sadath A. Sayeed (2006), pp. 600–610.

61 Although for the competent patient, these factors can form part of the benefit and burden assessment.

62 T. K. Koogler, B. S. Wilfond and L. F. Ross (2003), pp. 37–41.

63 Both are usually jointly withheld.

64 'Usually' is a necessary qualification indicating the absence of extraordinary conditions that would render provision quite untenable, for example, a poor society with heavily stretched marginal resources.

65 See, for example, Germain Grisez (1993), pp. 284–6, 524–32; William E. May *et al.* (1987) and (1997); Robert Barry (1989), pp. 1–30.

66 David Oderberg (2001), pp.103–12 and (2004c), pp. 50–56, regards the provision of food and nutrition via tubes as nothing other than ordinary everyday care and not treatment.

67 Oderberg (2001) and (2004). See also the viewpoint of Robert Truog and T. I. Cochrane (2005), pp. 2574–6, who question the very relevancy of treatment versus non-treatment in the first place as a significant distinction for overall quality-of-life decision making.

68 On advanced directives and surrogate decision making see Sara Travis *et al.* (2001), pp. 493–500; D. J. Doukas and D. W. Gorenflo (1993), pp. 41–5; M. J. Karel (2000), pp. 403–22; L. L. Emanuel and E. J. Emanuel (1989), pp. 3288–93.

69 See J Stone (1994), pp. 223–46; Elysa R. Koppelman (2002), pp. 65–85; Cynthia B. Cohen (2004), pp, 291–314.

70 Grisez (1993) and May (1990).

71 Joseph Boyle (1997), p. 198.

72 On the Schiavo case see T. Koch (2005), pp. 76–8; Darren P. Mareiniss (2005), pp. 233–59.

73 Bryan Jennett (1997), p. 179.

74 See Paulo Cattorini and Massimo Reichlin (1997), pp. 263–81; G. L. Gigli (2002), pp. 251–4. Compare Andrew Batavia (2002), pp. 219–33, who argues for exclusionary rationing for PVS patients because of revised futility criteria. No future consciousness equates to no claim on medical resources.

75 Jonathan Glover (1977), pp. 191–2, contemplates involuntary euthanasia, out of mercy, to save a person from awful future prospects that would make life not worth enduring.

76 On utilitarianism and the grounds for killing see Tom Carson (1983). He argues that many forms of utilitarianism can justify involuntary killing for reasons of profound unhappiness as well as for substantial benefits to third parties.

Chapter 7

State Intervention and the Common Good

7.1 Introduction

In the preceding chapters, I have presented to the reader my natural law arguments for holding that it is always a grave moral wrong to intentionally kill an innocent person, whether oneself or another, regardless of a further appeal to consequences or motive. Cases of suicide, assisted suicide or euthanasia, I have argued, are all shaped by choices to intentionally kill a material innocent as a means to an end and are wrong on that count. As of yet, however, certain questions centering on the interface between morality, politics and jurisprudence—especially the use of coercive legal sanctions prohibiting certain forms of human conduct—still need to be addressed. Put simply, choices to commit suicide, assisted suicide or euthanasia may be thought immoral but should they be subject to legal prohibition? If the condition of immorality alone is not sufficient justification for legal prohibition, what further justification might be needed in order to subject certain kinds of wrongful conduct to the force of legal sanction?

The first part of this chapter proceeds with a critical assessment of the arguments of the anti-perfectionists—H. Tristram Engelhardt, John Rawls and Ronald Dworkin—that it is not the 'business of the state' to enforce deep or substantive conceptions of what constitutes the 'good life' upon its citizens. The state is denied any such grand foundation for its constitutive authority. Instead, especially given the reality of contemporary pluralism, state authority is based on a decidedly more limited framework of justification.

Having proceeded to challenge the anti-perfectionist approach to state authority, I then turn to look at the claim that legitimate state authority need not be based on the call to anti-perfectionism. Liberals themselves challenge anti-perfectionism and seek to defend a perfectionist *raison d'être* for state authority centered on key liberal values. While I accept their use of the key idea of perfectionism—that the purpose of the state it to promote the authentic well-being of its citizens—I mainly disagree with the way in which personal autonomy is exalted as the key constitutive value informing this brand of perfectionism.

My natural law account of perfectionism encourages the active pursuit of many worthwhile forms of life. It stresses 'good lives' not merely the 'good life.' Whilst embracing an array of pluralism, however, it insists that authentic pluralism is built upon and fosters respect for all the primary goods of persons. Legal regulations ultimately derive their legitimacy from the extent to which they promote and do not radically undermine a conception of the common good based on respect for these primary aspects of human well-being. I argue that a natural law conception of the person in society, centered on the common good, provides a solid framework by which to assess the justification for, as well as place limits on, the use of legal coercion to enforce some moral requirements.

The concluding part of this chapter briefly examines 'slippery slope' reasoning in order to help understand the potential impact that the legalisation of assisted suicide or euthanasia may have on the common good of society. In short, my appeal to slippery slope reasoning seeks to make the point that, as a last resort, it may yet provide a basis for those who would otherwise endorse or tolerate these practises to recognize a prudential case for maintaining their ongoing legal prohibition.

7.2 Anti-Perfectionism and State Authority

Engelhardt, Rawls and Dworkin, as we saw in Chapter 2 (s. 2.7), seek to limit the reach of state power by restraining its authority to endorse and support a substantive (perfectionist) theory of the good. In the face of considerable disagreement concerning what a 'good life' might actually consist of, and the 'fractious nature' of the power of human reason to demonstrate the truth of its propositions to others, the state needs to be neutral in its regulation of public life together.

Engelhardt proposes a retreat to a minimalist state concerned with the basic conditions of peaceful toleration—a toleration made possible by the adoption of minimalist demands and maximum permissiveness. Further restrictions on the conduct of persons, for Engelhardt, are made possible only by resort to the power of agreement. The state cannot be constituted by a shared substantive theory of the good. Such substantive sharing is the sole preserve of various non-state associations and communities.[1]

Rawls conceives that the reach of the state is limited by appeals to what can be justified on the basis of 'public reason,' a form of reason that eschews any appeal to deep substantive or metaphysical doctrines in order to build up circles of overlapping consensus amongst citizens. Public reason, as a form of reason, preserves a strong role for negative liberty as well as providing some role for positive liberty via the promotion of 'thin goods'—goods that can serve as necessary conditions for the promotion of many different and diverse ends in life.[2]

Dworkin supports the key idea that equality of concern and respect for persons precludes the state from exercising its authority to privilege one robust conception of the good life over another. By so privileging one conception of the good life, especially when coercive power is used to enforce it, a state undermines its very legitimacy by failing to treat all of its citizens with equal concern and respect.[3]

Having endorsed the concept of state neutrality over different visions of the good—for the state is held to have no constitutive role in 'making men and women moral'—no essential role in seeking to 'perfect' persons—our anti-perfectionist authors make further appeal to variations of J. S. Mill's harm principle. The general grounds for restricting a person's exercise of liberty are (i) when the harm is other regarding and has not been consented to or (ii) where further restrictions are held to be justified by considerations of right—in Engelhardt's case by agreements based on the principle of permissiveness; in Rawls's case by consensus-based public reason;

in Dworkin's case by the benchmark of treating all citizens with equal concern and respect.

Although many significant details separate our authors' respective accounts of the authority of the state to regulate and control the affairs of its citizens, they nevertheless share a common scepticism concerning appeals to human reason to identify and support a perfectionist account of the good for the coordination of public life together. For Engelhardt, fissures in our moral reasoning are near complete and any contentful non-procedural reasoning is held to be entirely partisan in nature. For Rawls, there is only a limited form of content-based public reason that may be invoked in order to regulate public life together. For Dworkin, no religious or secular perfectionist account of the good can, without disrespecting the equality of persons, furnish us with a common framework for public life together.

Engelhardt, Rawls and Dworkin, of course, are not simply speaking to those who share their respective anti-perfectionist outlooks on public life, but are seeking to convince committed 'perfectionists,' those who have a 'thick theory' of the good (of what fulfills persons), that they should, for the sake of preserving legitimate state authority, follow them down their respective anti-perfectionist paths.[4] Having argued in Chapter 3 that the foundations of morality are indeed perfectionist—albeit perfectionist in more open and expansive ways than allowed for by traditional natural law ethics (for example, over topics in sexual ethics)—the key issue to be addressed here is whether a natural law perfectionist *need be drawn* into accepting their arguments against using contentful teleological reason to justify at least some forms of paternalistic state intervention. In turning now to examine each of our authors in more detail, I argue that their anti-perfectionist arguments do not succeed in convincing natural law perfectionists to abandon their appeal to substantive contentful reason in order to justify some morals legislation for the sake of promoting and protecting the political common good of society.

7.2a Engelhardt's Procedural Morality

Turning first to Engelhardt, it seems that the plausibility of his anti-perfectionist case depends on the conclusion that the only real alternatives left to Western societies, due to perceived failures of rationality, are (i) a decline into anarchy, (ii) the rise of authoritarianism or (iii) acceptance of the principle of permission with all it entails for limiting the reach of state authority.[5]

For Engelhardt, all non-formal reason is necessarily partisan in outlook. Only a retreat to a minimal procedural republic founded on a formal procedural pathway can hope to circumvent the disruptive forces of partisanship. His key claim is that we can have a formal procedural pathway to limited government—based on the principle of permission—that can avoid the 'sectarian' pitfalls of non-formal reasoning.[6]

When we start to look at the foundations of Engelhardt's contentless procedural project, however, we can in fact discern a 'smuggling in' of substantial non-formal kinds of reasoning, thereby undermining his claim that we can—as an alternative to 'discredited' contentful moralities—create a formal procedural pathway to limited state authority.[7]

Consider the foundational principle of permission itself. This idea is dependent on a whole array of substantive baggage concerning what it is to be a person. Persons are those who engage in complex processes of deliberation, negotiation and agreement. The edifice of Engelhardt's contractualism is actually built upon many non-formal assumptions drawn from contact theory as the normative paradigm for human conduct. Anyone with some knowledge of the development of mercantilism in the West will appreciate the controversial assumptions upon which the notion of 'free exchange' is premised. These are not mere innocent procedural assumptions that can be treated as light matter. [8]

Engelhardt repeatedly states that his secular political morality is purely procedural. It has 'inescapable rules but no content.'[9] Yet, his procedural method is actually underpinned by substantive assumptions. The standing he assigns to the principle of permission is predicated upon a contestable theory of persons. By examining the underbelly of his account of persons, Engelhardt's account starts to beg the question of its 'neutrality' *viz.* perfectionist moral and political theories that have different underpinnings.[10]

Consider Engelhardt's analysis of the morality of infanticide. He, as with other thinkers, states that infants are non-persons. Persons must have the exercisable deliberative capacities for negotiation and agreement. No exercisable capacities, no status of being a person.[11] Yet, we are entitled to ask, why are those held to be the determinate characteristics of persons granting immunity from intentional killing but not others? Just how is an appeal to the species principle condemned as being substantive and non-neutral but not his appeal to exercisable deliberative capacities for negotiation and agreement? (see s. 6.3). Once we start to contest Engelhardt's constitutive view of the human person and with it just why the 'principle of permission' should be granted the key normative status he accords to it, we can certainly start to find grounds for doubting the tenability of his formal procedural pathway towards the construction of a minimalist state.

In an earlier incarnation of his text, *Foundations of Bioethics*, he originally appealed to the positive value of autonomy, a notion with substantive normative baggage.[12] Yet the move to re-label the value of autonomy as the principle of permission, in the second edition, does not render it non-substantive as a starting point. Calling it the 'principle of permission' rather than the 'value of autonomy' changes the label used, but not, I think, his reliance upon this central value of persons as the substantive underpinning for his contractualist framework.

Consider now the question of assisted suicide. For Engelhardt, its legitimacy as a practise is heavily dependent on the principle of permission and further agreement. Since it is unlikely persons will give up the general right to control the manner and timing of their own deaths, they retain that right subject to other contractual duties (for example, the rights of third parties) that may need to be discharged first.[13] Yet, why should the natural law perfectionist be convinced—given the contestable view of the person upon which his account of permission is itself predicated—that there is any such 'reserved right' of persons to kill themselves in the first place? A perfectionist will simply not be taken in by the supposed neutrality of his appeal to a right to assisted suicide based on the principle of permission and further agreement—for Engelhardt's appeal ultimately begs the earlier question: just why should the governing principle of permission—underpinned as it is by substantive non-formal baggage—be viewed, in his terms, as being any less 'partisan' in its underlying foundation than other 'perfectionist' principles?

7.2b Rawls's Public Reason

Engelhardt's anti-perfectionist project was built on the assumption that the key principle of permission, together with the minimal authority it would grant the state under conditions of diverse pluralism, would avoid recourse to either anarchy or authoritarianism. However, is this really the extent of the alternatives facing Western society? Engelhardt, I think, is really offering us an unrealistic set of alternatives; a set that is in fact challenged by John Rawls's appeal to public reasonableness as the threshold standard for determining whether or not state authority is being legitimately exercised. For Rawls, consensual alliances and webs of association can be formed by appealing to public reason, thereby avoiding Engelhardt's contractual minimalism whilst also steering clear of the twin pitfalls of anarchism or authoritarianism.

The Rawls of *Political Liberalism* distances himself somewhat from the earlier Rawls who wrote *A Theory of Justice*.[14] Rawls now stresses a key difference between his earlier comprehensive philosophical liberalism and his restrained political liberalism—his attempt to accommodate the 'fact of reasonable pluralism.' Comprehensive liberalism is predicated on a substantive account of what fulfills persons. The political conception of liberalism, on the other hand, is said to be based on an open civic understanding of reason that all citizens can participate in and accept. Overlapping consensus must come about through appeals to public reason—meaningful discourse shared as ordinary citizens—and not through appeals to thick conceptions of the good grounded in comprehensive doctrines.[15] For Rawls, legislation that is held to be justified by comprehensive doctrine will generally not satisfy the requirements of public reason.[16]

Rawls's argument has many dimensions to it. I am not able in the space available to tackle it with the depth it merits. Yet there are, I think, a couple of weaknesses running through his defence of political liberalism that undermine his claim that he is operating within a purely political conception of reason held to be neutral between different comprehensive doctrines. Rawls is committed to the view that only public reasons can have justificatory force in the public realm. But here, I think, we must ask what epistemological assumptions implicitly inform and shape his account of public reason? Consider some of the arguments I have advanced in this book. I have, for example, defended the idea that profoundly damaged individuals—anencephalic infants and PVS patients—are still persons because they are individual members of the human family and have a rational nature (s. 6.3). I have offered the reader what I think are good arguments in defence of this proposition. If I were to take Rawls's account of public reason at face value, however, I would have to 'cut and tail' them to the point where their very intelligibility and integrity as arguments would be gravely affected.[17]

Now, I am not claiming some privileged revelatory point that God made all human beings as persons because it said so in a book of religion. Instead, I am making the claim that there are good secular reasons, accessible to others, that defend the truthfulness of the proposition that all individual human beings are persons. To deny to any citizen the public legitimacy of appealing to comprehensive secular arguments in defence of a crucial proposition, a proposition judged to be objectively true, would be to treat all comprehensive truth claims as if they were merely the equivalent of 'faith-based assertions.'[18]

The reason why appeals to comprehensive reasons are being ruled out of public consideration, for Rawls, is because their exclusion is thought to be justified by *de facto* scepticism resulting from the clash of different comprehensive truth claims. In simple terms, if B disagrees with the comprehensive reasons advanced by C to support proposition X, because B finds convincing other comprehensive reasons not to support X, appeals to comprehensive reasons are useless for resolving controversial questions. Even if X is true, as long as B has comprehensive reasons for not assenting to X, B cannot be converted or persuaded into accepting the truth of X. Comprehensive reasons, due to their limited acceptance and their inability to persuade others from different comprehensive backgrounds, then, must be bracketed out of open and accessible political decision making processes.

Rawls effectively denies that comprehensive truths can be known and found to be rationally persuasive between persons from different traditions and backgrounds. All comprehensive reasons are really just the equivalent of 'faith claims' from a public reason standpoint. When the Rawlsian idea of public reason is opened up to further scrutiny, however, we start to encounter a conception of public reason that cannot be endorsed by any thoughtful citizen who seriously maintains (a) there is substantive comprehensive truth to be had in morality and politics, and (b) evidence and arguments supporting these truths can function as accessible public justifications in civic discourse.[19] Those who do not accept that dissent invalidates all appeals to comprehensive reasons in the public square, will also reject the notion that pubic reason must be restricted only to those 'ordinarily accessible' and 'less demanding' forms of justification alone judged suitable for spreading agreement by consensus building. I doubt, for example, that slavery would have been challenged quite so profoundly in the present century had appeals to comprehensive doctrine emphasizing the basic dignity of all persons not been legitimately permitted as part of 'open' and 'accessible' public dialogue.

Rawls's version of public reason is really plausible only to those of like mind who are willing to endorse the fact of disagreement and dissent as a valid ground for setting aside all appeals to comprehensive truth claims in public discourse. For the natural law perfectionist, support for Rawls's position on public reason could only be advanced at the price of gravely undermining the very intelligibility of its key arguments. Natural law ethics cannot be readily divided up into (a) the non-doctrinal and public and (b) the doctrinal and non-public without damaging and distorting its very understanding of persons and what contributes to their well-being.[20] No natural law ethicist or Kantian or utilitarian thinker for that matter could begin to accept Rawls's account of what public reason entails and yet seriously remain a committed natural law ethicist or a Kantian or a utilitarian. Natural law ethics without comprehensive doctrine is simply not natural law ethics. Those who think that there really is substantive truth in morality and politics, truth that is in principle accessible to all, will not embrace Rawls's conception of public reason. Instead, they will favor some alternative account of reason-based dialogue that does not seek to exclude all significant appeals to comprehensive doctrine from the public square.

There are many reasonable differences which arise in public life that reflect legitimate differences in commitment. The range of authentic pluralism is large. A 'thick' theory of the human good does not necessarily entail a theory of the common good that is narrowly framed and deeply corporatist in its perfectionism. Pluralistic perfectionism, for example, celebrates goodness instantiated in many different and incompatible ways of life. But in relation to some important matters, for example, the protection of innocent human life from intentional, negligent or reckless killing, the natural law ethicist will claim that there are some right answers that are true and accessible to all, and ought to, notwithstanding the fact of disagreement, inform and shape our public life together.

Once it is conceded that wider appeals to comprehensive reason do significantly contribute to an understanding of public problems, those wider appeals must inevitably help shape what constitutes a reasonable ordering of values and principles in the public domain. It is interesting to note that Rawls, despite his strictures over appeals to comprehensive doctrine, cannot, it seems, remove some of his own public policy positions from implicit reliance on comprehensive liberal doctrine. Such reliance, I think, raises doubts as to whether his own methodological strictures can be consistently and faithfully adhered to when attempting to analyze and justify important public policy stances on controversial topics like abortion and assisted suicide.

While, in *Political Liberalism*, Rawls only mentions abortion in a footnote, it is intended to illustrate how his notion of public reason expresses a reasonable balance of political values. In that footnote he considers the case of a well-ordered society in which an adult woman requests an abortion. Rawls claims that any publicly reasonable balance of the values of 'due respect for human life, the ordered reproduction of political society over time, including the family, in some form, and finally the equality of women as equal citizens' requires that society accord to the woman 'a duly qualified right to decide whether or not to end her pregnancy during the first trimester.'[21] My reason for mentioning this footnote is not to argue the ethics of abortion. Instead, I seek to make the point that it is untenable to assert on entirely 'non-comprehensive grounds' that any reasonable assessment of the values at stake must accord to the woman a right to a first trimester abortion. Why is an appeal to the equality of woman a non-doctrinal public reason for justifying first trimester abortion but any mention of the status and rights of the foetus would be discounted as 'doctrinal' and 'non-public' reasoning? The reality, I think, is that Rawls is implicitly trading on liberal comprehensive reasoning in order to assist his weighing and balancing of the values at stake in the abortion issue. Both positions, however, are really being informed by comprehensive reasoning. One cannot 'reasonably' be included in the ballpark of the 'publicly reasonable' but not the other. The inclusion of one but the exclusion of the other is not neutral and impartial, for both positions depend on substantive comprehensive assumptions regarding the critical interests of the woman and her foetus. As Robert George and Christopher Wolfe point out, it is deeply suspicious that 'Public reason ... almost always has the effect of making the liberal position the winner in morally charged political controversies. It does this in effect by ruling out of bounds substantive moral argument on behalf of nonliberal positions.'[22]

Consider, now, the question of assisted suicide. Rawls, a signatory to *The Philosphers' Brief*, would appeal to public reason in order to justify the conclusion that there is a right to assisted suicide for those who are terminally ill, suffering and who are competent.[23] Yet the point of contestation here, is why the 'autonomy' and 'life' values at stake should be valued and balanced in the way he thinks. Why is an emphasis on autonomy over life regarded as a publicly reasonable and non-comprehensive account of these values but emphasis on the continuing value of life over autonomy is regarded as doctrinal and non-public?[24] The reality, I think, is that both accounts entail appeals to forms of comprehensive reasoning in order to justify their different approaches. The doctrinal and non-public labels seem to be utilized in order to discount assessment according to one comprehensive account while the non-doctrinal and public labels are being utilized to implicitly endorse another comprehensive account.[25] If arguments concerning the continuing protection of innocent life from intentional killing are deemed doctrinal, then so too should arguments advanced on behalf of personal autonomy that defend a right to certain forms of consensual killing. The content of public reasoning is, in effect, being 'fleshed out' with underlying assumptions supplied from comprehensive liberal doctrine. As John Haldane states, when faced with disagreement over controversial topics, 'Rawls's true position reveals itself to be far from neutral: try for an overlapping consensus, but where it is not available and where important issues are at stake, affirm your own comprehensive doctrine.'[26]

7.2c Dworkin's Equal Concern and Respect

As we saw in Chapter 2 (s. 2.7b), Ronald Dworkin has argued for the existence of a moral right of people to determine for themselves profound questions of meaning and to act upon those conceptions.[27] He derives a robust moral right from what he thinks it must mean to treat citizens with equal concern and respect. Citizens are not accorded equal concern and respect if one account of the good life is held to be privileged by the state and other competing conceptions of the good life are discounted. Such privileging results in a deep sense of inferiority and unworthiness for those who do share the theory of the good adopted by the state.[28]

For Dworkin to prevent a person from being assisted in committing suicide, in conditions of considerable pain and suffering, is said to represent an unwarranted devaluing of the worth and dignity of that person, even if his or her own assessment of life's worth is judged by others to be morally wrong. Out of respect for the equal worth of persons, person X has a moral right that Y not interfere with X's choice to Z. Prohibiting the making of such a choice would be to attack a person's deep sense of dignity and worth. Such is the significance of the requirement that persons be equally treated and respected by the state, it generally trumps other competing considerations.[29]

Now, I agree with Dworkin that the state has an important duty to treat all of its citizens with equal concern and respect. This is a fundamental requirement of fairness and justice. Where I depart from his judgment, however, is over the question of whether the promotion of natural law perfectionism by the state must be antithetical to treating persons with equal concern and respect.[30] On the contrary, I think natural law perfectionism is committed to a deep sense that citizens must be treated with equal concern and respect. Natural law perfectionism is concerned to respect the equal standing and dignity of all persons to pursue and promote their well-being.

Take, for example, the issue of heroin addiction. I do not doubt that some heroin addicts deeply value their addiction. It may have profound meaning for them. They may argue that prohibitions against the use of heroin make them feel as if their values do not count and that they are being treated as second class citizens. Against this claim of a moral right not to be interfered with, however, I would argue that concern for the equal worth and respect of all citizens can mandate positive intervention in order to prevent heroin addicts from falling prey to their drug dependency and self-abandonment. Intervention is justified because of a deep egalitarian sense that every human life is of radical worth and truly worth saving. Respect for the critical interests of all persons sometimes requires that we act to affirm those critical interests—notwithstanding subjective perceptions of being treated as inferiors. Not to intervene would be to abandon our egalitarian commitment to help promote their objective well-being as persons.

It is not apparent, then, that acting out of a deep sense of equal concern and respect for persons is incompatible with natural law perfectionism. Denying that X has a moral right against Y to Z need not necessarily entail that X is being denied equal concern and respect. While I would certainly argue that some conduct may be condemned by perfectionism as being morally unworthy, and some unworthy conduct, due to its impact on the common good, may be subject to legal sanction, it does not follow that a judgment is being made that any person *qua* person is being deemed less worthy of respect than any other person.[31] It seems too stretched a claim for Dworkin to assert that in seeking to prohibit assisted suicide, for example, the state necessarily manifests disrespect for the suicide and his or her assister rather than the unworthiness of the choice *qua* choice. Still, it may be retorted, if people are not allowed to determine and act upon profound questions of existence for themselves, are they not really being 'infantilized' and thus disrespected in their right to equal concern and respect?

Consider the example of a brutal contest to fight to the death.[32] All of the fighting participants freely consent to participate. They all love the thrill of violent deadly combat. It has profound meaning for them—to live and die in a manner of their own choosing. It is a closed contest. Only freely consenting adults pay to watch the ensuing spectacle. Dworkin, it seems, would have to uphold the 'moral right' of the fighters to maim and beat themselves to death because their freely made choices have profound value and meaning to them. If he does not endorse their moral right to pursue such a course of action, he would seem, on his own terms, to be committed to depriving the fighters of their right to equal concern and respect. I would argue that the common good interest of the state in upholding and protecting human life does not equate to the unequal treatment of the fighters as persons because the state legally prohibits them from fighting to the death. The fighters would only be treated unequally as persons if they were being deprived of their exercise of choice without good justificatory reason.[33] Simply because X does not accept that there is good justificatory reason for the state to prohibit X from doing Z, does not mean that X is being treated unequally by the state. Preventing the mutual infliction of injury and death for sporting purposes, is, I submit, a good justificatory reason to prohibit the exercise of the choice, notwithstanding any subjective sense of deprivation as to worthiness that may be experienced by the fighters. In time, perhaps, they might come to realize the 'good sense' behind the prohibition.

Clearly those who are prohibited from exercising certain choices may be psychologically affected by the prohibition. They may think that they are being treated as inferior persons. First, in reply, it should be pointed out that while certain choices are not being honored, this is not equivalent to the proposition that the state is necessarily dishonoring the radical dignity and worth of those who are subject to a prohibition. Our fighters, for example, may have a claim to unequal treatment if their form of killing was discriminated against but other forms of consensual killing— dueling; assisted suicide; voluntary euthanasia; Russian roulette—were being permitted. By subjecting all citizens to a general ban on consensual killing, however, the fighters are not being singled out for arbitrary or unfair treatment. Second, the appeal to subjective perceptions of inferiority in order to oppose the prohibition of choices would concede far too much by way of denying the state any appeal to good justificatory reasons where (i) persons do not accept those good reasons and (ii) where they feel they are being disrespected.[34]

Consider the case of George. He is a libertarian. Freedom to earn money and dispose of it as he sees fit has profound meaning to him. He views reasons to impose personal income tax as mere rationalizations for state licensed robbery. George feels demeaned and wronged by the enforcement and collection of personal income tax. I submit that notwithstanding (i) his rejection of good justificatory reasons used to impose personal income tax and (ii) his subjective feelings of being robbed by the state, he is not being denied equal concern and respect by the state through the enforcement of income tax collection.

If there really is no moral right to commit a moral wrong, what does need to be recognized, however, is the existence of political and legal rights not to be interfered with in the performance of many wrongdoings.[35] Consider the case of Pamela. She is very wealthy. She has a great deal of disposable income. She spurns all charitable efforts. She is motivated by material greed. Despite her immoral behavior—she does not have a moral right to be callous to the needs of others—she nevertheless has a political and legal right enforceable against others not to be coerced into making charitable donations.

For the sake of upholding important goods, and necessary freedoms to pursue those goods, many morally bad choices need to be permitted, subject only to forms of non-coercive disapprobation, for example, family or community censure. The coercive force of the law is something of a blunt power that needs to be exercised cautiously and with restraint. Thus, for example, X has a political and legal right of non-interference, under many circumstances, to lie to others where others have a moral right to the truth. Even with lying, however, the state has many interests in maintaining communicative truthfulness that can justify the use of its coercive power to restrain the scope of X's general political and legal right not to be interfered with while lying. Thus, X cannot lie in court thus committing perjury and perverting the course of justice; X cannot lie in order to defraud people into investing in a sham retirement scheme; X cannot lie in order to commit bigamy when X is legally married, and so on.

7.3 Liberal Perfectionism

Perfectionist liberals like Joseph Raz and William Galston challenge the very idea that anti-perfectionism can credibly hope to justify liberal policies.[36] They argue that it is necessary to focus on a substantive theory of the good—the key values that are truly constitutive of human well-being. Those values are perfectionist, for it is the very pursuit of them that truly makes life fulfilling and rewarding. Crucially, liberal perfectionists discount the possibility of founding political structures neutrally. Liberal values must be embraced as part of a comprehensive theory of the good. A key value is the value of personal autonomy. It is a substantive value of key defining worth for liberal perfectionists. It is effectively a master value. It cannot be adequately grounded or protected by an appeal to the idea of neutrality. Instead, if respect for autonomy in society is to be adequately constituted and defended, it requires a perfectionist justification.[37]

What is refreshing in perfectionist accounts of liberalism is the need to embrace and found state concerns on what is necessary for the promotion of human well-being. Only by embracing and promoting values can we begin to legitimize the exercise of state power in a way that credibly respects the nature of persons. The true worth of a political regime is ultimately to be determined by the authentic value of the lives that are cultivated under it.[38] Liberal perfectionist accounts, therefore, have structural similarities with accounts of natural law ethics, at least to the extent that they seek to promote a contentful theory of what it is to flourish as a person. Such questions are of central concern to society and the state. State action cannot be neutrally based. Liberal perfectionists reject the claim that important civil liberties will necessarily be jeopardized if the state positively seeks to promote and cultivate authentic human well-being.[39] Where they differentiate themselves from natural law perfectionism, however, is over their concern that natural law ethics fails to recognize and appreciate the full significance of personal autonomy as a master good of human well-being.[40]

I would admit that traditional natural law theory has historically paid a lack of attention to the legitimate concerns of both liberal anti-perfectionists and perfectionists that some important human liberties—freedom of religious worship; freedom of speech; freedom of association; certain sexual freedoms—have either not received a robust enough defence at the hands of traditional natural law or have been openly attacked.[41] I would agree that some paternalistic interventions by states are unwarranted curtailments or interferences with the exercise of individual autonomy. My revised account of natural law ethics rejects monism and embraces a pluralistic understanding of the good. There is no one form of good living. There are many different and divergent life narratives that can be positively pursued and promoted. The coercive power of the law is often a blunt instrument by which to seek to regulate individual human conduct. Appeals to it must be very carefully circumscribed, undertaken as a last resort, and only embarked upon where important common good interests are at stake. Where I do think liberal perfectionism goes astray, however, concerns its over emphasis on the key value of personal autonomy at the expense of adequately recognizing the standing and status of other objective and primary goods—especially human life—other goods that are basic and indispensable ingredients of human well-being.[42]

Autonomy is an important facilitative good of persons. It is an important precondition for all worthwhile action. The power to authentically constitute life plans and projects is also a vital aspect of the primary good of practical rationality itself. Guiding free choice by the requirements of reason is the perfection of the capacity to choose. Together we have the key idea of reason-guided moral autonomy (see s. 5.6a). It facilitates and promotes all manner of worthwhile choices. Choices that are profoundly bad, mistaken, and destructive however, by virtue of the very content of the choice, do not rightfully claim our respect and therefore do not generate a moral right to non-interference (see s. 7.2).

It is sometimes reasonable to intentionally limit the individual exercise of this important enabling good in order to prevent harm or destruction to the standing and worth of other vital goods. Human life, as we have seen, is a primary good of persons. It is a *per se* good. It is an ultimate reason for action. Such a primary good generates both positive and negative demands. Negatively, its normative force requires that we never intentionally violate innocent life, regardless of appeals to further consequences or motive. It is never practically reasonable to intentionally seek to destroy innocent life in order to promote other worthwhile goods, even the enabling good of personal autonomy.

It is in relation to the standing and priority given to personal autonomy *viz.* primary goods, then, that the respective paths of liberal perfectionism and natural law perfectionism can be seen to diverge. Revised natural law ethics cautiously maintains that gravely destructive or degrading choices are not inherently valuable and need not be treated as worthy objects of respect (the choice *never* the person) merely because those choices are made autonomously. Gravely destructive or degrading choices do not have a moral right to non-interference and may be subject to legal prohibition if they clearly undermine or impede the ability of the state to foster and maintain the common good of society.

Regarding assisted suicide, some liberal perfectionists certainly support such a right. Joseph Raz, for example, thinks that the dominion of personal autonomy can stretch to the state sanctioning of assisted suicide pacts between suffering terminally ill patients and their physicians.[43] Yet, it seems to me even a liberal perfectionist defender of the value of personal autonomy might endorse the right in principle but oppose adoption in practice due to prudential 'slippery slope' concerns that a legal policy of assisted suicide would inevitably lead to unacceptable slippage towards the adoption of non-consensual forms of euthanasia (see s. 7.4).

7.4 Natural Law Ethics and the Common Good

In my revised natural law ethics, the *raison d'être* of state authority is to secure and promote the well-being of the individuals who comprise a given political society. Societies exist at various levels and with varying degrees of overlap—families, networks of friends, parishes, etc. Wherever there is a society of persons we can talk of a common good of that society. Family life has a common good—reciprocal love, care and support between family members. Groups of friends too share in the common good of their inter-personal relationships built upon a sense of mutual regard. Wider forms of society are built on the commonality of mutual shared objectives.

Political society embraces a wider more expansive sense of common good. Intrinsically, political society enhances the life of its members via commitment to mutual concern and reciprocity. It is really an outgrowth of a more expansive form of friendship known as civic friendship.[44] The bonds of mutual concern and reciprocity give rise to the good of justice, of ensuring among the members of a political society that each and every person is (i) fundamentally respected as a member of the political society and is (ii) given his or her rightful due as an equal member of that society. Instrumentally, the political common good directs decision making towards the promotion of social, economic and political conditions that help facilitate the pursuit of human well-being by all individual members of society.[45] Thus, members of a political society endeavor to work cooperatively together in order to provide for such things as: a police force and a military in order to resist unjust internal and external acts of aggression; infrastructure that supports wealth generation via trade and commerce; infrastructure aimed at the education of the young; infrastructure aimed at the treatment and care of the sick; institutions that advance cultural pursuits such as museums, parks and libraries.[46] The list goes on.

The 'political common good' is not synonymous with the state. The common good of political society is antecedent to the existence of the state. The ultimate rationale for the existence of the state is its very ordination to serving the political common good. Serving and promoting the political common good ultimately underpins and legitimizes the power of the state to coordinate and regulate ways and means of promoting and protecting important societal objectives.[47]

A key strength of natural law ethics—regardless of the form of government operative in a given political society—monarchical; democratic; dictatorial, etc.—is that it furnishes accessible moral and political standards by which to scrutinize and assess the fairness and justice of a given regime's enactments.[48] A dictatorial regime that kills and tortures minorities because of their religious beliefs fails to serve the political common good of that society. A democratic regime that permits the enslavement of some persons for the sake of the 'greater good,' whereby a minority can be subjugated and exploited for the sake of the majority, also fails to act for the sake of the political common good because it violates one of its central tenets—a failure in justice to respect the equal dignity and worth of all persons.[49]

7.4a Goods of Persons and the Common Good

A fundamental requirement of state action in furtherance of the political common good is that its policies promote and do not undermine respect for the primary goods of persons. An authentic sense of the political common good cannot be set in opposition to these primary commonalities of well-being. The ultimate ends of life are primary goods. They are irreducibly plural in nature. They are fundamental to the well-being of all members of a political society. State actions that set aside, ignore or otherwise disregard the standing and significance of any primary good, appearances to the contrary notwithstanding, are not being correctly ordered towards the authentic common good of political society.[50] To the extent that a state enactment grossly undermines respect for primary goods, it fails to act justly and begs the question of the extent to which—depending on the gravity of the injustice—persons are bound, in conscience, to obey the terms of an unjust enactment.[51]

The primary goods of persons are more fully realizable in political society. To be able to practically realize these goods, people, via the instruments of governance, need to cooperate in order to develop conditions conducive to promoting and protecting them.[52] If individuals are to have adequate opportunities to perfect themselves in all their authentic diversity, government must promote conditions that allow the primary goods of persons to be pursued in many diverse and incompatible ways. Authentic pluralism is written into the very structure of a revised natural law ethics. However, to the extent that the state—a body that ultimately derives its coercive and regulatory authority from its ordination to the political common good—does not respect certain delimiting boundaries on the promotion of authentic diversity, it undermines that common good and acts unjustly.[53]

Wherever there is state injustice, notwithstanding appearances, every member of society can be said to be harmed by the state's failure to recognize and act upon fundamental requirements of justice. For example, no member of a political society ought to be exposed to a state enactment that sanctions the intentional killing of any innocent person. Such a policy cannot be reconciled with an appeal to authentic diversity. The state, in sanctioning such killing, permits a wrong directed against the structural fabric of civil society. Actions that intentionally kill the innocent are being granted *official public standing and recognition* in the name of the political common good. All members of a society, whether or not they realize it, are being objectively harmed with regard to their interests by the very *incivility* of such an enactment. Due concern and respect for innocent human life is being officially and publicly devalued by the state. In such an enactment, every member of society is being exposed to an unjust weakening in state support for a fundamental moral and political tenet upon which genuine civil life together ought to be structured around and built upon.

7.4b Common Good not Greater Good

It is important to note here that the pursuit of the political common good is not simply the equivalent of some general maximization thesis— such as utilitarianism— to combine, amalgamate and add up the total preferences of persons in order to determine the shape of public policy. Let me make it clear that I am not opposed to the use of numerical aggregation where the legitimate preferences of citizens in appropriate areas of decision making can be pooled and coordinated.[54] Political society B may have stronger pooled preferences for primary health care than tertiary education. Society C may have stronger pooled preferences for road rather than rail transportation, and so on. I also recognize that questions of effectiveness and efficiency in pursuit of established goals are also very important. If society D is going to build a bridge to solve a mobility problem it ought to determine if it is the most effective and efficient solution to the problem and then build it as effectively and efficiently as possible.

Aggregation, then, has an important role to play in the field of public welfare. Appeals to aggregate preferences, however, cannot be invoked where the preferences being appealed to are themselves unfair or unjust. Since the political common good is informed by the requirement to promote and protect the genuine goods of each and every member of a political society—*all fully respected with regard to their fundamental dignity and worth*—this benchmark requirement cannot be violated in order to maximize the overall return of societal preferences.[55] A public policy that sanctions the intentional killing of disabled innocent persons, for example, because they are deemed to be an unacceptable economic burden on society, might be compatible with a preference-utilitarian notion of what constitutes the greater good for society, but it is deeply incompatible with a key requirement of the political common good that the promotion of overall welfare preferences can never be directly advanced at the price of violating a fundamental requirement of justice—*no innocent person may ever be intentionally killed in order to advance general welfare concerns* (see s. 4.5). Disregard for fundamental moral restraints cannot be reconciled with an informed civil understanding of the political common good.

7.4c Limits on Pluralism

The political common good is concerned to promote positive social, economic and political conditions required for human well-being. The state is an instrument of governance instituted to coordinate and regulate our pursuit of the political common good. A fundamental limitation on state authority is its fundamental obligation to recognize that there is no one good form of living but many forms of living that are properly compatible with a pluralistic conception of human well-being.[56] There are innumerable worthwhile life plans that can be chosen that reflect a myriad of possibility. State action is grossly unjust when reasonable scope for plurality in political society is unduly curtailed or thwarted. Such restrictions do not serve to secure, promote or otherwise enhance the political common good of a society.

The political common good is served by framing a set of reasonable conditions that can underpin responsible civil life together. The justification for state paternalistic authority primarily relates to the control of manifestly unreasonable choices that are particularly undermining of the political common good because they attack key conditions of fairness and justice.[57] Maintaining peaceable coexistence may, of course, require a considerable degree of state toleration and non-interference regarding many kinds of unreasonable choice. Yet, due exercise of wise prudential restraint on the use of coercive power does not render illegitimate all use of coercive power to restrain and control the making of certain bad choices, choices that are deemed especially egregious to the political common good.[58]

Am I not here simply endorsing heavy handed state paternalism? Can the use of legal coercion really be deployed for the sake of promoting 'virtue' and suppressing 'vice'? I shall now explain my position further by briefly engaging with Aristotle and Aquinas thereby helping to further clarify the 'paternalistic reach' of my own revised natural law position.

For Aristotle, the polity, through its regulatory function of law making, could use coercive force to further virtue and discourage vice in those lacking the requisite prudence to conduct themselves virtuously. Aristotle thought that the use of force could suppress vice, and in doing so create conditions whereby the average citizen could better respond to the calling of the virtuous life.[59] The influence of Aristotle is clearly reflected in Aquinas's understanding of the relationship between law and the service of the political common good. Aquinas argued in his *De Regno* that the king who wishes to fulfill his duty to lead people to virtue, must, as far as practicable, create conditions for virtuous living. The King, via his coercive power, ought to promote virtuous living by restraining temptations to wickedness.[60]

Two criticisms made of Aristotle's and Aquinas's coercive use of law to promote virtue and suppress vice are: (i) there is no one good life and both are therefore concerned to promote a narrowly perfectionist account of virtue; (ii) coercing people to conform does not make them morally better. It does nothing more that lead to conformity in their external signs of behavior.[61]

Regarding the first criticism, I agree that Aristotle and Aquinas have an unduly narrow sense of what the virtuous life consists of. Both are monistic perfectionists. Aristotle privileged the contemplative life. Aquinas privileged a life centered on religious faith and worship. Both, I think, failed to appreciate and embrace the diversity and richness of different forms of good living compatible with respect for primary goods.[62] In short, there are many ways of pursuing genuine perfection in life that are not ordered towards the contemplative or the holy. Forms of living compatible with pursuit of authentic well-being are rather more diverse. Other worthwhile forms of living should be fully respected as being no less worthy of being pursued and realized. The primary good of family life, for example, is truly compatible with a richer diversity of social arrangements based on fidelity and commitment than either Aristotle or Aquinas would have accepted. Pluralistic perfectionism is more structurally sensitive to the ways in which freedom to pursue a wide range of worthwhile personal attachments and commitments in life places real limits on the paternalistic power of the state.[63]

Regarding the second criticism, I agree with it to the extent it appears that Aristotle and Aquinas do, at times, seem to readily speak of the law as if it can lead people directly into the 'open arms' of virtuous living. Too much 'power of conversion' is being claimed.[64] Nevertheless, there are, I think, three aspects informing Aristotle's and Aquinas's use of legal coercion that have validity and support some use of state coercive power to control unvirtuous conduct deemed to be especially undermining of the common good. First, if the law promotes some external conformity of behavior, this is surely a good. If B lives because C does not kill B although C wants to kill B but does not do so because he is afraid of the legal consequences, this is a positive thing. Perhaps, in time C will come to see that his reason for killing B lacks merit and may come to appreciate the wisdom behind the sanction that deterred him from killing B. Second, law can be used to set a moral example to others—conduct X is a deeply unworthy object of choice and ought not to be regarded as a legitimate object of pursuit. The law can create a 'moral tone' by taking a committed stance against the permissibility of certain forms of human conduct. Third, use of legal coercion may help restrain the actions of third parties who would take non-proscription of a given practice as license to promote and facilitate that practice.

7.4d Implications for Suicide, Assisted Suicide and Euthanasia

Reflecting on the requirements of the common good, and the efficacy of legal sanction to influence and moderate conduct, I would argue that an intentional act of suicide, whilst objectively immoral, cannot be subjected to any form of criminal legal sanction. Past laws that confiscated property or denied the suicide proper burial did not have deterrent value and unjustly punished the family.[65] Suicides are often undertaken in conditions of severe distress and disturbance of the mind. There may be little or no subjective culpability present. Punishment is grossly unwarranted where the burden of punishment is borne by the family who are denied rights of inheritance or who are denied the right to say goodbye to their loved one in a dignified manner. Mercy and compassion, not punishment, ought to inform our understanding of those who have committed suicide or are tempted to commit suicide.

Cases of assisted suicide and voluntary active euthanasia, however, are of a different order. The willingness of third parties to help suicides end their lives, renders such acts more probable by virtue of the knowledge people will have that third parties can legally render assistance either by supplying lethal pills (assisted suicide) or by executing the final lethal act (voluntary active euthanasia). Third party B who shares in the intentional killing of patient C generally concurs with the view of C that C's life lacks inherent worth. No one really assists in the execution of a suicide request unless the life in question is deemed to fall within a broad range of unacceptable lives not worth living. No person can have such a publicly sanctioned right to facilitate or execute the intentional killing of another, however, without undermining the common good requirements of civil/friendly society. The state has a paramount interest in upholding the *radical equality and worth of all innocent life*. Consent does not validate the intentional killing of the innocent (s. 5.6). Humanitarian relief of pain and suffering does not validate the intentional killing of the innocent as a means (s. 5.3). The state sanctioning of assisted suicide or voluntary active euthanasia would communicate the uncivil message to all of its citizens (especially the sick, weak and vulnerable) that not all innocent human life, in the eyes of the state, is truly of equal worth and dignity. Were a state to permit such practices, it would, I think, be engaged in the perpetration of an act of uncivil abandonment towards those who reasonably look to the state to foster and promote laws and societal conditions that reinforce and uphold rather than undermine this key requirement of the political common good.

Cases of non-voluntary (especially involuntary) active euthanasia abandon the idea that genuine informed consent of the one being killed is really shaping the decision to intentionally kill. Third parties take it upon themselves to decide that the very life of X (a profoundly impaired 'non-person') is not worth living and can be ended by means of a lethal causal agent. Yet, the state has a paramount interest in preventing the uncivil devaluation of human life at the hands of third parties, especially when such devaluation is utilized in order to deliberately end X's 'pointless and futile' life for the benefit of others, for example, via organ harvesting. No state can sanction willed killing of this kind without undermining its legitimate instrumental role in serving the political common good by advancing conditions that help to protect and not undermine due respect for all innocent life.

What of cases of voluntary passive euthanasia undertaken by the withholding or withdrawal of treatment? Here, I would argue that the law needs to respect and maintain a wide sphere of choice for patients to make benefit and burden assessments. Considerable variations in treatment decisions reflect the different dispositions of different patients. Many decisions to withhold or withdraw treatments, even life sustaining treatments, are compatible with an intention only to be free of the burdens of treatment. Preserving wide patient discretion in order not to impinge on reasonable choices will inevitably entail the toleration of some manifestly unreasonable choices in treatment decision making. Toleration, here, is informed by acting for the common good of patients, since over interference and disregard for discretion in treatment decision making may result in many bad and unwelcome side-effects for patients. Such a policy of toleration, however, is not the equivalent of tacitly or openly endorsing a policy of intentional killing by means of withholding or withdrawing treatment. Rather, it reflects a prudent recognition that the power of the law can only do so much to protect persons from intentionally or recklessly killing themselves. Forcing competent patients to undergo treatment against their will, apart from it being very likely ineffective, would have a destructive impact on the bonds of trust that must exist between physicians and patients in order to generally promote the good of health.

What of cases of non-voluntary passive euthanasia? Here, I think, laws need to be framed in order to prevent profoundly impaired never-competent or incompetent persons for being treated as 'non-persons' and being denied all significant treatment options on the ground that their very lives are deemed to lack inherent worth. Where patients' values and commitments are not known, best interests standards must inform treatment decisions. Best interests can never be informed by a surrogate judgment that a person's very life is not worth living and should therefore be passively killed. For certain categories of permanently unconscious patients, for example, anencephalic infants or PVS patients—where prior values and commitments are either unformed or unknown—hydration and nutrition, for example, should not be permitted to be withheld or withdrawn unless (i) patients are no longer able to metabolize them, (ii) they are immanently dying, or (iii) the fair allocation of critically stretched health resources— without unjustly discriminating against these patients on the grounds that their lives are pointless or futile—serves to restrict the overall time span of their continuing treatment.

7.5 Slippery Slopes

Above, I have argued that the protection of innocent life from all intentional or reckless killing is foundational to the idea of the common good. To the extent that respect for life is undermined by the state-sanctioned policies of assisted suicide or euthanasia, the common good of political society is weakened. In order to further assess what negative impact state sanctioned policies of assisted suicide or voluntary euthanasia might have on the common good, it is necessary to prudentially consider slippery slope questions. Further considerations of this kind need to be addressed because it is still possible, I think, to appeal to prudential dialectic in order to persuade those who might find assisted suicide or voluntary euthanasia morally acceptable in principle to nevertheless oppose their legal sanctioning in practice.

Policy makers in both the UK and the US, in the past, have found slippery slope concerns to be sufficiently compelling to uphold existing laws that prohibit the practices of assisted suicide or voluntary active euthanasia.[66] Such reasoning cannot simply be set aside as the last ill-conceived attempt of a 'sanctity-of-life' ethic to impose its moral imperatives on the free deliberations of contemporary pluralistic society. Any adequate consideration of the common good of society requires that slippery slope considerations be seriously addressed. As Philip Devine points out, no prudential agent, despite protestations, can ignore slippery slope concerns, for they are not mere 'obscurantist flim-flam.'[67]

7.5a Forms of Slippery Slope

There are two basic forms of slippery slope reasoning. One is logical and the other is empirical.[68] The first logical form states that if no significant conceptual difference between X and Y can be identified, the justification used to support X will also support justification for Y. If Y is unacceptable, X should also be unacceptable due to its lack of conceptual distinction from Y. The second empirical slippery slope takes the form of the likelihood of X sliding towards Y due to the operation of psychological, cultural and social factors that will erode boundaries between X and Y.

Whilst, again, I would readily concede that slippery slope arguments are based on prudential considerations—of trying to anticipate what might happen if a given policy is adopted—we cannot avoid reckoning with them. There are, of course, occasions when slippery slope arguments have been abused, amounting to little other than reactionary scare tactics in order to entrench an existing *status quo* position—for example gun lobbyists who argue that any significant restrictions placed on the ownership of firearms by citizens will eventually lead to the banning of all citizen owned firearms. As Sissela Bok rightly points out, however, abuse in some settings does not justify a blanket rejection of slippery slope reasoning in other more appropriate settings. She concludes that the assisted suicide/euthanasia debate is an appropriate setting. For Bok, any attempt to revise existing assisted suicide/euthanasia policy will need to fairly scrutinize the potential for change to bring about unacceptable negative effects.[69]

7.5b Weak Conceptual Boundaries

Central to the case of those who support only the legalization of assisted suicide but not active voluntary euthanasia is an attempt to point to a clear conceptual difference between the two. There will be no 'slippage' from X to Y because of the conceptual distance that separates X from Y. In physician-assisted suicide, the last fatal act is said to be performed by the patient, not the physician. It is argued, therefore, assistance by a physician in suicide does not entail the active killing of the patient by the physician. The two are quite distinct. A key question of real concern, however, is whether such a distinction is conceptually strong enough to hold the legal line that would be drawn between a policy of assisted suicide and a policy of voluntary active euthanasia. *The Philosophers' Brief*, composed by some leading liberal philosophers, made such an assurance central to their case for legalizing assisted suicide in the US.[70] R. G. Frey also states that such a conceptual differentiation plus appropriate safeguards can allay fears that a policy of assisted suicide would result in slippage from X to Y.[71] Yet many supporters of physician-assisted suicide view the enactment of assisted suicide legislation as being but one logical stepping stone on the progressive path to embracing voluntary active euthanasia. What crucial distinction, they argue, really separates an act of intimate assistance from the direct administration of lethal means? It cannot be a question of intent, for morality and the law have historically considered such intimate complicity a sharing of common purpose. Due to the sharing of intent and the adoption of a common plan, an appeal to who performs 'the last act' in a 'shared chain' is really a weak distinction not a strong one. Acceptance of X, due to reliance on a distinction lacking any significant moral or legal import, advances also the logical case for acceptance of Y.

The position that a significant distinction of real import between assisted suicide and voluntary active euthanasia cannot be credibly maintained, can be further strengthened by examining the reach of the values that inform appeals to assisted suicide—relief of pain and suffering and respect for personal autonomy. Once X is viewed within the logic of the values that are driving the advocacy of X, those very values also underwrite the acceptability of Y. Within such a value framework it seems decidedly contrived and artificial to say that patient B can be the beneficiary of suicide because he or she is able to execute the final act for herself, but patient C, who may be physically incapable of doing so, cannot be a beneficiary and only has the option of passive euthanasia. When viewed against the backdrop of the wider principles informing the assisted suicide debate, there is little by way of convincing conceptual difference to justify support for a policy of assisted suicide but not voluntary active euthanasia.[72] Acceptance of X, due to the logic of the values informing both X and Y, leads to acceptance of Y.

Let us assume now that a policy of voluntary active euthanasia is also supported. The consensual element is stressed. Both sets of policy will nevertheless face conceptual challenges over limitations placed on who can benefit from either policy.[73] Consider a policy stating that patients, in order to benefit, should have six months or less to live and that they should be afflicted with severe pain. Why only six months or less to live? Why only cases of severe pain? What of the chronically ill who have severe pain but who may live for many months or years? Why should they be denied merciful release from a life they judge not worth living? What of those who are said to be terminally ill but experience little pain? Should they not be able simply to point to other factors—suffering, indignity, economic considerations, burdens on others—to justify their intention to end their lives? What of those who persistently suffer but who are neither terminally ill nor in severe pain? Why should they be denied the option of merciful release? Arbitrary boundary stipulations are unobjectionable when determining a policy, say, of whether the speed limit is 70 mph or 65 mph; of whether to drive on the left or the right hand side of a road, and so on. They are dynamically unstable in this area, however, when we are determining whether B but not C can avail himself or herself of a fundamental equal right to end his or her own life. The logic driving mercy killing does not end with the relief of those who have six months or less to live and who endure considerable pain in that time frame.

Critics of a policy banning the legalization of assisted suicide or voluntary active euthanasia point to the 'state licensing of passive killing' in many hospital wards as a key reason to reject 'fraught arguments' over conceptual boundaries.[74] Here, however, I would argue that people widely and with good reason accept the validity of a distinction between 'letting die' and 'killing' that has conceptual strength, so many decisions to withhold or withdraw treatments are not cases of voluntary passive euthanasia at all. Secondly, people also recognize that only so much, other than by persuasion, can be done to keep patients alive against their will. They recognize that a policy of toleration is one that should not be equated with the 'back door' encouragement or endorsement of voluntary euthanasia by passive means. They realize that the reach of the law can only do so much in the health care context to protect innocent life from decisions to intentionally procure death by passive means.

Person/non-person is another distinction used in the discussion of non-voluntary euthanasia that is conceptually weak. The criteria typically established for determining personhood are arbitrary and vague (see s. 6.3). Given the vague and arbitrary criteria used to establish a distinction between persons and non-persons, I can see little hope of conceptually limiting the reach of the non-person class only to those who are deemed 'permanently and irreversibly unconscious.' Patients with advanced dementia, for example, due to weak conceptual boundaries, may well start to slip from the class of persons into the class of non-persons and thereby become 'ripe' candidates for non-voluntary euthanasia of both the passive and the active sort.

Sadly, the non-voluntary passive euthanasia of anencephalic infants and PVS patients is already being practised in both the UK and US.[75] If they are non-persons, however, why should they not simply be actively killed in a controlled manner in order to harvest their organs for the benefit of others? Since the lives of non-persons are not really worth living why should this be a problem? When persons are deprived of their status as persons, the conceptual case for resisting the adoption of non-voluntary active euthanasia becomes threadbare.

7.5c Empirical Erosion of Boundaries

In addition to the logical form of the slippery slope that points towards acceptance of a widespread right to voluntary active euthanasia as well as assisted suicide, empirical evidence from both the US and the Netherlands supports the contention that regulations used to draw various boundary lines in the formulation of assisted suicide/euthanasia policy suffer from vagueness or arbitrariness. Vagueness or arbitrariness in the framing of boundaries, when pressed by the cumulative weight of physiological, sociological and cultural pressures that challenge them, facilitates slippage towards assisted suicide or euthanasia practices deemed unacceptable.

Consider Oregon's *Death with Dignity Act*. Over the last few years, Oregon has permitted physician assisted suicide for competent terminally ill patients over 18 who are faced with burdens of severe pain and suffering. As many of the essays in Kathleen Foley's and Herbert Hendin's collection point out, however, whether or not patients have six months or less to live, because they suffer from incurable conditions, is a vague and arbitrary stipulation.[76] Empirical evidence shows that estimating life expectancy is fraught with uncertainty. Life expectancy is not reducible to ready calculation. Many incurable conditions defy accurate estimates in terms of months. Moreover, the question arises, is the six month period to be assessed with or without treatment or partial treatment that may delay the course of the irreversible condition?[77]

Given Oregon's tight control of information concerning patients and conditions, we do not really know how the time frame is being used and whether or not it will in fact be treated as a floating threshold that sympathetic physicians can use to squeeze in cases under its auspices. It is difficult to see why physicians disposed towards mercy killing would not be tempted to do so given that the stipulated time fame is so malleable and arbitrary in the first place. Why not four months? Why not eight months? Why exclude those who are chronically ill and who suffer considerably but who will likely live well beyond the threshold of six months?

Consider further the question of motive informing assisted suicide. As Neil Gorsuch points out, the Oregon legislation, despite the popular rhetoric of patients facing uncontrollable pain, places no such restriction, and patients often justify their suicide by appealing to dignity concerns. Reviewing the evidence, he concludes it is reasonable to infer that patients who will (a) live beyond six months or (b) who are not in severe pain are being assisted in suicide. The class of potential candidates, Gorsuch contends, actually turns out to be very malleable.[78] Reports do not yet indicate that physicians in Oregon have been involved in active voluntary euthanasia.[79] However, this may simply indicate that the relative newness of the practice, compared to the Dutch experience, has not permitted the 'voluntarist ethos' enough time to gather momentum in the minds of physicians, patients and the general public.

Given inevitable rounds of state and federal court challenges from patients who do not perceive these present Oregonian stipulations to be anything other than arbitrary—especially (i) those patients who cannot be smuggled in under the six months or less to live clause and yet have chronic illnesses that generate severe pain and suffering; and (ii) those patients who are not able to administer the final lethal dose of pills for themselves and who cannot therefore benefit from assisted suicide—it is surely only a matter of time before the boundaries of those who can benefit from intentionally procured death will be further widened.[80]

Turning now to the Netherlands, they have had a policy of not prosecuting physicians who actively or passively kill patients with their consent since 1984.[81] 'Due care' regulations were adopted by the Royal Dutch Medical Association and these regulations applied until 2001, when euthanasia was formally legalized.[82] The distinction between assisted suicide and voluntary euthanasia, from the outset, was held to be of relevance only for statistical reporting purposes (although, as a matter of fact, the Dutch strongly favor euthanasia over assisted suicide). The Dutch experience strongly presses the question why should patients not have the option of either practice given the lack of any clear moral or legal distinction between the two? Why should individual preferences not be accommodated?

Prior to 1993, it was held to be a breach of the Dutch regulations to kill a patient who was not terminally ill and who was not experiencing intolerable pain. By 1994, however, those regulations had become so watered down by a series of court challenges as to scope, that neither terminal illness nor severe pain were deemed grounds upon which to restrict the availability of euthanasia.[83] So much for the attempt of the earlier Dutch regulations to restrict the class of beneficiary in the face of court challenges over boundaries for inclusion and exclusion. If B can benefit from euthanasia because he is terminally ill and in severe pain then why not C who is terminally ill but is faced with severe suffering? If D is not terminally ill but faces chronic pain why should D be excluded? If E is not terminally ill but suffers greatly why should E be excluded?

Even more disturbing is evidence from official reports over the incidence of non-voluntary and involuntary killing where the express consent of competent patients has not been granted. Non-voluntary or involuntary euthanasia has occurred in approximately 900 cases per annum from 1995 though to 2001—between 0.7% and 0.6% of all deaths. Roughly half of these cases involved patients who made no mention of any prior wish to be euthanized.[84] The only reason that can account for the presence of such a significant statistic, despite prior regulation to the contrary, it the independent dynamic that is generated when physicians themselves, acting on their own judgment, start to decide whether or not patients in their care should live or die, either because (i) they would be 'better off dead' having such low 'quality-of-life' or (ii) because their deaths would relieve burdens/procure benefits for third parties or some combination of the two.

Once it becomes state-sanctioned to actively intend the death of a patient, it is not a mere 'scare tactic' to observe a creeping 'overall worth of life' dynamic at work that tacitly encourages physicians, despite regulation to the contrary, to kill patients without their express consent. It is not necessary to appeal to any fanciful Orwellian nightmare in order to illustrate the reality of clear empirical slippage in the Netherlands from the voluntary to non-voluntary and beyond.

Space, alas, will not permit a further assessment of empirical slippery slopes. I would recommend that the reader further consult Neil Gorsuch's sound analysis of empirical slippage in both the US and the Netherlands.[85] I believe, however, I have said enough on this topic to demonstrate to the reader that—far from being 'obscurantist flim-flam'—both the logical and empirical forms of slippery slope reasoning have to be taken very seriously by those who assert on moral grounds (a) the acceptability of assisted suicide X but not voluntary active euthanasia Y; or (b) by those who accept the full import of the appeal to autonomy and defend voluntary active euthanasia X but who seek to avoid further descent down the slippery slope towards the unacceptable practices of non-voluntary active euthanasia and involuntary active euthanasia.

Notes

1   H. Tristam Engelhardt (1996).
2   John Rawls (1993).
3   Ronald Dworkin (1990).
4   Joseph Boyle (1994), pp. 184–200.
5   Engelhardt (1996), pp. 3–16, 67–9.
6   Søren Holm (1998), pp. 75–7.
7   Holm (1998). See further discussion of his procedural foundationalism in Tom L. Beauchamp (1997), pp. 96–100.
8   Michael Wreen (1998), pp. 73–88; Thomas J. Bole (1999), pp. 169–76.
9   Engelhardt (1996), p. 69.
10 Wreen (1998), pp. 80–2.
11 Engelhardt (1996), pp. 135–54. For discussion of Engelhardt's views on the status of children see J. C. Moskop (1997), pp. 163–74.
12 Engelhardt (1986).
13 Engelhardt (1996), pp. 340–54.
14 Rawls (1993), pp. xvii–xx.
15 Rawls (1993), pp. 144–50.
16 Rawls (1993), pp. 174–8.
17 John Haldane (1996), pp. 64–9.
18 David McCabe (2000), pp. 326–7.
19 See Robert P. George and Christopher Wolfe (2000), p. 54.
20 David McCabe (2000), p. 324.
21 Rawls (1993), pp. 243–4, fn 32.
22 George and Wolfe, eds (2000), 'Introduction,' p. 2.
23 Ronald Dworkin *et al.* (1997).
24 Adapted from his footnote concerning abortion, (1993), pp. 243–4. See also John Finnis (2000), pp. 78–84; Haldane (1996), pp. 67–9.
25 What perfectionists need not do, then, is abandon appeals to their own substantive accounts of reason. See Michael J. White (1997), pp. 17–28.
26 Haldane (1996), p. 68, discussing Rawls's intrinsic life exclusion in the abortion argument.
27 Dworkin (1977), pp. 177–81, 272–3. The moral right to do a moral wrong is succinctly expressed by J. L. Mackie (1978), p. 351, 'If someone, A, has the moral right to do X, not only is he entitled to do X if he chooses—he is not morally required not to do X—but he is also protected in his doing of X—others are morally required not to interfere or prevent him.'
28 Dworkin (1985), pp. 190–91, 205–6, 364–7.
29 Dworkin (1993), ch. 7.
30 My thought here is in general accord with the liberal perfectionist William Galston who states that 'We show others respect when we offer them, as explanation, what we take to

be our true and best reasons for acting as we do.' See Galston (1991), p. 109. Quoted by David McNabe (2000), p. 326.

31 Rejecting the 'sin' not the 'sinner.' As Augustine of Hippo classically stated '*cum dilectione hominum et odio vitiorum*' (with love for mankind and hatred of sins). See further John Finnis (1987), pp. 433–7.

32 An example adapted from a different context by Irving Kristol (1994), p. 47.

33 Galston (1991), p. 109. See also (1983), pp. 320–24.

34 David McCabe (2000), pp. 326–7.

35 For discussion of different rights see Philip Devine (2000b), pp. 110–12.

36 Joseph Raz (1986) and (2001); William Galston (1991) and (1995).

37 See Patrick Neal (1994), pp. 25–58.

38 See George Sher (1997), pp. 89–96.

39 William M. Sullivan (1990), pp. 148–66.

40 Christopher Wolfe (2006), ch. 5.

41 My account of the good of the family (see s. 3.6d), for example, does not endorse traditional natural law condemnations of contraception or committed homosexual relationships.

42 Wolfe (2006), ch. 9.

43 Raz (2001), chs 3–4.

44 Michael Smith (1995a), p. 36 states, 'Where there is justice, friendship is possible. And where there is friendship, there is the pursuit of the common good.' See also Smith (1995b), pp. 111–25.

45 See John Finnis (1998), 222–8. Giving his unique interpretation of a specifically instrumental political common good in Aquinas.

46 Michael Pakaluk (2001), p. 57, lists instrumental goals like these but challenges Finnis's account that the political common good is entirely instrumental. I agree that the political common good, based on civic friendship, has an intrinsic dimension to it.

47 Wolfe (2006), ch. 11.

48 See Jacqueline A. Laing (2004), pp. 184–216; Robert George (1990), pp. 1415–29.

49 Classical natural law theory, alas, failed to appreciate that slavery was a condition radically incompatible with the inherent dignity and worth of persons.

50 Finnis (1980), ch. 6.

51 Finnis (1980), ch. 12. See also Jack Donnelly (1980), pp. 520–35.

52 See Smith (1995b), pp. 111–25.

53 Robert George (1993), pp. 189–92.

54 Finnis (1983), pp. 80–84, rightly takes to task preferences without prior respect for objective goods and principles. Where preferences do not conflict with prior moral standards, however, I cannot see why they would not be an important means of helping to shape the contours of public policy. My position is very different from preference-utilitarianism because preferences, to count, must satisfy all prior moral standards of practical reason. No appeal can be made to immoral preferences.

55 See Mark Murphy (2006), ch. 3, for discussion of a non-reductionist sense of aggregation, respecting intrinsic goods, within a natural law framework.

56 See Robert George (1993), for a discussion of important freedoms encouraged by pluralistic perfectionism.

57 George (1993), pp. 42–7.

58 Jacqueline Laing (2004).

59 Aristotle (1941), 1179b–1180a.

60 Aquinas (1949), I 15/16.

61 For discussion of perfectionism and coercion in Aristotle and Aquinas see, for example, George (1993), ch. 1; Christopher Wolfe (2006), ch. 8; Richard A. Crofts (1973), pp.

155–73; M. Cathleen Kaveny (1997), pp. 132–49; Danny Scoccia (2000), pp. 53–71; Peter Redpath (1995), pp. 332–41.

62 Douglas B. Rasmussen and Douglas J. Den Uyl (2005), ch. 8, have an interesting account of individualism and the common good. I appreciate their discussion of pluralism. I differ from them over the scope for authentic pluralism. Rasmussen and Uyl overstress the master value of autonomy in framing the common good.

63 Robert George (2001), pp. 91–109.

64 Kaveny (1997), pp. 132–49.

65 See Glanville Williams (1968), pp. 254–64.

66 Although Margaret Otlowski (1997) does not accept the prudential force of slippery slope arguments, she recognizes their considerable influence in public debate and on the minds of legislators in the UK and US. See chs 1–2.

67 Philip Devine (1978), p. 185, quoting Anthony Flew.

68 On the different forms of slippery slope and how they function in discourse David Lamb (1988), pp. 1–19; John Woods (2000), pp. 107–34.

69 Sissela Bok (1998), pp. 112–18.

70 Dworkin *et al.* (1997).

71 R. G. Frey (1998), pp. 43–63.

72 John Keown (2002), pp. 76–80

73 See Yale Kamisar (1997), pp. 225–60.

74 Helga Kuhse (1998), pp. 371–4.

75 D. Wilkinson (2006).

76 Kathleen Foley and Herbert Hendin (2002). See especially the essay by Felicia Cohn and Joanne Lynn, pp. 238–60.

77 Neil M. Gorsuch (2006), pp. 115–24.

78 Gorsuch (2006), pp. 116–18.

79 Susan Okie (2005), 1627–30.

80 John D. Arras (1997), pp. 361–89.

81 The Alkmaar case. A doctor euthanized a 95 year old woman whose health was deteriorating. See Mason L. Allen (2006), pp. 549–50.

82 Allen (2006), p. 551; Keown (2002), pp. 83–8.

83 The Chabot case. Dr Chabot killed his patient because she was suffering from inconsolable psychological distress without prospect for improvement. See Keown (2002), p. 87.

84 See Keown (2002), pp. 91–5 for discussion of the Remmelink Report and the Van der Maas Survey. Also Gorsuch (2006), pp. 109–12, discussing official statistics reported by the Dutch government. For the third survey covering 2001 see R. Fenigsen (2004), 73–9.

85 Gorsuch (2006).

Conclusion

From the outset of the book it was stressed that the framework for engaging important moral and legal concerns arising from the practises of suicide, assisted suicide and euthanasia, would be a natural law based ethics. Such an approach to ethical discourse has not been prominent in 'mainstream' ethics due to the widespread suspicion that natural law merely serves to operate as a kind of 'cloaking device' shrouding what really amounts to an attempt to impose 'divine imperatives' on an otherwise liberated secular society. Dispense with the legitimacy of privileged appeals to religion, it is said, and the case for a natural law ethics starts to look decidedly threadbare.

In response to this common point of view, I set about the task of seeking to justify a natural law based ethics whose fundamental structure was not derived either from appeals to religion or from appeals to quasi-religious metaphysical constructs. I have argued for a secular basis for natural law that is open and publicly accessible in its reasoning. My natural law framework, defended in Chapter 3, has provided the subsequent basis for building my sustained response to the case for assisted suicide and euthanasia as detailed in Chapter 2.

In my natural law ethics I have 'unfashionably' adhered to non-naturalism, a version of intuitionalism, a defence of the fact/value distinction, and irreducible goods pluralism. I am convinced, however, with respect to my natural law colleagues, that my reasons for departing from a more traditional naturalistic framework are justified and bear fruit. The reader must determine whether they think my 'meta-ethical' claims hold water or not.

At the heart of my opposition to the moral and legal case for assisted suicide and euthanasia has been my defence of a key concrete moral absolute: it is always and everywhere wrong to intentionally kill an innocent person regardless of any further appeal to consequences or motive. I am well aware that a defence of such a concrete moral absolute is also deeply 'unfashionable' in the contemporary ethical climate. Nevertheless, I have sought to argue that such a principle is generated from the wellsprings of our capacity for practical rationality. Practical rationality grasps an array of irreducible primary goods that ultimately establishes a dynamic polyteleology of all worthwhile action. One of the key shaping requirements of practical rationality is to respect and not violate the normative demands generated by any of the primary goods of persons. Different primary goods generate different positive and negative normative demands. I have sought to argue, however, that due respect for the negative normative demands generated by the good of human life will not admit to any 'compelling reason' that would permit the intentionally killing of any human innocent as a means to an end.

In order to flesh out the scope and meaning of this concrete moral absolute, it was necessary to defend a number of key concepts that were invoked to justify its practical application as an exceptionless norm-guiding choice. I have sought to defend a number of key distinctions judged crucial to sustainability of the principle: double effect reasoning; action types; actions and omissions; the meaning of innocence; the determination of death; persons and non-persons. Again, it is for the reader to decide whether my account of the requirements of practical rationality and my defence of this concrete moral absolute is convincing or not.

In further explaining the scope of this concrete moral absolute, I have argued that it covers all actions that intentionally kill a materially innocent person, whether oneself or another. Self-killing is included within the scope of the prohibition as are all actions of third parties that would seek to intentionally kill another materially innocent person for the sake of ending their pain and suffering. Omissions are also brought under the scope of illicit killing. Good ends cannot justify the election of an immoral means by action or omission or by some combination of the two. Notwithstanding the allure of 'disaster escape clauses' current in contemporary deontology, I have argued that any appeal to 'grave' or 'critical' consequences cannot invalidate a fundamental structural defect in the moral quality of an action pertaining to means. An appeal to consequences cannot 'override' or 'set aside' the continuing bindingness of this strategic exceptionless agent-centered side-constraint that protects all materially innocent human beings (persons) from being intentionally killed.

Clearly, the fields of law and morality are not identical in scope. As I have argued, however, it is important to realize that natural law ethics is not just concerned with any overly constrictive interpretation of what constitutes the 'moral domain.' As an approach to ethics, it is also fundamentally concerned with wider questions of how individual decisions impact the common good of society. Persons are not regarded as 'little islands' unto themselves. In short, a natural law based approach has political and jurisprudential implications for how we order society. For natural law ethics, there is a necessary connection between the conduct of individuals and the wider moral environment of a society. Contrary to the anti-perfectionist arguments of H. Tristram Engelhardt, John Rawls and Ronald Dworkin, I have argued that natural law has a reasonable and publicly accessible corpus of principles to draw upon that can justify the legitimacy of certain powers of the state, in the service of the common good, to limit certain actions that would attack or undermine central constitutive requirements of the common good.

An important part of the state's role in promoting the common good is to protect due respectfulness for the commonality of the primary human goods. Contrary to those who would argue that the toleration of intentional killing entailed by assisted suicide and voluntary active euthanasia would not undermine any 'balanced set of societal conditions,' I have argued that the state sanctioning of such practices would openly propagate and encourage the 'deep incivility' of 'officially devaluing' societal respect and protection for the radical worth and dignity of all innocent persons. The state, by virtue of its ordination to serve and uphold the common good of society, cannot permit appeals to 'consent' or to bold 'quality of life assessment' to empower a culture that licenses the intentional procurement of death without also undermining part of its very reason for being—to promote and protect conditions that facilitate and do not undermine plans and projects that are compatible with the respect for the ultimate purposes of human well-being.

Even if my natural law approach to the political requirements of the common good is not found convincing by some perfectionists, for example, Joseph Raz and William Galston, I have sought to point out, as a kind of last resort, that there are still good prudential grounds flowing from slippery slope kinds of reasoning to provide a plausible warrant to justify maintaining and enforcing legal prohibitions on those kinds of actions.

As a concluding caveat, with reference to the winds of prevailing change that seem to be blowing in the contemporary UK, US and elsewhere, I can only state that time will tell whether or not legislators and citizens will be assisted by the thrust of ideas defended in this book and in other sources, such that they will seek to resist proposals for legalizing physician assisted suicide and voluntary active euthanasia. If, as I have argued, the reader accepts that assisted suicide and euthanasia policies are not *pro bono publico*, I hope that he or she too will try and have some influence as a citizen over the direction of state policies in order to (a) resist pressure to legalize those practises and (b) to focus real attention on the development of better humanitarian means, especially improvements in the provision of palliative and hospice care, to better respond to the challenge of supporting the sick and ill who are in pain and who suffer.

Bibliography

Alexander, Larry (2000), 'Deontology at the Threshold,' *San Diego Law Review*, **37**, 893–912.

Allen, Mason L. (2006), 'Crossing the Rubicon: The Netherlands Steady March towards Involuntary Euthanasia,' *Brooklyn Journal of International Law*, **31**, 535–75.

Alvarez, Alfred (1972), *The Savage God: A Study of Suicide*, New York, N.Y.: Random House.

Anscombe, G. E. M. (1958), 'Modern Moral Philosophy,' *Philosophy*, **33, 1–28.** [Reprinted in various anthologies as well as her *Collected Philosophical Papers.*]

——— (1963), *Intention*, 2nd edn, Ithaca, N.Y.: Cornell University Press.

——— (1970), 'War and Murder,' in *War and Morality*, Richard Wasserstrom (ed.), Belmont, Calif.: Wadsworth, pp. 41–53. [Reprinted in various anthologies as well as her *Collected Philosophical Papers.*]

——— (1975), 'The First Person,' in *Mind and Language*, Samuel Guttenplan (ed.), Oxford: Clarendon Press, pp. 45–65.

——— (1981), *The Collected Philosophical Papers of G. E. M. Anscombe*, 3 vols, Oxford: B. Blackwell.

——— (1990), 'A Comment on Coughlan's "Using People",' *Bioethics*, **4**, 62.

——— (1994), 'Sins of Omission: The Non-Treatment of Controls in Clinical Trials,' in *Ethical Issues in Scientific Research: An Anthology*, Edward Erwin, Sidney Gendin, and Lowell Kleiman (eds), London; New York, N.Y.: Garland, pp. 219–24.

——— (2005), *Human Life, Action and Ethics: Essays by G. E. M. Anscombe*, Mary Geach and Luke Gormally (eds), Exeter: Imprint Academic.

Aquinas, Thomas (1948), *Summa Theologica*, trans. English Dominican Fathers, New York: Benziger.

——— (1949), *On Kingship*, trans. Gerald B. Phelan, Toronto: Pontifical Institute of Mediaeval Studies.

Aristotle (1941), *Nicomachean Ethics. The Basic Works of Aristotle*, trans. W. D. Ross; Richard McKeon (ed.), New York: Random House.

Arjoon, Surendra (2007), Ethical Decision-Making: A Case for the Triple Font Theory,' *Journal of Business Ethics*, **71**(4), 395–410.

Arkes, Hadley (1997), 'Autonomy and the Quality of Life: The Dismantling of Moral Terms,' *Issues in Law and Medicine*, **2**, 421–33.

Arras, John D. (1984), 'Toward an Ethic of Ambiguity,' *Hastings Center Report*, **14**(2), 25–33.

——— (1997), 'Physician-Assisted Suicide: A Tragic View,' *Journal of Contemporary Health Law and Policy*, **13**, 361–89.

Ashley, Benedict M. (1994), 'What is the End of the Human Person? The Vision of God and Integral Human Fulfilment,' in *Moral Truth and Moral Tradition: Essays in Honour of Peter Geach and Elizabeth Anscombe*, Luke Gormally (ed.), Dublin: Four Courts, pp. 68–96.

Asselin, Don T. (1995), 'A Weakness in the "Standard Argument" for Natural Immortality,' in *Freedom, Virtue, and the Common Good*, Curtis L. Hancock and Anthony O. Simon (eds), Notre Dame, Ind.: American Maritain Association, pp. 17–27.

Audi, Robert (1996), 'Intuitionism, Pluralism, and the Foundations of Ethics,' in *Moral Knowledge*, W. Sinnott-Armstrong and Mark Timmons (eds), Oxford: Oxford University Press, pp. 101–36.

Aulisio, Mark P. (1995), 'In Defense of the Intention/Foresight Distinction,' *American Philosophical Quarterly*, **32**, 341–54.

——— (1996), 'On the Importance of the Intention/Foresight Distinction,' *American Catholic Philosophical Quarterly*, **70**, 189–205.

Bales, R. E. (1971), 'Act-Utilitarianism: Account of Right-Making Characteristics or Decision Procedures?' *American Philosophical Quarterly*, **8**, 257–65.

Ball, Steven W. (1988), 'Reductionism in Ethics and Science: A Contemporary Look at G. E. Moore's Open Question Argument,' *American Philosophical Quarterly*, **25**, 197–213.

Bambrough, Renford (1981), *Moral Scepticism and Moral Knowledge*, London: Routledge.

Baron, Marcia (1984), 'The Alleged Moral Repugnance of Acting from Duty,' *Journal of Philosophy*, **81**(4), pp. 197–220.

Barnett, Randy E. (1986) 'Contract Remedies and Inalienable Rights,' *Social Philosophy and Policy*, **4**(1), 179–202.

Barry, Robert, 'Feeding the Comatose and the Common Good in the Catholic Tradition,' *Thomist*, **53**, 1–30.

——— (1994), *Breaking the Thread of Life*, New Brunswick, N.J.: Transaction.

Battin, Margaret P. (1998), 'Ethical Issues in Physician-Assisted-Suicide,' in *Last Rights: Assisted Suicide and Euthanasia Debated*, Michael M. Uhlmann (ed.), Washington, D.C.: Ethics and Public Policy Center, pp. 111–45.

——— (2005), *Ending Life: Ethics and the Way We Die*, New York, N.Y. Oxford University Press.

Beauchamp, Tom L. (1976), 'An Analysis of Hume's Essay "On Suicide",' *Review of Metaphysics*, **30**, 73–95.

——— (1986), 'Suicide,' in *Matters of Life and Death: New Introductory Essays in Moral Philosophy*, 2nd edn, Tom Regan (ed.), New York, N.Y.: Random House, pp. 77–124.

——— (1997), 'Engelhardt's Foundations,' *Reason Papers*, **22**, 96–100.

——— (2001), 'The Failure of Theories of Personhood,' in *Personhood and Health Care*, David C. Thomasma, Christian Hervé, and David N. Weisstub (eds), London; Dordrecht: Springer, pp. 59–70.

——— and Arnold Davidson, (1979), 'The Definition of Euthanasia,' *Journal of Medicine and Philosophy*, **4**, 294–312.

—— and James F. Childress (1994), *Principles of Biomedical Ethics*, 4th edn, New York, N.Y.: Oxford University Press.

Bennett, Jonathan (1968), 'Whatever the Consequences,' in *Ethics*, J. J. Thompson and Gerald Dworkin (eds), New York, N.Y.: Harper and Row, pp. 211–36.

—— (1981), 'Morality and Consequences,' in *Tanner Lectures on Human Values*, vol. 2, S. M. McMurrin (ed.), Salt Lake City, Utah: University of Utah, pp. 47–116.

—— (1995), *The Act Itself*, Oxford: Oxford University Press.

Bentham, Jeremy (1979), *An Introduction to the Principles of Morals and Legislation. Utilitariarism,* Mary Warnock (ed.), London: Fontana, 1979 [primary text published 1789].

Bernat J. L. (1998), 'A Defense of the Whole Brain Concept of Death,' *Hastings Center Report*, **28**, 14–23.

Blázquez, Niceto (1985), 'The Churches' Traditional Moral Teaching on Suicide,' in *Suicide and the Right to Die*, Jacques Pohier and Dietmar Mieth (eds), Edinburgh: T. & T. Clark, pp. 63–74.

Bognar, Greg (2005), 'The Concept of Quality of Life,' *Social Theory and Practice*, **31**(4), 561–80.

Bok, Sissela (1998), 'Euthanasia,' in *Euthanasia and Physician-Assisted-Suicide*, Gerald Dworkin, R. G. Frey and Sissela Bok (eds), Cambridge: Cambridge University Press, pp. 107–27.

Bole, Thomas J. (1999), 'Faulting Engelhardt's Libertarianism by Default,' *Southwest Philosophy Review*, **15**, 169–76.

Boyle, Joseph M. (1977a), 'Double-Effect and a Certain Type of Embryotomy,' *Irish Theological Quarterly*, **44**, 303–18.

—— (1977b), 'On Killing and Letting Die,' *New Scholasticism*, **51**(4), 433–52.

—— (1989), 'Sanctity of life and Suicide: Tensions and Developments within Common Morality,' in *Suicide and Euthanasia: Historical and Contemporary Themes*, Baruch Brody (ed.), Dordrecht; Boston: Kluwer, 221–50.

—— (1992), 'Natural Law and the Ethics of Traditions,' in *Natural Law Theory*, Robert P. George (ed.), Oxford: Clarendon Press, pp. 3–30.

—— (1994), 'Radical Moral Disagreement in Contemporary Health Care,' *Journal of Medicine and Philosophy*, **19**, 184–200.

—— (1997), 'A Case for Sometimes Tube-Feeding Patients in PVS,' in *Euthanasia Examined: Ethical, Clinical and Legal Perspectives*, John Keown (ed.), Cambridge: Cambridge University Press, pp. 189–99.

—— (1998), 'An Absolute Rule Approach,' in *A Companion to Bioethics*, Helga Kuhse and Peter Singer (eds), Oxford; Malden, Mass.: Blackwell, pp. 72–9.

—— (2002) 'Personal Responsibility and Freedom in Health Care: A Contemporary Natural Law Perspective,' in *Persons and Their Bodies: Rights, Responsibilities, Relationships*, Mark J. Cherry (ed.), London; Dordrecht: Springer, 111–41.

—— (2004), 'Medical Ethics and Double Effect: The Case of Terminal Sedation,' *Theoretical Medicine and Bioethics*, **25**(1), 51–60.

—— and Thomas D. Sullivan (1977), 'The Diffusiveness of Intention Principle: A Counter Example,' *Philosophical Studies*, **31**, 357–60.

Bradley, Gerard V. (1998), 'No Intentional Killing Whatsoever: The Case of Capital Punishment,' in *Natural Law and Moral Inquiry*, Robert P. George (ed.), Washington, D.C.: Georgetown University Press, pp. 155–73.

Bratavia, Andrew I. (2002), 'Disability versus Futility in Rationing Health Care Services: Defining Medical Futility Based on Permanent Unconsciousness—PVS, Coma, and Anencephaly,' *Behavioral Sciences & the Law*, **20**(3), 219–33.

Braine, David (1993), *The Human Person: Animal and Spirit*, London: Duckworth.

Brandt, Richard B. (1980), 'The Rationality of Suicide,' in *Suicide: The Philosophical Issues*, Margret P. Battin and David Mayo (eds), New York, N.Y.: St. Martin's Press, pp. 117–32.

Bratman, Michael (1987), *Intention, Plans and Practical Reason*, Cambridge, Mass.: Harvard University Press.

Brock, Dan W. (1973), 'Recent Work in Utilitarianism,' *American Philosophical Quarterly*, **10**, 241–76.

——— (1984), 'The Use of Drugs for Pleasure, Some Philosophical Issues,' in *Feeling Good and Doing Better, Ethics and Nontherapeutic Drug Use*, Thomas Murray, Willard Gaylin, and Ruth Macklin (eds), Clifton, N.J.: Humana, pp. 83–106.

——— (1986), 'The Value of Prolonging Human Life,' *Philosophical Studies*, **50**, 401–28.

——— (1993), *Life and Death: Philosophical Essays in Biomedical Ethics*, New York, N.Y.: Cambridge University Press.

——— (1998), 'Medical Decisions at the End of Life,' in *A Companion to Bioethics*, Helga Kuhse and Peter Singer (eds), Oxford; Malden, Mass.: Blackwell, pp. 231–41.

——— (1999), 'A Critique of Three Objections to Physician-Assisted Suicide,' *Ethics*, **109**, 519–54.

Brock, Steven L. (1998), *Action and Conduct: Aquinas and the Theory of Action*, Edinburgh: T & T. Clark.

Brody, Howard (1992), 'A Compassionate Response to Medical Failure,' *New England Journal of Medicine*, **327**, 1384–8.

——— (1993), 'Causing, Intending and Assisting Death,' *Journal of Clinical Ethics*, **4**, 112–25.

Brown, Ron M. (2001), *The Art of Suicide*, London: Reaktion Books.

Buckle, Stephen (2005), Peter Singer's Argument for Utilitarianism,' *Theoretical Medicine and Bioethics*, **26**,(3), 175–94.

Byrne, Peter (1990), 'Homicide, Medical Ethics and the Principle of Double Effect,' in *Ethics and Law in Health Care and Research*, Peter Byrne (ed.), Chichester; New York, N.Y.: John Wiley, pp. 131–60.

Calder, Gideon (2006), Ownership Rights and the Body,' *Cambridge Quarterly of Healthcare Ethics*, **15**, 89–100.

Callahan, Joan. C. (1987), 'On Harming the Dead,' *Ethics*, **97**(2), 341–52.

Cameron, James M. (1994), 'On Death and Human Existence,' in *Language, Metaphysics, and Death*, 2nd edn, John Donnelly (ed.), New York, N.Y.: Fordham University Press, pp. 30–42.

Cameron, Nigel M. de S. (1996), 'Autonomy and the Right to Die,' in *Dignity and Dying,* John F. Kilner, Arlene B. Miller and Edmund D. Pellegrino (eds), Grand Rapids, Mich.: Eerdmans, pp. 23–33.

Campbell, Courtney S. (1992), 'Body, Self, and the Property Paradigm,' *Hastings Center Report*, **22**(5), 34–42.

———— (2001), 'A No-Brainer: Criticisms of Brain-Based Standards of Death,' *Journal of Medicine and Philosophy*, **26**(5), 539–51.

Cantor, Norman L. (2005), *Making Medical Decisions for the Profoundly Mentally Disabled*, Cambridge, Mass.: MIT Press.

Carr, Craig L. (1991), 'Duress and Criminal Responsibility,' *Law and Philosophy*, **10** (2), 161–88.

Carrick, Paul (2001), *Medical Ethics in the Ancient World*, Washington, D.C.: Georgetown University Press.

Carson, Tomas L. (1983), 'Utilitarianism and the Wrongness of Killing,' *Erkenntnis*, **20**(1), 49–60.

———— (1986), 'Hare's Defense of Utilitarianism,' *Philosophical Studies*, **51**(1), 97–115.

———— (1993), 'Hare on Utilitarianism and Intuitive Morality,' *Erkenntnis*, **39**(3), 305–31.

Cassem, E. H. (1995), 'Depressive Disorders in the Medically Ill,' *Psychosomatics*, **36**, S2–S10.

Cattorini, Paulo and Massimo Reichlin (1997), 'Persistent Vegetative State: A Presumption to Treat,' *Theoretical Medicine and Bioethics*, **18**(3), 263–81.

Cavanaugh, Thomas A. (1996), 'The Intended/Foreseen Distinction's Ethical Relevance,' *Philosophical Papers*, **25**, 179–88.

———— (1997) 'Double Effect and the Ethical Significance of Distinct Volitional States,' *Christian Bioethics*, **3**, 31–41.

———— (1998a), 'Act Evaluation, Willing and Double Effect,' *Proceedings of the American Catholic Philosophical Association*, **72**, 243–53.

———— (1998b), 'Currently Accepted Practices That Are Known to Lead to Death, and PAS: Is There an Ethically Relevant Difference?,' *Cambridge Quarterly of Healthcare Ethics*, **4**, 375–81.

———— (1999), 'Double Effect and the End-not-means Principle: A Response to Bennett,' *Journal of Applied Philosophy*, **16**, 181–5.

———— (2006), *Double-Effect Reasoning: Doing Good and Avoiding Evil*, Oxford: Clarendon Press.

Celesia, Galstone G. (1997), 'Persistent Vegetative State: Clinical and Ethical Issues,' *Theoretical Medicine and Bioethics*, **18**(3), 221–36.

Chang, Ruth (1997), 'Introduction,' in *Incommensurability, Incomparability and Practical Reason*, R. Chang (ed.), Cambridge, Mass.: Harvard University Press, pp. 1–38.

Chappell, Timothy D. J. (1997a), 'In Defence of Speciesism,' in *Human Lives: Critical Essays on Consequentialist Bioethics*, David S. Oderberg and Jacqueline A. Laing (eds), New York, N.Y.: St. Martin's Press, pp. 96–108.

———— (1997b), 'Reductionism about Persons,' *Proceedings of the Aristotelian Society*, **97**, 41–57.

—— (1998), *Understanding Human Goods: A Theory of Ethics*, Edinburgh: Edinburgh University Press.

—— (1999), 'Ethics in an Age of Self-Interest: Critical Notice of Peter Singer, "How Should One Live?"', *New Blackfriars*, January, 530–36.

—— (2001a), 'The Implications of Incommensurability,' *Philosophy*, **76**, 137–48.

—— (2001b), 'Option Ranges,' *Journal of Applied Philosophy*, **18**(2), 107–18.

—— (2002), 'Two Distinctions that do make a Difference: The Action/Omission Distinction and the Principle of Double Effect,' *Philosophy*, **22**, 211–33.

—— (2003), 'Practical Rationality for Pluralists about the Good,' *Ethical Theory and Moral Practice*, **6**(2), 161–77.

—— (2004), 'The Polymorphy of Practical Reason,' in *Human Values: New Essays on Ethics and Natural Law*, David S. Oderberg and T. D. J. Chappell (eds), London: Palgrave Macmillan, pp. 102–26.

Charlesworth, Max. *Bioethics in a Liberal Society*. Cambridge: Cambridge University Press, 1993.

Chisholm, Roderick (1970), 'The Structure of Intention,' *Journal of Philosophy*, **67**, 636–52.

Cohen, Cynthia B. (2004), 'Philosophical Challenges to the Use of Advance Directives,' in *Handbook of Bioethics: Taking Stock of the Field from a Philosophical Perspective*, George Khushf (ed.), London; Dordrecht: Springer, pp. 291–314.

Cohn, Felicia and Joanne Lynn (2002), 'Vulnerable People: Practical Rejoiners to Claims in Favor of Assisted Suicide,' in *The Case against Assisted Suicide: For the Right to End-of-Life Care*, Kathleen M. Foley and Herbert Hendin (eds), Baltimore, Md.: Johns Hopkins University Press, pp. 238–60.

Cranor, C. F. (1983), 'On Respecting Human Beings as Persons,' *Journal of Value Inquiry*, **17**, 103–17.

Clark, Michael (2000), 'Self-Defence Against the Innocent,' *Journal of Applied Philosophy*, **17**(2), 145–55.

Costa, Michael J. (1986), 'The Trolley Problem Revisited,' *Southern Journal of Philosophy*, **24**, 437–49.

—— (1987), 'Another Trip on the Trolley,' *Southern Journal of Philosophy*, **25**, 461–66.

Coughlan, Michael J. (1990), 'Using People,' *Bioethics*, **4**, 55–61.

Crimmins, James E. (1990), *Secular Utilitarianism: Social Science and the Critique of Religion in the Thought of Jeremy Bentham*, Oxford: Clarendon Press.

Crisp, Rodger (1996), 'Naturalism and Non-Naturalism in Ethics,' in S. Lovibond and S. G. Williams (eds), *Identity, Truth and Value*, Oxford; Malden, Mass.: Blackwell, pp. 113–29.

Crofts, Richard A. (1973), 'The Common Good in the Political Theory of Thomas Aquinas,' *Thomist*, **37**, 155–73.

Crowe, Michael B. (1977), *The Changing Profile of the Natural Law*, The Hague: Nijhoff.

Culver, Charles M. and Gert, Bernard (1982), *Philosophy in Medicine*, New York, N.Y.: Oxford University Press.

Dancy, Jonathan (1993), 'An Ethic of Prima Facie Duties,' in *A Companion to Ethics*, Peter Singer (ed.), Oxford: Blackwell, pp. 219–29.

D'Arcy, Eric (1963), *Human Acts: An Essay in their Moral Evaluation*, Oxford: Clarendon Press.

Darwell, Stephen, (1977), 'Two Kinds of Respect,' *Ethics*, **88**, 36–49.

Daube, David (1972), 'The Linguistics of Suicide,' *Philosophy and Public Affairs*, **1**, 387–437.

Davis, Nancy A. (1991), 'Contemporary Deontology,' in *A Companion to Ethics*, Peter Singer (ed.), Oxford: Blackwell, pp. 205–18.

DeGrazia, David (2004), 'Biology, Consciousness, and the Definition of Death,' in *Death and Dying: A Reader*, Thomas A. Shannon (ed.), Lanham, Md.: Rowman & Littlefield, pp. 1–8.

Denyer, Nicholas (1997), 'Is Anything Absolutely Wrong?' in *Human Lives: Critical Essays on Consequentialist Bioethics*, David S. Oderberg and Jacqueline A. Laing (eds), New York, N.Y.: St. Martin's Press,1997, pp. 39–57.

Destro, Robert A. (1986), Quality-of-life Ethics and Constitutional Jurisprudence: The Demise of Natural Rights and Equal Protection for the Disabled and Incompetent,' *Journal of Contemporary Health Law and Policy*, **2**, 71–130.

Devine, Philip E. (1974), The Principle of Double Effect,' *American Journal of Jurisprudence*, **19**, 44–60.

———— (1978), *The Ethics of Homicide,* Ithaca, N.Y.; London: Cornell University Press.

———— (1998), 'Homicide, Criminal Versus Justifiable,' in *Encyclopedia of Applied ethics,* vol. 2, Ruth F. Chadwick (ed.), San Diego, Calif.: Academic, pp. 587–95.

———— (2000a), 'Capital Punishment and the Sanctity of Life,' *Midwest Studies in Philosophy*, **XXIV**, 228–42.

———— (2000b), *Natural Law Ethics*. Westport, Conn.: Greenwood Press, 2000.

Dinello, Daniel (1971), 'On Killing and Letting Die,' *Analysis*, **31**, 84–6.

Dolan, John M. (1999), 'Judging Someone Better Off Dead,' *Logos*, **2**, 48–67.

Donagan, Alan (1969), 'The Scholastic Theory of Moral Law in the Modern World,' in *Aquinas: A Collection of Critical Essays*, Anthony J. P. Kenny (ed.), London: Macmillan, pp. 325–39.

Donnelly, John (1978), 'Suicide and Rationality' in *Language, Metaphysics, and Death*, John Donnelly (ed.), New York, N.Y.: Fordham University Press, pp. 87–105.

———— (1977), *The Theory of Morality*, Chicago: University of Chicago Press.

Donohue-White, Patricia and Kateryna F. Cuddeback (2002), 'The Good of Health: An Argument for an Objectivist Understanding,' in *Person, Society and Value: Towards a Personalist Concept of Health*, Paulina Taboada, Kateryna F. Cuddeback and Patricia Donohue-White (eds), London; Dordrecht: Springer, pp. 165–96.

Doukas, D. J. and D. W. Gorenflo (1993), 'Analyzing the Values History: An Evaluation of Patient Medical Values and Advance Directives,' *Journal of Clinical Ethics*, **4**(1), 16–20.

Driver, Julia (1992), 'The Suberogatory,' *Australasian Journal of Philosophy*, **70**(3), 286–95.

Dubois, James M. (2002), 'Is Organ Procurement Causing the Death of Patients,' *Issues in Law and Medicine*, **8**(1), 21–41.

Duff, R. A. (1973), 'Intentionally Killing the Innocent,' *Analysis*, **34**(1), 16–19.

——— (1983), 'Socratic Suicide,' *Proceedings of the Aristotelian Society*, **83**, 48–56.

Dupré, Louis (1988), 'A Thomistic Argument Against the Ban on Contraception,' in *St. Thomas Aquinas on Politics and Ethics*, Paul E. Sigismund (ed.), New York, N.Y.: W. W. Norton, pp. 241–4.

Durkheim, Émile (1951), *Suicide*, trans. J. A. Spaulding and G. Simpson, Glencoe, Ill.: Free Press.

Dworkin, Gerald (1972), 'Paternalism,' *Monist*, **56**, 64–84.

——— (2005) 'Moral Paternalism,' *Law and Philosophy*, **24**(3), 305–19.

———, (ed.) (1997), *Mill's On Liberty: Critical Essays*. Lanham, Md.: Rowman & Littlefield.

Dworkin, Ronald (1977), *Taking Rights Seriously*, Cambridge, Mass.: Harvard University Press.

——— (1985), *A Matter of Principle*. Cambridge, Mass.: Harvard University Press.

——— (1990), 'Foundations of Liberal Equality,' in *The Tanner Lectures on Human Values*, vol. 11, Grethe B. Peterson (ed.), Salt Lake City, Utah: University of Utah, pp. 1–119.

——— (1993), *Life's Dominion: An Argument about Abortion and Euthanasia*, London: Harper Collins; New York, N.Y.: Alfred Knopf.

——— (1996), *Freedom's Law: The Moral Reading of the American Constitution*, Cambridge, Mass.: Harvard University Press.

——— *et al.* (1997) 'Assisted Suicide: The Philosophers' Brief,' *New York Review of Books* (27 March), 41–7.

Eberl, Jason T. (2005), 'A Thomistic Understanding of Human Death,' *Bioethics*, **19**(1), 29–48.

Ellis, Anthony (1992), 'Deontology, Incommensurability and the Arbitrary,' *Philosophy and Phenomenological Research*, **52**(4), 855–75.

Elster, Jon (1982), 'Sour Grapes: Utilitarianism and the Genesis of Wants,' in *Utilitarianism and Beyond*, A. Sen and B. Williams (eds), Cambridge: Cambridge University Press, pp. 219–38.

Emanuel L. L. and E. J. Emanuel (1989), 'The Medical Directive. A New Comprehensive Advance Care Document,' *Journal of the American Medical Association*, **261**, 3288–93.

Engelhardt, Jr., H. Tristram (1986), *The Foundations of Bioethics*, New York, N.Y.: Oxford University Press.

——— (1996), *The Foundations of Bioethics*, 2nd edn, New York, N.Y.: Oxford University Press.

——— (1997), 'The Foundations of Bioethics: Liberty and Life with Moral Diversity,' *Reason Papers*, **22**, 101–8.

Erde, Edmund L. (2001), 'Personhood: The Vain and Pointless Quest,' in *Personhood and Health Care*, David C. Thomasma, Christian Hervé and David N. Weisstub (eds), London; Dordrecht: Springer, pp. 71–90.

Evans. David W. (1988), 'The Demise of "Brain Death" in Britain,' in *Beyond Brain Death: The Case Against Brain Based Criteria for Human Death*, Paul A. Byrne,

Richard G. Nilges and Michael Potts (eds), London; Dordrecht: Kluwer, pp. 139–58.

Fehige, Christoph and Ulla Wessels (1998), 'Preferences: An Introduction,' in *Preferences*, C. Fehige and Ulla Wessels (eds), Berlin; New York, N.Y.: Walter de Gruyter, pp. xx–xliii.

Feinberg, Joel (1978), 'Voluntary Euthanasia and the Inalienable Right to Life,' *Philosophy and Public Affairs*, **7**(2), 93–123.

——— (1986), *Harm to Self*, New York, N.Y.: Oxford University Press.

——— (1989), 'Autonomy,' in *The Inner Citadel: Essays on Individual Autonomy*, John Christman (ed.) New York, N.Y.: Oxford University Press, pp. 27–53.

——— (1992), *Freedom and Fulfillment: Philosophical Essays*, Princeton, N.J.: Princeton University Press.

Feldman, Fred (1991) 'Some Puzzles about the Evil of Death,' *Philosophical Review*, **100**(2), 205–27.

——— (1995), 'Adjusting Utility for Justice: A Consequentialist Reply to the Objection from Justice,' *Philosophy and Phenomenological Research*, **55**(3), 567–85.

Fenigsen, R. (2004), 'Dutch Euthanasia: The New Government Ordered Study,' *Issues in Law and Medicine*, **20**(1), 73–9.

Finnis, John M. (1980), *Natural Law and Natural Rights*, Oxford: Clarendon Press, 1980.

——— (1983), *Fundamentals of Ethics*, Washington, D.C.: Georgetown University Press.

——— (1987a), 'The Act of the Person,' in *Persona Verità, e Morale: Atti del Congresso Internazionale di Teologia Morale*, Aurelio Ansaldo (ed.), Roma: Città Nuova Editrice, pp. 159–75.

——— (1987b), 'Legal Enforcement of "Duties to Oneself": Kant v. the Neo–Kantians,' *Columbia Law Review*, **87**, 433–56.

——— (1991a), *Moral Absolutes: Tradition, Revision, and Truth*, Washington, D.C.: Catholic University of America Press.

——— (1991b), 'Intention and Side-Effects,' in *Liability and Responsibility: Essays in Law and Morals*, R. G. Frey and Christopher W. Morris (eds), Cambridge: Cambridge University Press, pp. 32–64.

——— (1993), 'Bland: Crossing the Rubicon?,' *Law Quarterly Review*, **109**, 329–37.

——— (1994), 'Law, Morality, and "Sexual Orientation",' *Notre Dame Law Review*, **69**, 1049–76.

——— (1995), 'Intention in Tort Law,' in *Philosophical Foundations of Tort Law*, David Owen (ed.), Oxford: Oxford University Press, pp. 229–48.

——— (1997), 'The Good of Marriage and the Morality of Sexual Relations: Some Philosophical and Historical Observations,' American Journal of Jurisprudence, **42**, 97–134.

——— (1998), *Aquinas: Moral, Political, and Legal Theory*, Oxford: Oxford University Press.

——— (2000), 'Abortion, Natural Law, and Public Reason,' in *Natural Law and Public Reason*, George and Wolfe (eds), Washington, D.C.: Georgetown University Press, pp. 75–105.

Foley, Kathleen M., and Herbert Hendin (eds) (2002), *The Case against Assisted Suicide: For the Right to End-of-Life Care*, Baltimore, Md.: Johns Hopkins University Press.

Foot, Philippa (1978), 'The Problem of Abortion and the Doctrine of Double Effect,' in her *Virtues and Vices and Other Essays in Moral Philosophy,* Berkeley, Calif.: University of California Press, pp. 19–32 [originally in *Oxford Review*, **5**, 1967, 5–15]; Also her 'Euthanasia,' pp. 33–61.

———— (1984), 'Killing and Letting Die,' in *Abortion: Moral and Legal Perspectives*, Joy L. Garfield and Patricia Hennessy (eds), Amherst, Mass: University of Massachusetts Press, pp.177–85.

Ford, Norman M. (2002), *The Prenatal Person: Ethics from Conception to Birth*, Oxford: Blackwell.

Frey, R. G. (1975), Some Aspects of the Doctrine of Double Effect,' *Canadian Journal of Philosophy*, **5**, 259–83.

———— (1978), 'Did Socrates Commit Suicide?,' *Philosophy*, **53**, 106–8.

———— (1998), 'The Fear of a Slippery Slope,' in *Euthanasia and Physician-Assisted-Suicide*, Gerald Dworkin, R. G. Frey and Sissela Bok, Cambridge: Cambridge University Press, pp. 43–63.

———— (1999), 'Hume on Suicide,' *Journal of Medicine and Philosophy*, **24**, 336–51.

Fried, Charles (1978), *Right and Wrong*, Cambridge, Mass.: Harvard University Press.

Friedman, Roger F. (1995), 'It's My Body and I'll Die If I Want To: A Property-Based Argument in Support of Assisted Suicide,' *Journal of Contemporary Health Law and Policy*, **12**, 183–213.

Furrow, Barry L. *et al.* (2000), *Health Law*, St. Paul, Minn.: West Group.

Galston, William A. (1983), 'On the Alleged Right to Do Wrong: A Response to Waldron,' *Ethics*, **93**(2), 320–24.

———— (1991), *Liberal Purposes*: *Goods, Virtues, and Diversity in the Liberal State*, Cambridge: Cambridge University Press.

———— (1995), 'Two Concepts of Liberalism,' *Ethics*, **105**, 516–34.

Garcia, J. L. A. (1990), 'The Intentional and the Intended,' *Erkenninis*, **33**, 191–209.

———— (1991), 'On the Irreducibility of the Will,' *Synthese*, **86**, 349–60.

———— (1993), 'Better Off Dead?,' *APA Newsletter on Philosophy and Medicine*, **92**(1), 85–88.

———— (1995a), 'Intention-Sensitive Ethics,' *Public Affairs Quarterly*, **9**(3), 201–13.

———— (1995b), 'Intentions and Wrongdoings,' *American Catholic Philosophic Quarterly*, **69**, 605–17.

———— (1997), 'Intentions in Medical Ethics,' in *Human Lives: Critical Essays on Consequentialist Bioethics*, David S. Oderberg and Jacqueline A. Laing (eds), New York, N.Y.: St. Martin's Press, pp. 161–81.

———— (1999), 'Are Some People Better Off Dead? A Reflection,' *Logos*, **2**, 68–81.

—— (2007), 'Health Versus Harm: Euthanasia and Physicians' Duties,' *Journal of Medicine and Philosophy*, **32**(1), 7–24.

Gay, Robert (1985), 'Ethical Pluralism: A Reply to Dancy,' *Mind*, **94**, 250–62.

Geach, Peter (1977), *The Virtues*, Cambridge: Cambridge University Press.

Geddes, Leonard (1973), 'On the Intrinsic Wrongness of Killing Innocent People,' *Analysis*, **33**(3), 93–7.

Geisler, Norman L., and J. P. Moreland (1990), *The Life and Death Debate: Moral Issues of our Time*, New York, N.Y.: Greenwood Press.

George, Robert P. (1989), 'Moral Particularism, Thomism, and Traditions,' *Review of Metaphysics*, **42**, 593–605.

—— (1990), 'Moralistic Liberalism and Legal Moralism,' *Michigan Law Review*, **88**, 1415–29.

—— (1993), *Making Men Moral: Civil Liberties and Public Morality*, Oxford: Clarendon Press.

—— (1999), *In Defense of Natural Law*, Oxford: Clarendon Press.

—— (2001), *The Clash of Orthodoxies*, Wilmington, Del.: ISI Books.

—— and Christopher Wolfe (2000), 'Natural Law and Public Reason,' in *Natural Law and Public Reason*, George and Wolfe (eds), Washington, D.C.: Georgetown University Press, pp. 51–74.

Gert, Bernard, Charles Culver, and K. Danner Clouser (1997), *Bioethics: A Return to Fundamentals*, New York, N.Y.: Oxford University Press.

Gewirth, Alan (1978), *Reason and Morality*, Chicago, Ill.: University of Chicago Press.

Gigli, G. L. (2002), 'Persistent Vegetative State: Let's not Blow out the Candle,' *Neurological Sciences*, **23**(5), 251–4.

Glenn, Gary D. (1984), 'Inalienable Rights and Locke's Argument for Limited Government: Political Implications of a Right to Suicide,' *The Journal of Politics*, **46**(1), 80–105.

Glover, Jonathan (1977), *Causing Death and Saving Lives*, Harmondsworth: Penguin.

Gómez-Lobo, Alfonso (1985), 'Natural Law and Naturalism,' *Proceedings of the American Catholic Philosophical Association*, **59**, 232–49.

—— (1989), 'The Ergon Inference,' *Phronesis*, **34**, 170–84.

—— (2002), *Morality and the Human Goods*, Washington, D.C.; Georgetown University Press.

Gordijn, Bert (1999), 'The Troublesome Concept of the Person,' *Theoretical Medicine and Bioethics*, 347–59.

Gormally, Luke (1992), The Aged: Non-Persons, Human Dignity and Justice,' in *The Dependent Elderly: Autonomy, Justice, and Quality of Care*, Luke Gormally (ed.), New York, N.Y.: Cambridge University Press, pp. 181–8.

—— (ed.) (1994), *Moral Truth and Moral Tradition: Essays in Honour of Peter Geach and Elizabeth Anscombe*, Dublin: Four Courts Press.

Gorsuch, Neil M. (2006), *The Future of Assisted Suicide and Euthanasia*, Princeton, N.J.: Princeton University Press.

Green, Michael B. and Daniel Wikler (1980), 'Brain Death and Personal Identity,' *Philosophy and Public Affairs*, **9**(2), 105–33.

Grisez, Germain G. (1970), 'Toward a Consistent Ethic of Killing,' *American Journal of Jurisprudence*, **15**, (1970), 64–96.

―――― (1978), 'Against Consequentialism,' *American Journal of Jurisprudence*, **23**, 21–72.

―――― and Joseph Boyle (1979), *Life and Death with Liberty and Justice: A Contribution to the Euthanasia Debate*, Notre Dame, Ind.: University of Notre Dame Press.

―――― (1993), *Living a Christian Life*, Quincy, Ill.: Franciscan Press.

Grover, Dorothy (1989), 'Posthumous Harm,' *Philosophical Quarterly*, **39**, 334–53.

Guevin, Benedict (2001), 'The Conjoined Twins of Malta: Direct or Indirect Killing?,' *The National Catholic Bioethics Quarterly*, **1**(3), 397–405.

Haldane, John (1996), 'The Individual, the State, and the Common Good,' *Social Philosophy and Policy*, **13**, 59–79.

Hampton, Jean (1989), Should Political Philosophy Be Done Without Metaphysics?,' *Ethics*, **99** (4), 791–815.

Hanink, James G. (1975), 'Some Light on Double Effect,' *Analysis*, **35**, 147–51.

Harcourt, Edward (1998), 'Integrity, Practical Deliberation and Utilitarianism,' *The Philosophical Quarterly*, **48**, 189–98.

Hardie, W. F. (1971), 'Willing and Acting,' *The Philosophical Quarterly*, **21**, 193–206.

Harris, John (1985), *Value of Life*, London: Routledge & Kegan Paul.

―――― (1997), 'Euthanasia and the Value of Life,' in *Euthanasia Examined: Ethical, Clinical and Legal Perspectives*, John Keown (ed.), Cambridge: Cambridge University Press, pp. 6–22.

―――― (2001), 'The Concept of the Person and the Value of Life,' in *Personhood and Health Care*, David C. Thomasma, Christian Hervé and David N. Weisstub (eds), London; Dordrecht: Springer, pp. 99–114.

Harrison, Ross (1983), *Bentham*, London: Routledge.

Harsanyi, John .C. (1988), 'Problems with Act-Utilitarianism and with Malevolent Preferences,' in *Hare and Critics: Essays on Moral Thinking*, D. Seanor and N. Fotion (eds), Oxford: Oxford University Press, pp. 89–99.

Häyry, Matti (1991), 'Measuring the Quality of Life: Why, How and What?,' *Theoretical Medicine*, **2**, 97–116.

―――― (1994), *Liberal Utilitarianism and Applied Ethics*, London: Routledge.

Hick, John (1994), *Death and Eternal Life*, Westminster, Md.: John Knox Press.

Hicks, D. C. (1971), 'Respect for Persons and Respect for Living Things,' *Philosophy*, **46**, 346–48.

Hittinger, Russell (1987), *A Critique of the New Natural Law Theory*, Notre Dame, Ind.: University of Notre Dame Press, 1987.

―――― (1993), 'Does Liberalism Need Natural Rights?,' *Reason Papers*, **18**, 79–88.

―――― (1994), 'Political Liberalism' *Review of Metaphysics*, **3**, 585–602.

Hodgson, D. W. (1967), *Consequences of Utilitarianism*, Oxford: Oxford University Press.

Holm, Søren (1998), 'Secular Morality and its Limits,' *Medicine, Healthcare and Philosophy*, **1**(1), 75–7.

Holtug, Nils (2002), 'The Harm Principle,' *Ethical Theory and Moral Practice*, **5**(4), 357–89.

Honnefelder, Ludger (1996), 'The Concept of a Person in Moral Philosophy,' in *Sanctity of Life and Human Dignity*, Kurt Bayertz (ed.), London; Dordrecht: Kluwer, pp. 139–60.

Hooff, Anton J. L. Van (1990), *From Autothanasia to Suicide: Self-Killing in Classical Antiquity,* London; New York, N.Y.: Routledge.

Horgan, Terence, and Mark Timmons, (1990–91), 'New Wave Moral Realism Meets Moral Twin Earth,' *Journal of Philosophical Research*, **16**, 447–65.

Hospers, John (1980), 'Libertarianism and Legal Paternalism,' *Journal of Libertarian Studies*, **4**(3), 255–65.

Houlgate, Laurence D. (ed.) (1999), *Morals, Marriage, and Parenthood: An Introduction to Family Ethics*, Belmont, Calif.: Wadsworth.

——— (1992), 'Troubles for New Wave Moral Semantics: The Open Question Argument Revived,' *Philosophical Papers*, **21**, 153–75.

Hume, David (1998), *Dialogues Concerning Natural Religion: The Posthumous Essays of the Immortality of the Soul and of Suicide*, 2nd edn, Indianapolis, Ind.: Hackett [originally published 1783].

——— (2000), *A Treatise of Human Nature*, new edn, David Fate Norton and Mary J. Norton (eds), Oxford: Oxford University Press [originally published 1739].

Igneski, Violetta (2006), 'Perfect and Imperfect Duties to Aid,' *Social Theory and Practice*, **32**(3), 439–66.

Jennett, Bryan (1997), 'Letting Vegetative Patients Die,' in *Euthanasia Examined: Ethical, Clinical and Legal Perspectives*, John Keown (ed.), Cambridge: Cambridge University Press, pp. 169–88

Johnstone, Brian V. (1985), 'The Sanctity of Life, The Quality of Life,' *Linacre Quarterly*, **53**, 58–70.

Jones, David Albert (2000), Metaphysical Misgivings about "Brain Death",' in *Beyond Brain Death: The Case Against Brain Based Criteria for Human Death*, Paul A. Byrne, Richard G. Nilges, and Michael Potts (eds), London; Dordrecht: Kluwer, pp. 91–120.

Jones, Karen (2005), 'Moral Epistemology,' in *The Oxford Handbook of Contemporary Philosophy*, Frank Jackson and Michael Smith (eds), Oxford: Oxford University Press, pp. 63–85.

Jordan, Jeff (1990), 'The Doctrine of Double Effect and Affirmative Action,' *Journal of Applied Philosophy*, **7**, 213–16.

Kaczor, Christopher R. (2005), *The Edge of Life: Human Dignity and Contemporary Bioethics*, London; Dordrecht: Springer.

Kamisar, Yale (1997), 'Physician-Assisted Suicide: The Last Bridge to Active Voluntary Euthanasia' in *Euthanasia Examined: Ethical, Clinical and Legal Perspectives*, John Keown (ed.), Cambridge: Cambridge University Press, pp. 225–60.

Kamm, Frances Myrna (1993), *Morality, Mortality: Volume 1: Death & Whom to Save from It*, Oxford: Oxford University Press.

Karel, M. J. (2000), 'The Assessment of Values in Medical Decision Making,' *Journal of Aging Studies*, **14**(4), 403–22.

Kass, Leon (2002), *Life, Liberty, and the Defense of Dignity: The Challenge for Bioethics*, San Francisco, Calf.: Encounter Books.

Kaveny, M. Cathleen (1997), 'The Limits of Ordinary Virtue,' in *Choosing Life*, Kevin Wm. Wildes and Alan C. Mitchell (eds), Washington, D.C.: Georgetown University Press, pp. 132–49.

Kay, Richard S. (2006), 'Causing Death for Compassionate Reasons in American Law,' *American Journal of Comparative Law*, **54**, 693–716.

Keown, John, (2002), *Euthanasia, Ethics, and Public Policy: An Argument against Legalisation*, Cambridge: Cambridge University Press.

———— (2005), 'A Futile Defence of Bland,' *Medical Law Review*, **13**, 393–402.

Kegan, Shelly (1991), *The Limits of Morality*, New York, N.Y.: Oxford University Press.

Kenny, Anthony J. P. Kenny (1973), 'The History of Intention in Ethics,' in his *Anatomy of the Soul: Historical Essays in the Philosophy of Mind*, Oxford: Blackwell, 1973, pp. 129–47.

———— (2001), *Essays on the Aristotelian Tradition*, Oxford: Oxford University Press.

Klimchuk, D. (2004), 'Three Accounts of Respect for Persons in Kant's Ethics,' *Kantian Review*, **8**, 38–61.

Kluge, E. W. (1975), *The Practice of Death*, New Haven, Conn.: Yale University Press.

Koch. T. (2005), 'The Challenge of Terri Schiavo: Lessons for Bioethics,' *Journal of Medical Ethics*, **31**, 376–8.

Kohl, Marvin (1974), *The Morality of Killing*, New York, N.Y.: Humanities Press.

Koogler, T. K., B. S. Wilfond, and L. F. Ross (2003), 'Lethal Language, Lethal Decisions,' *Hastings Center Report*, **33**(2), 37–41.

Koppelman, Elysa R. (2002), 'Dementia and Dignity: Towards a New Method of Surrogate Decision Making,' *Journal of Medicine and Philosophy*, **27**(1), 65–85.

Kristol, Irving (1994), 'Pornography, Obscenity, and the Case for Censorship,' in *Morality, Harm and the Law*, Gerald Dworkin (ed.), Boulder, Colo.: Westview Press, pp. 46–9. [Reprint of a 1971 New York Times article.]

Kuflik, Arthur (1984), 'The Inalienability of Autonomy,' *Philosophy and Public Affairs*, **13**(4), 271–98.

Kukathas, Chandran (ed.) (2003), *John Rawls: Critical Assessments of Leading Political Philosophers*, London: Routledge.

Kuhse, Helga (1987), *The Sanctity-of-Life Doctrine in Medicine: A Critique*, Oxford: Clarendon Press.

———— (1998), 'Why Killing Is Not Always Worse—and is Sometimes Better—Than Letting Die,' *Cambridge Quarterly of Healthcare Ethics*, **7**, 371–4.

———— and Peter Singer (1985), *Should the Baby Live? The Problem of Handicapped Infants*. Oxford: Oxford University Press.

Kupfer, Joseph (1990), 'Suicide: Its Nature and Moral Evaluation,' *The Journal of Value Inquiry*, **24**, 67–81.

Laing, Jacqueline A. (2004), 'Law, Liberalism, and the Common Good' in *Human Values: New Essays on Ethics and Natural Law*, David S. Oderberg and T. D. J. Chappell (eds), London: Palgrave Macmillan, pp. 184–216.

Lamb, David (1985), *Death, Brain Death, and Ethics*, Albany, N.Y.: State University of New York Press.

——— (1988), *Down the Slippery Slope: Arguing in Applied Ethics*, London: Croom Helm.

Lanfear, Ray (1986), Moral Autonomy and Reason, *Journal of Value Inquiry*, **20**(3), 183–93.

Larson, Edward J., and Darrel W. Amundsen (1998), *A Different Death: Euthanasia and Christian Tradition*, Downers Grove, Ill: InterVarsity Press.

Lee, Patrick (1997), 'Is Thomas's Natural Law Theory Naturalist?,' *American Catholic Philosophical Quarterly*, **71**(4), 567–87.

——— (1998), 'Human Beings Are Animals,' in Natural Law and Moral Inquiry, Robert P. George (ed.), Washington, D.C.: Georgetown University Press, pp. 135–51.

Levine, Susan (1984), 'The Moral Permissibility of Killing a "Material Aggressor" in Self-Defense,' *Philosophical Studies*, **45**, pp. 69–78.

Li, Jack (2002), *Can Death be a Harm to the Person Who Dies?*, London; Dordrecht: Kluwer.

Lichtenberg, Judith (1982), 'The Moral Equivalence of Action and Omission,' *Canadian Journal of Philosophy*, **8**, 19–36.

Linehan, Elizabeth A. (1984), 'The Duty Not to Kill Oneself,' *Proceedings of the American Catholic Philosophical Association*, **58**, 104–11.

Lisska, Anthony J. (1996), *Aquinas's Theory of Natural Law: An Analytical Reconstruction*, Oxford: Clarendon Press.

Locke, Don (1982), 'The Choice Between Lives,' *Philosophy*, **57**, 453–75.

Locke, Kohn (1961), *Essay Concerning Human Understanding*, London: Dent.

Lombardi, Louis G. (1983), 'Inherent Worth, Respect, and Rights,' *Environmental Ethics*, **5**, 257–70.

Loewy, Erich H., and Roberta Loewy (2004), *Textbook of Healthcare Ethics*, London; Dordrecht: Kluwer.

Lynch, Tony and David Wells (1998), 'Non-Anthropocentrism? A Killing Objection,' *Environmental Values*, **7**(2), 151–64.

Lustig, Andrew B. (2001), 'Theoretical and Clinical Concerns About Brain Death: The Debate Continues,' *Journal of Medicine and Philosophy*, **26**(5), 447–55.

MacIntyre, Alison (2001), 'Doing Away with Double Effect,' *Ethics*, **111**(2), 219–55.

MacIntyre, Alistair (1981), *After Virtue*, London: Duckworth.

Mack, Mary P. (1963), *Jeremy Bentham: An Odyssey of Ideas*, New York, N.Y.: Columbia University Press.

Mackie, J. L. (1977), *Ethics: Inventing Right and Wrong*, Harmondsworth: Penguin.

——— (1978), 'Can There Be a Right-based Moral Theory?' *Midwest Studies in Philosophy*, **3**, 350–59.

MacLean, Anne (1993), *The Elimination of Morality: Reflections on Utilitarianism and Bioethics*, London: Routledge.

Mappes, Thomas A. (2003), 'Persistent Vegetative State, Prospective Thinking, and Advance Directives,' *Kennedy Institute of Ethics Journal*, **13**(2), 119–39.

Mareiniss, Darren P. (2005), 'A Comparison of Cruzan and Schiavo: The Burden of Proof, Due Process, and Autonomy in the Persistently Vegetative Patient,' *Journal of Legal Medicine*, **26**(2), 23–59.

Margolis, James (1975), *Negativities: The Limits of Life*, Columbus, Ohio: Charles Merrill.

Maritain, Jacques (1951), *Man and the State*, Chicago, Ill.: University of Chicago Press.

Martin, Robert (1980), 'Suicide and Self-Sacrifice,' in *Suicide: The Philosophical Issues*, Margaret P. Battin and David J. Mayo (eds), New York: St. Martin's Press, pp. 48–68.

Mason, J. K., Alexander McCall Smith, and G. T. Laurie (2005), *Mason & McCall Smith's Law and Medical Ethics*, Oxford; Oxford University Press.

May, William E. (1989), *Moral Absolutes: Catholic Tradition, Current Trends, and the Truth*, Milwaukee, Wis.: Marquette University Press.

———— *et al.* (1987), 'Feeding and Hydrating the Permanently Unconscious and Other Vulnerable Persons,' *Issues in Law and Medicine*, **3**, 203–17.

———— *et al.* (1997), 'Caring for Persons in the Persistent Vegetative State,' *Anthropotes: Rivista di Studi sulla persona e la famiglia*, **13**, 317–31.

McCabe, David (2000), 'Knowing about the Good: A Problem with Antiperfectionism,' *Ethics*, **110**, 311–38.

McConnell, Terrance (1984), 'The Nature and Basis of Inalienable Rights,' *Law and Philosophy*, **3**(1), 25–59.

McInerny, Ralph (1992), *Aquinas on Human Action*, Washington, D.C.: Catholic University of America Press.

———— (1997), *Ethica Thomistica: The Moral Philosophy of Thomas Aquinas*, Rev. edn, Washington, D.C.: Catholic University of America.

McMahan, Jeff (1995), 'The Metaphysics of Brain Death,' *Bioethics*, **9**(2), 91–126.

Megone, Christopher (1990), 'The Quality of Life: Starting from Aristotle,' in *Quality of Life: Perspectives and Policies*, S. Baldwin, C. Godfrey ,and C. Propper (eds), London , Routledge, pp. 28–39.

Mellema, Gregory (1991), *Beyond the Call of Duty: Supererogation, Obligation, and Offence*, Albany, N.Y.: State University of New York.

Merrill, Kenneth R. (1999), 'Hume on Suicide,' *History of Philosophy Quarterly*, **16**, 395–412.

Metz, Thaddeus (2001), 'The Concept of a Meaningful Life,' *American Philosophical Quarterly*, **38**(2), 137–53.

———— (2002), 'Recent Work on the Meaning of Life,' *Ethics*, **112**(4), 781–814.

Midgley, Mary (1985), 'Persons and Non-persons,' in *In Defense of Animals*, Peter Singer (ed.), Oxford: Blackwell, pp. 52–62.

———— (2003), 'Is a Dolphin a Person?,' in *The Animal Ethics Reader*, Susan Armstrong and Richard Botzler (eds), London: Routledge, pp. 166–74.

Mill, John Stuart (1962), *Utilitarianism. On Liberty*, Mary Warnock (ed.), London: Fontana.

Miller, Alexander (2003) *An Introduction to Contemporary Metaethics*, Cambridge; Malden, Mass.: Polity Press.

Miller, Arthur R. (1987), 'Acts and Consequences: Squeezing the Accordion,' *Metaphilosophy*, **18**, 200–207.

Miller, R. G. (1992) 'Hospice Care as an Alternative to Euthanasia,' *Law Medicine and Health Care*, **20**, 127–32.

Minogue, Brendan, Gabriel Palmer-Fernandez, and James E. Reagan (eds) (1997), *Reading Engelhardt: Essays on the Thought of H. Tristram Engelhardt, Jr*, Dordrecht; Boston: Kluwer Academic.

Momeyer, Richard W. (1983) 'Medical Decisions Concerning Noncompetent Patients,' *Journal Theoretical Medicine and Bioethics*, **4**(3), 275–90.

Moskop, J. C. (1997), 'Persons, Property or Both? Engelhardt on the Moral Status of Young Children,' in *Engelhardt: Essays on the Thought of H. Tristram Engelhardt, Jr*, Brendan Minogue, Gabriel Palmer-Fernandez and James E. Reagan (eds), Dordrecht; Boston: Kluwer Academic, pp. 163–74.

Moore, George Edward (2002), *Principia Ethica*, 2nd edn, Thomas Baldwin (ed.), Cambridge: Cambridge University Press [originally published 1903].

Morgan, Michael L. (1992), 'Plato and the Greek Religion,' *Cambridge Companion to Plato*, Cambridge: Cambridge University Press, pp. 227–47.

Müller, Anselm W. (1977), 'Radical Subjectivity: Morality Versus Utilitarianism,' *Ratio*, **19**, 115–32.

——— (2004), 'Acting Well,' in *Modern Moral Philosophy*, Anthony O'Hear (ed.), Cambridge: Cambridge University Press, pp. 15–46.

Munby, James (2004), 'Consent to Treatment: Incompetent Patient,' in the *Principles of Medical Law*, Andrew Grubb (ed.), Oxford: Oxford University Press, pp. 205–310.

Murphy, Jeffrie G. (1973), 'The Killing of the Innocent,' *The Monist*, **57**(4), 527–50.

Murphy, Mark C. (2001), *Natural Law and Practical Rationality*, Cambridge: Cambridge University Press.

——— (2006), *Natural Law in Jurisprudence and Politics*, Cambridge: Cambridge University Press.

Nagel, Thomas (1979), *Mortal Questions*, Cambridge: Cambridge University Press.

——— (1986a), *The View From Nowhere*, Oxford: Oxford University Press, 1986.

——— (1986b), 'Death,' in *Applied Ethics*, Peter Singer (ed.), Oxford: Oxford University Press, pp. 9–18.

Narveson, Jan (1983), 'Self-Ownership and the Ethics of Suicide,' *Suicide and Life-Threatening Behavior*, **13**(4), 240–53.

——— and Susan Dimock (2000), 'Liberal Neutrality,' in *Liberalism: New Essays on Liberal Themes*, Dordrecht ; Boston: Kluwer Academic.

Neal, Patrick (1994), 'Perfectionism with a Liberal Face? Nervous Liberals and Raz's Political Theory,' *Social Theory and Practice,* **20**, 25–58.

Nielsen, Kai (1990), *Ethics Without God*, revised edn, Amherst, N.Y.: Prometheus.

——— (1999), *Moral Matters*, 2nd edn, Orchard Park, N.Y.: Broadview Press.

Nielsen, W. H. (1999), 'The Slippery Slope Argument against the Legalization of Voluntary Euthanasia,' *Journal of Social Philosophy*, **18**, 12–27.

Nozick , Robert (1974), *Anarchy, State and Utopia*, New York, N.Y.: Basic Books.

Oakley, Justin and Dean Cocking (1994), 'Consequentialism, Moral Responsibility, and the Intention/Foresight Distinction,' *Utilitas*, **6**, 201–16.

Oddie, Graham, (1977), 'Killing and Letting Die: Bare Differences and Clear Differences,' *Philosophical Studies*, **88**(3), 267–87.

Oderberg, David S. (2000a), *Moral Theory: A Non-Consequentialist Approach*, Oxford: Blackwell.

——— (2000b), *Applied Ethics*, Oxford: Blackwell.

——— (2000c), 'Is there a Right to be Wrong?,' *Philosophy*, **75**, 517–37.

——— (2001), 'Starved to Death by Order of the Court,' *Human Life Review*, Summer, 103–12.

——— (2004a), 'The Structure and Content of the Good,' in *Human Values: New Essays on Ethics and Natural Law*, David S. Oderberg and T. D. J. Chappell (eds), London: Palgrave Macmillan, pp. 127–65.

——— (2004b), 'The Ethics of Co-operation in Wrongdoing,' in *Modern Moral Philosophy*, Anthony O'Hear (ed.), Cambridge: Cambridge University Press, 203–27.

——— (2004c), 'Ordinary Duties, Extraordinary Means,' *Human Life Review*, Winter, 50–56.

Okie, Susan (2005), 'Physician-Assisted Suicide—Oregon and Beyond,' *New England Journal of Medicine*, **352**, 1627–30.

Olver, Ian N. (2002), *Is Death Ever Preferable to Life*, Dordrecht; Boston: Kluwer.

O'Neill, Onora (2002), *Autonomy and Trust in Bioethics*, Cambridge: Cambridge University Press.

Oshana, Marina (2003), 'How Much Should We Value Autonomy,' in *Autonomy*, Ellen Frankel Paul, Jeffrey Paul, and Fred Dycus Miller (eds), Cambridge: Cambridge University Press, pp. 99–126.

Otlowski, Margaret, (1997), *Voluntary Euthanasia and the Common Law*, Oxford: Clarendon Press.

Pakaluk, Michael (2001), 'Is the Common Good of Political Society Limited and Instrumental?,' *Review of Metaphysics*, **55**(1), 57–94.

——— (2005), *Aristotle's Nicomachean Ethics: An Introduction*, Cambridge: Cambridge University Press.

Pallis, Christopher (1999), 'On the Brainstem Criterion of Death,' in *The Definition of Death: Contemporary Controversies*, Stuart J. Youngner and Robert M. Arnold (eds), Baltimore, Md.: Johns Hopkins University Press, pp. 93–100.

Pannier, Russell (1987), 'Finnis and the Commensurability of Goods,' *New Scholasticism*, **61**, 427–39.

Partridge, Ernest (1981), 'Posthumous Interests and Posthumous Respect,' *Ethics*, **91**(2), 243–64.

Paterson, Craig (2000), 'On "Killing" versus "Letting Die" in Clinical Practice: Mere Sophistry with Words?,' *Journal of Nursing Law*, **6** (4), 25–44.

——— (2000b), 'On Justifying a Right to Adequate Health Care,' *Providence: Studies in Western Civilization*, **5**, 51–72.

——— (2003a), 'On Clarifying Terms in Applied Ethics Discourse: Suicide, Assisted Suicide, and Euthanasia,' *International Philosophical Quarterly*, **43** (3), 351–8.

——— (2003b), 'A Life Not Worth Living?,' *Studies in Christian Ethics*, **16**(2), 1–20.

——— (2006), 'Aquinas, Finnis and Non-naturalism,' in Craig Paterson and Matthew S. Pugh (eds), *Analytical Thomism: Traditions in Dialogue*, Aldershot; Burlington, Vt.: Ashgate, pp. 171–93.

Pellegrino, Edmund D. (1992), 'Doctors Must not Kill,' *Journal of Clinical Ethics*, **3**, 95–102.

——— (2000), 'Decisions to Withdraw Life-Sustaining Treatment: A Moral Algorithm,' *Journal of the American Medical Association*, **283**(8), 1065–67.

Pence, Gregory E. (2004), *Classic Cases in Medical Ethics*, Boston, Mass.: McGraw-Hill.

Plato (1997), *Complete Works: Phaedo*, trans. John M. Cooper, Indianapolis, Ind.: Hackett.

Potts, Michael, Paul A. Byrne, and Richard G. Nilges (2000), 'Introduction: Brain Death,' in *Beyond Brain Death: The Case Against Brain Based Criteria for Human Death*, Paul A. Byrne, Richard G. Nilges, and Michael Potts (eds), London; Dordrecht: Kluwer, pp. 1–20.

Postema, Gerald J. (1986), *Bentham and the Common Law Tradition*, Oxford: Clarendon Press.

Pullman, Daryl (2002), 'Human Dignity and the Ethics and Aesthetics of Pain and Suffering,' *Theoretical Medicine and Bioethics*, **23**(1), 75–94.

Quill, Timothy E. 'The Ambiguity of Clinical Intentions,' *New England Journal of Medicine*, **329**(14), 1039–40.

———, R. Dresser, and Dan W. Brock (1997), 'The Rule of Double Effect—A Critique of Its Role in End-of-Life Decision Making,' *New England Journal of Medicine*, **337**(24), 1768–71.

Quinn, Warren S. (1989a), 'Actions, Intentions, and Consequences: The Doctrine of Doing and Allowing,' *Philosophical Review*, **98**(3), 287–312.

——— (1989b), 'Actions, Intentions, and Consequences: The Doctrine of Double Effect,' *Philosophy and Public Affairs*, **18**(4), 334–51.

Rachels, James (1975), Active and Passive Euthanasia,' *New England Journal of Medicine*, **292**, 78–80.

——— (1986), *End of Life: Euthanasia and Morality*, New York, N.Y.: Oxford University Press.

——— (1993), 'Euthanasia,' in *Matters of Life and Death*, 3rd edn, Tom L. Beauchamp and Tom Regan (eds), New York, N.Y.: McGraw-Hill, pp. 30–68.

Ramsey, Paul (2002), *The Patient as Person*, New Haven, Conn.: Yale University Press [reprint].

Rasmussen, Douglas B. (1999), 'Human Flourishing and the Appeal to Human Nature,' *Social Philosophy and Policy*, **16**(1), 1–43.

——— and Douglas J. Den Uyl, (2005), *Norms of Liberty: A Perfectionist Basis for Non-Perfectionist Politics*, University Park, Pa.: Pennsylvania University Press.

Rawls, John, (1971), *A Theory of Justice*, Harvard, Mass. Harvard University Press.

——— (1985), 'Justice as Fairness: Political not Metaphysical,' *Philosophy and Public Affairs*, **14**, 223–51.

────── (1993), *Political Liberalism*, New York, N.Y.; Columbia University Press.

Raz, Joseph (1986), *The Morality of Freedom*, Oxford: Clarendon Press.

────── (1990), Facing Diversity: The Case of Epistemic Abstinence,' *Philosophy and Public Affairs*, **19**(3), 3–52.

────── (2001), *Value, Respect, and Attachment*, Cambridge: Cambridge University Press.

Redpath, Peter (1995), 'Private Morality and Public Enforcement,' in *Freedom, Virtue, and the Common Good*, Curtis L. Hancock and Anthony O. Simon (eds), Notre Dame, Ind.: American Maritain Association, pp. 332–41.

Reeve, Andrew F. (1997), 'Incommensurability and Basic Values,' *Journal of Value Inquiry*, **31**(4), 545–52.

Reynolds, Terrence (1985), 'Moral Absolutism and Abortion: Alan Donagan on the Hysterectomy and Craniotomy Cases,' *Ethics*, **95**, 866–73.

Richards, David A. J. (1981), 'Autonomy and Rights,' *Ethics*, **92**, 3–20.

────── (1982), *Sex, Drugs, Death and the Law*, Totowa, N.J.: Rowman & Littlefield.

────── (1986), *Toleration and the Constitution*, New York: Oxford University Press.

────── (1987), Kantian Ethics and the Harm Principle,' *Columbia Law Review*, **87**, 457–71.

Richardson, Henry S. (2004), 'Incommensurability and Basic Goods: A Tension in the New Natural Law Theory,' in *Human Values: New Essays on Ethics and Natural Law*, David S. Oderberg and T. D. J. Chappell (eds), London: Palgrave Macmillan, pp. 70–101.

Rhonheimer, Martin (2000), *Natural Law and Practical Reason*, trans, Gerald Malsbary, New York, N.Y.; Fordham University Press.

Rommen, Heinrich (1947), *The Natural Law*, St. Louis, Mo: Herder, 1947.

Ross, W. D. (1930), *The Right and the Good*, Oxford: Clarendon Press.

────── (1939), *Foundations of Ethics*, Oxford: Oxford University Press.

Rousseau, Mary (1979), 'Elements of a Thomistic Philosophy of Death,' *Thomist*, **43**, 582–601.

Sachs, G. A. *et al.* (1995), 'Good Care of Dying Patients: The Alternative to Physician-Assisted Suicide and Euthanasia,' *Journal of the American Geriatric Society*, **43**(5), 553–62.

Sadurski, Wojciech (1990), *Moral Pluralism and Legal Neutrality*, Dordrecht; Boston, Mass.; Kluwer Academic.

Sayeed, Sadath A. (2006), 'The Marginally Viable Newborn: Legal Challenges, Conceptual Inadequacies, and Reasonableness,' *The Journal of Law, Medicine & Ethics*, **34**(3), 600–610.

Scanlon, Thomas M. (1998), *What We Owe to Each Other*, Cambridge, Mass.: Harvard University Press.

Scarlett, Brian (1997), 'The Moral Uniqueness of the Human Animal,' in *Human Lives: Critical Essays on Consequentialist Bioethics*, David S. Oderberg and Jacqueline A. Laing (eds), New York, N.Y.: St. Martin's Press, pp. 77–95.

Scarre, Geoffrey (1996), *Utilitarianism*, London: Routledge.

Scheffler, Samuel (1994), *The Rejection of Consequentialism*, revd edn, Oxford: Oxford University Press.

Schier, Flint (1993), 'The Kantian Gulag: Autonomy and the Liberal Conception of Freedom,' in *Virtue and Taste*, Dudley Knowles and John Skorupski (eds), Oxford: Blackwell, pp. 1–18.

Schneewind, J. B. (1991), 'Natural Law, Skepticism, and Methods in Ethics,' *Journal of the History of Ideas*, **52**, 289–301.

Schneider, Angela and Robert Butcher (2001), 'Ethics, Sport, and Boxing,' in *Ethics in Sport*, William J. Morgan, Klaus V. Meier, and Angela Schneider (eds), Champaign, Ill.: Human Kinetics, pp. 357–69.

Scoccia, Danny (2000), 'Moral Paternalism, Virtue, and Autonomy,' *Australasian Journal of Philosophy*, **78**(1), 53–71.

Scott, Russell (1981), *The Body as Property*, London: Allen Lane.

Seifert, Josef (2002), 'What is Human Health?: Towards Understanding its Personalist Dimensions,' in *Person, Society and Value: Towards a Personalist Concept of Health*, Paulina Taboada, Kateryna F. Cuddeback, and Patricia Donohue-White (eds), London; Dordrecht: Springer, pp. 109–45.

Sen, Amartya and Bernard Williams (1982), 'Introduction: Utilitarianism and Beyond,' in *Utilitarianism and Beyond*, A. Sen and B. Williams (eds), Cambridge: Cambridge University Press, pp. 1–22.

Shafer-Landau, Russ (2006), 'Ethics as Philosophy: A Defense of Ethical Nonnaturalism,' *Metaethics After Moore*, Terry Horgan and Mark Timmons (eds), Oxford; New York, N.Y.: Oxford University Press, pp. 209–32.

Shaw, Joseph (2006), 'Intention in Ethics,' *Canadian Journal of Philosophy*, **36**(2), 187–224.

Sher, George (1997), *Beyond Neutrality: Perfectionism and Politics*, Cambridge: Cambridge University Press.

Shewmon, D. Alan (1985), 'The Metaphysics of Brain Death, Persistent Vegetative State and Dementia,' *Thomist*, **49**(1), 24–80.

––––––– (2001), 'Brain Stem Death, Brain Death, and Death,' *Journal of Medicine and Philosophy*, **26**(5), 457–78.

Silverstein, Harry (1980), 'The Evil of Death,' *Journal of Philosophy*, **77**, 401–24.

Simmons, Lance (1997), 'On Not Destroying the Health of One's Patients,' in *Human Lives: Critical Essays on Consequentialist Bioethics*, David S. Oderberg and Jacqueline A. Laing (eds), New York, N.Y.: St. Martin's Press, pp. 144–60.

Singer, Peter (1983), 'Sanctity of Life or Quality of Life,' *Pediatrics*, **72**(1), 128–9.

––––––– (1987), 'Life's Uncertain Voyage,' in *Metaphysics and Morality: Essays in Honour of J. J. C. Smart*, P. Pettit, R. Sylvan, and J. Norman (eds), Oxford: Blackwell, pp. 154–72.

––––––– (1993), *Practical Ethics*, 2nd edn, New York, N.Y.: Cambridge University Press.

––––––– (1994), *Rethinking Life and Death: The Collapse of Our Traditional Ethics*, New York, N.Y.: St. Martin's Press.

––––––– (1995), 'Is the Sanctity of Life Ethic Terminally Ill?,' *Bioethics*, **9**, 327–42.

––––––– (1998), 'Possible Preferences' in *Preferences*, Christoph Fehige and Ulla Wessels (eds), Berlin; New York: Walter de Gruyter, pp. 383–98.

———— (2002), *Unsanctifying Human Life: Essays on Ethics*, Helga Kuhse (ed.), Oxford; Malden, Mass.: Blackwell.

———— and Helga Kuhse (1993), 'More on Euthanasia,' *The Monist*, **76**, 158–74.

Smart, J. J. C. (1973), 'An Outline of a System of Utilitarian Ethics,' in *Utilitarianism: For and Against*, J. J. C. Smart and Bernard Williams (eds), Cambridge: Cambridge University Press, pp. 1–25.

Smith, Janet E. (1997), 'The Pre-eminence of Autonomy in Bioethics,' in *Human Lives: Critical Essays on Consequentialist Bioethics*, David S. Oderberg and Jacqueline A. Laing (eds), New York, N.Y.: St. Martin's Press, pp. 182–95.

Smith, Michael (1980), 'Did Socrates Kill Himself?,' *Philosophy*, **55**, 253–4.

———— (1995a), *Human Dignity and the Common Good in the Aristotelean-Thomistic Tradition,* Lewiston, N.Y.: Edwin Mellen Press.

———— (1995b), 'Common Advantage and Common Good,' *Laval théologique et philosophique*, **51**, 111–25.

Somerville, Margaret, (2001), *Death Talk: The Case Against Euthanasia and Physician-Assisted Suicide*, Montreal; Ithaca: McGill-Queen's University Press.

Stell, Lance K. (1979), 'Dueling and the Right to Life,' *Ethics*, **90**, 7–26.

Stern-Gillet, Suzanne (1987), 'The Rhetoric of Suicide,' *Philosophy and Rhetoric*, **20**, 160–70.

———— (1995), *Aristotle's Philosophy of Friendship*, Albany, N.Y.: State University of New York Press.

Stith, Richard (2004), 'The Priority of Respect: How our Common Humanity can Ground our Individual Dignity,' *International Philosophical Quarterly*, **44**, 165–84.

Stone, Isidor F. (1988), *The Trial of Socrates*, Boston: Little, Brown & Co.

Stone J. (1994), 'Advance Directives, Autonomy and Unintended Death,' *Bioethics*, **8**(3), 223–46.

Stratton-Lake, Philip (2002), 'Introduction,' in *Ethical Intuitionalism: Re-evaluations*, Philip Stratton-Lake (ed.), Oxford: Oxford University Press, pp. 1–28.

Sullivan Rodger J. (1989), *Immanuel Kant's Moral Theory*, Cambridge: Cambridge University Press.

Sullivan, William M. (1990), 'Bringing the Good Back In,' in *Liberalism and the Good*, R. Bruce Douglas, Gerald M. Mara and Henry S. Richardson (eds), London: Routledge, pp. 148–66.

Sulmasy, Daniel P., and Edmund D. Pellegrino (1999), 'The Rule of Double Effect: Clearing Up the Double Talk,' Archives of Internal Medicine, **159**, 545–50.

Sundstrom, P. (1995), 'Peter Singer and "lives not worth living",' *Journal of Medical Ethics*, **21**(1), 35–8.

Taurek, John (1977), 'Should the Numbers Count?,' *Philosophy and Public Affairs*, **6**, 298–316.

Teichman, Jenny (1985), 'The Definition of Person,' *Philosophy*, **60**, 175–85.

———— (1992) 'Humanism and the Personism: The False Philosophy of Peter Singer,' *Quadrant*, **36**(12), 26–9.

———— (1993), 'Humanism and the Meaning of Life,' *Ratio*, **6**(2), 155–64.

———— (1996), *Social Ethics*, Oxford: Blackwell.

Ten, C. L. (1968), 'Mill on Self-Regarding Actions,' *Philosophy*, **43**, 29–37.

―――― (1980), *Mill on Liberty*, Oxford: Clarendon Press.

Theron, Stephen (1984), 'Two Criticisms of Double Effect,' *New Scholasticism*, **58**, 67–83.

Thomson, Judith Jarvis (1985), 'The Trolley Problem,' *Yale Law Journal*, **94**, 1395–415.

―――― (1991), 'Self-Defense,' *Philosophy and Public Affairs*, **20**(4), 283–310.

Timmons, Mark (2002), *Moral Theory: An Introduction*, Lanham, Md.: Rowman & Littlefield.

Tindale, Christopher W. (2005), 'Tragic Choices: Reaffirming Absolutes in the Torture Debate,' *International Journal of Applied Philosophy*, **19**(2), pp. 209–22.

Tolhurst, W. E. (1983), 'Suicide, Self-sacrifice, and Coercion,' *Southern Journal of Philosophy*, **21**, 109–21.

Tooley, Michael (1987), 'Abortion and Infanticide,' in *Applied Ethics*, Peter Singer (ed.), Oxford: Oxford University Press, pp. 57–86.

―――― (1994), 'An Irrelevant Consideration: Killing Versus Letting Die,' in *Killing and Letting Die*, 2nd edn, Bonnie Steinbock and Alastair Norcross (eds), New York, N.Y.: Fordham University Press, pp. 103–11.

―――― (1995) 'Voluntary Euthanasia: Active Versus Passive, and the Question of Consistency,' *Revue Internationale de Philosophie*, **49**(3), 305–22.

Trammell, Richard L (1975), 'Saving Life and Taking Life,' *Journal of Philosophy*, **72**(5), 131–7.

―――― (1976), 'Tooley's Moral Symmetry Principle,' *Philosophy and Public Affairs*, **5**(3), 305–13.

―――― (1979), 'The Nonequivalency of Saving Life and Not Taking Life,' *Journal of Medicine and Philosophy*, **4**(3), 251–62.

Travis, Sara *et al.* (2001), Guidelines in Respect of Advance Directives: The Position in England,' *International Journal of Palliative Nursing*, **7**(10), 493–500.

Troug, Robert D. (1997), 'Is It Time to Abandon Brain Death?' *Hastings Center Report*, **27**(1), 29–37.

―――― and T. I. Cochrane (2005), Refusal of Hydration and Nutrition: Irrelevance of the "Artificial" vs "Natural" Distinction,' *Archives of Internal Medicine*, **165**(22), 2574–6.

Tywcross, Robert (1997), 'A View from the Hospice,' in *Euthanasia Examined: Ethical Clinical and Legal Perspectives*, John Keown (ed.), Cambridge: Cambridge University Press, pp. 141–68.

Uniacke, Suzanne M. (1984), 'The Doctrine of Double Effect,' *The Thomist*, **48**, 188–218.

―――― (1994), *Permissible Killing: The Self-Defence Justification of Homicide*, Cambridge: Cambridge University Press.

Veatch Henry B. (1971), *For and Ontology of Morals*, Ivanston, Ill.: Northwestern University Press.

―――― (1990), *Swimming Against the Current in Contemporary Philosophy*, Washington, D.C.: Catholic University of America Press.

Veatch, Robert M. (1975), 'The Whole-Brain-Oriented Concept of Death: An Outmoded Philosophical Formulation,' *Journal of Thanatology*, **3**(1), 3 30.

—— (1993), 'The Impending Collapse of the Whole-Brain Definition of Death,' *Hastings Center Reports*, **23**(4), 18–24.

—— (2004), 'Abandon the Dead Donor Rule or Change the Definition of Death?' *Kennedy Institute of Ethics Journal*, **14**(3), 261–76.

Veenhoven, Ruut (2000), 'The Four Qualities of Life,' *Journal of Happiness Studies*, **1**(1), 1–39.

Waldron, Jeremy (2005), 'Moral Autonomy and Personal Autonomy,' in *Autonomy and the Challenges to Liberalism: New Essays*, John Philip Christman and Joel Anderson (eds), Cambridge: Cambridge University Press, pp. 307–29.

Wall, Ian (2006), 'Consent to Medical Treatment,' in *Medicolegal Essentials*, Jason Payne-James, Ian Wall and Peter Dean (eds), Cambridge: Cambridge University Press, pp. 39–50

Wall, Steven (1998), *Liberalism, Perfectionism and Restraint*, Cambridge: Cambridge University Press.

Walter, James J. and Thomas A. Shannon (eds) (1990), *Quality of Life: The New Medical Dilemma*, New York, N.Y.: Paulist Press.

Walton, Richard E. (1980), 'Socrates' Alleged Suicide,' *Journal of Value Inquiry*, 14, 287–99.

Warren, Mary Anne (1997), 'On the Moral and Legal Status of Abortion,' in *Ethics in Practice*, H. Lafollette (ed.), Oxford: Blackwell, pp. 79–90.

Wasserman, David (1987), 'Justifying Self-Defense,' *Philosophy and Public Affairs*, **16**, 356–78.

Watt, Helen (2001), 'Conjoined Twins: Separation as Mutilation,' *Medical Law Review*, **9**(3), 237–45.

—— (2004), 'Beyond Double Effect: Side-Effects and Bodily Harm,' in *Human Values: New Essays on Ethics and Natural Law*, David S. Oderberg and T. D. J. Chappell (eds), London: Palgrave Macmillan, pp. 236–51.

Weinreb, Lloyd L. (1987), *Natural Law and Justice*, Cambridge, Mass.: Harvard University Press.

Werth, James L. (1999), *Contemporary Perspectives on Rational Suicide*, Philadelphia, Pa.: Brunner/Mazel.

Westberg, Daniel (2002), 'Good and Evil in Human Acts (Ia IIae, pp. 18–21),' in *The Ethics of Aquinas*, Washington, D.C.: Georgetown University Press, pp. 90–102.

Westerman, Pauline C. (1998), *The Disintegration of Natural Law Theory: Aquinas to Finnis*, Leiden; New York, N.Y.: E. J. Brill.

Westmoreland, Robert (1999), 'The Truth about Public Reason,' *Law and Philosophy*, **18**(3), 271–96.

White, Michael J. (1997), *Partisan or Neutral? The Futility of Public Political Theory*, Lanham, Md.: Rowman and Littlefield.

Wilder, Alfred. (1995), 'The Meaning and Place of the Principle of Double Effect in St. Thomas Aquinas,' in *Sanctus Thomas De Aquino Doctor Hodiernae Humanitatis*, Leo Elders (ed.), Rome: Pontificia Accademia di S. Thommaso, pp. 571–80.

Wildes, Kevin Wm. (1998), Libertarianism and Ownership of the Body,' in *Ownership of the Human Body: Philosophical Considerations on the Use of the Human Body*, Jos V. M. Welie and H. Ten Have (eds), London; Dordrecht: Kluwer, pp. 143–57.

———— (2006), 'Whose Nature? Natural Law in a Pluralistic World,' in *The Death of Metaphysics; The Death of Culture: Epistemology, Metaphysics, and Morality*, Mark J. Cherry (ed.), London; Dordrecht: Springer, pp. 29–37.

Wilkinson, D. (2006), 'Is it in the Best Interests of an Intellectually Disabled Infant to Die?,' *Journal of Medical Ethics*, **32**, 454–9.

Williams, Bernard (1973), 'A Critique of Utilitarianism,' in *Utilitarianism: For and Against*, by J. J. C. Smart and Bernard Williams, Cambridge: Cambridge University Press, pp. 77–150.

———— (1985), *Ethics and the Limits of Philosophy*, London: Fontana.

Williams, Glanville Llewelyn (1968), *The Sanctity of Life and the Criminal Law*, New York, N.Y. Alfred Knopf [reprint from 1957].

Wolfe, Christopher (2006), *Natural Law Liberalism*, Cambridge: Cambridge University Press.

Woods, John (2000), 'Slippery Slopes and Collapsing Taboos,' *Argumentation*, **14**(2), 107–34.

Woodward, P. A. (2001), *The Doctrine of Double Effect*, Notre Dame, Ind.: University of Notre Dame Press.

Woozley, A. D. (1983), 'A Duty to Rescue: Some Thoughts on Criminal Liability,' *Virginia Law Review*, **69**(7), 1273–300.

Wreen, Michael (1986), 'My Kind of Person,' *Between the Species*, **2**, 23–8.

———— (1987), 'The Logical Opaqueness of Death,' *Bioethics*, **1**, 366–71.

———— (1996), 'Importune Death a While,' *Public Affairs Quarterly*, **17**, 153–62.

———— (1998), 'Nihilism, Relativism, and Engelhardt,' *Theoretical Medicine and Bioethics*, **19**, 73–88.

Youngner Stuart J., and Robert M. Arnold (2001), 'Philosophical Debates About the Definition of Death: Who Cares?,' *Journal of Medicine and Philosophy*, **26**(5), 527–37.

Zanardi, William J. (1998), 'Why Believe in the Intrinsic Dignity and Equality of Persons?,' *Southwest Philosophy Review*, **14**, 151–68.

Zeis, John (2005), 'Killing Innocents and the Doctrine of Double Effect,' *Proceedings of the American Catholic Philosophical Association*, **78**, 133–44.

Index

abortion, Rawls on 161
absolutist prohibitions
    concrete 77
    formal 77
action
    elements 76–7
    end of 76
    moral quality, examples 76
    re-description 74–5
    see also double effect reasoning
action types 74–5
    examples 75
Alvarez, Alfred 7
anencephalic infants 130, 132, 139, 140–3,
    175
    medical treatment 142–3, 172
    organ harvesting 131
    person status 133, 139
    retained dignity 140–1
anencephaly, and death 130, 131
Anscombe, G.E.M. 86
anti-perfectionism, and the state 15–16,
    156–65
    see also perfectionism
Aquinas, Thomas 2, 5, 6
    on capital punishment 37fn9
    on practical reasoning 45
    self-defence analysis 27
    on sexual practices 45
    on state use of force 170
    on suicide 45
    supreme good 60
    works
        De regno 170
        Summa theologiae 27
Aristotle 6, 137
    on state use of force 170
assisted suicide
    and the common good 171
    current debates 1–2
    definitions 9–11
    Engelhardt on 158–9

euthanasia, distinction 174–5
    as homicide 103–4
    House of Lords decision on 1
    with morphine 120–1
    natural law approach 1–2
    contestability 36–7
    Netherlands 1, 177
    Oregon 1, 176
    Philosophers' Brief anthology 35, 162,
        174
    and public reason 162
    and self-determination 166
    and the state 171
    UK 1, 149, 173
    US 1, 149, 173

Battin, Margaret 17, 26
Beauchamp, Tom 19, 95
    and Arnold Davidson, on euthanasia
        11–12
    on suicide 9
beauty, as primary good 55
Bennett, Jonathan 29, 74
Bentham, Jeremy 29
    on suicide 18
'better off dead' argument 104, 105–6, 141,
    148–9
Boethius, definition of person 136
Bok, Sissela 173
boxing, and negative demands on health
    80–1
Boyle, Joseph 108
Brandt, Richard, on suicide 8
Brock, Dan 16
burning man case, killing 28, 122

capital punishment
    Aquinas on 37fn9
    permissibility 85
    and sanctity-of-life doctrine 17
Chappell, T.D.J. 93
Childress, James 19, 95, 96

Clouser, Danner 19, 20
the *cogito*, Descartes 133
common good
    and assisted suicide 171
    and natural law ethics 167–72
    realization of 169
    and suicide 171
    vs greater good 168–9
'condition of the soul' argument, and suicide
        42, 67fn2
consequentialism
    and deontology 19, 95–6
    double effect reasoning 31, 90
    and sanctity-of-life doctrine 18
    shortcomings 74
constrained partiality, human life 65, 78–9
contemplation, as primary good 52
conventionalism 4
Culver, Charles 19, 20, 131

Davidson, Arnold *see* Beauchamp
death
    and anencephaly 130, 131
    brain-stem 129–30
    criteria for 129–32
    declaration of, and organ harvesting 131
    deprivation account of 105–6
    higher-brain 130–1, 132, 139
    and personhood 131, 132
deontology
    and consequentialism 19, 95–6
    and sanctity-of-life doctrine 21
Descartes, René, the *cogito* 133
Devine, Philip 173
'dominion of life' argument, and suicide 42
Donagan, Alan 30
double effect reasoning 15, 27–32, 85
    absence of moral absolutes 28–9
    acts/omissions 31–2
    distinction 92–5
    Aquinas' self defence analysis 27
    basic method, challenge to 29
    Bentham's critique 29
    causal ordering 30–1, 88–90
    consequentialism 31, 90
    criteria 27–8
    intention/foresight 30
    examples 85–8
    and killing 85–95
    and morphine use 121
    principle 27

side-effects, responsibility for 90–2
Socrates' suicide 39fn69
    see also action
drugs, negative demands on health 80
Dupré, Louis 32
Durkheim, Emile, on suicide 8
duties, conflicts 19
Dworkin, Ronald 107, 155, 156, 157, 182
    equal concern and respect 23–4, 34–5,
        156, 157, 162–5
    critique 163–5
    mixed rights-based system 21
    politically reasonable discourse 34–5
    works
        Life's Dominion 24, 35
        Taking Right Seriously 23

Ellis, Anthony 96
Engelhardt, H. Tristram 130, 155, 157, 182
    on assisted suicide 158–9
    Foundations of Bioethics 158
    on the minimalist state 156
    permission principle 36, 158, 159
    on persons 158
    procedural rationality 35–6, 157–9
        critique 158
Epicureans 18
equal concern and respect
    Dworkin 23–4, 34–5, 156, 157, 162–5
        critique 163–5
    and natural law perfectionism 163
equality, and self-determination 23–4
euthanasia
    assisted suicide, distinction 174–5
    current debates 1–2
    definitions 11–12
        Beauchamp/Davidson 11–12
        Dutch Supreme Court decision 1
        as homicide 104
        House of Lords decision 1
    natural law approach 1–2
        contestability 36–7
    non-voluntary 148–50
        permissibility 143–4
        and the state 172
    Oregon 1, 176
    US Supreme Court decision 1

facts, and possibility 46
family life, as primary good 53–4
Feinberg, Joel 24–5, 113

Harm to Self 25
Feldman, Fred 105
Foot, Philippa 91
Frey, Roger G. 124, 174
Fried, Charles 19, 95
friendship, as primary good 54

Galston, William 165, 183
George, Robert 161
Gert, Bernard 19, 20, 131
Glover, Jonathan 20, 28, 106, 122
Golden Rule, practical rationality 91
'good lives' approach 6, 32–3, 36, 108
  see also sanctity-of-life doctrine
Gorsuch, Neil 176, 177
Grisez, Germain 108
gun lobbyists, 'slippery slopes' argument
  173

Haldane, John 162
Hare, R.M. 60
harm principle
  Mill 22, 113–14, 115, 156
  and self-determination 113–14, 115
Harris, John 20–1, 106, 107, 108
homicide
  assisted suicide as 103–4
  euthanasia as 104
  suicide as 103
human beings, persons, interchangeability
  135–6
human life/health
  constrained partiality 65, 78–9
  instrumental aspect 73–4, 108, 132
  negative demands 79–81
    boxing example 80–1
    drug example 80
    intentional harm, to preserve life
      79–80
    priorities 81
  positive demands 78–9
  as primary good 51, 78, 140, 166
  value 15, 126fn13
  see also sanctity-of-life doctrine
Hume, David
  'is/ought' distinction 43
  On Suicide 16
  Treatise of Human Nature 43

innocence, and killing 82–5
'is/ought'

distinction, Hume 43
transition, practical rationality 63

Kant, Immanuel 3, 46
  on persons 137–8
  self-determination concept 25, 112
killing
  burning man example 28, 122
  case studies 120–5
  and double effect reasoning 85–95
  and innocence 82–5
  intentional 81–2, 148
    examples 110–11
    with morphine 121
    non-permissibility 181–2
    Oates example 122–3
    and self-determination 112–20
    Socrates example 124–5
    soldier under torture 124
  justified 82–3
  non-intentional 82, 90
    examples 111
    with morphine 121
  self-defence 17, 27, 83–4
  state 17
  Stoics, justification 18
  unjustified 19–20
  see also homicide
knowledge, as primary good 51–2
Kohl, Marvin 17
Kuhse, Helga 16, 17, 20, 106, 107, 108

Lamb, David 131
laws of nature, natural law, distinction 2–3
liberalism, secularism, association 3
Lichtenberg, Judith 31, 32, 92, 94
life *see* human life/health
Lisska, Anthony, *Aquinas's Theory of
  Natural Law* 47
Locke, John
  on persons 133, 136
  property rights 23

McInerny, Ralph 44, 45
Mackie, John 30
Margolis, James 26
Maritain, Jacques 44, 45
medical treatment
  anencephalic infants 142–3, 172
  of never-competent persons 141
  non-provision 108

Baby Doe case 141–2, 152fn57
Baby K case 143
examples 108–9
self-determination 109, 126fn22,
  139
Terry Schiavo case 146
and personal dignity 141
PVS patients 143–7, 172
and quality of life assessments 141
Midgley, Mary 135
Mill, J.S. 112
harm principle 22, 113–14, 115, 156
On Liberty 21
mixed rights-based system, Dworkin 21
Moore, G.E.
Principia Ethica 44
on reductionism 44
moral autonomy
meaning 116
and self-determination 112–13, 116
morphine
assisted suicide 120–1
and double effect reasoning 121
intentional killing 121
non-intentional killing 121

Nagel, Thomas 95, 105
Narveson, Jan, on suicide 23
natural law
assisted suicide 1–2
  contestability 36–7
euthanasia 1–2
  contestability 36–7
laws of nature, distinction 2–3
meaning 6
and objective morality 5
objectivism 4–5
perfectionism 5–6, 36, 157
  equal concern and respect 163
religious associations 3, 32, 41, 181
secular approach 2, 3, 42
trans-culturalism 4–5
transcendence 4–5
as universalist 4
natural law ethics 2–7
absolutist prohibitions 77
Catholic Church support 32, 41
and the common good 167–72
intentional killing, non-permissibility
  181–3
non-naturalism 181

see also double effect reasoning
naturalism, non-naturalism 6–7
naturalistic fallacy
denial of 45–6, 47
support for 46
nature, dynamic properties 47
negative demands
and concrete moral absolutes 81–5
human life/health 79–81
Netherlands, assisted suicide 1, 177
normative theory, and pluralism 59–63
Nozick, Robert 95
on self-ownership 23

Oates case, suicide 122–3
objectivism, natural law as 4
Oderberg, David 137
Oregon
assisted suicide 1, 176
euthanasia 1, 176
organ harvesting
anencephalic infants 131
and declaration of death 131
PVS patients 131, 138

pain, as secondary good 58
perfectionism
liberal 165–6
  critique 166
meaning 5
natural law 5–6, 36, 157
  and equal concern and respect 163
pluralistic 6
see also anti-perfectionism
permission principle, Engelhardt 36, 158,
  159
personal autonomy *see* self-determination
personhood
and death 131, 132
'mask' origins of term 151fn30
persons
anencephalic infants as 132, 133, 139
definition
  Boethius' 136
  class attributes 136–7
Engelhardt on 158
human beings, interchangeability 135–6
intentional killing, protection from
  138–9
Kantian 137–8
Locke on 133, 136

never-competent, medical treatment 141
non-persons, distinction 150fn18, 175
    PVS patients as 131, 132, 139
    and rights 133
    threshold theories
        arbitrariness 134–5
        problems 133–9
    see also anencephalic infants; PVS
        patients
Philosopher's Brief, assisted suicide 35,
    162, 174
Plato, *Phaedo* 67fn2, 124
play, as primary good 55
pleasure, as secondary good 57–8, 80
pluralism 1–2, 3, 6
    limits on 169–71
    and normative theory 59–63
    value 116, 117
politically reasonable discourse, Dworkin
    34–5
possibility, and facts 46
power, as secondary good 56
practical rationality
    first principle 48–50
    Golden Rule 91
    'is/ought' transition 63
    key requirements 63–7
        constrained partiality 65, 78–9
        control maintenance 64
        normative demands, discernment
            66–7
        primary goods, respect for 65–6
        primary/secondary goods, objective
            status 64
        structured life narrative 64–5
    meaning 48
    pluralist vs monistic approach 60
    as primary good 52–3, 63
    self-evidentiality 49
    and utilitarianism 62
    see also practical reasoning; primary
        goods
practical reasoning
    Aquinas on 45
    meaning 44, 48
    see also practical rationality
primary goods 50–5
    Aristotelian-Thomist teleology 60–1
    beauty 55
    contemplation 52
    family life 53–4

friendship 54
human life/health 51, 78, 140, 166
irreducibility 60–1
knowledge 51–2
objective status 64, 73
play 55
plurality 59
    in political society 168
practical rationality 52–3, 63
priorities 59–60, 78
respect for 65–6
state, fostering by 168, 182
truth 51
Utilitarian teleology 61–3
work 54–5
see also secondary goods
procedural rationality, Engelhardt 35–6,
    157–9
    critique of 158
property rights
    and self-ownership 118–20
    and suicide 23
    see also self-ownership
public reason
    and assisted suicide 162
    Rawls 33–4, 156, 157, 159–62
        critique of 159–62
PVS patients 130, 135–6, 143–8, 175
    medical treatment 143–5, 143–7, 147–8,
        172
        dignity issues 145–6
        Terry Schiavo case 146
    organ harvesting 131, 138
    person status 131, 132, 139
    surrogate decision makers 147–8

quality of life assessments
    and medical treatment 141
    and sanctity-of-life doctrine 20–1
    and self-determination capacity 20–1,
        106–8

Rachels, James 20, 29, 31, 88, 92, 106
Rawls, John 3, 155, 182
    on abortion 161
    public reason 33–4, 156, 157, 159–62
        critique of 159–62
    works
        A Theory of Justice 33, 159
        Political Liberalism 33, 159, 161
Raz, Joseph 165, 166, 183

reciprocity principle 33–4
reductionism, Moore on 44
Regina v. Dudley and Stephens 9
Richards, David A. J., on self-determination
      25–6, 112
rights
      and persons 133
      and self-determination 25–6
Rommen, Heinrich 44, 45
Ross, W.D., influence 19

sanctity-of-life doctrine 16
      and capital punishment 17
      challenges to 16–18, 32, 95
            deontological tradition 21
            Epicureans 18
            Hume's 16
            quality-of-life assessments 20–1
            Stoics 18
      and consequentialism 18
      inconsistencies 15, 17
      religious basis 15, 16, 95
      and self-defence 17
      and utilitarianism 18–19
      see also 'good lives' approach
Schiavo, Terry 146
secondary goods 55–9
      material goods 56
      objective status 64
      pain 58
      pleasure 57–8, 80
      power 56
      self-determination 58–9
      see also primary goods
secularism
      liberalism, association 3
      and publicly accessible reason 3–4
self-defence
      analysis, Aquinas 27
      killing 17, 27, 83–4
      and sanctity-of-life doctrine 17
self-determination (personal autonomy)
      arguments 15, 21–6
      and assisted suicide 166
      capacity, and quality of life assessments
            20–1, 106–8
      compromised 117–18
      concept 24
      Kantian origins 25, 112
      and equality 23–4
      formation 24–5

and harm principle 113–14, 115
and intentional killing 112–20
libertarian defence of 114
limitations on 113–15, 117, 166
medical treatment, non-provision 109,
      126fn22, 139
and moral autonomy 112–13, 116
non-libertarian defence of 114–16
perfectionist justification 165, 166
positive value of 113–16
Richards on 25–6, 112
and rights 25–6
as secondary good 58–9
and self-ownership 22–3
and state sovereignty 25
and suicide 115–16
self-ownership
      contestability of concept 118–19
      Nozick on 23
      and property rights 118–20
      and self-determination 22–3
sexual practices, Aquinas on 45
Silverstein, Harry 105
Singer, Peter 18–19, 20, 31, 90, 106, 108
      on higher-brain death 131
'slippery slopes' arguments 173–8
      forms
            empirical 173
            logical 173
      gun lobbyists 173
Smart, J.J.C. 18
society
      levels 167
      political 167, 168
            and primary goods 168
Socrates, suicide
      as double effect reasoning 39fn69
      as intentional killing 124–5
state
      anti-perfectionist view 15–16, 156–65
      and assisted suicide 171
      authority, limits on 169
      killing by 17
      minimalist, Engelhardt on 156
      and non-voluntary euthanasia 172
      primary goods, fostering 168, 182
      purpose 167, 169
      sovereignty, and self-determination 25
      use of force
            Aquinas on 170
            Aristotle on 170

legitimate 170–1
Stoics 18
Stone, Isidor F. 124
subjectivism 4
suicide
    Aquinas on 45
    Bentham on 18
    and the common good 171
    and 'condition of the soul' argument 42,
        67fn2
    definitions 7–9, 103
        Beauchamp's 9
        Brandt's 8
        Durkheim's 8
    direct/indirect 14fn15
    and 'dominion of life' argument 42
    as homicide 103
    Hume on 16
    Narveson on 23
    Oates case 122–3
    permissibility 112, 171
    and property rights 23
    'rational' 26
    religious arguments against, critique of
        16–17
    soldier under torture 124
    soldier/hand grenade 123

Teichman, Jenny 137
Thomism, teleology, and primary goods
    60–1
Thomson, Judith Jarvis, trolley problem
    91–2
Tooley, Michael 31, 92, 94
trolley problem, Thomson 91–2
Truog, Robert 131

UK, assisted suicide 1, 149, 173
universalism, natural law as 4
US, assisted suicide 1, 149, 173
utilitarianism
    critique 62
    and practical rationality 62
    preference 18–19
    and sanctity-of-life doctrine 18–19
    teleology, and primary goods 61–3

Veatch, Henry 44, 45
Veatch, Robert 130
vitalism 108, 126fn24
    see also sanctity-of-life doctrine

Williams, Glanville 30
Wolfe, Christopher 161
work, as primary good 54–5